Plants Grown Up

Projects for Sons on the Road to Manhood

Pam Forster

Doorposts, 5905 SW Lookingglass Dr., Gaston, OR 97119

To Daniel, Joseph, and Benjamin,
three of the plants in our garden,
as we labor together toward the harvest

ISBN 978-1-891206-28-3

Doorposts
5905 SW Lookingglass Dr., Gaston, OR 97119
www.doorposts.com

That our sons may be as plants grown up in their youth; that our sons may be as corner stones, polished after the similitude of a palace:

That our garners may be full, affording all manner of store: that our sheep may bring forth thousands and ten thousands in our streets:

That our oxen may be strong to labour; that there be no breaking in, nor going out; that there be no complaining in our streets.

Happy is that people, that is in such a case: yea, happy is that people, whose God is the LORD.

(Psalms 144:12-15)

"...And beside this, giving all diligence,
add to your faith virtue;
and to virtue knowledge;
and to knowledge temperance;
and to temperance patience;
and to patience godliness;
and to godliness brotherly kindness;
and to brotherly kindness charity.

For if these things be in you, and abound,
they make you that ye
shall neither be barren nor unfruitful
in the knowledge of our Lord Jesus Christ."

(2 Peter 1:5-8)

Table of Contents

"And to temperance PATIENCE"

"And to patience GODLINESS"

"And to godliness BROTHERLY KINDNESS"

"And to brotherly kindness CHARITY"

Our Greetings to You

"...That our sons may be as plants grown up in their youth; that our sons may be as corner stones, polished after the similitude of a palace" (Psalm 144:12).

Sixteen years ago we realized we needed a plan. God had blessed us with three sons and three daughters, precious "plants" in the "garden" He had entrusted to our care. How would we, by God's grace, guide these children to godly adulthood? Our sons were already eight, six, and four. How could we ever teach them everything they needed to learn before they left our home to start their own families?

We prayed for wisdom and strength, and the idea for this book was born. Its purpose was simple. **We wanted to prepare our sons to faithfully serve God as young men, as husbands, as fathers, as church members, and as leaders in their community.** (Similarly, *Polished Cornerstones* was born out of a desire to see our daughters become godly women.)

Now, sixteen very fast years later, we thank God for His grace and mercy. Ever-faithful to His Word, God continues to work in our lives, and we praise Him for the evidences of His grace at work.

Those three sons, just little boys only yesterday, are now godly young men, committed to serving God in their homes, their careers, and their church.

This book is part of our journey – a journey that centered on God's Word. Perhaps these ideas will be a help to you, as well. May you continually turn to God and His Word as you disciple your sons. May you rejoice in the years to come, when you see the fruit of your labor and the evidence of God's faithfulness in strong and vigorous "plants grown up," godly sons with courage and commitment, joyfully bearing fruit for Christ's kingdom.

In His Grace,
Pam, for all the Forsters

The Purpose of "Plants Grown Up"

Preparing Boys to Be Godly Men

We put this book together to use with our own sons. Its ideas focus on preparing our sons for godly manhood.

We desire to see our sons grow not only in body and intellect, but also in spirit. We want them to follow the example of Jesus in His youth, increasing "in wisdom and stature, and **in favour with God** and man" (Luke 2:52).

There are plenty of books that encourage the development of the intellect, the gathering of information. The purpose of this book is to provide specific projects that will encourage the growth of deep godly character in our sons. Without wisdom, the ability to apply God's truth to life, all academic endeavors will be fruitless for God's kingdom.

The projects that follow in this book aim to prepare our sons to be:

- Godly young men
- Godly single men
- Godly workers
- Godly husbands
- Godly fathers
- Godly friends
- Godly church members
- Godly neighbors
- Godly citizens and/or government leaders

Preparing Boys to Be Godly YOUNG Men

Psalm 144:12 prays, *"...That our sons may be as plants grown up in their youth..."*

Our sons can be as "plants grown up" **in their youth.** This means that **in their teens** their lives can be **bearing fruit!** Gone is the myth that the teen years must be years of turmoil and rebellion! They can be years of harvest, years when a mature plant begins to bear fruit for its Master!

If we are faithful in caring for these little plants that God places in our gardens, if we water and feed and protect and weed, God will bring them to greater maturity in their **youth.** Scripture promises that we will "reap if we faint not"

(Galatians 6:9). The years that so many parents dread can become years of joy and fruitfulness.

> *"The father of the righteous shall greatly rejoice: and he that begetteth a wise child shall have joy of him. Thy father and thy mother shall be glad, and she that bare thee shall rejoice"* (Proverbs 23:24-25).

Growing Together

But we must look at the rest of Psalm 144. It goes on to conclude in verse 15, "Happy is that people, that is in such a case; yea, happy is that people, whose God is the Lord."

Happy are the parents who see their sons come to fruitfulness in their youth. Happy are the parents **who have made God their Lord.**

Raising godly sons requires a commitment on the part of both sons and parents. First, there must be a commitment to our Lord and Savior. Next, there must be a commitment to studying and obeying God's Word. This commitment will encompass all aspects of life -- family relationships, friendships, the music we listen to, the books we read, the education we receive, the church we attend. Every part of our lives must come under the lordship of Christ.

This book is a plan for **discipleship**, working side by side with our sons, advancing **together** in our walk with the Lord.

Parents and sons will be studying the Bible, searching for God's answers, examining their hearts by God's standard, learning from mature saints, working together, reaching out together, practicing the skills that equip them for serving the King in the way He has called them to serve.

A Help to Single Mothers and Wives of Unbelievers

This material is not designed exclusively for fathers and sons. Obviously, God's ideal is for the father to set a godly example for his son to follow. But sin has marred God's perfect plan.

Part of the purpose of *Plants Grown Up* is to make the job of the single mother easier as she strives to raise her sons to be godly young men. We hope the ideas in this book will give you direction and help you consider the many areas in which a boy needs guidance as he matures.

Mom, you can study the Bible with him. You can pray with him and work alongside him. You can pray for the presence of godly men in your son's life. You can seek out assistance in discipling him.

Our Heavenly Father has promised to be a "father to the fatherless." He can bring your son to spiritual maturity, even without the presence of an earthly father.

The same is true for the wife whose husband is an unbeliever, or whose Christian husband is not committed to investing his time and energy into personal growth or the discipling of his sons. God is still faithful.

You can pray. You can come alongside your sons. You can study the Word with them. You can work through these projects with them. You can pray for other godly influences in their lives.

Timothy's father, we are told in Acts 16:1, was a Greek. His mother was a believer. But in 2 Timothy 1:5, Paul recalls "the unfeigned faith that is in thee, which dwelt first in thy grandmother Lois, and thy mother Eunice; and I am persuaded that in thee also."

Mothers, God is not limited to working only through faithful, God-fearing fathers. And the absence of that type of husband does not excuse us from our own accountability to God. Your "chaste conversation coupled with fear," your "meek and quiet spirit, which is in the sight of God of great price" (1 Peter 3:1-4), may win your husband someday. It can also greatly influence the direction of your sons' lives.

"Let us not be weary in well doing: for in due season we shall reap, if we faint not" (Galatians 6:9).

How To Use "Plants Grown Up"

Read the Instructions Carefully

A book like *Plants Grown Up*, with pages and pages full of lists and projects, is dangerous! It tempts its owner to start doing the projects without reading the instructions first. This approach will almost always end in frustration.

This chapter is designed to help you use *Plants Grown Up* more effectively. It will save you time and confusion, and help you make the most of the investment you made in this book. However, for those of you who insist on diving right in, please read the following summary points. The rest of the chapter will expand on these main points:

- Use this book with all ages.
- Don't do all the projects. Don't even try to do half of the projects. Choose ones that fit your needs.
- Suggested resources are only suggestions. Use the ones that interest you and ignore the rest.
- Use planning sheets to help you organize.
- Do many of the projects with your son.
- Evaluate and encourage your son's progress.

For Boys of All Ages

The projects in *Plants Grown Up* are designed for sons of all ages. As soon as your little boys can memorize, you can start using this book with them. You can also start completing the projects at any age; you don't need to start when your sons are very young. Simply select projects that interest you and that are appropriate for the age and maturity of each of your sons.

The projects in each chapter are divided into four different sections. These roughly correspond to the following age groups:

- Memory verses, for all ages
- Beginner, 4-9 year-olds
- Intermediate, 10-14 year-olds
- Advanced – 15 years and older

However, **these are only general guidelines** for people who want guidelines. The age guidelines might help you narrow your choices, if the number of projects in this book overwhelms you, but don't let the age guidelines dictate your choices. If you look at a project in the intermediate section and believe your younger son would benefit from it, give it a try. Adapt it, if you think it will work better. Shorten it. Talk about it together instead of assigning a written paper.

If you see a project in the beginner section that seems to fit your older son's needs, don't reject it because you believe he's too old for it. Many projects listed in the beginner section are designed for younger boys to do with their parents. They are very appropriate for older sons to do on their own.

If you start using *Plants Grown Up* when your son is older, **you should use some of the projects in the younger age categories**. Earlier projects cover ideas and principles that the older sons will still benefit from.

The goal is to help your son grow. Use the projects that you believe will best accomplish that, and modify them to fit your needs.

Don't Try to Do It All!

Try to approach *Plants Grown Up* in the same way you would approach a road trip with your family. This book is not designed to start at the beginning, working your way straight through to the end. You would not start your family vacation by steering onto the closest interstate freeway and taking every exit ramp you see for the next 200 miles. You wouldn't get off the freeway to explore every restaurant, gas station, store, and tourist attraction.

A road trip is full of potential. There are usually lots of things to see and do between your departure point and your destination. Weeks before your trip, you might get online and research the tourist attractions along your route, selecting the ones you think your family would most enjoy. You might calculate mileage and plan how far to travel each day, planning specific stops and reserving motel rooms along the way. But you wouldn't be able to take advantage of every opportunity along your route. You would have to choose some activities and bypass others.

This book, like the route you travel on your trip, is full of possibilities. It's designed to give you as many choices as possible. But you will only do **a few projects in each chapter**, and these will be completed over the course of several years.

You approach a family vacation with limited time and limited resources. You should approach this book in the same way. You only have a few years before your son will leave home to start his own family, and you only have a small amount of time each day, or perhaps a short time each week, to invest in these projects. Just the first chapter could take you more than a year to complete if you invested an hour each day and tried to complete every project in the chapter!

So be a wise "traveler"!

- **It helps to know what you're trying to accomplish.** You wouldn't pack the car and start driving 400 miles a day for the next week if your family needs a time to rest and relax together. You wouldn't stop to visit every site along the way if you need to reach your destination as quickly as possible.

  What does your son need? In what areas would you like to see him grow? What weaknesses does he have? What are his needs? What are his interests? Turn to a chapter that will help you disciple your son in his specific areas of need and interests.

- **It helps to remember the ages of your fellow travelers.** You wouldn't plan a long road trip, driving many hours each day, if you have a car full of toddlers. You probably wouldn't point your car toward Sesame Place if your children are all teenagers.

  How old is your son? How mature is he? Do you need to select projects from the beginner level of *Plants Grown Up*, or is he mature enough for intermediate, or even advanced projects? You'll want to invest your time and his time in projects that will match his maturity level and that will be successfully completed.

- **It helps to remember your family's interests**. No need to spend money on concert and play tickets if you have an action-loving family who would rather be on the ski slopes. Scuba diving at the beach is great unless your family would be happier poking their way through historical museums and book shops.

  What does your son like? How does he learn best? Is he the kind of person who likes to read and write, or does he learn best by doing? Does he work well by himself, or will he do best by working with you, his parents? Select (or modify) *Plants Grown Up* projects to best fit his learning style.

- **It helps to follow a map.** Looking at a map points you in the right direction and helps you find your way to the amusement park or vacation site.

  Study this book. Learn your way around. Read **all** of the section on "How to Use Plants Grown Up." It is written to help you make the best use of all the rest of the material in the book. Peruse the table of contents. Browse through several chapters. Circle projects that you find particularly interesting.

- **It helps to set limits.** You won't be able to see and do everything on your trip. You'll have to make some choices in order to have time and money for the things you want to do most.

  To get started in *Plants Grown Up,* choose one chapter that fits your goals and needs. Skim the project ideas, circling ones that look appealing to you. Then review your circled projects and pick just one to start on with your son. This will get you started! Don't worry about having a year-long plan all drawn up before you can start working on projects. While he starts working, you can draw up more detailed plans.

- **It helps to plan ahead.** You won't spend all of your vacation budget on attractions and souvenirs, or you won't have any money for meals or lodging. You won't spend all two weeks at your first stop if you are hoping to see several other attractions before your return home. An itinerary helps you make the best use of your time, and a budget will help you use your money in a purposeful way. Without plans, it is easy to wander about, distracted by one thing after another, without actually accomplishing your goal.

  Pray for God's guidance as you start to use *Plants Grown Up* with your son. Take time to think about your family goals, his strengths and weaknesses, and your available time. Then follow the instructions for planning. Use the planning sheets in this book (pages 32 and 34) to help you list and schedule potential chapters and projects for your son. Instructions for planning and scheduling are included on pages 26 -29.

It might also help to think of this book like you would think about a buffet restaurant. Buffets are designed to give you many, many choices – several kinds of meat; mashed, baked, or fried potatoes; a variety of salads; a tantalizing array of breads and desserts. An attempt to sample everything usually ends in misery. The meal is much more pleasant if you limit your choices, picking and choosing what you like most from the many food selections.

From the hundreds of projects described in this book, you will select ones that fit your son's needs and temperament and your family's style and budget. If your budget is limited, select projects that fit that budget. Treat projects that require additional resources like high-fat desserts in the potluck line. Try one or two, but not **all** of them!

Take Advantage of the Seasons

With the exception of the chapter titled "Home Skills," each chapter in *Plants Grown Up* is divided into three sections – beginner, intermediate, and advanced.

The three categories of projects in each chapter are designed to correspond to three seasons of development in a boy's life.

Beginner Level: The Young Collector

Any astute parent with sons knows a young boy's enthusiasm for acquiring facts! Our boys went through "binges," devouring everything they could read about bugs, then about seashells, then about World War II, and on and on. They memorized scientific names, quizzed each other from field guides, studied the unique characteristics of every Allied and Axis airplane, and learned how to organize collections.

And, while they gathered the facts, they also gathered the real thing, lining shelf upon shelf with beach treasures, jars full of creepy, crawly and slithery things, combing the thrift stores for anything olive drab, and filling the skies over their beds with model fighters and bombers.

They were (and still are) hungry for facts. They memorized quickly. They loved to gather, arrange, display, and admire!

This is prime time for memorizing Scripture and catechisms, hearing Bible stories over and over, learning basic facts about how to treat others, how to organize their room, how to perform various tasks. This is a good season for role-playing, simulating actual situations, and rehearsing proper behavior in each situation.

The early years are also the time for laying the foundation for character development. A young boy needs to learn good habits of orderliness, obedience, and self-control. He needs to develop a proper respect for and fear of God and his parents.

The early projects in each chapter of this book focus on memory work, Bible stories, working and learning alongside parents, and basic training in obedience.

Intermediate Level: The Analyst

Boys always seem to want to know "why." That seems to be a constant question as long as there is a toddler in the family! But there comes an age when a boy seems to take "why" into his own hands, and begins to do his own research, his own analyzing, a weighing of alternatives and theories.

His ability to reason improves. He studies diagrams and illustrations. He sorts similar objects into different categories. He enjoys science experiments, magic tricks, and riddles.

This is the season for **studying** the Bible with Dad and/or Mom, researching what God says about particular topics, grouping proverbs into various categories, keeping journals, creating notebooks, drawing up charts, studying the proof texts of catechisms, deeper study of doctrines, interviewing and compiling data.

Advanced Level: The Maturing Leader

As a boy matures into young manhood, he is ready to take on more responsibility and leadership. He enjoys expressing his ideas and opinions (perhaps a little too much at times). He forms stronger ideas about how he will perform his duties as a husband and father.

In these years of young manhood, we have suggested projects that will give our sons opportunity to practice the skills they will need as the leaders of their family: leading family worship, thinking through their future wives' role in the home, writing essays on family-related topics, practicing repair skills, more actively planning and organizing their time, listing goals, becoming involved in community affairs, etc.

Suggested Resources

Although many other resources are suggested in *Plants Grown Up*, it is **not necessary to purchase any additional material** in order to use this book. **You can simply select projects that do not use other books**.

The projects largely focus on the study of God's Word. This is because we want to help our sons form their beliefs and opinions, their actions and goals, from the truth and wisdom of Scripture. The book of Proverbs was written for sons; it is a key resource in the projects included in this book.

To train your son in personal Bible study, two reference books will be extremely helpful. *Nave's Topical Bible*, by Orville Nave, and *Strong's Exhaustive Concordance of the Bible*, by James Strong, are very good study tools to have. Many projects suggest reading stories from the Bible about specific people. A concordance will help you locate these stories. It will also help you study specific words. The topical Bible will aid you in studying particular subjects.

You do not need to purchase either of these. Both are available for use online, but if you prefer a printed version, they may also be purchased in bound book form from Doorposts or at most Christian bookstores. The printed version of *Nave's Topical Bible* contains all the text for each reference. Online versions only list references to click on, which makes it harder to quickly skim through verses.

In addition to the personal study of Scripture, believers should also learn from each other:

- God has gifted many people with the ability to study, write, and teach. God can teach us through these people, while we continually weigh their words against the truths of God's Word.

- Our sons will be learning to seek and accept the counsel and wisdom of others as they read these books.

- They will acquire the joy of searching out a matter and learning all they can about it.

- If books are purchased (many can be purchased used to save money), your son will be building his own personal library of study books.

- Sons will gain a wealth of information and wisdom from older and wiser believers.

Many projects in this book refer to other books that will be helpful to your son. **You may or may not choose to use these books.** But your sons will gain much wisdom by reading these additional books. If you do choose to use some of them, many can be borrowed without cost from libraries. Most will also be found easily online, both new and used, some even free at *www.books.google.com.*

Even if you are on a limited budget, or choose not to read most of the books mentioned in this book, **please consider at least purchasing some of the following five books,** depending on the age of your son:

- *Leading Little Ones to God,* by Marian Schoolland. This is a foundational book for young children. It explores basic doctrines of the faith in easy-to-understand language and includes questions for further discussion.

- *For Instruction in Righteousness,* by Pam Forster. A topical listing of dozens of sins, offering biblical patterns for disciplining sinful behavior and rewarding godly behavior.

- *Discipline: The Glad Surrender,* by Elisabeth Elliot. Thought-provoking insights on surrendering our lives to God in order to do His will.

- *Disciplines of a Godly Man,* by R. Kent Hughes. A clear summary of the disciplines a man of God will exercise in his life.

- *The Exemplary Husband,* by Stuart Scott. A practical and Bible-saturated approach to the duties of husbands.

Memorizing Verses

Each chapter includes a list of possible memory verses related to the chapter's topic. Easier verses are listed in italics; longer, more difficult verses are in standard type. Select the verses you would like your son to memorize. **He doesn't need to memorize every verse that is suggested in this book.**

Committing verses to memory is a key element in discipling our sons. God's Word is "quick, and powerful, and sharper than any two-edged sword, piercing even to the dividing asunder of soul and spirit, and of the joints and marrow, and is a discerner of the thoughts and intents of the heart" (Hebrews 4:12).

And all Scripture is "profitable for doctrine, for reproof, for correction, for instruction in righteousness: **that the man of God may be perfect, thoroughly furnished unto all good works**" (2 Timothy 3:16-17). God's Word alone has the power to change hearts. We want that Word in our sons' hearts!

Scripture memorization does not need to be drudgery. Make it fun and challenging!

Here are a few ideas to help children memorize more effectively:

- Read the verse aloud together and discuss its meaning and application.

- Draw pictures to illustrate each verse.

- Paraphrase each verse.

- Write and draw rebus-type sentences, using pictures for sounds and words in the verse. Give the rebus to another child in the family to identify.

- Write verses out by memory.

- Write a summary paragraph explaining the verse's meaning.

- Have a "Memory Verse Bee," calling out verse references for each child to recite instead of spelling words to spell.

- Have children recite a memory verse as their "ticket" to a meal.

- Write the words to a verse in large letters on paper, and cut the verse into pieces, with one word on each piece. Put the words all back in order like a puzzle.

- Go around the table at mealtimes, reciting verses together, with one child saying one word, another child saying the next word, etc.

- See how many verses you can recite together while going for a walk with your son.

- Memorize the verses **together with your son**. Quiz each other, review together, **apply** them in daily life together.

Hide God's Word in Young Hearts, by Joan Kosmachuk, is full of creative ideas to make memorizing easier and more enjoyable.

Make Discipleship a Priority

The main resource your son needs while he uses *Plants Grown Up* is you! Young boys will need your help memorizing, reading, and learning. As your son matures, however, he will still need you. The projects in this book will bear much greater fruit, in your son's life and in yours, if you make the time to study with him, and if you encourage him to discuss his own studies with you.

Obviously, to share in these projects with your sons will require an investment of time and energy. We have to make choices as parents. The season of parenting young children is short when viewed within the entire span of our lifetime. We must choose to sow seed in the planting season God has given us. God reminds us in Scripture,

> *"Be not deceived; God is not mocked: for whatsoever a man soweth, that shall he also reap. For he that soweth to his flesh shall of the flesh reap corruption; but he that soweth to the Spirit shall of the Spirit reap life everlasting"* (Galatians 6:7-8).

- We must **set aside other desires and activities** in order to devote the time needed to really **know** our children and to diligently train them for righteous living. If certain activities are preventing us from faithfully raising up our children, those activities are probably not God's will for our lives at this time. He will not require more of us than we can faithfully perform.

- We may have to **postpone some dreams**. The years when our children are home is the only season we will be given for training them. We may have to wait for another season of life to pursue some activities that would seem to promote God's kingdom, but would pull our hearts away from loving and discipling our own children.

> *"Though I speak with the tongues of men and of angels, and have not charity, I am become as sounding brass, or a tinkling cymbal.*
>
> *And though I have the gift of prophecy, and understand all mysteries, and all knowledge; and though I have all faith, so that I could remove mountains, and have not charity, I am nothing.*
>
> *And though I bestow all my goods to feed the poor, and though I give my body to be burned, and have not charity, it profiteth me nothing"* (1 Corinthians 13:1-3).

- We may have to **choose to live with fewer material goods**. It is foolish to invest our energies into acquiring "treasures on earth" if we are forfeiting "treasures in heaven."

- We may have to **rethink our approach to the academic education** of our children. If the acquiring of man's knowledge about the world leaves no time for acquiring the wisdom of the Creator about His creation, then man's knowledge has become too important. God's Word and His wisdom, helping us interpret our limited knowledge of His creation, need to be our **priority**. "For the wisdom of this world is foolishness with God" (1 Corinthians 3:19a).

- We should also draw on the wealth of love and experience that **grandparents** offer to our children. Their wisdom is precious. Enlist interested grandfathers to help in the discipling of your sons. Even unbelieving grandfathers can help train your sons in practical skills such as car repair, household maintenance, and animal care. Besides the tremendous help their contribution of time and knowledge can be to you as you seek to balance your many responsibilities, most grandfathers will also be eager to share more time with their grandsons.

Make Plants Grown Up Part of Your School Day

These projects can easily be incorporated into a traditional academic curriculum. While your son learns to read, he will also learn from God's Word. While he learns composition skills, he will also meditate on the truths of Scripture. While he learns to speak clearly, he will also learn how to instruct her future children. While learning research skills, he will also learn how to study the Bible.

Use some of these projects **in place of assignments** in your homeschool curriculum. At the end of each idea, the related academic subjects are noted. If you would like to use projects from this book for part of your school curriculum, you can look through each chapter and see which would tie in with reading lessons, which would be appropriate for composition assignments, etc.

Adapt Projects to Fit Your Needs

Many projects can easily be **changed** to incorporate different academic skills. If you have a son who is an especially gifted speaker, allow him to present his research and thoughts in speeches instead of written papers. The same would be appropriate if your son struggles with written assignments. Don't burden him with too much writing. He could benefit from many projects by simply doing his research and then sitting down to discuss it with you.

If you would like to have your son work on certain projects that exceed his academic skills (in writing and reading, for example), work on those projects with him, or study those areas together as a family. Take the ideas in this book and **adapt** them to fit your family needs!

You will also want to add your own ideas, unique to your own son's needs and your own family's goals. The content of this book is only the beginning of all we could do to disciple our sons. Our goals for ourselves and our children will grow as we grow. The list of ideas will never be complete. When you think of a potential project for your son, note it in the appropriate chapter of the book.

Schedule Time to Work Together

Try to set aside a time each day, or at least two or three times a week, that you can dedicate to working with your son on these projects. Sunday afternoons can be a good time for Bible study and prayer together.

You can also meet together early in the morning before everyone else is up, or in the evening before bed. A weekend away, just one parent and one son, can be a very profitable time of planning, studying, talking, and playing together. A weekly burger and fries at the local drive-in, or an occasional early morning breakfast or hour at the coffee shop can help you find time to work on these ideas together.

We can almost always find time for the things that are important to us. God will give us the time if we choose to make the discipling of our sons one of our highest priorities. Page 36 includes a "Daily Checklist for Sons" that you may choose to have your son complete each day. If you help him establish the daily habit of reading the Bible, praying, memorizing, etc., many of the projects in this book can be done during that time.

Doorposts' *Family Circles* may also help you set aside the time for *Plants Grown Up* projects. This simple organizing tool is designed to help parents spend individual time with each child in their family each day. It can help you have a designated time at least once or twice a week for individual Bible study, prayer, projects, memorizing Scripture, walks, etc. with each child. If you are having difficulty setting aside time for discipling your son, you might want to try this out, or devise your own system of rotating times with your children.

Planning Projects for Your Son

Plants Grown Up can be approached in many different ways. Some families may want to plan ahead for an entire year of projects. Some will choose one project at a time as the need arises. Use the planning system that works best for you. We designed this book to use with our own sons, and **the system that worked best for us was a monthly planning session**.

One month's worth of plans made it much **easier to faithfully work on projects**, because we didn't have to decide over and over what to have the boys do. Once the monthly plan was finished, we were set. We could simply look at our plans, adjust them if necessary after some unforeseen change in daily activities, and assign projects as we wrote out our weekly school assignment page.

A monthly plan allowed for **flexibility**. As different issues and needs arose throughout the year, we could tailor our projects to address those needs. As unanticipated events occurred in the household, we did not have to modify an entire year's plans to accommodate the changes.

A monthly plan was **simpler** when we needed to assign different projects to sons of different ages. Planning for an entire year would have been overwhelming and would not have allowed for the growing maturity and changing interests of the boys over the course of a year.

How To Plan for a Month of Projects

Dad and Mom, you will need to discuss what approach will work best for you. Is Dad going to be completely responsible for *Plants Grown Up* assignments? Is he going to make all the project selections, assign them, complete them with your sons, and hold your sons accountable for the work? Or would he like Mom's help with some of the administrative details? Would he like her to browse through the book and give him a list of suggested projects that he can then make choices from? Would he like both of you to hold a monthly planning session together, or would he like to sit down with your son to draw up plans? Are you going to include some of the projects in your school day? Will Dad correct the work, or does he want Mom's help with some projects? What will you do to establish regular times of studying and working with your son?

When you have worked up a basic plan, use photocopies of the "Project Page" (page 32) and the calendar (page 34) as you work through the following steps. Samples of each sheet filled out are also included on pages 33 and 35.

1. Decide **how much time** you are planning to devote to *Plants Grown Up* projects each week. Will you work on projects on the same days at the same time each week, or will it need to vary some from week to week?

2. **Select a chapter or two that seem appropriate for the month**. When you have selected the chapter, note its title and page number on a "Project Page,"

using one page for each chapter. Ask yourself the following questions as you choose the chapter.

- **Is there an area in which your son especially needs instruction?** (For example, if he is disobeying you, the chapter on submission might be helpful.)

- **Is there an area that your son would especially enjoy?** If you always assign topics that your son is struggling with, he may be tempted to resent the projects. Look for topics that will also be a delight to him. We all have areas to grow in, but sometimes it is encouraging to work in an area of our strength.

- **Does the month include a holiday or family celebration that would make certain projects more practical?** (December, for instance, might be a good month to focus on hospitality or finances.)

- **Does the season of the year present opportunities that you will not be able to take advantage of during the rest of the year?** (Outdoor home repairs will be more pleasant to complete in the spring and summer, for example.)

- **Are any major events or changes occurring during the month that might impact your schedule significantly?** (You might want to tackle home skills if you're remodeling or moving during the month, or you might choose to focus on mercy if a grandparent will be having surgery or moving in with you during the month.)

  In general, at least while your sons are young, it is easiest to have all your boys working on projects from the **same chapter**. By doing this, you can memorize the same verse together and discuss the same general topic throughout the month. Older sons can also help their younger brothers with some of their projects, which will reinforce what they are learning in their own projects.

3. **Select at least one memory verse from the chapter(s).** Note it on your planning page. Sons of all ages should be memorizing verses from the chapter lists. This can easily become part of your family worship time together.

4. **Skim over the list of projects, marking ones that interest you.** At this point you are simply noting potential projects. You will not necessarily assign all these projects during the month. Search online for descriptions of recommended books to help you better understand the project and its suitability for your son.

When you read a project description that interests you, note on the project page the following information:

- Initials of the son you want to complete this project (if you are planning projects for more than one son) in the "Name" column.

- The project's identifying letter and page number

- Any notes you want to record (necessary preparation, books to obtain, etc.)

- Estimated amount of time needed to complete the project

- Details in the "How" column, such as who might do the project with him, what time of day, etc. Some projects could take place during your family worship time, at bedtime, in the car while you are traveling, and during other times besides your designated *Plants Grown Up* project time. This will help you disciple throughout the day, save you time, and help you cover more material in the book.

5. **Use the calendar to schedule the projects for the month.**

- Record the days of the month on the calendar page.

- Note any major events you know will occur during the month. Some of these might affect your project plans. You won't want to assign a more complicated or messy project on a busy day. You might want to assign independent work on days when you will not have as much time to work with them. Your older son's assignment might be to help a younger brother on a day when you know you will be unavailable.

- At the top of the calendar, note the month and the topic or topics you will be emphasizing for the month.

- At the bottom, right hand corner of the calendar note memory verses that you intend to work on during the month.

- From your list of potential projects, choose ones to assign to appropriate days on the calendar, allowing for the number of days you are devoting to each project. Be sure to schedule time for memorizing verses and studying them with some of the methods suggested at the beginning of each verse list.

    You will probably not use every project that you listed as a possibility. Keep your project sheet to refer to next month, or the next time you want to do projects from this chapter again.

- Identify projects for different sons with their initials or some other identifying mark.

6. Use the calendar to help you assign projects. You can tell your sons the assignment each day, give them a copy of your calendar, enter assignments on your weekly school assignment page, or simply introduce the project when you meet together.

If you would like to get a head start on your planning for the year, follow steps 1 through 4 as you browse through each chapter of the book. Keep these project sheets in a notebook for future reference.

Evaluating Progress

At the end of each chapter we have provided a series of questions to help you evaluate how well you and your son are doing. These can be used in several ways:

- Mom and Dad, read through them together, to help you pinpoint weak areas in your training or in your son's character. Use this knowledge to help you plan the projects you want to work through with your son over the next year.

- You can read through them together with your son, as an evaluation tool and as a means of bringing up weak areas to discuss with him.

- You can give the page to your son to read through, think over, and write in answers. In doing this, he is working with his own conscience under the conviction of the Holy Spirit.

- You could do a yearly evaluation, dating each page, and keeping them in the notebook as a testimony of the progress your son is making.

- You could also give selected pages of questions to an extended family member, employer, teacher, or others who know your son well. These folks could offer another view into your son's character.

- Use these completed question forms as a list to pray from when you approach the throne of grace on behalf of your son.

Use an occasional Sunday afternoon to review your goals and evaluate your progress. A special dinner out near your son's birthday, or some quiet time on New Year's Eve or New Year's Day can also become regular checkpoints for reviewing progress over the past year.

Celebrating Milestones

You might want to consider having a party at some point in your son's pre-teen years. Invite extended family members, your pastor, close Christian friends, perhaps even some unbelieving neighbors.

Orally quiz your son on his memory work. Ask him to recite specific verses, and to answer specific questions from the catechisms. Let him display his work thus far. Give him a special gift as you publicly commend him for his diligence.

We have given each of our sons an ounce of gold when he could successfully recite two verses from each chapter of *Plants Grown Up.* "The law of thy mouth is better unto me than thousands of gold and silver" (Psalms 119:72). Because he has chosen to seek after knowledge and commit himself to hiding God's Word in his heart, we choose to reward him with something of high earthly value, though it pales in comparison to the eternal value of what is in his heart.

A notebook filled with your son's Bible study notes, his essays, his prayer journal, his financial records, your yearly evaluations, and so forth, can function as a sort of "portfolio." It -- and more importantly, his life -- will serve as testimony to the years of work he has devoted to preparing for the responsibility of a family of his own.

Imagine how you would feel if a potential suitor approached you for permission to court your daughter, with a notebook under his arm, stuffed full of evidence of his commitment and training! Imagine how your future in-laws will feel when your son can show them **his** work, either in the physical form of a notebook or in the fruit of his life.

Perhaps, if God leads your son into marriage, at his engagement, you would like to have another party. Replace the traditional "bachelor party" with an advice night. Invite fathers, grandfathers, and the men of the church to celebrate with you. Have lots of good food, time for fellowship and a time for guests to share godly wisdom about marriage and family with your son. What an encouraging and edifying time this could be!

These are ideas. God will lead you and your unique family in ways to encourage and reward your son as he grows toward manhood.

Claiming His Promises

2 Peter 1:5-7 admonishes us as believers to diligently add to our faith,

> *"virtue; and to virtue **knowledge**; and to knowledge **temperance**; and to temperance **patience**; and to patience **godliness**; and to godliness **brotherly kindness**; and to brotherly kindness **charity**."*

These are the goals that we aim for in this book. These are the areas of character we desire to encourage in the lives of our sons.

In our great desire to build godly character into the lives of our children, we must remember that all these godly qualities are to be added to **faith**. We must first be diligent to lead these precious souls to the cross. We must pray for their salvation. We must point them to the saving grace of Christ's death and resurrection and ascension.

Unless we build on the foundation of faith, unless our children come under the lordship of the Saviour, our efforts will be in vain. 2 Peter 1:3 reminds believers that,

> *"His divine power hath given unto us all things that pertain unto life and godliness, through the knowledge of him that hath called us to glory and virtue"* *(2 Peter 1:3).*

If we do, with the Holy Spirit's guidance, lead our believing children toward godly maturity, 2 Peter goes on to promise,

> *"For if these things be in you, and abound, they make you that ye **shall neither be barren nor unfruitful** in the knowledge of our Lord Jesus Christ. But he that lacketh these things is blind, and cannot see afar off, and hath forgotten that he was purged from his old sins.*
>
> *Wherefore the rather, brethren, give diligence to make your calling sure; for if ye do these things, **ye shall never fall**"* *(2 Peter 1:8-10).*

Let's be diligent in the calling our Lord has given us! He has promised to uphold us!

Project Page

Chapter_____ Page _____

Memory verse _____

Name	Project	Page	Notes	Time	How
_____	_____	___	_____	_____	_____
_____	_____	___	_____	_____	_____
_____	_____	___	_____	_____	_____
_____	_____	___	_____	_____	_____
_____	_____	___	_____	_____	_____
_____	_____	___	_____	_____	_____
_____	_____	___	_____	_____	_____
_____	_____	___	_____	_____	_____
_____	_____	___	_____	_____	_____
_____	_____	___	_____	_____	_____
_____	_____	___	_____	_____	_____
_____	_____	___	_____	_____	_____

Project Page

Memory verse _D- Isa. 58:13-14 / J&B- Ps. 118:24, Hab. 2:20 / All- Ex. 20:8-11_

Name	Project	Page	Notes	Time	How
J&B	B	317	"Leading Little Ones"	Bible time	w/Mama
J&B	C	"	Paper, crayons/felt pens	½ hr.	School
J&B	D	"	Use white board. List days	15 min.	Family worship
All	E	"	Write & post in dining room	Daily	Dinnertime
All	G	"	Help J&B / Check D	Sat. aft.	Done before dinner
All	H	"	Make indiv. lists	1 hr.	School
All	J	"	Materials, books of ideas	2 hr.	School
All	K	"	Mail order, $40 budget	1 hr.	Fri. eve.
D	N	318	Choose & prepare activity	Weekly	Fridays
D	O	"	For company on Sunday	1½ hrs.	School
All	P	"	Family activity w/treats	Afternoon	Sun. tog.
D	Q	"	Plan menu, oversee bros.	1 hr.	w/Daddy & popcorn
All	S	"	Plan ahead, discuss ideas	Weekly	After service

Projects for the Month of _____

Emphasis: _____

Sun	Mon	Tue	Wed	Thurs	Fri	Sat

Memory Verse(s): _____

Notes : _____

Projects for the Month of __April__   Emphasis: __Honoring God's Day of Rest__

Sun	Mon	Tue	Wed	Thurs	Fri	Sat
				1] J4B 317B	2] GOOD FRIDAY Watch Easter story video	3] All-317G 318S Discuss video
4] EASTER Help someone All-319BB Memorize Isa.58:13/Ps.116:24 →	5] J4B-317D Tell about helping @church	6]	7] D-Shop for notebook for sermon notes	8] D-318U	9] Family time 317K D-318N	10] All-317G
11] Refer to checklist Help someone, D's activity D-Take notebook Memorize Isa.58:14/Mem. Hab 2:20	12] J4B-317C Tell about helping @church	13]	14] All-317H	15] D-318Q w/Daddy + popcorn	16]	17] All-317G
18] Refer to checklist Help someone D's dinner w/J4B Bring out Sun. box!	19] Tell about helping @church Review verses →	20] → D- memorize WC No.115-116	21] All-317J	22] All-317J	23] D-318N	24] All-317G
25] Refer to checklist D's activity All-318P game Help someone Review verses →	26] Tell about helping at church	27] → D-Finish WC No.115-116	28]	29]	30] All-recite all verses (prizes)	

Notes: __D-Memorize WC No.115-116, discuss sermon each week w/D, order Easter video in March, compile__
__meal ideas before 4/15, materials for game-making by 4/24__ Memory Verse(s): __All-Ex.20:8-11, D-Isa.58:13-14__
__Sun.__ __J4B-Ps.118:24/Hab. 2:20__

Daily Checklist for Sons

_____
Month

	READ BIBLE	PRAY	MEMORIZE	REVIEW VERSES	WORK ON PROJECTS FROM PLANTS GROWN UP
1	_____	_____	_____	_____	_____
2	_____	_____	_____	_____	_____
3	_____	_____	_____	_____	_____
4	_____	_____	_____	_____	_____
5	_____	_____	_____	_____	_____
6	_____	_____	_____	_____	_____
7	_____	_____	_____	_____	_____
8	_____	_____	_____	_____	_____
9	_____	_____	_____	_____	_____
10	_____	_____	_____	_____	_____
11	_____	_____	_____	_____	_____
12	_____	_____	_____	_____	_____
13	_____	_____	_____	_____	_____
14	_____	_____	_____	_____	_____
15	_____	_____	_____	_____	_____
16	_____	_____	_____	_____	_____
17	_____	_____	_____	_____	_____
18	_____	_____	_____	_____	_____
19	_____	_____	_____	_____	_____
20	_____	_____	_____	_____	_____
21	_____	_____	_____	_____	_____
22	_____	_____	_____	_____	_____
23	_____	_____	_____	_____	_____
24	_____	_____	_____	_____	_____
25	_____	_____	_____	_____	_____
26	_____	_____	_____	_____	_____
27	_____	_____	_____	_____	_____
28	_____	_____	_____	_____	_____
29	_____	_____	_____	_____	_____
30	_____	_____	_____	_____	_____
31	_____	_____	_____	_____	_____

And Add to Your Faith,

VIRTUE

Leadership: Justly Judging in Discipline Situations

"Give therefore thy servant an understanding heart to judge thy people, that I may discern between good and bad: for who is able to judge this thy so great a people?" (1 Kings 3:9)

By following Scripture while training our sons, we not only raise them to be godly men, but we also provide them with an example to follow when they become fathers themselves. We can help them become righteous judges by setting an example as a righteous judge.

We should base our discipline on Scriptural principles. When we discipline, we should read from the Bible and explain why an action or attitude must be disciplined. We should hold up as our standard God's perfect standard.

We need to resist the temptation to ignore misbehavior and disagreements. If we will faithfully uphold justice, carefully investigating with the purpose of helping our children repent and reconcile, our children will be better prepared to act as judge for their own children someday. They will also be better equipped to serve God in all other areas of life.

We need to teach our sons the Biblical principles of godly reproof. If they learn to properly confront peers who have wronged them, with the purpose of restoring them, they will be much better prepared to confront their own children when they transgress God's law.

A. Select verses from the list below, and use some or all of the following suggestions to help you study and better understand their meaning (easier verses are listed first, in italics):

1) Copy the passage.

2) Read it in several different translations of the Bible.

3) Read the passage and several of the verses before and after it to gain a better understanding of the context of the passage.

4) Rewrite the passage in your own words. What does it mean?

5) Record a specific way in which you can change your actions or attitudes based on the teaching of this passage.

6) Memorize the passage.

Proverbs 3:12
Proverbs 19:18
Proverbs 24:23
John 7:24
1 Kings 3:9
Proverbs 17:15
Proverbs 18:17
Zechariah 8:16
(BIBLE / SPEECH)

Beginner

B. Read through the *If Then Chart* with your parents. Talk about the verses and the consequences that your parents have agreed to enforce when you misbehave. *(BIBLE / LAW / FAMILY)*

C. Memorize the verses on the *If-Then Chart*. *(BIBLE)*

D. Read about Jethro's advice to Moses in Exodus 18. Narrate the story back to your father or mother. What did Jethro suggest to Moses to make his job easier? Act out this story with your siblings or with toys. *(BIBLE / SPEECH / DRAMA)*

E. Read the story of Solomon's judgment in 1 Kings 3:16-28. Act out the story with your siblings or with toys. *(BIBLE / DRAMA)*

F. Illustrate the story of Solomon in 1 Kings 3:16-28. *(BIBLE / ART)*

G. If you have sisters who play with dolls, volunteer to act as the father when they play house and their "children" misbehave. Decide how they should be disciplined, based on Scripture. *(BIBLE / LAW)*

H. Write out the Ten Commandments and post them on a wall in your room. Each time you are disciplined, each time you have sinned, read through the commandments. Identify which commandments you have transgressed. *(BIBLE)*

I. Study *The Brother-Offended Checklist* with your parents. Follow the steps on the chart when someone wrongs you. If you learn how to settle disagreements and reprove wrongdoers in a godly way now, as a child, it will be much easier for you to lovingly reprove your own children in the future. *(BIBLE / FAMILY / SOCIAL SKILLS)*

J. Study, with your parents, the last section of *The Brother-Offended Checklist*, "What the Bible Tells the 'Judge' To Do." Explain how the Bible says to deal with a false witness and with a person who rejoices in the wrongdoing of another. Discuss the steps involved in being a just judge. Role-play different discipline situations, with you acting as judge. Use Biblical principles! *(BIBLE / LAW / FAMILY / SOCIAL SKILLS)*

K. Ask your parents to give you a list of Bible verses that deal with a particular area of sin with which you are struggling. Study these verses together with your parents. What does God say about this sin? What does Scripture say should happen to you if you continue to sin in this way? Work with your parents in deciding how you should be disciplined when you sin in this way. Write out a list of disciplines and put it up on the wall to help you remember what the consequences of sinning will be. Illustrate the list if that will help you. *(BIBLE / READING / HANDWRITING)*

Intermediate

L. Find a Scripture passage to support each of the rules listed in *21 Rules of This House,* by Gregg and Joshua Harris. *(BIBLE / RESEARCH)*

M. Under your father's direction, find Scripture about a particular discipline problem to share and comment on during a mealtime. *(BIBLE)*

N. Ask your parents to write up or describe hypothetical behavior problems and discipline situations. Study the Bible for appropriate discipline action. Use a topical Bible and concordance to help you discover what God says will happen to people who lie, cause trouble, complain, etc. Then write down these ideas to keep in a notebook. Discuss these ideas with your parents. Are they based on Biblical principles? *(BIBLE / RESEARCH / READING)*

O. Ask your father to include you during actual episodes which call for discipline. He could take you aside when he comes across a problem during the day, and you could discuss together what you think God would want you to do when someone has sinned in a certain way. How do you think the offender should be disciplined? Why? Keep notes! *(BIBLE / FAMILY)*

P. Discuss as a family what the appropriate punishment should be for various offenses. Base your decisions on Scripture. Write down your ideas, and the Scripture verses to support them. *(BIBLE / FAMILY)*

Q. With your parents, study Jesus' example of dealing with Pharisees, His disciples, and others when they were in sin. List each situation, the Scripture passage that describes it, His response, and how we might apply the principles observed from His example in our daily discipline problems. (Use copies of the form on page 45.) *(FAMILY / LOGIC)*

R. Doorposts sells a chart called the *If-Then Chart*, which lists offenses, relevant Scriptures, and appropriate consequences. Design your own *If-Then Chart*. In the left hand column, list different common offenses that occur in your home. In the center column, write down Bible verses that tell why each offense is wrong. In the right hand column, write down what you think an appropriate discipline would be for each offense. Base your decisions on Scripture. (See form on page 46.) *(BIBLE / RESEARCH / LOGIC)*

S. Design a *Blessing Chart*. List godly character qualities. Then look up verses that describe God's blessings for those who have these qualities. Patterned after these verses, make a list of ways to encourage and reward children who show progress in developing these character qualities. *(BIBLE / FAMILY)*

T. 1 Peter 2:14 says that governors are sent to punish evildoers, and to praise them that do well. Think about ways to encourage children when they do well. Make a list of ideas, based on Scripture. *(BIBLE / LOGIC / FAMILY)*

U. Study the chapter in *For Instruction in Righteousness,* by Pam Forster, that addresses a particular sin with which you are struggling. List commandments about the sin, consequences of the sin, blessings of resisting the sin, things to which the Bible likens the sin, etc. Write a plan for how you would discipline a son of your own who sinned in this way. How would you encourage and reward him when he improves? *(BIBLE / READING / LOGIC)*

V. Read through the book of Proverbs, and make a list of the ways we are to punish the wicked and reward the righteous. Categorize according to different areas of sin. (Use the form on page 47.) *(BIBLE / READING / RESEARCH)*

W. Memorize Questions 123-130 and their answers from *The Westminster Larger Catechism* that address the roles of "superiors" and "inferiors." *(DOCTRINE)*

Advanced

X. Write a list of rules of behavior for a household. Base your rules on Scriptural principles. *(FAMILY / HANDWRITING)*

Y. Read the account of Moses' problems with judging the Israelites in Exodus 18. If you have younger siblings, ask your father if you could take on the responsibility of an "under-judge." Ask for authority to act as the hearer for disagreements between two particular children in your family. They would come to you first with any grievances they have been unable to settle by themselves. You would hear both sides, help them see their errors, and take them through Biblical steps of reconciliation. Take any cases you cannot handle, or which require disciplinary measures to your parents. You will want to go through *The Brother-Offended Checklist* with your father first. *For Instruction in Righteousness,* by Pam Forster, would also be a helpful tool as you talk to your siblings. *(LAW / BIBLE / FAMILY)*

Z. Discuss Jethro's advice to Moses (Exodus 18) with your father or write a short paper: How will you, when you become a husband and father, implement this advice in your household? *(BIBLE / FAMILY / MANAGEMENT)*

AA. If you have problems with people not cooperating with you when you are given authority over them, ask God to help you discern the reasons this might be happening. Are there sinful attitudes in your heart that might be leading people to resist your leadership? Are there sinful attitudes among those placed under you? Discuss the problem with them. Ask them what you could do to improve the situation. Ask forgiveness for any wrongs you have committed against them. Basing your decisions on Scripture, what can you do to exercise your authority in a more effective and godly manner? Write out your thoughts. *(LOGIC / HANDWRITING)*

BB. Observe a courtroom trial or follow a trial in the news. Is true justice being upheld? Do you agree with the final sentence? How does the Bible say the offender should be punished? *(BIBLE / LAW / CURRENT EVENTS)*

CC. Study 1 Peter 2:13-15 and other related passages on authority. What is the responsibility of those in authority? Who has granted them their authority? How will this affect your actions as a parent? How should it affect your responses as a son? Write out your findings. *(BIBLE / RESEARCH)*

DD. Complete the study "Discipline Faithfully" in Chapter 7 of *Prepare Thy Work,* by Daniel Forster. *(BIBLE / RESEARCH / FAMILY)*

EE. Read *Teach Them Diligently: How To Use the Scriptures in Child Training,* by Lou Priolo. Take careful notes to keep for future reference. What principles especially stand out to you in this book? In what ways will it change the way you want to train your children in the future? Use Appendix B, "Questions That Help Bring Conviction," to examine your own heart each day and to help you address wrongdoing with younger siblings. Purchase a copy of this book to use in your future home. *(BIBLE / FAMILY)*

FF. Read *Shepherding a Child's Heart,* by Tedd Tripp and *Instructing a Child's Heart,* by Tedd and Margy Tripp. Write a paper comparing and summarizing the two books. What are the main points of both? What principles from both books do you want to apply in your own family someday? *(BIBLE / FAMILY / ENGLISH COMPOSITION)*

GG. Accept positions of authority: baby-sitting, teaching a class, overseeing a project, etc. Use Biblical principles as you exercise your authority. *(TEACHING)*

HH. Read Part 6, "Building a Heritage," in *The Family: God's Weapon for Victory,* by Robert Andrews. If possible, read the book with your father, and discuss together the discussion questions at the end of each chapter. Finish reading the entire book, if you have not already done so. *(FAMILY)*

II. Study in the Bible: What are the dangers of delaying or overlooking discipline when it is needed? What happens to the child who has misbehaved? What happens to the parent who does not fulfill his responsibility as disciplinarian? Write out your findings. (Study Proverbs, Exodus, and Deuteronomy, and read about the families of David and Eli.) *(BIBLE / RESEARCH / FAMILY)*

Additional ideas:

Jesus' Example of Reproving

(See instructions in Project Q.)

EFERENCE	SITUATION	RESPONSE	PRINCIPLES TO APPLY

An "If-Then" Chart

(See instructions in Project R.)

MISBEHAVIOR	SCRIPTURE	CONSEQUENCE

Punishing the Wicked & Rewarding the Righteous

(See instructions in Project V.)

REFERENCE	REWARD RIGHTEOUS	PUNISH WICKED

Parents:

Consider and discuss with your son the following questions:

- Can he explain why an action is wrong?

- Can he explain why you discipline as you do?

- Does he understand that his misbehavior is sin against God?

- Does he recognize God's Word as **the** authority in all matters of justice?

- Is he able to find and refer to specific verses and scriptural principles that apply to particular discipline situations?

- Can he recite the Ten Commandments?

- Does he understand that God curses disobedience and blesses obedience?

- Can he think of appropriate discipline actions for children that would parallel the curses and discipline of God when we disobey Him?

- Does he have a basic sense of justice?

- Does he recognize God's mercy as well as His justice? Does he realize that God has not disciplined us as we truly deserve, but has given His Son to pay the penalty for our sin?

- How does he do when given authority? Does he treat those under him fairly? Does he show favoritism? Does he neglect to correct those who need correcting?

- Does he make an issue of every infraction, or is he willing to overlook minor offenses?

- Does he pass by when he knows a sibling or younger child is doing something wrong, or does he take time to correct him and explain why the action is wrong?

- Does he enjoy seeing others get into trouble?

- Does he get angry at siblings who wrong him, or is he able to reprove them in a loving, edifying way?

- When he corrects someone, is he doing it with a sincere desire for their good or is his correction motivated by annoyance or a critical spirit?

- When he is given authority over others, does he encourage and praise them, as well as correcting them when necessary?

- Is he a peacemaker? (He'll **have** to be as a father!)

Leadership: Overseeing Household Duties

"One that ruleth well his own house..." (1 Timothy 3:4).

After marriage our sons will have the lifelong job of overseeing all aspects of their households. We have the clear responsibility to train our sons in this skill!

Delegate responsibility to your sons, and hold them responsible for completion of the duties you have given them. Bring them alongside you as you plan your day, as you oversee the many aspects of home life, as you organize and lead those under you.

Many chapters in this book are dealing with different aspects of managing a household. This chapter focuses on the area of delegation and overseeing chores and maintenance duties in the home. A good husband, father, and family leader will instill a sense of teamwork in his wife and children. His leadership and wise management will inspire loyalty and motivate others to do their best for him.

A. Select verses from the list below, and use some or all of the following suggestions to help you study and better understand their meaning (easier verses are listed first, in italics):

1) Copy the passage.

2) Read it in several different translations of the Bible.

3) Read the passage and several of the verses before and after it to gain a better understanding of the context of the passage.

4) Rewrite the passage in your own words. What does it mean?

5) Record a specific way in which you can change your actions or attitudes based on the teaching of this passage.

6) Memorize the passage.

   Proverbs 12:24
   Proverbs 27:23
   1 Timothy 3:4
   1 Peter 5:2-3
   (BIBLE / SPEECH)

Beginner

B. Read about Joseph in Genesis 39. What job did he have in Potiphar's household? Draw a picture of him doing his job. How did he end up in prison?

Did he quit being a good worker when he was put in prison? Draw another picture of him working in the prison. Why do you think Potiphar and the prison keeper both gave Joseph authority and responsibility? Act out this story in your play time. *(BIBLE / ART / DRAMA)*

C. Make and post an illustrated list of the tasks that are required to keep your bedroom in order. Complete these tasks each day. *(ART)*

D. Make illustrated charts that list the tasks and chores that your parents want you and each of your younger siblings to complete each day. Post these on the wall where they will help each of you remember your responsibilities. *(ART / BUSINESS)*

E. Pick a project to do with your father or mother. Before starting the project, discuss the steps required to complete it, the materials needed, and the amount of time if might take. Gather any necessary supplies, and then complete the project. *(BUSINESS)*

F. Ask your parents to set up their own chore assignment system that you can use to assign and oversee chores done by your younger siblings. *(BUSINESS / FAMILY)*

G. Ask your parents to give you a list of tasks to be done by all the children by dinner time. As their delegated overseer, take the list, assign tasks, and see that all the jobs are completed. *(FAMILY / TEACHING / BUSINESS)*

H. Ask your parents to give you responsibility over an area of your household -- animals, room cleaning, car care, etc. Plan together with them all the basic tasks you will be responsible for, and then accept full responsibility for this area. Observe the results of your diligence or negligence. *(HOME SKILLS / AGRICULTURE / MECHANICS, ETC.)*

I. Take responsibility for keeping the inside of your family's car clean. Dust and vacuum it regularly. Make sure people throw away trash and take their things out when you come home from traveling in the car. *(HOME SKILLS / AUTO)*

J. Ask your parents to put you in charge of paying family members for chores if you are paid for some chores. (We had our oldest son keep track of all paid chores each day, total them at the end of the week, count out the pay and put it into each child's budget categories.) *(MATH / BUSINESS / BOOKKEEPING)*

Intermediate

K. Ask your parents to grant you authority over a particular household task (dishwashing, mowing the lawn, washing the car, etc.). Outline the steps required to complete the project, schedule out the various steps, assign the workers, and see the project to completion. Be sure to delegate responsibilities; a leader can't do all the work by himself. *(BUSINESS / TEACHING / FAMILY)*

L. Teach a new skill, or procedure for completing a new chore, to a younger sibling or other child. *(TEACHING)*

M. With your parents' permission, devise a method of organizing chores, and then put your plan into action. *(BUSINESS)*

N. Ask your parents to grant you authority over a particular area of your house or yard (garden, garage, basement, bedroom). Take responsibility for the upkeep of this area and enlist the assistance of others in your family. Oversee periodic cleanup times, if necessary. *(HOME SKILLS / BUSINESS)*

O. Work with your parents to schedule regular maintenance and seasonal jobs on a calendar. How often would you replace the furnace filter, change the oil in the car, clean out the gutters, lubricate appliances? When should you prune the trees and shrubs, order the garden seeds, put on the snow tires, add antifreeze to the car radiator, fill out the tax forms, etc.? Help complete these tasks as they become necessary. *(HOME SKILLS / PHYSICAL SCIENCE / MECHANICS / AGRICULTURE / BUSINESS)*

P. Act as the "man of the house" whenever your father is gone overnight or for an extended period of time. Assume responsibility for overseeing household duties, leading family worship time, supporting your mother when she is tired, etc. *(FAMILY)*

Q. Study the Bible for all instructions given to masters or those who exercise authority over those who work for them. What principles can you find? How can they be applied in daily life? (Look up "Master, Scriptures Relating to Masters of Servants" in *Nave's Topical Bible.*) *(BIBLE / RESEARCH / BUSINESS)*

R. Interview a manager of a store or other business. Make a list of questions you can ask about organizing tasks, overseeing others, etc. (i.e., "What do you do if someone is doing careless work?"). Tape record your interview, or take thorough notes so that you can summarize your findings in a report. What can you learn and apply in your own dealings with others? *(BUSINESS / ENGLISH COMPOSITION)*

S. Read the following chapters in *Emilie's Creative Home Organizer.* (Although this book is written by a woman and addressed primarily to women, these chapters contain information and hints that are helpful to men as well.)

- Storage
- The Garage
- The Automobile
- Time Savings
- Moving

(FAMILY / HOME SKILLS)

Advanced

T. Read pages 176-181 in *All the Way Home,* by Mary Pride. These pages offer creative ideas for encouraging and rewarding children who work hard at their chores and other work. Take notes. Try out some of the ideas you think are best. *(FAMILY / BUSINESS)*

U. Read the book *401 Ways to Get Your Kids to Work at Home*, by Bonnie Runyan McCullough and Susan Walker Monson. Try out some of the ideas with your younger siblings or with other children who need to work under you. *(READING / FAMILY / BUSINESS)*

V. Accept responsibility for a particular project at your church (maintenance, cleaning, organizing an event, etc.). Organize a team of people to complete the task and oversee their work until the job is finished. *(BUSINESS / COMMUNITY SERVICE)*

W. Find a project that your grandparents or an elderly neighbor would like to have completed. Organize a plan for completing the project and oversee the job to its completion. *(BUSINESS / COMMUNITY SERVICE)*

X. Accept full responsibility for one or more regular or seasonal maintenance projects at the home of your grandparents or an elderly neighbor (i.e. cleaning out gutters, raking leaves, putting up Christmas lights, changing oil in the car, cutting firewood). Schedule the jobs on your calendar, initiate the work, and make sure it gets completed. *(HOME SKILLS / BUSINESS / COMMUNITY SERVICE)*

Y. Discuss with your parents what your mother's role is in the family. How does she help your father? What areas of responsibility has he delegated to her? What are you looking for in a wife? How will she help you? How will you lead her? What areas do you think you will delegate to her? What will be your responsibility in areas that you have delegated to your wife? Write a paper explaining your ideas. *(FAMILY / COMPOSITION)*

Additional ideas:

Parents:

Consider and discuss with your son the following questions:

- Can you give him a job with the confidence that he will complete it properly?

- Can he organize and lead others in completing a job?

- Can he give clear instructions?

- Is he able to break a large job into a list of smaller tasks?

- Can he complete a short-term project without becoming distracted?

- Can he complete a long-term project without much oversight on your part?

- Can he evaluate work he and others have done and pinpoint areas that need improvement?

- Does he see a job through until it is completely finished?

- Does he lead workers under him in a humble way, or does he lord his authority over them?

- Does he work alongside those he is overseeing, or does he only watch and command?

- Does he assume leadership when no one else is leading?

- Does he view himself as part of the team in your family?

Notes and comments:

Leadership: Faithfulness in Family Worship

"...The father to the children shall make known thy truth" (Isaiah 38:19b).

Family worship is central to a healthy, spiritually growing family. Obviously, the first step in training our sons to be effective leaders in family worship is to have a consistent family worship time with our own family each day. Make this a priority. Make it a meaningful and worshipful time of bringing your family to God's Word. Spend time reading and discussing Scripture, singing psalms and hymns together, and praying together.

We should involve our sons and give them growing responsibility in leading the family in worship. Have them read Scripture, lead songs, lead in prayer, choose Scripture passages, plan special activities.

A. Select verses from the list below, and use some or all of the following suggestions to help you study and better understand their meaning (easier verses are listed first, in italics):

1) Copy the passage.

2) Read it in several different translations of the Bible.

3) Read the passage and several of the verses before and after it to gain a better understanding of the context of the passage.

4) Rewrite the passage in your own words. What does it mean?

5) Record a specific way in which you can change your actions or attitudes based on the teaching of this passage.

6) Memorize the passage.

   Isaiah 38:19
   Hebrews 3:13
   Deuteronomy 6:6-7
   Colossians 3:16
   James 5:16
   (SPEECH / BIBLE)

Beginner

B. Recite your memory verses once a week during family worship time. *(SPEECH / BIBLE)*

C. Under your father's direction, present a flannelgraph story for family worship time. *(SPEECH / TEACHING / BIBLE)*

D. Direct a family Bible drama time. Ask your father for a Bible story that he would like acted out during family Bible time. Organize your siblings, gather costumes and props, and oversee the performance. *(DRAMA / ART / BIBLE)*

E. Ask your father to allow you to read the Bible aloud for the family at a mealtime or family worship time. Practice reading the passage so that you can read it clearly. *(READING / SPEECH / BIBLE)*

F. Ask your father to allow you to lead in singing, playing the guitar or piano, praying, reading the Bible, etc. during family worship times. *(MUSIC / BIBLE / FAMILY)*

G. Proverbs has 31 chapters. If you start reading chapter one on the first of each month, you will have one chapter for each day of the month throughout the year. With your father's permission, select and read a Proverb from the day's chapter at breakfast each day. *(READING / BIBLE / SPEECH)*

H. Take responsibility to keep a current list of prayer requests from extended family members and friends. Ask about their particular needs and keep these in a list that the family can refer to when praying during family worship time. *(FAMILY / HANDWRITING)*

I. Under your father's direction, read from the Bible or from Bible storybooks for your younger siblings during family Bible study time. *(READING / BIBLE / FAMILY / TEACHER ED)*

J. Create a family hymnal for use in family worship time. Put sheet protectors into a small 3-ring notebook, and then slip copies of favorite hymns into the pages. Use this to help your family learn the words to hymns that are sung in your church. *(MUSIC / ART)*

K. Ask your father for the responsibility of recording prayer requests and answers to prayer in a family prayer journal. *(FAMILY / HANDWRITING / SPELLING)*

Intermediate

L. Thank your father for his commitment to leading the family in worship. Respectfully discuss the things you like and dislike about family worship. What could make your worship times more worshipful? What changes might you make? *(HANDWRITING)*

M. Under your father's direction, look for Scripture passages to be read on a certain topic for upcoming family worship times. *(RESEARCH / BIBLE)*

N. Discuss with your father: Why do you have family worship? If you don't have family worship, respectfully ask him why you don't. If he is interested, study the topic together. Read books about family worship and discuss them. Work together to make and implement plans for family worship in your home. *(FAMILY)*

O. If you do not already have one, create a family prayer journal. Use an empty book or spiral notebook, and divide pages into 2 columns -- one for requests and one for answers. You could also have separate pages for different family members, for missionaries, church family, etc. *(HANDWRITING / SPELLING / ART)*

P. Ask your father to give you a specific topic, and then plan and lead a family worship time that centers on that topic. *(RESEARCH / BIBLE)*

Q. Lead family worship time whenever your father is absent. *(FAMILY / BIBLE / MUSIC)*

R. Ask your father to give you regular responsibility for family worship time once a month. *(FAMILY / BIBLE)*

S. Work together with your father in planning activities for a week of family worship times or for Sunday afternoons. *(TEACHING / BIBLE / FAMILY)*

T. Teach your family a new song. Help them learn the words and lead them in singing it. *(MUSIC / TEACHING)*

U. Ask your father if you could select the songs to sing during some family worship times. Ask him to tell you what passage he will be reading from ahead of time, so that you can work at picking songs that would further expand on the meaning of the Scripture reading for the day. *(RESEARCH / MUSIC / BIBLE)*

V. Read the questions and answers on family worship at *www.FamilyWorshipGuide.net* and discuss them with your father. *(FAMILY)*

Advanced

W. Listen with your father to *The Joy of Family Worship: A Key to Healthy Body Life,* by R. C. Sproul, and discuss it together. *(FAMILY)*

X. Listen with your father to Steve Maxwell's talks, *Feed My Lambs: A Practical Guide to Daily Family Bible Time.* Discuss these talks with your father. What have you learned that will influence the way you lead your future family in worship? *(READING)*

Y. Read *Family-Driven Faith*, by Voddie Baucham, Jr., focusing especially on Chapter 7, "Mark the Home as God's Territory." Discuss with your father seven steps the author lists for beginning family worship and seven blessings families will experience when they worship together. *(FAMILY / TEACHER ED)*

Z. Complete the study "Make a Habit of Family Worship" in Chapter 7 of *Prepare Thy Work*, by Daniel Forster. *(BIBLE / RESEARCH / FAMILY)*

AA. Read and discuss with your father articles on family worship from the website for The Council on Biblical Manhood and Womanhood, *www.cbmw.org*. What is the biblical basis for family worship? What is the father's role in leading his family in worship? What message do we communicate to children when family worship is not a priority? *(RESEARCH / FAMILY)*

BB. Read "Implementing Family Worship," by Joel Beeke at *www.TruthforYourFamily.com*. Outline its main points. Which ideas might be helpful in your family's worship time? Which points do you want to remember when you lead your own future family? Discuss this with your father. *(RESEARCH / FAMILY / TEACHER ED)*

CC. Read "Family Worship," by A.W. Pink, at *www.TruthforYourFamily.com*. Outline Mr. Pink's main points and discuss them with your father. *(FAMILY / RESEARCH)*

DD. Study the section entitled "Bible Study on Family Religion," (pages 86-87) in Wayne Mack's book, *A Homework Manual for Biblical Living, Vol. 2*. *(BIBLE / RESEARCH / HANDWRITING)*

EE. Interview other Christian fathers. Ask them what they do for family worship, how they encourage Bible reading in their home, how they encourage singing, etc. Compile your findings into a report. *(FAMILY / ENGLISH COMPOSITION)*

FF. Keep a list of recommended Bible commentaries and study aids that you can refer to for help when you teach your future family from Scripture. Ask for recommendations from your father and other men. Locate reliable commentaries online. Start collecting print copies of the best for your personal library. *(RESEARCH / TEACHER ED)*

GG. Read and discuss with your father the last portion of James Alexander's book, *The Family*, which is entitled "Thoughts on Family Worship." Chapters 14-18 are especially helpful in discussing the reasons for, and elements of, family worship. Work together on implementing your conclusions. *(READING / FAMILY / BIBLE)*

HH. Read about and examine different books and helps that could be used for family worship times. Choose from those listed below or search for others online. Which ones appeal the most to you?

What materials can help you more effectively teach from Scripture? What can you use to help you lead them in singing? What helps could you enlist if you think you can't sing well? Make a list of the best resources and keep it in a notebook or on your computer for future reference. With your father's permission, use at least one of your favorites to occasionally lead your family in worship.

- *Advent and Christmas in Family Worship,* by Doug and Amy Hayes
- *The Book of Psalms: The Heart of the Word,* by Kevin Swanson
- *The Book of Psalms for Singing,* published by Crown and Covenant Publications
- *Cantus Christi* and 4-part accompaniment CD set, published by Canon Press
- *Disciplines of a Godly Man,* by R. Kent Hughes (Appendices D through I provide daily reading lists, a topical reading list, and hymn and chorus recommendations.)
- *The Family Worship Book: A Resource Guide for Family Devotions,* by Terry Johnson
- *Family Worship for the Christmas Season,* by Ray Rhodes, Jr.
- *Family Worship for the Reformation Season,* by Ray Rhodes, Jr.
- *FamilyWorshipGuide.net*
- *Family Worship Hymnal,* published by Christian Liberty Press
- *Hidden Treasures,* by Pam Forster
- *Hymns for Kith and Kin,* piano accompaniments to hymns recorded by Rebecca Serven
- *Morning and Evening,* by Charles Spurgeon
- *Table Talk,* published by Ligonier Ministries
- *Training Hearts, Teaching Minds,* by Starr Meade

(FAMILY / MUSIC / BIBLE / RESEARCH)

II. Subscribe to *www.FamilyWorshipGuide.net* to receive a daily guide for family worship, which lists Scripture passages for reading, hymns to sing, verses and catechism to memorize, and prayer suggestions. Explore the website for other aids. *(MUSIC / TEACHER ED.)*

JJ. Read Chapter 2, "Worship of God in Families: Is It by Divine Appointment?" in *The Godly Home,* by Richard Baxter. Outline the chapter and then discuss it with your father, summarizing Baxter's main theses and supporting arguments. *(FAMILY / RESEARCH / HISTORY)*

KK. Search online for resources that you could use when you lead your future family in worship. *(FAMILY / RESEARCH)*

Additional ideas:

Parents:

Consider and discuss with your son the following questions:

- Does he sit attentively during family worship time?

- Does he sit in a respectful way?

- Does he do things that distract others?

- Does he show respect for the reading of God's Word?

- Does he show respect in the way he handles the Bible?

- Does he read clearly when reading the Bible aloud for the family?

- Does he ask meaningful questions?

- Does he answer questions?

- Does he sing?

- Does he show reverence during times of prayer?

- Does he willingly pray aloud?

- Does he pray thoughtfully or mechanically?

- Does he willingly lead during family worship when you ask him to?

- Does he understand the importance of leading family worship in his own future household?

- Is he committed to leading family worship in his own future family and is he gathering knowledge and resources that will equip him to effectively do so?

Notes and comments:

Leadership: Providing a Godly Example

"...I will walk within my house with a perfect heart." (Psalm 101:2b).

Our exemplary lives before our children will be among the most powerful ways **they** learn to become good examples to others. (It seems like helping our children mature keeps requiring maturity from us, doesn't it?)

Are we setting a godly example before our sons? Are we setting one standard for our children while we live by another? Are our friends and their children people we want our children to emulate?

In an age of the movie superhero, we can help our sons develop true godly heroes by pointing out the godly men in their lives, telling them stories of great men in history, directing them to well-written biographies, and providing them with books, costumes and props that will encourage them to reenact the lives of these men in their play.

We can also help our sons realize how much others are watching them. Point out younger children who look up to them. Help them see when they have influenced others for good and for evil. And we can guard our sons' hearts as they choose their friends, their heroes, and their reading material.

A. Select verses from the list below, and use some or all of the following suggestions to help you study and better understand their meaning (easier verses are listed first, in italics):

1) Copy the passage.
2) Read it in several different translations of the Bible.
3) Read the passage and several of the verses before and after it to gain a better understanding of the context of the passage.
4) Rewrite the passage in your own words. What does it mean?
5) Record a specific way in which you can change your actions or attitudes based on the teaching of this passage.
6) Memorize the passage.

   Psalm 101:2
   Proverbs 4:11
   1 Corinthians 11:1
   Philippians 4:9
   John 13:14-15

Philippians 3:17
1 Timothy 4:12
Titus 2:7-8
1 Peter 2:21-24
(SPEECH / BIBLE)

Beginner

B. Draw a picture of your favorite hero. Is he someone you would want to be like? Why? Is he the kind of person God wants you to become? *(ART)*

C. Discuss with your father: Who are your heroes? Who do you imitate? Are you learning good habits from these heroes? Does your father have any suggestions of heroes you should admire? *(HISTORY / CURRENT EVENTS / ETC.)*

D. Discuss with your parents: What kind of example do you provide for those who watch you -- siblings, younger children, etc.? Do you lead them in doing what is right or in doing what is wrong? Write down plans for needed change. *(HANDWRITING)*

E. Read Matthew 5:14. Go with your parents to a dark place at night where you can see the light of a house or of a city up on a hill. How can you be a light on a hill in a dark world? *(BIBLE)*

F. Read with your parents Matthew 5:15-16. Draw a picture to illustrate the passage. How can you be like a candle on a candlestick in your household? *(BIBLE / ART)*

G. Read accounts of great men and heroes in Scripture (Noah, Abraham, Joseph, Moses, Joshua, David, etc.) What can you learn from their examples? What can you imitate in their lives that will enable you to be a better example to those who imitate you? *(BIBLE)*

H. Read one or all of the books in the *Lightkeepers* series, by Irene Howat:

- *Ten Boys Who Changed the World*
- *Ten Boys Who Didn't Give In*
- *Ten Boys Who Made a Difference*
- *Ten Boys Who Made History*
- *Ten Boys Who Used Their Talents*

What can you learn from each of these boys? *(HISTORY / READING)*

Intermediate

I. Study the word **leaven** as it is used as a picture of sin and evil influence in Scripture. What is leaven? How can it be like sin? *(CHEMISTRY / RESEARCH / BIBLE)*

J. Study how **salt** and a **light on a hill** are both used as examples of having a positive influence on those around us. Read commentaries on Matthew 5:13-16. What do these verses mean? *(CHEMISTRY / PHYSICAL SCIENCE / BIBLE / RESEARCH)*

K. Interview children with older brothers. What do they admire most in their big brothers? Why? What can you learn from their answers? Record your findings. *(SPEECH / WRITING)*

L. With the help of your parents, create your own **Checklist for Sons.** Write up a list of character qualities that you want to develop in your life. Write out questions that will help you examine yourself in light of what Scripture says about each of those qualities. Use this checklist to examine yourself at least once each week (perhaps on Sunday). In areas that you see weakness, try to write down specific actions and goals that you can attempt to complete during the week. *(BIBLE / HANDWRITING)*

M. Interview children, asking them to tell you the traits they most admire and value in their fathers. Record your findings. Are these traits ones that are present in your life? *(SPEECH / WRITING)*

N. Interview adults, asking them to tell you the traits they have most admired and valued in their fathers. Write up your findings. Are these traits ones that are present in your life? *(SPEECH / WRITING)*

O. Read all four volumes of *Hero Tales,* by Dave and Neta Jackson. What can you learn from the example of each of these people? *(READING / HISTORY)*

P. 1 Timothy 4:12 admonishes us to be examples in **word, conversation, charity, spirit, faith, and purity.** Evaluate your life in each of these areas. Are you following Jesus' example? Are you following the teaching of Scripture? Are you setting a **good** example for those around you? List specific goals and actions for improvement in each area. Share these with your parents, and pray with them for God's enabling power to change. *(BIBLE)*

Q. Make a list of the men in your life -- in your family, church, neighborhood, place of work, your "heroes," and the men you "know" through books, stories, and movies. Which ones are good examples? Which ones are bad examples? Why? Some of these men you can choose to not associate with if they are a bad influence. Others who are not a good example, you can learn from as you seek God's protection from their influence. And others, who are good and godly examples, you can follow, imitate, and thank for their faithfulness. *(HANDWRITING)*

R. Study Chapter 3, "Who Are the Men in Your Life?" and Chapter 38, "How do You Choose Your Heroes?" in *Christian Manhood* by Gary Maldaner. *(BIBLE)*

S. Interview wives, asking them to tell you what traits they value most in their husbands. *(SPEECH / WRITING / FAMILY)*

T. Write up a "character reference," as though you were applying for a job. Ask questions about your character. Are you honest, trustworthy, prompt, diligent, respectful, obedient, self-controlled, etc.? Give this reference to adults who know you well. Ask them to fill it out and give it to your parents. Ask your parents to fill it out as well. Discuss the answers with your parents. *(BUSINESS / WRITING)*

U. Read biographies of famous godly men. Keep a list of the books you read. Keep notes of lessons you learn from the lives of these men. *(READING / HISTORY)*

V. Choose one godly leader to study in detail. Read all you can about him. Share what you have learned about him with others. Write a paper, compile a notebook, or create a video presentation on the life of this man. *(READING / HISTORY)*

W. Look up the word "influence" in *Nave's Topical Bible.* Read through all the verses. What can you learn from these verses? Write a summary of your thoughts. *(BIBLE / RESEARCH)*

X. Ask your parents to observe your example. Keep a journal of their observations in the following areas:
- Peacemaking
- Charity/Kindness
- Patience
- Obedience
- Self-Control
- Orderliness

(WRITING)

Y. Study the effect of the examples set for you by siblings, friends, parents, elders. How have their examples affected your life? Are all their examples good ones, or have some had a negative effect on your life? Thank God for all the people He has sovereignly put in your life and for what He is teaching you through each of them. *(WRITING)*

Z. Think of men who have been godly examples to you. List the character qualities that you have admired in them. Interview them, and ask them how God has built these traits into their lives. Can they remember specific trials and experiences that God has used to help them mature in their Christian life?
(WRITING / SPEECH)

AA. Study the following verses that tell us about Christ's example. Write out your observations and specific actions that you can take in your life to follow His example.

Mark 10:43-45
Luke 22:27
John 13:13-17 and 34
Romans 15:2-7
2 Corinthians 8:9
Ephesians 5:1-2
Philippians 2:5-8
Colossians 3:13
Hebrews 12:2-3
1 Peter 2:21-25
1 John 2:6
Revelation 3:21
(BIBLE / WRITING)

BB. Conduct a word study in the Bible on the following words: **example, imitate, follow.** *(RESEARCH / BIBLE / GRAMMAR / FOREIGN LANGUAGE)*

CC. Study the lives of leaders in the Bible -- Abraham, Moses, Gideon, Joshua, David, and others. What can you learn from each of them about leading others? *(GOVERNMENT / FAMILY / BIBLE)*

Advanced

DD. Read one or all of the following biographies of great men from the *Leaders in Action* series:

- *All Things for Good: The Steadfast Fidelity of Stonewall Jackson,* by J. Steven Wilkins

- *Apostle of Liberty: The World-Changing Leadership of George Washington,* by Stephen McDowell

- *Call of Duty: The Sterling Nobility of Robert E. Lee,* by J. Steven Wilkins

- *Carry a Big Stick: The Uncommon Heroism of Theodore Roosevelt,* by George Grant
- *A Divine Light: The Spiritual Leadership of Jonathan Edwards,* by David Vaughan
- *For Kirk and Covenant: The Stalwart Courage of John Knox,* by Douglas Wilson
- *Forgotten Founding Father: The Heroic Legacy of George Whitefield,* by Stephen Mansfield
- *Give Me Liberty: The Uncompromising Statesmanship of Patrick Henry,* by David Vaughan
- *Glory and Honor: The Music and Artistic Legacy of Johann Sebastian Bach,* by Gregory Wilbur
- *A Heart Promptly Offered: The Revolutionary Leadership of John Calvin,* by David Hall
- *Never Give In: The Extraordinary Character of Winston Churchill,* by Stephen Mansfield
- *Not a Tame Lion: The Spiritual Legacy of C.S. Lewis,* by Terry Glaspey
- *Then Darkness Fled: The Liberating Wisdom of Booker T. Washington,* by Stephen Mansfield
- *Statesman and Saint: The Principled Politics of William Wilberforce,* by David Vaughan
- *A Place to Stand: The Word of God in the Life of Martin Luther,* by Gene Edward Veith

(HISTORY / READING)

EE. Study the examples of these men. What effect did they have on others? What can you learn from their examples?

Solomon

Nadab

Ahab

Ahaziah

Jeroboam

Manasseh

(HISTORY / BIBLE / GOVERNMENT)

FF. Study these men, and note the good influence they had on others:

Jonathan

Jehoshaphat

Azariah

Jotham

(HISTORY / BIBLE / GOVERNMENT)

GG. Study Christ's example. Read through the Gospels, listing passages that demonstrate the fruit of the Spirit (as listed in Galatians 5:22-23) in Jesus' life. Read also 2 Corinthians 8:7-9, Philippians 2:5-8, Colossians 3:13, 1 Peter 2:21-23, 1 John 3:3. List each Bible reference and the quality exhibited. *(BIBLE)*

HH. Complete the study "Set and Follow Good Examples" in Chapter 2 of *Prepare Thy Work*, by Daniel Forster. *(BIBLE / RESEARCH)*

II. Read through the following verses, noting Paul's example before others. Could you honestly say these things? Could people follow your example? Why or why not?

Acts 20:35

1 Corinthians 4:16

1 Corinthians 7:7-8

1 Corinthians 11:1

Philippians 3:17

Philippians 4:9

2 Thessalonians 3:7-10

1 Timothy 1:16

2 Timothy 1:13

(BIBLE)

JJ. Study the qualifications for elders that are listed in 1 Timothy 3:1-7 and Titus 1:5-9. Elders are supposed to be an example to those they lead. As a young man in leadership roles, and as a husband and father, you will need to be an example to those under you. Do you possess the qualities in your life that are listed in these passages? List the qualities that you do not possess. Then list ways to help build those qualities into your life. *(BIBLE / HANDWRITING)*

Additional ideas:

Parents:

Consider and discuss with your son the following questions:

- Does he admire godly or ungodly men?

- Does he look to Jesus as his example in life?

- Does he act in a way that you would want younger children to emulate?

- What habits and traits does he have that you would **not** want someone else to imitate? What can you do about it?

- Does he read books about men who provide a godly example?

- Does he consciously seek to set a good example to his peers?

- Does he consciously seek to set a good example for younger children?

- Does he lead others to sin or to greater righteousness?

- Does he understand the seriousness of leading others astray?

- Does he have a sincere desire to be a "light on a hill," living a godly life before others and pointing them to Christ?

Notes and comments:

Leadership: Exercising Initiative

"Therefore to him that knoweth to do good, and doeth it not, to him it is sin" (James 4:17).

A husband and father, if he is going to lead his family in the way God instructs *him, will need to exercise a great deal of initiative. As the head of his own family,* a son will be **leading**! That means he will initiate ideas, actions, discipline, projects, changes, etc. So **we** have the responsibility to train him!

A husband and father must have convictions and goals, based on godly principles, and then live his life in obedience to God as he pursues those goals. That requires initiative. He must choose to build his relationship with the Lord. He must choose to study the Word. He must choose to take action on what he learns from Scripture. He must choose to lead in a godly direction that will lead those under his authority to greater maturity.

His life will be full of decisions and circumstances that will require him to take action when no one else is telling him to. So he had better learn how to as a boy and as a young man!

The man is also the primary initiator in the marriage relationship, seeking and pursuing a wife, just as God chooses and pursues us. We can prepare our sons for a responsible and protective approach to courtship and marriage by teaching them to honor women and girls, especially their mother and sisters.

One of the best ways to train our sons to take initiative is to give them the opportunity! Teach them proper behavior, let them know what is expected of them, and then be willing to step back and let them make their decisions. If they do what is right of their own initiative, encourage and reward them. If they choose to ignore their responsibilities, let them suffer the consequence, correct them, and give them more opportunities to choose the right actions.

Make lists of daily required tasks. Then hold your sons responsible for their completion, without any reminders from you. We must resist the temptation to be constantly reminding our children of what they are supposed to be doing. But we must also be watchful and diligent to discipline them when they fail to discipline themselves.

A. Select verses from the list below, and use some or all of the following suggestions to help you study and better understand their meaning (Easier verses are listed first, in italics):

1) Copy the passage.

2) Read it in several different translations of the Bible.

3) Read the passage and several of the verses before and after it to gain a better understanding of the context of the passage.

4) Rewrite the passage in your own words. What does it mean?

5) Record a specific way in which you can change your actions or attitudes based on the teaching of this passage.

6) Memorize the passage.
   Proverbs 21:25
   Proverbs 26:13-14
   James 4:17
   Proverbs 6:6-8
   Proverbs 30:24-28
   Ecclesiastes 11:4
   Ecclesiastes 11:6
   Isaiah 6:8
   Luke 12:47
   1 Corinthians 9:24
   Galatians 6:10
   (SPEECH / BIBLE)

Beginner

B. Read with your parents the story of David and Goliath in 1 Samuel 17. Act out the story with your siblings, friends, or toys, or draw a picture to illustrate the story. Did anyone ask David to fight Goliath? Why did he do it? *(BIBLE / ART)*

C. Read Proverbs 6:6-8 with your parents. Then find some ants outside. Drop some small crumbs on the ground or pavement and watch to see what the ants will do. *(SCIENCE)*

D. Draw a picture to illustrate Ecclesiastes 10:18. *(BIBLE / ART)*

E. How can you be a helper in your home? Ask your parents to help you make a list of ideas and draw a picture next to each idea. Post this list on a wall, and use it to help you remember ways to be helpful without being asked. *(ART / HOME SKILLS)*

F. Do all your chores in a day before someone tells you to do them! *(HOME SKILLS)*

G. Do all your schoolwork in a day before someone tells you to do it! *(TIME MANAGEMENT)*

H. See how many things you can pick up and put away in a day without being told. Keep count. Try to do even better tomorrow! *(HOME SKILLS)*

I. See if you can be the first to be the peacemaker in disagreements throughout the day. *(SOCIAL SKILLS)*

J. Purchase or start your own ant farm. Watch the ants. What do they do? Do certain ants do particular tasks? Who directs the activities of the ants? How can you be like an ant? *(SCIENCE)*

K. Write your own daily checklist. List each regular task or activity you have each day, make columns for each day of the week, and check off when you complete each task. *(HANDWRITING)*

L. Work on learning to initiate. On one day, try to initiate at least **one** thing. Write down what it was. On the next day, initiate at least **two** things. On the next day, initiate **three** things, etc. Keep a record of what you have done. *(HANDWRITING)*

M. With your parents, study the chapter on "Laziness" in *For Instruction in Righteousness,* by Pam Forster. *(BIBLE)*

N. Make a list of specific people in your family, church, and neighborhood. List specific things you can do to encourage and help them. Then start doing some! *(HANDWRITING / COMMUNITY SERVICE)*

O. See how many things you can do during the day before someone tells you to do them! *(FAMILY / HOME SKILLS)*

P. Learn to initiate reading your Bible every day. Set a goal of reading your Bible **every day** for an entire year. Give yourself some sort of reward (or maybe your parents can!) if you succeed. *(BIBLE / READING)*

Intermediate

Q. Look for a problem in your household and solve it! *(LOGIC / ECONOMICS / CARPENTRY, ETC.)*

R. Study Proverbs 30:24-28. Then study ants, conies, locusts, and spiders. How does each show initiative? Record all that you learn about them, and how you can apply what you learn. *(BIOLOGY / RESEARCH / WRITING)*

S. Watch your father for a day. Write down everything you see him do that no one told him to do. *(FAMILY / HANDWRITING)*

T. Keep notes on your own activities for a day. Or ask someone else to observe you. Write down everything you do without anyone else telling you to. *(HANDWRITING)*

U.   Learn to **see** things that need to be done. You can't initiate an action unless you see that it needs to be done. On one day watch specifically for ways to help keep the house clean. On another, watch for ways to encourage others. Devote separate days to looking for specific ways to share, ways to show honor, ways to make peace, ways to help parents, and so on. Write down everything you think of, and then start **doing** the things you have listed!
(FAMILY / HOME SKILLS)

V.   Compliment your sisters, tell them you love them, help them with tasks, hug them, protect them, and treat them politely. This will not only encourage your sisters; it will also prepare you to be the initiator in expressing care and affection for your future wife. *(FAMILY / SOCIAL SKILLS)*

W.   Study James 4:13-17 with your parents. What does it say about doing what is right? Write a short essay about the meaning and application of this verse.
(BIBLE / ENGLISH COMPOSITION)

X.   Study how these Bible characters exercised initiative. What might have happened differently if they had not shown initiative?

Jacob in reconciling with Esau

Joseph in Egypt

Jethro with Moses

Abigail

The Good Samaritan

Ruth

Jael

(BIBLE / READING)

Y.   Study the chapter entitled "Initiative" in *Christian Character*, by Gary Maldaner, pages 70-75. *(READING / BIBLE / WRITING)*

Z.   If you are homeschooling, ask your parents to give you a weekly list of assignments for school. Work on completing the assignments by the end of the week without any reminders from your parents. *(TEACHING)*

AA.   Plan ahead for a holiday or birthday. Take initiative in preparing and planning for a day that will be special for others. *(MANNERS / ART / HISTORY, ETC.)*

BB.   When your parents give you a project or job to complete, ask them to give you a deadline, or set a deadline for yourself. Work on the job until it is complete, without any reminders. *(BUSINESS EDUCATION)*

CC. Work at initiating conversation. When visitors attend your church, go and speak to them. Initiate a polite greeting to adults. Politely ask questions when you need help. Place the order in a restaurant. Make phone calls to find prices, etc. Keep a record of these times. (See form on page 77.) *(MANNERS / SPEECH / HANDWRITING)*

DD. Find something in your house that needs to be repaired. Ask your father for instructions, or learn how to make the repairs from a book. Then fix it! *(HOME SKILLS / FAMILY)*

EE. Read *Do Hard Things: A Teenage Rebellion Against Low Expectations,* by Alex and Brett Harris. Discuss the book with your parents or friends. What hard things is God calling you to do? Are you doing them? What can you do to start? *(READING)*

FF. Follow The Rebelution's blog at *www.therebelution.com/blog.* Read past posts and discuss them with your family and friends. *(READING / SOCIAL SKILLS / COMPUTER)*

GG. Read *Generation Change: Roll Up Your Sleeves and Change the World,* by Zach Hunter. What has God impressed most on your mind after reading this book? Write down your thoughts and any goals you would like to set. *(READING)*

Advanced

HH. If you are working outside the home or busy with studies and social activities, be sure to continue to take initiative at home. Look for ways to contribute to the household. Fix things that need fixing. Put things away that are out of place. Help with household chores. Commit to devoting time and attention to these tasks without being asked. *(TIME MANAGEMENT / HOME SKILLS / FAMILY)*

II. Study the "Parable of the Talents," in Matthew 25:14-30 and Luke 19:12-27. Write a paper on how it relates to the responsibility of taking initiative. *(BIBLE / ENGLISH COMPOSITION)*

JJ. Write a short paper or discuss with your parents or a friend: How useful is talent alone? What do we need to add to God-given abilities to make them useful for His kingdom? *(ENGLISH COMPOSITION)*

KK. Complete the study "Take Initiative" in Chapter 2 of *Prepare Thy Work*, by Daniel Forster. *(BIBLE / RESEARCH)*

LL. Think about the following questions and record your answers: What talents has God given you? Are you being a good steward of His gifts? What specific steps can you take to better use your gifts? *(CAREER ED)*

MM. Study through the chapter. "Problem Solving" (pages 152-153) in Wayne Mack's book, *A Homework Manual for Biblical Living, Vol. 1.* *(LOGIC / WRITING / BIBLE)*

NN. Study the chapter, "Sorting Out Responsibilities," (pages 29-32) in Wayne Mack's book, *A Homework Manual for Biblical Living, Vol. 2.* Answer the questions according to how you think household responsibilities should be divided between you and your future wife. Are you preparing yourself for the responsibilities that will be yours? *(FAMILY / BUSINESS)*

OO. Study **election** and **predestination.** Organize your notes into a paper. How does God's choosing us before we loved Him demonstrate initiative? How can a young man picture this when he seeks and marries a wife? *(DOCTRINE / FAMILY)*

PP. Study Christ's life. In what ways did He demonstrate initiative? Summarize your observations in a short essay. In what ways can you imitate Him in your daily life? *(BIBLE)*

Additional ideas:

Record of Initiated Conversations

(See instructions in Project CC.)

DATE	WITH WHOM	WHERE	WHAT I SAID

Parents:

Consider and discuss with your son the following questions:

- Does he wait to be told -- to clean his room, do his chores, brush his teeth, do his schoolwork, etc.?

- Has he trained himself to **see** needs?

- Does he do something when he sees a need? (i.e. helping others, picking up things on the floor, fixing something)

- How does he behave when you are not around?

- Does he only work when someone is watching him?

- When you ask "someone" in the family to do a task, does he volunteer or try to look invisible?

- Does he wait for someone else to do a needed job?

- Does he ask questions when he needs to know what to do next, or does he use ignorance as an excuse for inaction?

- Does he try to come up with a solution to a problem, or does he only complain?

- Does he greet people first, or wait until after they have addressed him?

- Does he seek to be the peacemaker in disagreements?

- Can you assign him tasks or give him a series of instructions, and know that he will complete them without further prodding?

- Can he do regular daily chores without being reminded?

Notes and comments:

Leadership: Making Godly Decisions

"Trust in the LORD with all thine heart; and lean not unto thine own understanding. In all thy ways acknowledge him, and he shall direct thy paths" (Proverbs 3:5-6).

Every man's life is full of decisions. A godly man must decide again and again to say "no" to his flesh and "yes" to his Lord. His decisions affect not only his life, but also the lives of those around him.

We need to be sure we give our sons the opportunity to make decisions. How will they ever learn to make wise choices if they never get to practice? We need to disciple our sons in this area. It often seems easier to make a decision for them, than to take the time to train them in the steps that will lead them to making their own wise decision.

A husband who has never learned to make decisions will turn to his wife to lead the family in this area. A husband who has never built the principles of God's Word into his life will make unwise and harmful decisions. As a son matures, after years of diligent training, he should be granted more and more freedom in making his own well-counseled, godly decisions.

When a son has transgressed your law (and God's), it is good to remind him that he **decided** to do this. He has chosen cursing over blessing when he disobeys. He is personally responsible for his actions and their consequences.

A. Select verses from the list below, and use some or all of the following suggestions to help you study and better understand their meaning (easier verses are listed first, in italics):

1) Copy the passage.
2) Read it in several different translations of the Bible.
3) Read the passage and several of the verses before and after it to gain a better understanding of the context of the passage.
4) Rewrite the passage in your own words. What does it mean?
5) Record a specific way in which you can change your actions or attitudes based on the teaching of this passage.
6) Memorize the passage.

   Psalm 32:8
   Psalm 119:66

Proverbs 3:5-6
Proverbs 9:10
Proverbs 11:3
Matthew 6:24
John 16:13
James 1:5-8
(BIBLE / SPEECH)

Beginner

B. Pray daily for your father who must make many decisions each day. Pray that God will give him wisdom. *(FAMILY / DEVOTIONS)*

C. Notice times throughout the day when you must make a decision. You decide how to respond when someone is unkind to you, when you want something you don't have, when you are told to do something, etc. Are you making good decisions? Are they the kind of decisions God wants you to make? *(SOCIAL SKILLS)*

D. Read with your parents James 1:5-8. What do these verses mean? Draw a picture to illustrate them.

E. When you have sinned and are being disciplined, learn to acknowledge your responsibility. Say, "I decided to do the wrong thing. It was a poor decision. Will you forgive me? I will do better next time." *(SOCIAL SKILLS)*

F. Read with your parents about Solomon's son, Rehoboam, in 1 Kings 12. Did Rehoboam make a wise decision? What was the result of his decision? *(BIBLE)*

G. Read with your parents about Lot's decision in Genesis 13. What was Lot deciding? Did he decide wisely? Read Genesis 19. Was Sodom a good place for Lot and his family to live? Draw a picture to illustrate what happened to Sodom and to Lot and his family. *(BIBLE / ART)*

H. Listen to your father read a chapter of Proverbs each day until you have heard the entire book of Proverbs. As you listen, notice each time a Proverb speaks about wisdom. Write down (or ask your father to write for you) the references and notes about each verse. When you have finished, review all the verses you have recorded and discuss what you can learn about wisdom and making wise decisions. *(BIBLE / WRITING)*

I. Pray for God's guidance when your family needs to make an important decision. Write down your prayer requests and record God's answers.
(HANDWRITING)

J. At the end of the day, review with your parents the decisions you made throughout the day. Talk about the good and bad decisions. What was the outcome of each? Which Biblical principles did you follow? Which did you violate? *(BIBLE / LOGIC)*

K. Read through the book of Proverbs with your parents. Use the form on page 85 to list each time a fool or wise man is mentioned. Write down the reference, what the verse says each man is like, and what the verse says will happen to him. *(BIBLE / RESEARCH / READING / WRITING)*

L. Study Proverbs 1-9 with your parents. What is the source of wisdom? What are the results of acquiring wisdom? To what is its value compared? What commands are given? *(HANDWRITING)*

M. Read the following verses about the fool.

Proverbs 12:15
Proverbs 18:2
Proverbs 26:11
Proverbs 27:22
Proverbs 28:26

Make a small booklet to illustrate these verses. What kind of decisions does the fool make? What can you do to avoid becoming a fool? *(BIBLE / RESEARCH)*

N. With your parents, study the chapter entitled "Easily Swayed/Double-Minded" in *For Instruction in Righteousness,* by Pam Forster. *(BIBLE)*

Intermediate

O. Read a chapter of Proverbs each day until you have read the entire book. As you read, notice each time a proverb speaks about planning, decisions, and counsel. Write down the references and notes about each verse. Review your list of verses and notes and then tell your father what you have learned about decision-making from Proverbs. *(BIBLE / WRITING)*

P. Make a list of godly people to whom you will go for counsel when making decisions. Write down their names and phone numbers (when needed) for easy reference. *(WRITING / RESEARCH)*

Q. Study the phrase "the fear of the Lord" in the Bible. Look up "Fear of God" in *Nave's Topical Bible.* What does it mean? What happens to the man who fears the Lord? Write out references where the phrase is found, read the verses, and summarize their meaning. *(BIBLE / RESEARCH / WRITING)*

R. Do a topical study in the Bible on **the will of God**. Look up "Will, Of God, the Supreme Rule of Duty," in *Nave's Topical Bible*. *(BIBLE / RESEARCH / WRITING)*

S. Look up verses that include the phrase "the will of God." All God's Word is a statement of His will, but these passages are drawing our attention to specific aspects of it. List each of these verses and what they state God's will to be. Review this list when making difficult decisions. *(BIBLE / RESEARCH / WRITING)*

T. Do a topical study in the Bible on **guidance**. *(BIBLE / RESEARCH / WRITING)*

U. Study Psalm 25:9. What does "meek" mean? What does God promise to the meek? Are you meek? *(BIBLE / RESEARCH / FOREIGN LANGUAGE)*

V. Study the chapter on "Decisiveness" in *Christian Character*, by Gary Maldaner, pages 14-17. *(BIBLE / READING / WRITING)*

W. When facing a decision, answer these questions: Will this action bring glory to God? Does the action I am considering contradict any known laws, commandments, prohibitions, or principles of Scripture? *(BIBLE)*

X. Interview fathers and others, asking them to give you accounts of God's guidance and provision in their lives. What can you learn from these stories? Tell some of these stories to your family. *(SPEECH / FAMILY / WRITING / HISTORY)*

Y. Interview fathers and others, asking them to give you accounts of times when they made bad decisions. What principles did they violate? What did they learn from their mistakes? What can you learn from them? Write a summary of your findings. *(SPEECH / FAMILY / WRITING / HISTORY)*

Z. Study the lives of the following men. Find points in their lives when they had to make a decision. What did each decide? Was it a good or bad decision? What was the result of the decision?

Abel
Noah
Abraham
Jacob
Joseph
Moses
Israelites in wilderness
Caleb
Balaam
Gideon
Joshua

David

Namaan

Jehu

Josiah

Nehemiah

(BIBLE / HISTORY / GOVERNMENT)

AA. Study the following verses and write down what they say about the results of meditating on God's commandments:

Psalm 119:9-11, 24, 66, 98-101, 104, 105, 130, 165

(BIBLE / HANDWRITING)

Advanced

BB. Complete the Bible study *How To Make Choices You Won't Regret,* by Kay Arthur and BJ and David Lawson. *(BIBLE / READING)*

CC. When facing a difficult decision, divide a paper into 2 halves. On one side list all the positive reasons for deciding a certain way. On the other side, list the negative reasons. *(LOGIC)*

DD. When facing a decision, pray for discernment as you write a list of the things you need or desire in this decision. Write down a specific description, and then take appropriate actions while praying for God to lead. (For example, if you are deciding on a college to attend, you might list: "1. Near a good, theologically sound church 2. Opportunity to live with a family 3. Scholarship 4. Within four hours of home. 5. Good program in my chosen field of study." Then while you pray, you would do your research.) *(WRITING)*

EE. When facing a decision, study the Bible to find the principles that apply. Use the wisdom of Scripture and the examples in Bible stories to help you make your decision. *(BIBLE / RESEARCH)*

FF. Work alongside your father when he is making decisions involving the family. Discuss pros and cons and the biblical principles that guide his decision. *(FAMILY)*

GG. Complete the study "Make Wise Decisions" in Chapter 2 of *Prepare Thy Work*, by Daniel Forster. *(BIBLE / RESEARCH)*

HH. Read *Step by Step,* by James C. Petty. What did God speak to you about most powerfully in this book? How will this affect your daily decision-making? *(READING)*

II.   Read *Just Do Something,* by Kevin DeYoung. Outline each chapter and then write a review of the book that you can share with others. *(READING / WRITING)*

JJ.   Study the chapter entitled "Problem Solving" (pages 152-153) in Wayne Mack's book, *A Homework Manual for Biblical Living, Vol. 1.* *(FAMILY / BIBLE)*

Additional ideas:

Comparing the Wise Man & the Fool

(See instructions in Project K.)

WHAT WISE MAN DOES	REF.	RESULTS	WHAT FOOLISH MAN DOES	REF.	RESULTS

Parents:

Consider and discuss with your son the following questions:

- Does he generally make wise decisions?
- Does he correctly choose between right and wrong?
- Does he avoid making decisions?
- Does he wait for someone else to decide for him?
- Does he blame poor decisions on someone else?
- Can he weigh the pros and cons of a decision?
- Does he know how to study the Bible for guidance in decision-making?
- Does he seek the counsel of those older and wiser than he?
- Does he have difficulty making simple decisions?
- Is he easily swayed by what he thinks someone else would want him to do?
- Does he make decisions based on conviction or on feelings?
- Does he pray for God's wisdom?

Notes and comments:

Leadership: Planning and Organizing

"...The prudent man looketh well to his going" (Proverbs 14:15b).

God is a God of order. He wants His children to reflect His character in their orderliness.

A disorganized life does not bring glory to God. It wastes the precious and brief time He has given us to do His will here on earth. It inconveniences and annoys others instead of putting their needs and desires before our own. It reflects a slothful spirit.

A son who has not learned the habit of organizing himself and his time will flounder as a leader in his home. How will he teach his children orderliness? How will he protect those under him if he has not learned to consider potential dangers and pitfalls? How will he set goals for maturity in the lives of those he leads, if he has no spiritual goals for himself? How will his family follow him if he has no goal toward which he is leading them?

As the saying goes, if we aim at nothing, we will hit it every time! If we desire God's best for our sons (and their families), we must teach them to discern God's will, motivate them to set goals in accordance with God's Word, and disciple them in the character and skills they will need to realize those goals.

A. Select verses from the list below, and use some or all of the following suggestions to help you study and better understand their meaning (easier verses are listed first, in italics):

1) Copy the passage.

2) Read it in several different translations of the Bible.

3) Read the passage and several of the verses before and after it to gain a better understanding of the context of the passage.

4) Rewrite the passage in your own words. What does it mean?

5) Record a specific way in which you can change your actions or attitudes based on the teaching of this passage.

6) Memorize the passage.

   Proverbs 16:9
   Proverbs 22:3
   Psalm 112:5
   Proverbs 13:16

Proverbs 14:15
Proverbs 19:2
Proverbs 24:27
(BIBLE / SPEECH)

Beginner

B. Read and talk about 1 Corinthians 9:24 with your parents. What prize do we as Christians seek to win? Draw a picture to illustrate the verse and post it in your room. *(BIBLE / ART)*

C. Put away your clothes at the end of the day. Put dirty clothes in a laundry hamper and clean clothes neatly in their proper places. *(HEALTH / HOME SKILLS)*

D. Read with your parents Proverbs 24:27. Act this proverb out with your siblings. What does it mean?

E. Put away toys and books before getting out new playthings. *(HOME SKILLS)*

F. Read with your parents in Genesis 41 the story of Joseph helping the Egyptians prepare for famine. What did Joseph do to save the Egyptians and his own people? Act this story out with your siblings or with toys. *(BIBLE / DRAMA)*

G. Read with your parents Luke 14:28-33. Discuss these words that Jesus spoke and draw an illustration. *(BIBLE / ART)*

H. Organize your personal belongings — drawers, closet, desk, toys, books, collections, etc. Ask for guidance if you are not naturally organized. Ask your parents to help label drawers, provide storage space, and inspect on a regular basis. *(HOME SKILLS)*

I. Work with your parents in listing tasks which must be completed in a day. Plan your day to complete these tasks. *(BUSINESS EDUCATION / WRITING)*

J. Save your money for a special purchase or project. Determine how long it should take to save the required amount. Ask your parents to help you plan ways to earn money. *(FINANCES)*

K. Ask your parents for a daily checklist of tasks which must be completed by a certain time each day. Agree on consequences for the times when tasks are not completed (extra chores, longer practicing time at the piano, etc.). Accept the responsibility for completing these tasks without reminders from your parents. Accept the consequences when you fail to complete your tasks. *(BUSINESS EDUCATION / FAMILY)*

L. With your parents' guidance, make a list of tasks that could be done in a day. Prioritize the tasks, from least to most important. *(TIME MANAGEMENT / FAMILY)*

M. With your parents' guidance, list the tasks you should do during the next week. Prioritize the tasks, then do them. *(BUSINESS EDUCATION / FAMILY)*

N. Under your parents' guidance, plan a family outing — where to go, what to take, etc. *(FAMILY)*

Intermediate

O. At the beginning of each week, list all major tasks you need to complete, along with appointments and other scheduled commitments. Then, at the beginning of each day, look at your list for the week and make a list of the day's tasks. Cross off each task as you complete it throughout the day. Review your list at the end of the day, and carry any uncompleted jobs on to the list for the following day. *(TIME MANAGEMENT)*

P. Work with your father and/or mother on organizing something. Start with a tool chest, tackle box, or bookshelf. Help clean and organize the basement, garage, or pantry. Offer creative ideas. Some suggestions may be used, and your parents can explain why others are impractical. *(HOME SKILLS)*

Q. With your parents' permission, plan a party — a birthday party for one of your siblings or a party for your friends. Ask for a budget to work within, and plan refreshments, games, decorations, etc. Or work to earn the money to pay for the party yourself. *(FAMILY / FINANCES / ART / P.E.)*

R. Help your mother with her homeschool record-keeping. *(TEACHING / BOOKKEEPING / BUSINESS)*

S. With your parents' guidance, select and faithfully use a method for organizing your responsibilities and schedule — calendar, notebook, planning book, etc. *(BUSINESS EDUCATION / FAMILY)*

T. Study the chapter on "Haste" in *For Instruction in Righteousness,* by Pam Forster. *(BIBLE)*

U. Ask for a list of school assignments which must be completed by the end of the week. Plan your time for completing them. Don't tempt your parents to nag you! (A younger son can start out by listing one day's assignments.) *(TEACHING / TIME MANAGEMENT)*

V.   Design a project with a deadline. List all elements of the project and schedule your time in order to finish by the deadline. (A younger son should ask for help with scheduling.) *(WRITING / MATH)*

W.   Choose one goal you would like to reach in your spiritual life (i.e., reading the Bible every day, learning to study the Bible, memorizing more Scripture, showing Christ-like love to others, overcoming a particular habitual sin). Make a list of steps you can take to reach that goal. *(BIBLE / WRITING)*

X.   Write a short-range plan to earn money to purchase a desired item. What are you working toward? Where is it? How much does it cost? When will you buy it? Why do you need it? How will you obtain it? *(RESEARCH / FINANCES / WRITING / MATH)*

Y.   Write a plan that will guide you in reading through the entire Bible in one year. *(BIBLE / READING)*

Z.   Ask to be involved in the selection and purchase of homeschool curriculum and the planning of the school year. Attend a homeschool curriculum exhibit with your parents. Ask your father for input. Make these plans for your own schooling or for one of your siblings. *(TEACHING / FINANCES)*

AA. Learn to plan school assignments for another child. Write out assignments, due dates, etc. *(TEACHING)*

BB. Plan an outing or field trip for your family. Make all necessary preparations and lead in cleanup tasks when the trip is completed. *(GEOGRAPHY / FAMILY / RESEARCH)*

CC. Plan activities to involve younger children during your mom's homeschool support group meeting. Organize other young people to help you lead the children in these activities. *(ART / P.E. / MUSIC / WRITING)*

DD. Plan a way to help and encourage each widow in your church, or each elderly couple, or each family with special needs. Write out your ideas and put at least a portion of your plan into action. If possible, get others involved. Lead in establishing a program to minister to these needy people. *(WRITING / FAMILY / COMMUNITY SERVICE)*

EE. Write a list of ways to fight abortion. Publish your list in your church newsletter or in the local paper. *(POLITICS / WRITING)*

FF. Plan a vacation trip (real or imaginary). Research, gather maps and information, write packing lists, prepare a budget, make reservations (or list phone numbers and dates if you are planning an imaginary trip). Figure mileage, costs, etc. *(GEOGRAPHY / RESEARCH / FINANCES / MATH)*

GG. Read *Clutter's Last Stand*, by Don Aslett. Take notes and implement ideas from the book. *(READING / WRITING / HOME SKILLS)*

HH. Work with your parents in planning projects and goals that are outlined in this book. Write in dates to show when you plan to work on memory work, studies, training in home skills, etc. *(FAMILY / WRITING)*

II. Write a long range plan to prepare for your lifetime vocation. Consider what career you might choose to pursue, and then outline training needs, volunteer opportunities and other ways to gain experience in the field, costs involved, etc. *(BUSINESS / FINANCES / RESEARCH)*

JJ. Study the word **prudent** as it is used in Scripture. *(GRAMMAR / FOREIGN LANGUAGE / WRITING / RESEARCH / READING)*

KK. Write out goals for courtship as you wait on the Lord to provide your lifelong mate. What kind of person are you seeking in a wife? What will be your approach to courtship/dating? *(WRITING / BIBLE / FAMILY)*

LL. Plan a business venture -- describe the product or service, plan the finances, outline the steps to bring your idea to fruition (how you will market it, what you will need, etc.). If possible, put this plan into action. *(BUSINESS EDUCATION / MATH / WRITING)*

Advanced

MM. Read and study Philippians 3:10-14. How should these verses influence the way you live your life? Write a list of life goals that are guided by the message of this passage. *(TIME MANAGEMENT / BIBLE / WRITING)*

NN. Write a list of specific actions you can take to grow in a particular area (social skills, public speaking, showing love to your siblings, etc.). Schedule at least one of these actions each week until you have completed your list. Reevaluate. Do you still need to grow in this area? List more actions you can take, and continue working through your list. *(SOCIAL SKILLS / FAMILY)*

OO. Write a list of goals that will help you prepare for marriage. Assign time frames to your goals. Work to reach your goals by the designated times. *(TIME MANAGEMENT)*

PP. Write out basic long term goals that you want to have as a future husband. *(BIBLE / FAMILY / WRITING)*

QQ. Write out basic long-term goals that you want to have as a future father. *(BIBLE / FAMILY / WRITING)*

RR. Read Chapter 10, "The Discipline of Time," in *Discipline: The Glad Surrender,* by Elisabeth Elliot. What points stand out most to you in this chapter? What one thing will you do differently after reading this? *(TIME MANAGEMENT)*

SS. Listen to Gregg Harris's *Seasons of Life Seminar* (on MP3 from *www.noblebooks.org*). Think through the various stages of your life -- boyhood, teen years, young adulthood, early marriage, fatherhood, grandfatherhood. Write down goals that you have for each of those seasons of life. *(FAMILY / BIBLE)*

TT. Listen to Gregg Harris's *Noble Planner Time Management Seminar* (on MP3 from *www.noblebooks.org*) which teaches Christian time-management principles. *(FAMILY / BIBLE / BUSINESS / FINANCES)*

UU. Design a form that will be useful to your family's business, your own business efforts, or a fictitious business (i.e., a form to help keep track of inventory, a checklist of tasks that must be completed on a regular basis, etc.) *(BUSINESS / WRITING / MATH / COMPUTER)*

VV. Practice writing a will using a common will kit, or ask to see and study your parents' will. *(FAMILY)*

WW. Study various options for life insurance. What are the advantages and disadvantages of each type? Which do you think is best? *(FAMILY / FINANCES)*

XX. Study the various options for retirement plans. Which one do you think is best? *(MATH / ECONOMICS / FAMILY)*

YY. Study through the chapter entitled "Planning and Priorities" (pages 132-143) in Wayne Mack's book, *A Homework Manual for Biblical Living, Vol. 1.* *(BIBLE / WRITING)*

Additional ideas:

Parents:

Consider and discuss with your son the following questions:

- Does he think ahead?

- Can he foresee dangers and pitfalls?

- Can he use his time wisely to meet deadlines, or is he always hurrying to complete tasks at the last minute?

- Can he think through the steps required to finish a project?

- Can he make a list of tasks, prioritize, and complete them?

- Can he break a large or long-term project into smaller, sequential steps that lead to completion?

- Can he find his clothes, school books, sports equipment, etc. when needed?

- Is he usually prompt?

- Does he leave messes behind him?

- Is his room orderly and clean?

- Can he prioritize a list of tasks, knowing which ones are most important, which to do first?

- Can he plan and carry out a solution to a problem?

- Can he keep track of appointments?

- Does he forget commitments he has made?

- Does he recognize his time and energy limits when making commitments?

Notes and comments:

Leadership: Influencing the Community

"When the righteous are in authority, the people rejoice: but when the wicked beareth rule, the people mourn" (Proverbs 29:2).

We should pray that our sons will be leaders in their communities, and that they will have the integrity and courage to play a part in the reformation of this nation. They must turn to God's Word as the final authority on how a government should operate under God's sovereign rule.

They must gain a clear understanding of America's history, appreciating the godly foundation on which our nation and its laws were built. We must lead our sons in political and community involvement. Our families should be praying for our leaders. We should discuss issues and seek to apply Scripture to ethical questions. We should be involved in our communities in practical and life-changing ways, seeking to show the love of Christ while upholding God's law as the standard for all of life.

A. Select verses from the list below, and use some or all of the following suggestions to help you study and better understand their meaning (easier verses are listed first, in italics):

   1) Copy the passage.

   2) Read it in several different translations of the Bible.

   3) Read the passage and several of the verses before and after it to gain a better understanding of the context of the passage.

   4) Rewrite the passage in your own words. What does it mean?

   5) Record a specific way in which you can change your actions or attitudes based on the teaching of this passage.

   6) Memorize the passage.

   Proverbs 21:1
   Proverbs 29:2
   Acts 5:29
   2 Chronicles 7:14
   Proverbs 25:5
   Proverbs 28:2
   Daniel 2:20-21
   Matthew 5:13-16

Romans 13:1-2
1 Timothy 2:1-2
1 Peter 2:13-17
(BIBLE / SPEECH)

Beginner

B. Read with your parents the story of Josiah in 2 Kings 22 and 23. How old was he when he became king? What kind of king was he? What did he do during his reign? Make an illustrated book about the life of Josiah, or act out his life with friends or with toys. *(BIBLE / ART/ DRAMA)*

C. Set up an imaginary kingdom with Legos, Playmobil, stuffed animals, or other toys. Help the king rule in a godly way, exercising biblical justice in his kingdom. *(GOVERNMENT / DRAMA)*

D. Read with your parents and illustrate Proverbs 29:2. *(BIBLE / ART)*

E. Study Deuteronomy 17:14-20 and Hosea 8. What are the qualifications for a king? If you were called to rule, would you qualify? In what areas do you fail to qualify? *(BIBLE / GOVERNMENT)*

F. Subscribe to *Early Edition* or *Taking Off* (current events magazines from a Christian perspective for children, available from *www.gwnews.com*). Read and discuss each issue with your parents. *(POLITICS / GEOGRAPHY)*

G. Go with your parents to the election booth and help them punch their ballots. *(POLITICS / GOVERNMENT)*

H. Study and memorize the basic hierarchy of state and federal government. *(GOVERNMENT / LAW / RESEARCH)*

I. Read with your parents Acts 5:12-32. What should you do if an authority tells you to disobey God and do something that you know is wrong? *(BIBLE / LAW / GOVERNMENT)*

Intermediate

J. Find and summarize the verses that describe the duties of a ruler or king. List the duties. *(GOVERNMENT / BIBLE / RESEARCH)*

K. Read through Old Testament history. List all the good kings and bad kings along with their deeds. Note what happened to each king. What can we learn from them? Draw up a chart or timeline to illustrate what you learn. *(HISTORY / ART / READING)*

L. Study the following passages. What does each say about the duties of citizens? *(BIBLE / GOVERNMENT)*

Exodus 22:28
Ezra 6:10
Ezra 7:26
Proverbs 24:21
Proverbs 25:15
Ecclesiastes 8:2-4
Ecclesiastes 10:4 and 20
Jeremiah 29:7
Matthew 17:24-27
Matthew 22:17-21
Romans 3:1-3, 5-7
1 Timothy 2:1-2
Titus 3:1
1 Peter 2:13-17

M. Subscribe to *News Current* or *Top Story* (current events magazines from a Christian perspective for young people, available at *www.gwnews.com*). Read each issue and discuss it with your family. *(POLITICS / GEOGRAPHY)*

N. Compile a list of all local government positions and their responsibilities. Then find the names of the people who fill those positions and pray for them at least once a week. *(LAW / GOVERNMENT / RESEARCH)*

O. Study your state's education code. What are the laws about compulsory attendance, home education, etc.? *(LAW / TEACHING)*

P. Study Acts 5:12-42. Read commentaries on the passage. Discuss it with your father and pastor. What should we learn from Peter and the other apostles? *(BIBLE / RESEARCH)*

Q. During an election season, study the voter's guide. How would you vote? Why? Discuss your decisions with your father. Are your choices based on Scripture? *(POLITICS / LAW / BIBLE)*

R. Outline the basic philosophy of each political party. *(POLITICS)*

S. Listen to a TV or radio political talk show. Discuss how principles of Scripture relate to the topic discussed. *(BIBLE / POLITICS)*

T.   Read biographies of Christian men who stood for the truth in their countries' governments (William Wilberforce, Patrick Henry, George Washinton, etc.) Pick one man to study further, and write a report on his life. *(HISTORY / GOVERNMENT / RESEARCH / WRITING)*

U.   Become involved in some action against abortion -- petition signing, volunteer carpentry work in a Pregnancy Resource Center, letters to a newspaper editor or to stores whose profits help support Planned Parenthood, etc. *(COMMUNITY SERVICE / ENGLISH COMPOSITION / CARPENTRY / ETC.)*

V.   Teach a Bible class to children in your neighborhood.   *(TEACHING / BIBLE / COMMUNITY SERVICE)*

W.   Read Chapter 6 in *The Homeschooling Father,* by Michael Farris. Do some of the activities suggested. *(POLITICS)*

X.   Look up *"Rulers, Character and Qualifications of"* in *Nave's Topical Bible* and study the verses that explain the qualifications of kings and civil leaders. List the qualifications. *(BIBLE / RESEARCH / GOVERNMENT)*

Y.   Explore *www.Congress.org*, and learn how to:
- Read about legislation being debated by Congress
- Track recent votes
- Identify your representatives
- Send an e-mail to your lawmakers.

(RESEARCH / GOVERNMENT / COMPUTER SKILLS)

Z.   Find instructions in books or online for writing effective letters to your congressmen. Following those instructions, write a letter to your congressmen about a particular issue. Send a handwritten letter via postal service, if possible, or send an email to your congressman at *www.Congress.org*. *(RESEARCH / ENGLISH COMPOSITION / GOVERNMENT)*

AA.   Fill in the names of each of the following government officials and pray for them specifically at least once a week. Pray for their conversion, if they are not believers. Pray for them to submit to and promote God's laws. Pray for them to be honest and morally pure. Pray for them to vote wisely about legislative issues. *(GOVERNMENT)*

President:_____

Vice-President:_____

U.S. Senator:_____

U.S. Senator:_____

U.S. Congressman:_____

U.S. Congressman:_____

Supreme Court Justices:_____

_____

Governor:_____

District Representatives:_____

Mayor:_____

BB. Obtain the addresses and phone numbers of each of the government officials listed above. Keep a list in your home for easy use in contacting these people with opinions about political actions and proposals being considered. *(RESEARCH)*

CC. Participate in political action groups that are involved with family and education issues. *(POLITICS / FAMILY / TEACHING)*

DD. Attend public testimony hearings in legislative sessions. *(LAW / GOVERNMENT)*

EE. Read *WORLD* magazine. Discuss with your parents at least one article each issue. Initiate conversations about articles at the meal table. *(READING / CURRENT EVENTS / POLITICS / GEOGRAPHY)*

FF. Watch the news at least once a week with your father and discuss what you hear. What worldviews are presented? What solutions does the Bible offer for the problems in the world? What truths of Scripture are being demonstrated in the events of the world? How can you respond appropriately to what you hear? *(POLITICS / GOVERNMENT / GEOGRAPHY)*

GG. Participate in a political campaign. *(POLITICS)*

HH. Write letters to the editor of your local newspaper. *(ENGLISH COMPOSITION)*

Advanced

II. Spend a day with a policeman. What problems does he deal with? What are some possible solutions? *(LAW / WRITING)*

JJ. Spend a day with a public school teacher. What problems does he deal with? What are some possible solutions? *(TEACHING / LAW)*

KK. Study the role of Christians in the armed forces. Should Christians be conscientious objectors or should they serve in the military? Study Scripture, read books, talk to your father, pastor, and other leaders. Write a paper stating your conclusions. *(BIBLE / LAW / HISTORY / WRITING)*

LL. Visit *www.fightpp.org* to learn more about corporate supporters of Planned Parenthood. Purchase their boycott list and write to companies on the list. Express your opinions and your intention to not do business with them. *(HANDWRITING / ENGLISH COMPOSITION)*

MM. Study the platforms of current political parties. Then write out a political platform for a potential Christian party. *(BIBLE / RESEARCH / GOVERNMENT / WRITING)*

NN. Follow *World Magazine's* blog at *www.onlineworldmag.com* and discuss posts with your father or with your family at mealtimes. *(POLITICS / GEOGRAPHY / COMPUTER)*

OO. Write a paper on what the Bible says about submitting to the laws of the land, and rebelling against authority. What are the principles Scripture gives? When is it right to not submit to government authorities? *(ENGLISH COMPOSITION / BIBLE / GOVERNMENT)*

PP. If you are old enough, register to vote, and then participate in every election. *(POLITICS / CITIZENSHIP)*

QQ. Study with your father *God and Government,* by Gary DeMar. Discuss the questions at the end of each chapter together or write out your answers. *(READING / GOVERNMENT / LAW / WRITING)*

RR. Discuss with your father and other Christian men: Should we vote for an unbelieving political candidate in order to keep a worse candidate from winning? Or should we vote for a Christian candidate that stands biblically on issues, even though he may not win and his loss might mean the victory of the most liberal candidate? *(POLITICS / BIBLE / ETHICS)*

SS. Read *By This Standard: The Authority of God's Law Today,* by Greg Bahnsen. What is the role of God's law in society today? Discuss the book with your father. *(BIBLE / POLITICS / LAW)*

TT. Study what the Bible says about the following moral issues. God's Word should determine your beliefs on these issues and should guide your campaigning and voting. *(BIBLE / GOVERNMENT / LAW / RESEARCH)*

Abortion:

Genesis 1:27	Psalm 100:3	Isaiah 59:7
Genesis 9:6	Psalm 106:38	Jeremiah 1:5

Exodus 2:2,3

Exodus 20:13

Exodus 21:22-23

Exodus 23:7

Numbers 35:33

Deuteronomy 5:17

Deut. 27:17, 19, 25

Deuteronomy 30:19

2 Kings 21:6

Job 31:15

Psalm 113:9

Psalm 127:3-5

Psalm 128:3-4

Proverbs 6:16-19

Proverbs 24:11-12

Ecclesiastes 11:5

Isaiah 5:20-21

Isaiah 8:18

Isaiah 44:24

Isaiah 49:1

Jeremiah 7:31

Hosea 9:11

Amos 1:13

Matthew 2:18

Matthew 18:1-6

Matthew 18:10

Matthew 19:14

Matthew 25:44-45

Luke 1:41-44

Luke 18:15-17

Infanticide:

2 Kings 17:16-20

Psalm 127:3

Proverbs 24:11-12

Jeremiah 22:3

Matthew 25:37-40

Euthanasia:

Genesis 9:6

Exodus 20:12

Exodus 20:13

Exodus 23:7

Leviticus 19:32

Leviticus 24:17

Leviticus 19:32

Leviticus 24:17

Deut. 30:15-19

Psalm 8:2

Psalm 139:13-17

Proverbs 16:31

Proverbs 23:22

Isaiah 3:5

Matthew 5:21

Matthew 18:10

Matthew 19:14

1 Corinthians 3:16-17

AIDS:

Exodus 15:26

Leviticus 26:21

Deuteronomy 7:15

Deut. 28:58-62

2 Chronicles 21:18

Ezekiel 18:26-28

Galatians 6:7-8

James 1:14-15

Balanced Budget/Debt:

Leviticus 19:36	Proverbs 16:11	Romans 13:1-2
Deuteronomy 5:13-15	Proverbs 17:18	Romans 13:6-7
Psalm 37:21	Proverbs 22:3-4	1 Peter 2:13-14
Proverbs 6:1-3	Proverbs 22:26-27	
Proverbs 11:1	Proverbs 27:23-24	

Capital Punishment:

Genesis 9:4-6, 12	Leviticus 24:17-21	Ecclesiastes 8:11
Exodus 21:12-15	Numbers 16:9-34	Luke 23:40-41
Exodus 21:16	Deuteronomy 21:22	Acts 25:10-12
Exodus 21:23-25	Deuteronomy 24:7	Romans 13:3-4

Taxation:

2 Kings 23:35	Isaiah 47:6	Romans 13:6-7
2 Chronicles 10:6-10	Mark 12:14-17	
Ezra 4:20	Luke 2:1-5	

Pornography:

Job 31:1	1 Corinthians 6:9-10	2 Timothy 2:22
Ezekiel 23:14, 20	2 Corinthians 12:21	1 Peter 2:11
Matthew 5:27-28	Galatians 5:19-21	1 Peter 4:3-5
Mark 7:20-23	Ephesians 4:19-24	2 Peter 2:14
Romans 1:21-32	Ephesians 5:11-12	1 John 2:16-17
Romans 13:13-14	1 Thessalonians 5:22	
1 Corinthians 3:16-17	1 Timothy 1:9-10	

Homosexuality:

Genesis 1:27	Leviticus 20:13	1 Timothy 1:9-11

Genesis 19:4-5, 24   1 Kings 14:24   2 Peter 2:6

Leviticus 18:22   Romans 1:24-32   Jude 7

UU. Read as many as possible of the following books on controversial social issues. Take notes and use what you have learned to intelligently discuss the issues with unbelievers and other Christians.

- *Pro-Life Answers to Pro-Choice Arguments,* by Randy Alcorn
- *Welfare Reformed,* edited by David Hall
- *Same Sex Controversy: Defending and Clarifying the Bible's Message About Homosexuality,* by James White and Jeffrey Niell

(ETHICS / BIBLE / GOVERNMENT)

VV. Attend a local school board meeting. Write a paper about your observations or discuss them with your parents. How could a Christian make a difference in this position? *(GOVERNMENT / TEACHING)*

WW. Read *Is Christianity Good for the World?* By Christopher Hitchens and Douglas Wilson. Discuss this book with your father. What are the basic arguments of both men? Who do you think presents the best argument? What can you learn from Mr. Wilson's example? (You may also want to watch the movie *Collision,* which documents the debates between Douglas Wilson and Christopher Hitchens.) *(RELIGION / DEBATE)*

Additional ideas:

Parents:

Consider and discuss with your son the following questions:

- Can he identify the president, senators, congressmen, and representatives that govern him?

- Can he outline basic government hierarchy?

- Does he have a basic understanding of the platform of the different political parties?

- Has he ever participated or seen you participate in lobbying or other political activities?

- Does he understand the campaign and election process?

- Does he pray for government leaders?

- Does he hear you pray for government leaders?

- Is he aware of the laws and political proposals that undermine the family?

- Is he aware of current events in our nation?

- Can he spot misleading humanist thinking in the media?

- Can he explain Biblical principles that apply to political and ethical issues?

- Does he show proper respect for government leaders, even those who display ungodly beliefs and actions?

- Does he respect and obey the laws of our country?

- Is he a witness for Christ in your neighborhood?

Notes and comments:

Honesty

"The just man walketh in his integrity: his children are blessed after him" (Proverbs 20:7).

It is important for our sons to build the virtue of honesty into their lives. Without honesty they will be unable to admit their fallen, sinful state and their need of Christ's redemptive work on the cross. They will be unable to accept responsibility for their sinful actions and thoughts.

We all struggle with the deception of our own hearts when it comes to facing our sins. A young man who has matured physically while nursing the sin of dishonesty will have a difficult time growing spiritually, because he will not honestly evaluate his heart and actions in light of Scripture. Instead he will make excuses for his actions and deny the sinfulness of what he has done.

A dishonest husband and father seriously harms his relationship with his wife and children. Integrity is essential in building strong, loving relationships.

A father who has not allowed the Spirit to help him gain victory over the sin of dishonesty in his life will have a much harder time instilling the virtue of honesty in the lives of his children.

A. Select verses from the list below, and use some or all of the following suggestions to help you study and better understand their meaning (easier verses are listed first, in italics):

1) Copy the passage.

2) Read it in several different translations of the Bible.

3) Read the passage and several of the verses before and after it to gain a better understanding of the context of the passage.

4) Rewrite the passage in your own words. What does it mean?

5) Record a specific way in which you can change your actions or attitudes based on the teaching of this passage.

6) Memorize the passage.

> *Proverbs 12:22*
> *Proverbs 20:7*
> *Colossians 3:9*
> Psalm 24:3-5
> Psalm 63:11

Ephesians 4:25
Philippians 4:8
1 Peter 2:12
(BIBLE / SPEECH)

Beginner

B. Read with your parents the story of Achan in Joshua 7. In what way was Achan dishonest? How did his dishonesty affect others? How did his dishonesty affect him? Draw a picture to illustrate this story. *(BIBLE / ART)*

C. Read Proverbs 6:16-19 with your parents. What seven things does God hate? Draw a picture to illustrate each of these seven things. *(BIBLE / ART)*

D. Read Colossians 3:9-10 with your parents. Why should we not lie, according to these verses? Draw a picture to illustrate the old self and the new self, and post it in your room. Are you living and speaking like your old self or your new self? *(BIBLE / ART)*

E. Ask your parents and other adults to recount stories of when they chose to be honest. What were the results? *(FAMILY)*

F. Ask your parents and other adults to recount stories of when they chose to be dishonest. What were the results? *(FAMILY)*

G. Tell a story about a time when you chose to be honest, and the results of that honesty in your life. *(SPEECH / ENGLISH COMPOSITION)*

Intermediate

H. Write about times when you have lied, and the results of those lies in your life. *(ENGLISH COMPOSITION)*

I. Make several copies of page 109 to form a small journal. Use this journal to record situations in which you were tempted to lie. Write down the circumstances, whom you were with, and why you were tempted to lie. Then find a verse in the Bible that you can use to combat temptation the next time you are in a similar situation. Write out the verse and memorize it. *(WRITING / BIBLE / RESEARCH / HANDWRITING)*

J. With your parents, study the chapters on "Lying" and "Theft" in *For Instruction in Righteousness,* by Pam Forster. *(BIBLE / READING)*

K. Study **honesty** and **lying** in the Bible. What are the consequences of each? What are the blessings of honesty? *(BIBLE / RESEARCH / READING)*

L. Study the chapter on "Honesty" in *Christian Character,* by Gary Maldaner, pages 59-63. *(RESEARCH)*

M. Do topical and/or word studies on the following words:

Deceit
False witness
Flattery
Hypocrisy
(BIBLE / FOREIGN LANGUAGE / WRITING)

N. Study the lives of Abraham, Isaac, Jacob, and Jacob's sons. Notice the pattern of dishonesty in their lives. Take notes on the different occasions when each man chose to lie. Why did each man lie? Read commentaries on these stories. Do all commentators have the same interpretations of these accounts? Did they offer any explanations for the dishonesty of these men? *(BIBLE / READING)*

O. Read the following passages about people in the Bible who deceived others in order to accomplish good. Use the form on page 110 to help you study each account. Why did each of them deceive? What were the results? Based on these accounts, do you believe it is ever right to purposely deceive someone? When, if ever, is it appropriate?

Exodus 1:15-22, Hebrew midwives
Exodus 2, Moses's parents
Joshua 2, Rahab
Judges 4:17-22, Jael
Judges 3:15-30, Ehud
1 Samuel 21:10-15, David
2 Kings 11:2-4, Jehosheba
(BIBLE / ETHICS)

P. Look up the word "falsehood" in *Nave's Topical Bible.* Read the verses under the subsection entitled "Instances of..." Write down each instance, the reference from the Bible, and the motivation behind the dishonesty. Was the liar motivated by fear, personal gain, revenge, etc.? (See form on page 111.)
(RESEARCH / BIBLE)

Advanced

Q. Memorize the answers to Questions 143-145 of *The Westminster Larger Catechism.*

R. List each sin that is delineated in the answer to Question 145 of *The Westminster Larger Catechism.* Study what each of these means and list examples of the ways in which you might commit these specific sins of dishonesty. Repent of sins you have committed and pray for God to give you the grace to become more honest. *(RESEARCH)*

S. Study Lesson 47 in *The Westminster Shorter Catechism for Study Classes*, by G.I. Williamson.   *(BIBLE)*

T. Study the chapter entitled "Blameshifting" (pages 16-21) in Wayne Mack's book, *A Homework Manual for Biblical Living, Vol. 1.* *(BIBLE / WRITING)*

U. Study Proverbs 26:28. How does the lying tongue demonstrate hatred toward those afflicted by it? Write an essay on this subject.   *(BIBLE / ENGLISH COMPOSITION)*

V. Discuss with your parents: Is it ever right to lie or deceive? *(ETHICS / BIBLE)*

W. Read James Jordan's *Primeval Saints,* focusing on Chapter 7, "Faith and Tyranny: the Stories of Isaac and Rebekah." (In addition to print copies, this book is also available at *www.books.google.com.*) What five types of lies does Jordan list? According to him, when is it appropriate to use deception? What reasons does he give for each man's lying? Do you agree with Mr. Jordan? Why or why not?   *(ETHICS / BIBLE)*

Additional ideas:

Record of Temptation to Dishonesty

(See instructions in Project I.)

CIRCUMSTANCE	COMPANIONS	MOTIVATION	SCRIPTURE TO MEMORIZE

Is It Ever Right to Lie?

(See instructions in Project O.)

REFERENCE	PERSON	WHAT HE/SHE DID	RESULTS
Exodus 1:15-22			
Exodus 2			
Joshua 2			
Judges 4:17-22			
Judges 3:15-30			
1 Samuel 21:10-15			
2 Kings 11:2-4			

Falsehood in the Bible

(See instructions in Project P.)

PERSON	REFERENCE	SITUATION	MOTIVATION

Parents:

Consider and discuss with your son the following questions:

- Do you know that you can trust him to tell you the truth?
- Does he tell "half-truths"?
- Does he make excuses?
- Does he deceive with his actions?
- Does he omit information or deceive by **not** speaking?
- Does he fabricate stories?
- Does he exaggerate (to impress others, for instance)?
- Does he keep promises?
- Does he follow through on commitments he makes?
- Is he repentant when caught in a lie, or does he tell more lies in an attempt to cover his wrong?
- Does he admit and quickly repent of sin?
- Does he hide information (when he is in trouble, for instance)?
- Does he take or use things that do not belong to him without permission from the owner?
- Does he return what he has borrowed?
- Is he honest with himself in regard to his time limits, relationships, plans, thoughts, attitudes? Does he deceive and justify himself?
- Does he flatter others so that he can benefit from them?
- Does he promise special favors or make threats to get someone else to do what he wants?
- Does he say he was "teasing" when caught in a lie or in troublemaking?
- Does he give false reports about others' wrongdoings?
- Does he gossip about others?

Notes and comments:

Courage

"Watch ye, stand fast in the faith, quit you like men, be strong" (1 Corinthians 16:13).

If our sons are going to mature into men who will be strong leaders in their homes and communities, they must learn to be courageous -- not in their own strength, but with a spirit of faith in the unfailing character of our all-powerful and sovereign God.

A fearful man will be afraid to lead his family. He will be afraid to stand up for what is right when family members do wrong. He will be afraid to confront those under him about their sins. He will be afraid to risk failure or embarrassment.

We must not be afraid to let our sons experience frightening situations. We must not yield to the temptation to shield our children from any experience that will cause them fear. We can breed a spirit of fear in our sons by overprotecting them and keeping them from launching into areas that we fear ourselves. Facing fear, and learning to do the right thing in spite of it, is part of growing up.

We must also not be afraid to let our sons fail. If we shield them from failure or express dismay at their failures they will become afraid to try anything that would risk failure. A fear of failure will greatly hinder a man's ability and willingness to lead.

A. Select verses from the list below, and use some or all of the following suggestions to help you study and better understand their meaning (easier verses are listed first, in italics):

1) Copy the passage.

2) Read it in several different translations of the Bible.

3) Read the passage and several of the verses before and after it to gain a better understanding of the context of the passage.

4) Rewrite the passage in your own words. What does it mean?

5) Record a specific way in which you can change your actions or attitudes based on the teaching of this passage.

6) Memorize the passage.

Proverbs 28:1
2 Timothy 1:7
Hebrews 13:6

1 Peter 5:7
Proverbs 29:25
Matthew 6:34
Luke 12:22-31
1 Corinthians 16:13
Philippians 4:6-7
(BIBLE / SPEECH)

Beginner

B. Draw a picture to illustrate Proverbs 28:1. *(BIBLE / ART)*

C. Read with your parents the story of Gideon in Judges 6 and 7. Was Gideon naturally a brave man? How do you know? How did God assure him of victory over the Midianites? How did he defeat the Midianites? Can God use us even when we are tempted to be afraid? *(BIBLE)*

Set up some tents in the back yard or make tents with sheets in your house, and act out the story of Gideon and his victory over the Midianites. *(BIBLE / DRAMA)*

D. Read with your parents the story of the Israelite spies that Moses sent in to the land of Canaan. How many men thought they should go in and conquer the Canaanites? How many thought they shouldn't? What reasons did they give for their opinions? How did the Israelite people respond to their reports? What happened to the spies who gave the bad report? What happened to the people? What happened to Joshua and Caleb? *(BIBLE)*

Act out this story with your friends and/or siblings or with your toys. *(BIBLE / DRAMA)*

E. Read with your parents about some of David's mighty men:
Josheb-basshebeth or the Tachmonite, 2 Samuel 23:8
Eleazar, 1 Chronicles 11:12-14
Shammah, 2 Samuel 23:11-12
Abishai, 2 Samuel 23:18-19
Benaiah, 2 Samuel 23:20-23, 1 Chronicles 11:22-25

Act out the courageous deeds of these men with your siblings and/or friends or with your toys. *(BIBLE / P.E.)*

F. Draw pictures of David's mighty men (see Project E) and post them in your room or bind them into a book. *(BIBLE / ART)*

G. Talk with your parents about people and situations that cause you to be afraid. What attributes of God can you trust during those times? What verses can you memorize to recite to yourself when you are afraid? *(BIBLE / WRITING)*

H. Do something that you are afraid of doing (talking to someone you don't know, performing in front of an audience, going outside alone in the dark, etc.) Pray for God to give you courage, and thank Him when He does. *(SOCIAL SKILLS / PERFORMANCE / ETC.)*

I. Tell your family a story about a time you gave in to fear. What happened? Did God protect you? *(SPEECH)*

J. Tell your family a story about a time when you chose to trust God when you were afraid. *(SPEECH)*

Intermediate

K. Choose an area in which you are afraid, and take actions that will help you overcome that fear. (Examples: Take swimming lessons if you are afraid of water. Accept opportunities to speak in public if you are afraid to do that. Learn to go out in the dark.) Pray and memorize Scripture that will give you God's boldness in these situations. *(P.E. / SPEECH / BIBLE)*

L. Write out an account of a time you chose to trust in God and to be brave, and what the results were. *(ENGLISH COMPOSITION)*

M. Interview different men and ask them to recount episodes in their lives when they were tempted to be afraid. What happened when they gave in to their fear? What happened when they trusted God and were courageous? Write a summary of your findings. *(SPEECH / WRITING)*

N. Complete the study: *God, What's Your Name?* by Kay Arthur and Janna Arndt, from the "Discover 4 Yourself Children's Bible Study Series." How does each part of God's character enable us to be courageous? Write down your ideas, and review your list when you are tempted to be afraid. *(BIBLE / WRITING)*

O. Study the men of the Reformation -- men like Martin Luther, William Tyndale, John Knox, John Huss. What gave them the courage to stand up against the corrupt practices of the church when they knew such rebellion could cost them their lives? Copy quotes from Reformation leaders that explain the source of their courage. *(HISTORY / HANDWRITING / RESEARCH / READING)*

P. Read daily from one of the following devotionals that focus on courage and trusting God:

- *Battlefields and Blessings: Stories of Faith & Courage from World War II,* by Larkin Spivey, John Croushorn, and Jocelyn Green

- *Battlefields and Blessings: Stories of Faith & Courage from the War in Iraq and Afghanistan,* by Jane Hampton Cook, John Croushorn, and Jocelyn Green

- *Battlefields and Blessings: Stories of Faith and Courage from the Revolutionary War,* by Jane Hampton Cook

- *Battlefields and Blessings: Stories of Faith and Courage from the Civil War,* by Terry Tuley

(HISTORY / READING)

Q. Study the book of Joshua. Write down every incident that required courage from those involved. What were the results? (See form on page 119.) *(BIBLE / RESEARCH / WRITING)*

R. Study Bible characters who exhibited courage and faith in God, beginning with those mentioned in Hebrews 11. Make a chart listing each person, the Bible references, and what the person did. *(HANDWRITING / BIBLE / RESEARCH)*

S. Study cowardice in the Bible: Adam, Isaac, Jacob, the Israelites in the wilderness, the disciples, Peter, Pilate, etc. List each person, what they were afraid of, what actions they took, and what the results were. (Look up *"Cowardice, Instances of,"* in *Nave's Topical Bible.* Use the form on page 120.) *(RESEARCH / BIBLE / WRITING)*

T. Use a concordance to help you study the phrase "fear not" in Scripture. Using copies of the form on page 121, list each reference, who is speaking, who is being spoken to, the circumstances, and the reason given for not being afraid. When you have finished your reading, review your notes. Why should we not be afraid? *(BIBLE)*

U. Study the chapter on "Courage" in *Christian Character,* by Gary Maldaner, pages 10-13. *(BIBLE / READING / WRITING)*

V. Study the chapter on "Fear" in *For Instruction in Righteousness,* by Pam Forster. *(BIBLE)*

W. Study *Choosing Victory, Overcoming Defeat,* Kay Arthur's inductive study on Joshua, Judges and Ruth. *(BIBLE)*

Advanced

X. Study "the fear of the Lord." How does a proper fear of God enable us to be bold in the face of testing and temptation? Write out your insights and conclusions. (You can look up "Fear of God" in *Nave's Topical Bible*) *(BIBLE / RESEARCH / WRITING)*

Y. Study the chapter on "fear" (pages 72-74) in Wayne Mack's book, *A Homework Manual for Biblical Living, Vol. 1.* *(BIBLE / WRITING)*

Z. Research your family history. What can you find out about courage exhibited in your ancestors? How would your life be different now if they had not been brave in the face of danger? Write a story of your family's history, or compile what you discover into a notebook with photographs, letters, and stories. *(FAMILY / HISTORY / WRITING)*

AA. Read *Foxe's Book of Martyrs*. What gave these men and women the courage to die for their faith? *(READING / HISTORY)*

BB. Read the book of Acts, noting each demonstration of courage displayed by the apostles and early believers. What challenges did they face? How did they respond? What can you learn from their examples? Write a paper summarizing your observations. *(BIBLE / ENGLISH COMPOSITION)*

CC. Conduct word studies in the Bible on the following words:

Afraid
Bold
Courage
Faith
Fear
Trust

(BIBLE / RESEARCH / FOREIGN LANGUAGE / WRITING)

DD. Study the Psalms. As you read, note references to fear and to trusting God. Why could David be brave? On what did he base his courage and trust? List verses and insights. *(BIBLE / WRITING / RESEARCH)*

EE. Complete the study, *Lord, I Want to Know You,* by Kay Arthur. How can an understanding of God's character help you trust Him more? *(BIBLE)*

FF. Read *Courage to Stand: Jeremiah's Message for Post-Christian Times,* by Philip Graham Ryken. Answer the discussion questions for each chapter at the back of the book. What has God most strongly impressed on your mind after reading this book? What can you do about it? Write down a specific plan.

(BIBLE / READING / WRITING)

GG. Study the book, *Knowing God,* by J.I. Packer. Outline the book as you read, and write a summary when you have completed the book, or use the companion study guide to study the book with your parents or a friend. How does a true knowledge of God and His character enable us to be courageous?

(RESEARCH / BIBLE / READING)

Additional ideas:

Courage in the Book of Joshua

(See instructions in Project Q.)

PERSON	REFERENCE	INCIDENT	STATED REASONS FOR COURAGE	RESULTS

Cowardice in the Bible

(See instructions in Project S.)

COWARDLY PERSON	REFERENCE	WHAT THEY FEARED	ACTION TAKEN	RESULTS

A Study of "Fear Not"

(See instructions in Project T.)

REFERENCE	SPEAKER	HEARER	CIRCUMSTANCES	REASON TO NOT FEAR

Parents:

Consider and discuss with your son the following questions:

- Is he overly shy around adults or strangers?
- Is he afraid of personal harm?
- Is he afraid of talking to others?
- Is he afraid of people's opinion of him?
- Is he afraid to talk openly and express his feelings?
- Is he afraid to express his opinions?
- Is he afraid to try anything new?
- Is he afraid to fail?
- Is he afraid to try again when he fails?
- Does he put things off?
- Does he deny reality?
- Is he afraid to stand up for what is right?
- Is he afraid of the future?
- Is he afraid to say "no" when others encourage him to do wrong?
- Is he afraid to say "no" when others ask him to accept responsibilities that will cause him to over-extend himself?
- Does he have the courage to resolve disagreements and misunderstandings with friends, siblings, teachers, parents, etc.?
- Does he tend to become discouraged or give up when confronted with sin in his life?
- Does he accept criticism with a positive attitude?
- Does he have the courage to admit when he is wrong?
- Does he have the courage to ask forgiveness when he has wronged someone?
- Does he have the courage to humbly confront a friend who is sinning?
- Does he fear man more than God?
- Is he afraid to share Christ with others?

Notes and comments:

Add to Your Virtue,

KNOWLEDGE

Bible Skills

"Study to show thyself approved unto God, a workman that needeth not to be ashamed, rightly dividing the word of truth" (2 Timothy 2:15).

God's Word is our only standard for living, and our children should be immersed in it from an early age. The goal in this chapter is to give our sons the basic groundwork for effectively "finding their way around" in the Bible – teaching them the Bible's basic structure, its history, and how to truly study it. Teaching basic study methods can give the reader more direction and purpose, and makes God's Word even more exciting and life-changing as we and our children learn to dig for its treasures.

Our sons need to know how to study the Bible, and they will need to know how to examine what it really says when they accept the responsibility of leading their family. Men cannot lead their families in following God's Word, they cannot carry the principles of Scripture into the workplace, they cannot submit to the teachings of the Bible in their own lives, if they are not familiar with Scripture. They need to know how to study God's Word. They need to know how to find in the Bible the answers to their questions.

A. Select verses from the list below, and use some or all of the following suggestions to help you study and better understand their meaning (easier verses are listed first, in italics):

1) Copy the passage.

2) Read it in several different translations of the Bible.

3) Read the passage and several of the verses before and after it to gain a better understanding of the context of the passage.

4) Rewrite the passage in your own words. What does it mean?

5) Record a specific way in which you can change your actions or attitudes based on the teaching of this passage.

6) Memorize the passage.

> *Acts 17:11*
> Psalm 19:7-11
> Romans 15:4
> *(SPEECH / BIBLE)*

Beginner

B. Read with your parents Chapter 59, "God's Children Read the Bible," and Chapter 60, "God's Children Think About God," in *Leading Little Ones to God,* by Marian Schoolland. *(BIBLE / READING)*

C. Read each day with your mother or father from *The Early Reader's Bible*, by V. Gilbert Beers, or *The Beginner's Bible: Timeless Children's Stories*, by Kelly Pulley. *(BIBLE / READING)*

D. Read about the armor of God in Ephesians 6:13-17. List piece of the Christian's "armor." Why do you think God's Word is his sword? How can the Bible be your sword? Draw a picture of Christian with all of his armor. *(BIBLE / ART)*

E. Memorize books of the Bible in order, and memorize the categories into which the books are divided (i.e., law, history, prophets) For songs, games, and flashcards to help you memorize, go to *www.eBibleTeacher.com* and search on "Books of the Bible Memory Tools." *(BIBLE)*

F. As soon as you can read, get your own copy of the Bible in a translation you can understand. Read it each day. *(BIBLE / READING)*

G. Read through a Bible quiz book and test each other at meal times with your family. *(BIBLE / READING)*

H. Memorize the main theme of each book of the Bible. *What the Bible Is All About for Young Explorers* is a good book for this information. *(BIBLE)*

I. Have a "Sword Drill." Ask your parents to call out different Bible references for you to look up in the Bible. Have brothers and sisters or other friends join you, and see who is fastest. *(BIBLE / READING)*

Intermediate

J. Read *How the Bible Came to Us,* by Meryl Doney. Write a summary of the book's content. Do some of the activities suggested in the book. *(BIBLE / HISTORY / ART / WRITING / READING)*

K. Make a timeline of basic Biblical historical events and people. Use your Bible and a Bible handbook to help you. Add illustrations, if you desire. Post your timeline on a wall or bind it into a book. *(HISTORY / WRITING / ART)*

L. Complete the studies in *How to Study the Bible for Kids,* by Kay Arthur and Janna Arndt. *(BIBLE)*

M. Learn how to use a concordance and other study helps. Use aids from the following list to help you learn how to study the Bible.

- *7 Steps to Bible Skills,* by Dorothy Hellstern. Instructions for using several Bible study tools

- *Beauty and the Pig,* by Pam Forster. Step-by-step instructions for __ different types of study, while studying God's definition of true beauty

- *The Navigator Bible Studies Handbook,* published by NavPress. Instructions and ideas for 8 different methods of Bible study, along with reproducible forms

- Studies from the *Discover 4 Yourself Inductive Bible Studies for Kids*, by Kay Arthur and others:
  - *God's Amazing Creation*, Genesis Chapters 1-2
  - *Digging Up the Past,* Genesis, Chapters 3-11
  - *Abraham: God's Brave Explorer*
  - *Extreme Adventures with God: Isaac, Esau, and Jacob*
  - *Joseph: God's Superhero*
  - *Boy, Have I Got Problems*, James
  - *You're a Brave Man, Daniel,* Daniel 1-6
  - *Wrong Way, Jonah!*
  - *Jesus in the Spotlight*, John 1-10
  - *Jesus -- Awesome Power, Awesome Love*, John 11-16
  - *Jesus -- to Eternity and Beyond!* John 17-21
  - *Becoming God's Champion,* 2 Timothy

  (BIBLE / HISTORY / RESEARCH)

N. To gain a greater understanding of biblical geography, complete selected activities and map projects In *Trail Guide to Bible Geography,* by Cindy Wiggers and Dianna Wiebe. *(BIBLE / GEOGRAPHY / WRITING / DRAWING / RESEARCH)*

O. Explore *www.biblemap.org*. Enter the reference of a Bible passage you are reading, view it on Google maps and learn more about its geographical location. *(BIBLE / GEOGRAPHY)*

P. Search for online Bible atlases. Explore and compare the features of each site. Which one do you like best? Use it as you study your Bible. *(BIBLE / RESEARCH / GEOGRAPHY)*

Q. Download blank maps of Israel and other countries of the Bible. Label each map with the key cities, rivers, mountains, and other sites from biblical accounts. Use different maps for different Bible stories, if desired. Label each map with the Bible reference and story, and put them all together in a binder for easy reference. Use other blank maps to test your knowledge of the lands of the Bible. *(BIBLE / GEOGRAPHY / WRITING / MAP SKILLS)*

R. Explore *www.bibleplaces.com*. Use the site to view photographs of places mentioned in your Bible reading and study. *(BIBLE / RESEARCH / GEOGRAPHY)*

S. Read the *International Children's Bible Field Guide,* by Lawrence Richards, and complete some of the "To Think About and Do" activities at the end of each section. *(BIBLE)*

T. Write a report about one of the following men who contributed to the English translation of the Bible:

- John Wycliffe
- William Tyndale
- Miles Coverdale

(BIBLE / HISTORY / ENGLISH COMPOSITION / RESEARCH)

U. Find a reading schedule online that will help you read through the entire Bible in one or two years. To help you better understand your Bible as you read, also read the corresponding chapters in *The Victor Journey through the Bible,* by V. Gilbert Beers. *(BIBLE / HISTORY / GEOGRAPHY)*

V. Read through Kay Arthur's *How to Study Your Bible.* Then study your Bible using each of the following methods:

- Word study
- Topical study
- Character study
- Outline
- Summaries
- Inductive

(BIBLE / RESEARCH / WRITING / READING)

W. Pick a book of the Bible that you would like to study. Ask your pastor or father to recommend a good commentary on that book. Find it online, if possible, or purchase a print copy of it, and consult it for guidance as you study your Bible. *(BIBLE)*

X. Explore Bible reference websites such as:
> *www.biblestudytools.com*
> *www.biblegateway.com*
> *www.biblios.com*
> *www.e-sword.net*
> *www.bibleclassics.com*

Find out which commentaries and translations of the Bible are offered and what historical books, reference tools, and other helps are included on each site. Try out different sites while you study your Bible. Which one do you like best? *(BIBLE / RESEARCH)*

Y. Read *A Visual History of the English Bible: The Tumultuous Tale of the World's Bestselling Book,* by Donald Brake. Share what you learn from each chapter at the dinner table. *(BIBLE / HISTORY)*

Z. Read *Knowing Scripture,* by R. C. Sproul. Review with your parents or a friend the author's ten "practical rules of biblical interpretation," and seek to apply those rules in your reading and study of the Bible. *(BIBLE / GRAMMAR / HISTORY)*

Advanced

AA. Read *He Gave Us Stories: The Bible Student's Guide to Interpreting Old Testament Stories,* by Richard Pratt, Jr., or *A House for My Name: A Survey of the Old Testament,* by Peter Leithart. Complete the review questions and talk about discussion and "thought questions" with your parents or friends. *(BIBLE)*

BB. Read *Survey of the Bible: A Treasury of Bible Information,* by William Hendricksen. Read the first ten chapters to gain an overall understanding of the Bible – its history and formation, its chronology, organization, study, and interpretation. Study the charts and use the question manual at the back of the book to quiz yourself about dates and basic information. Then use the final section of the book, Part 3, which includes chapters 11-33, to guide you through a chronological study of all the books of the Bible. Work on this project throughout the year until you finish reading the entire Bible and the accompanying commentary. *(BIBLE / HISTORY)*

CC. To gain experience in using the inductive Bible study method, complete *Walking in Power, Love, and Discipline: 1 and 2 Timothy & Titus* (or one of the other studies) in Kay Arthur's *New Inductive Study Series. (BIBLE / WRITING)*

DD. Read *Living by the Book,* by Howard Hendricks and William Hendricks. Complete the "You Try It" exercises at the end of each chapter. Go through the companion video lessons and workbook with your family, or lead a study group of young men, going through the videos and lessons together. *(BIBLE)*

EE. Join a Bible study group in your church or neighborhood. *(BIBLE)*

FF. Lead a Bible study for children or young people in your church or neighborhood. *(BIBLE / SOCIAL SKILLS / TEACHER ED.)*

GG. Study a particular topic or book of the Bible and ask your father if you can share what you have learned with the rest of the family during family worship time. Or lead your family in studying the topic or book together. *(BIBLE / TEACHER ED.)*

HH. Consider a problem or question you have in your life. Using the study methods that you have learned, study your Bible to come up with practical answers you can apply to the situation. Discuss what you find with your parents. *(BIBLE)*

II. Study the Bible for answers to a controversial issue in politics, entertainment, or education. When you have completed your study, organize your notes into a paper on the topic or a letter to the editor of a newspaper or magazine. *(BIBLE / POLITICS / CITIZENSHIP / ENGLISH COMPOSITION)*

JJ. Volunteer to give a devotional talk at a rest home church service or an event at your church. Use your Bible study skills to help you prepare. *(BIBLE / TEACHER ED.)*

KK. Read *How To Read the Bible for All Its Worth,* by Gordon Fee and Douglas Stuart. Outline each chapter and apply these principles as you study the Bible. Read the appendix, "The Evaluation and Use of Commentaries," noting the commentaries that the authors recommend. Which ones can you find free online? Read reviews on others on book store websites. Make a list of the commentaries you think you would use most. *(BIBLE / RESEARCH)*

LL. Read *Let the Reader Understand,* by Dan McCartney and Charles Clayton. Take notes and write a summary of the book's message when you have finished reading. *(BIBLE)*

Additional ideas:

Parents:

Consider and discuss with your son the following questions:

- Can he list all the books of the Bible in order?

- Can he easily find a passage in the Bible?

- Can he identify the major divisions of the Bible (i.e., poetry, major prophets)?

- Can he tell you which division each book goes in?

- Does he have a basic grasp of Biblical history?

- Does he know how the Bible was written, compiled, and translated into various languages and versions?

- Does he know how to use a concordance?

- Does he know how to use a topical Bible?

- Does he know how to use cross-references?

Notes and comments:

Scriptural Manhood

"For the husband is the head of the wife, even as Christ is the head of the church: and he is the saviour of the body" (Ephesians 5:23).

This chapter focuses on godly masculinity and specifically, the specific roles of husband and father, roles that most men will eventually fill. Of course, the most effective teacher of godly manhood for any boy is his own godly father. This means that a father will be constantly challenged to conform more and more to the image of Christ, submitting himself to the authority of God's Word, and growing, by God's grace into the mature and godly man that his son can imitate. A godly father can further encourage his son with the projects listed in this chapter.

Because we live in a fallen world, many boys do not have a godly example to follow. Those boys, like all boys, can still look to their Heavenly Father for the perfect example of husbanding and fatherhood. As God loves them and cares for them, they can, by God's grace, grow into godly men who will be better pictures of God's care and protection to their own wives and children.

A. Select verses from the list below, and use some or all of the following suggestions to help you study and better understand their meaning (easier verses are listed first, in italics):

1) Copy the passage.

2) Read it in several different translations of the Bible.

3) Read the passage and several of the verses before and after it to gain a better understanding of the context of the passage.

4) Rewrite the passage in your own words. What does it mean?

5) Record a specific way in which you can change your actions or attitudes based on the teaching of this passage.

6) Memorize the passage.

   Ephesians 6:4
   Ephesians. 5:23-31
   1 Timothy 3:1-13 and Titus 1:5-9 (These are qualifications for church officers and are obviously good goals of maturity for all men to seek.)
   (SPEECH / BIBLE / FAMILY)

Beginner

B. Read *When I'm a Daddy: A Little Boy's Guide to Biblical Fatherhood,* by Ginger Fulton. If you would like, draw your own book of pictures to show what you will do when you are a daddy. *(ART)*

C. Take responsibility for the care of a family pet or farm animal. *(HOME SKILLS / AGRICULTURE / SCIENCE)*

D. Make a treat for your father, take it to him, and sit down with him and tell him all the things you like about him. Thank him for being a good father to you. *(FAMILY)*

E. Ask your father and mother both what they like best about their fathers. Ask your grandparents, too. *(FAMILY)*

F. Ask your mother what she likes best about your father. *(FAMILY)*

G. Read with your parents the story of Noah in Genesis 6-8. What does this passage say about Noah? Why did God spare him in the ark? How was Noah's family blessed by his righteousness? Will your future wife and children someday be blessed by your faithful obedience to God and His Word? Draw a picture to illustrate the story of Noah, or act it out with your friends or toys. *(BIBLE / ART)*

H. Read stories about families aloud with your parents and notice how the roles of husband and father are portrayed. Is the husband or father obeying God? Is he fulfilling his roles as a godly man? How do his actions affect the rest of his family? *(READING / FAMILY)*

Intermediate

I. Study the Scriptural qualifications for elders and deacons, as outlined in 1 Timothy 3:1-13 and Titus 1:5-9. These are qualities for which all men should strive. How many are present in your life? Which ones do you need to improve in? Make a list and discuss it with your parents. *(BIBLE / WRITING)*

J. Which men do you know who exhibit each of the traits listed in 1 Timothy 3:1-13 and Titus 1:5-9? Learn from their lives as you observe them, and take opportunities to get to know them better. *(SOCIAL SKILLS / BIBLE)*

K. List men from the Bible who possessed the character qualities listed in 1 Timothy 3:1-13 and Titus 1:5-9. How did God use their lives? List each man and his accomplishments. *(BIBLE / RESEARCH / HISTORY)*

L. Read through the Old Testament from Genesis through 2 Chronicles. List men mentioned (major characters), the passage, and whether they were godly or ungodly. *(BIBLE / HISTORY / WRITING)*

M. Do a Bible study with Dad on biblical manhood. What does God say a godly man is like? *(BIBLE / FAMILY)*

N. With your father, study and discuss the book, *Christian Manhood,* by Gary Maldaner. *(BIBLE)*

O. Study husbands in the Bible: Job, Abraham, Adam, Nabal, Ahab, Isaac, Jacob, Ananias, etc. Make a list, give Bible references, and then note what they did right or wrong and how their behavior affected their family. (Use the form on page 138.) *(FAMILY / BIBLE)*

P. Interview your father and/or other men you know who are godly examples as husbands and fathers. What advice do these men have? What lessons has God taught them? Write a series of questions you can ask and then report on your findings. *(SPEECH / FAMILY / WRITING)*

Q. Read a book that portrays a family. Explain how the husband and/or father does or does not exhibit the Scriptural characteristics of a godly husband or father. *(READING / BIBLE)*

R. Read *Letters to Young Men,* by W. B. Sprague. Make notes of what you learn, and how you can apply it to your life. *(READING / BIBLE / WRITING / FAMILY)*

S. Look up "husband" in *Nave's Topical Bible.* Read each verse in the section and note any commands and responsibilities that are given to husbands in Scripture. *(BIBLE / WRITING / RESEARCH)*

T. Study fathers in the Bible: Noah, Abraham, Lot, Isaac, Jacob, Eli, David, Abraham, Jacob, Isaac, the prodigal son's father. What did they do right? What did they do wrong? What were the results? (Use the form on page 139.) *(BIBLE / FAMILY / READING / RESEARCH)*

U. Choose one man in the Bible to study carefully. Observe his actions, his obedience, his failures. What can we learn from him? *(BIBLE / RESEARCH)*

V. Read the verses under the heading, "Parents" in *Nave's Topical Bible.* What are the responsibilities of a father according to Scripture? List your findings and discuss them with your parents. *(BIBLE / FAMILY / RESEARCH)*

Advanced

W. Do word studies from the Bible on the following words:

Admonition/Admonish
Dwell together
Nurture
Train up
(BIBLE / RESEARCH / FOREIGN LANGUAGE / WRITING)

X. Memorize Questions 129-130 from the *Westminster Larger Catechism.* (These deal with the responsibilities of those in authority.) *(BIBLE / FAMILY / SPEECH)*

Y. Complete the studies "Put God First" and "Embrace Your Christian Calling" in Chapter 1 of *Prepare Thy Work*, by Daniel Forster. *(BIBLE / RESEARCH)*

Z. Read Chapters 1-6 in *Discipline: The Glad Surrender,* by Elisabeth Elliot. Explain the following quote in a short paper:

"Discipline is not my claim on Christ, but the evidence of His claim on me. I do not 'make' Him Lord, I acknowledge Him Lord."

What does the author mean by this? What has God provided to help us obey Him? *(READING / ENGLISH COMPOSITION)*

AA. Subscribe to *Credenda Agenda* or read *Credenda Agenda* articles at www.credenda.org. Entire back issues of this magazine can be downloaded from PDF archives. Discuss the articles with your father. *(READING / FAMILY / BIBLE)*

BB. Study Ephesians 5:21-33. Compare the husband's role to that of Christ over the church. Compare the wife's role to that of the church. Use the worksheet provided in this section on page 140. *(BIBLE / FAMILY / WRITING)*

CC. Ephesians 5 says that the husband is to love his wife as Christ loves the church. How did Christ show love to His followers? Read through the Gospels, and note all the examples of Christ's love. What can you learn from this that you can apply to loving your future wife? (See form on page 141.) *(BIBLE / READING / RESEARCH / WRITING)*

DD. Study the lives of men in the Bible who were specifically described as godly men. Take notes as you read about each of them. What common traits do they share?

- Noah - "found favor in the eyes of the Lord," "a righteous man, blameless in his generation" (Genesis 6:8-9, ESV)

- Daniel - "blameless before [God]" (Daniel 6:22)

- Abraham - "He will command his children and his household after him, and they shall keep the way of the Lord, to do justice and judgment." (Genesis 18:19)

- Job - "blameless and upright, one who feared God and turned away from evil" (Job 1:1, ESV)

- Moses - "found favor in [God's] sight" (Exodus 33:12)

- David - "a man after [God's] own heart" (1 Samuel 13:14)

  (BIBLE)

EE. Read *The Disciplines of a Godly Man,* by R. Kent Hughes. Take notes and then outline a plan for living a more purposeful and disciplined life. Share your plan with your parents. *(TIME MANAGEMENT)*

FF. Read Puritan Thomas Watson's *The Godly Man's Picture.* Outline the book's main points and write a paper that summarizes the message of the book and how you plan to apply what you have learned to your life. *(READING / ENGLISH COMPOSITION)*

GG. Study 1 Peter 3:7 in the context of the rest of the passage. Study the meaning of the phrases, **dwell according to knowledge, giving honor, weaker vessel, heirs together,** and **hindered.** Read commentaries on this passage. What does it mean? How should it affect your relationship with your future wife? *(BIBLE / FOREIGN LANGUAGE / WRITING / RESEARCH / FAMILY)*

Additional ideas:

Husbands in the Bible

(See instructions in Project O.)

HUSBAND	REF.	RIGHT ACTIONS	WRONG ACTIONS	EFFECT ON FAMILY

Fathers in the Bible

(See instructions in Project T.)

FATHER	REF.	RIGHT ACTIONS	WRONG ACTIONS	RESULTS

Husband & Wife Compared to Christ & the Church

(See instructions in Project BB.)

HUSBAND	REFERENCE	CHRIST	REFERENCE

WIFE	REFERENCE	CHURCH	REFERENCE

Examples of Christ's Love

(See instructions in Project CC.)

REF.	SITUATION	WHAT JESUS DID	APPLICATION TO LOVING WIFE

Parents:

Consider and discuss with your son the following questions:

- What are his strong traits? In what areas is he doing well?

- Does he have specific character weaknesses that will hinder his effectiveness as an employ**ee**?

- Does he have specific character weaknesses that will hinder his effectiveness as an employ**er**?

- Does he have specific character weaknesses that will hinder his effectiveness as a husband?

- Does he have specific character weaknesses that will hinder his effectiveness as a father?

- What can you do to help him mature in the areas you have identified in the above questions?

- In reading through the qualifications for elders in 1 Timothy 3:1-13, are there areas where your son would not qualify?

- Is he striving to mature in his areas of weakness?

- Does he have specific goals for his life -- do they focus on vocation and family or personal pleasure?

Notes and comments:

Doctrine

"Let no man despise thy youth; but be thou an example of the believers, in word, in conversation, in charity, in spirit, in faith, in purity. Till I come, give attendance to reading, to exhortation, to doctrine" (1 Timothy 4:12-13).

Teaching our sons sound doctrine is essential. What we believe profoundly affects what we do. What our sons believe about the Bible and its teachings will greatly affect the actions they take and the future of the generations that follow us.

If our sons, as the leaders of their families, do not have a clear and accurate understanding of the Bible's teachings, they will not be able to pass on the faith to their children – our grandchildren. They must understand the basic tenets of the faith, and they must be able to clearly explain them to others. And they must be able to recognize false teaching when they or their families are exposed to it.

This chapter suggests the reading of many other books. Scripture is our ultimate authority, but God-fearing scholars and theologians can help us, through their writings, to better categorize and articulate the truths of Scripture. A thorough and systematic knowledge of the Bible will equip us to better obey it, reach others with it, and transform the world with it.

A. Select verses from the list below, and use some or all of the following suggestions to help you study and better understand their meaning (easier verses are listed first, in italics):

1) Copy the passage.

2) Read it in several different translations of the Bible.

3) Read the passage and several of the verses before and after it to gain a better understanding of the context of the passage.

4) Rewrite the passage in your own words. What does it mean?

5) Record a specific way in which you can change your actions or attitudes based on the teaching of this passage.

6) Memorize the passage.

   1 Thessalonians 5:21
   2 Thessalonians 2:15
   Galatians 5:1
   Colossians 2:6-8
   2 Timothy 1:12-13

2 Timothy 3:14-16
Titus 1:9
Hebrews 13:9
2 Peter 3:17-18
(BIBLE / SPEECH)

B. Memorize these verses on the way of salvation (easier verses in italics):

John 3:16
Romans 6:23
John 5:24
Romans 10:9
Ephesians 2:8-9
1 John 1:9
(BIBLE / SPEECH)

Beginner

C. Read and discuss with your parents the following books by R. C. Sproul:
- *The Lightlings*
- *The Priest with the Dirty Clothes*
- *The Prince's Poison Cup*
- *The King Without a Shadow*

(READING)

D. With your parents, read Parts 1-2 and 6-8 of *Leading Little Ones to God,* by Marian Schoolland. Discuss the questions at the end of each chapter. *(BIBLE / DOCTRINE)*

E. Study *The Catechism for Young Children,* illustrated by Vic Lockman. Look up each of the verses that are supplied with each question, and discuss with your father or mother. *(BIBLE / DOCTRINE)*

F. Memorize the answers to all the questions in *The Catechism for Young Children,* illustrated by Vic Lockman. Recite the catechism during meal times or in the car. *(BIBLE / DOCTRINE / SPEECH)*

G. Discuss with your parents when they were saved. When did they put their trust in Jesus? What were the circumstances? Who did God use in their lives to help them understand the gospel? How do they know they are saved? *(FAMILY HISTORY / DOCTRINE / EVANGELISM)*

H. Working with your parents, make a list of all the things you know about God. *(DOCTRINE)*

I. Listen to and memorize the songs on *Why Can't I See God?,* written and performed by Judy Rogers. Discuss the lyrics of the songs with your parents. *(BIBLE / MUSIC)*

J. Read, discuss, and do the activities with your parents in the following books:

- *The Big Book of Questions and Answers About Jesus,* by Sinclair Ferguson
- *The Big Book of Questions and Answers: A Family Guide to the Christian Faith,* by Sinclair Ferguson
- *Big Truths for Little Children: Teaching Your Children to Live for God,* by Richie and Susan Hunt

(BIBLE / DOCTRINE)

Intermediate

K. Ask your father what he believes and why. Listen carefully and ask questions. *(DOCTRINE / FAMILY)*

L. Read with your parents *Grandpa's Box: Retelling the Biblical Story of Redemption,* by Starr Meade. Summarize the story of redemption aloud to your parents when you have finished the book. *(BIBLE / DOCTRINE)*

M. Discuss the sermon each week with your father. Keep a notebook of your sermon notes for easy reference and review. *(BIBLE)*

N. Complete the studies in *God, What's Your Name?* in Kay Arthur's "Discover 4 Yourself Inductive Bible Studies for Kids." *(BIBLE / DOCTRINE)*

O. Write out an outline of the way of salvation that you could recall when sharing the Gospel with an unbeliever. *(BIBLE / EVANGELISM)*

P. Do a Bible study on the book of Romans. Use commentaries to help you better understand the meaning of the book. *(BIBLE / DOCTRINE / READING)*

Q. Read *Essential Truths of the Christian Faith,* by R. C. Sproul. Read the "Bible passages for reflection" that are included with each chapter, and copy each chapter's summary points into a notebook or journal. If you read one of the short sections each day, you will complete the book in less than four months. *(BIBLE / DOCTRINE)*

R. Clip or read excerpts from news articles to discuss at the dinner table. How does the presentation of the information reveal the writers' beliefs and presuppositions? Do the articles represent a biblical world view? *(JOURNALISM / POLITICS / LOGIC / READING)*

S. Compare coverage of the same news item in *World Magazine* and in a secular news magazine. How does their coverage differ? *(JOURNALISM / POLITICS / READING / LOGIC)*

T. Write a critique or review of a magazine article, book, movie, etc., explaining how it portrays or contradicts Biblical truth. *(JOURNALISM / ENGLISH COMPOSITION / BIBLE)*

U. Study *Lord, I Want to Know You*, by Kay Arthur. *(BIBLE / DOCTRINE)*

V. Attend an ordination exam. Listen carefully to the questions and answers. Take notes. *(DOCTRINE)*

W. Study your church's statement of faith. Is there anything in it that you do not understand? Ask your parents or pastor to help you answer your questions. *(DOCTRINE)*

X. Write your own "statement of faith." *(BIBLE / RESEARCH / ENGLISH COMPOSITION)*

Y. Study the basic differences between various religious groups, such as Mormons, Jehovah's Witnesses, etc. Where do these groups deviate from true Scriptural doctrine? *(BIBLE / DOCTRINE / RELIGION / RESEARCH / READING / HISTORY)*

Z. Read *Confronting the Cults,* by Gordon Lewis. Take notes and be prepared to use what you have learned to converse with those who have embraced false doctrines. *(BIBLE / DOCTRINE / RELIGION / READING / HISTORY)*

Advanced

AA. Read *Dug Down Deep: Unearthing What I Believe and Why It Matters,* by Joshua Harris, and discuss it with your father. *(BIBLE / DOCTRINE)*

BB. Interview your pastor and other men in your church. Ask them two questions:

- What do you believe?
- How does it affect how you live?

Then ask yourself the same question. What do **you** believe, and how does it affect **your** life? Compile the notes from your interviews into a report. *(ENGLISH COMPOSITION)*

CC. Write a paper entitled "What Is the Gospel?" *(BIBLE / DOCTRINE / ENGLISH COMPOSITION)*

DD. Sit in on men's discussions at church and at other church gatherings. *(DOCTRINE / SOCIAL SKILLS / SPEECH)*

EE. Participate in a membership class or other class offered at your church that discusses elements of your church doctrines. *(BIBLE / DOCTRINE)*

FF. Complete the study "Know What You Believe" in Chapter 1 of *Prepare Thy Work*, by Daniel Forster. *(BIBLE / RESEARCH)*

GG. Complete one or more of the following studies on the historic creeds, confessions, and catechism of the Church:

- *Faith of Our Fathers: A Study of the Nicene Creed,* by L. Charles Jackson
- *Heidelberg Catechism: A Study Guide,* by G. I. Williamson
- *The Westminster Shorter Catechism for Study Classes,* by G. I. Williamson

(BIBLE / DOCTRINE / HISTORY)

HH. Read *Defending the Faith,* by R. C. Sproul, and summarize each chapter. Discuss what you have learned with a parent or friend. *(BIBLE / DOCTRINE / APOLOGETICS)*

II. Read *Tearing Down Strongholds,* by R. C. Sproul, Jr. Take notes. As you read newspapers and magazines, identify false presuppositions and philosophies that influence the way the information is presented and interpreted. *(BIBLE / DOCTRINE / APOLOGETICS)*

JJ. Pretend you are talking to an atheist. Write out a dialogue between him and you, imagining what he might say and how you would respond. Ask him to support his arguments against the existence of God. Challenge his presuppositions. *(BIBLE / EVANGELISM / APOLOGETICS)*

KK. Read and outline *Is Christianity Good for the World?* By Christopher Hitchens and Douglas Wilson. Also watch *Collision,* featuring Christopher Hitchens and Douglas Wilson. What can you learn from Mr. Wilson's interactions with Mr. Hitchens? *(EVANGELISM / APOLOGETICS)*

LL. Read *Always Ready: Directions for Defending the Faith,* by Greg Bahnsen. Take notes and use what you have learned as you interact with unbelievers. *(EVANGELISM / APOLOGETICS)*

MM. Read through *The Heidelberg Catechism,* along with each question's Scriptural proofs. If you study two questions each day it will take you a little over a year to study the entire catechism. *(BIBLE / DOCTRINE / READING)*

NN. Research a doctrinal question. Study the meaning of a theological term, the interpretation of a difficult passage, etc. Use Bible study aids and commentaries to help you. Write a summary of your research. *(RESEARCH / BIBLE / WRITING)*

OO. Study Wayne House's *Charts of Christian Theology and Doctrine.* Explain the basic differences between different groups of believers. *(DOCTRINE / LOGIC / BIBLE)*

PP. Read *A Body of Divinity*, by Thomas Watson. Outline its basic content.
(READING / BIBLE / WRITING)

QQ. Enroll in a correspondence or online course on some aspect of Biblical doctrine. *(BIBLE / WRITING / RESEARCH / READING)*

RR. Study each of the following doctrinal subjects. Then ask your father to test you on them. How well can you explain and support what you believe about each topic?
The Fall
Salvation
The Trinity
The Holy Spirit
The attributes of God
The deity of Christ
The humanity of Christ
Inspiration and infallibility of Scripture
Creation
The Church
Baptism
Communion
Heaven and hell
End times
(BIBLE / DOCTRINE)

SS. Study Louis Berkhof's *Summary of Christian Doctrine.* Read each chapter, and write out the answers to the review questions at the end of the chapters.
(BIBLE / RESEARCH / WRITING)

Additional ideas:

Parents:

Consider and discuss with your son the following questions:

- Does he have a basic understanding of Biblical doctrine?

- Does he recognize false teaching in books, television, news media, etc.?

- Can he explain the way of salvation to an unbeliever?

- Can he explain the meaning of basic theological terms such as justification, grace, redemption, etc.?

- Can he explain what **he** believes about:
  The Fall
  Salvation
  The Trinity
  The Holy Spirit
  The attributes of God
  The deity of Christ
  The humanity of Christ
  Inspiration and infallibility of Scripture
  Creation
  The Church
  Baptism
  Communion
  Heaven and hell
  End times

- Can he support what he believes with specific Scripture passages?

- Does he argue over minor theological issues while neglecting obvious areas of Scriptural truth?

Notes and comments:

Teaching Skills

"And these words, which I command thee this day, shall be in thine heart: And thou shalt teach them diligently unto thy children, and shalt talk of them when thou sittest in thine house, and when thou walkest by the way, and when thou liest down, and when thou risest up" (Deuteronomy 6:7).

God has commanded us to teach our children. He has commanded our sons to teach **their** children. So we must diligently teach and prepare our sons to be good and responsible teachers.

We can do much toward teaching our children how to be good teachers by setting a godly example for them. We need to be diligent and creative in teaching them in all the areas of their lives. We need to be sensitive to their individual temperaments. We need to take our job as "trainers" seriously.

We also need to provide plenty of opportunities for our sons to practice teaching. Let them train a younger sibling to do a household chore. Enlist their assistance in homeschool lessons and plans. Encourage them to read the Bible and stories to younger children. Each of these experiences will make them more comfortable and prepared for teaching their own children in the future.

We should also prepare our sons for the overseeing of their children's education. Present the various educational options to them. Help them see the benefits and disadvantages of different approaches. If you are homeschooling, be sure your children know why you have chosen to teach them at home. If you have placed your children in private school, explain your reasons for this. If you have them in government schools, seriously examine your motives for leaving them there. Can you offer a biblical defense for this decision? Your sons, along with their wives, will someday be deciding how to educate their children. Explaining your educational choices to them now will help them make wise decisions in the future and further your vision for your family's future generations.

A. Select verses from the list below, and use some or all of the following suggestions to help you study and better understand their meaning (easier verses are listed first, in italics):

  1) Copy the passage.

  2) Read it in several different translations of the Bible.

  3) Read the passage and several of the verses before and after it to gain a better understanding of the context of the passage.

4) Rewrite the passage in your own words. What does it mean?

5) Record a specific way in which you can change your actions or attitudes based on the teaching of this passage.

6) Memorize the passage.

> *Proverbs 22:6*
> *Isaiah 38:19*
> Deuteronomy 6:6-9
> Psalm 78:5-8
> Proverbs 16:21
> Ephesians 6:4
> 1 Thessalonians 2:11
> *(BIBLE / SPEECH)*

Beginner

B. Read with your parents Deuteronomy 6:6-9. Divide a piece of paper into four sections and draw pictures to show the four times that parents should teach their children God's law. What do you think this means? Are there other times that parents do not need to be teaching their children God's Word? *(BIBLE / ART)*

C. Read with your parents Psalm 119:130. Where do we get wisdom and understanding? *(BIBLE)*

D. Ask a parent or grandparent to tell you a story. Remember the story and re-tell it to the rest of your family at the dinner table. *(FAMILY HISTORY / SPEECH)*

E. If you see a younger sibling doing something dangerous, explain why they should not do it. *(FAMILY / SAFETY)*

F. If a younger sibling asks your father or mother a question and you know the answer, ask your parent if **you** can tell them the answer (but be careful not to interrupt). *(TEACHER ED.)*

G. Let a sibling or other younger child work alongside of you while you work. Teach them how to do aspects of your job. *(HOME SKILLS / FAMILY)*

H. Teach a younger sibling or another child how to set the table. *(HOME SKILLS / TEACHER ED.)*

I. Teach a memory verse to one of your siblings. Help them practice and recite the verse. *(BIBLE / TEACHER ED.)*

J. Help teach a younger sibling to put away toys. Help him pick them up and teach him where they are stored. *(HOME SKILLS / TEACHER ED.)*

Intermediate

K. Tell Bible stories, using visuals or flannelgraph if you choose, to your own siblings, cousins, nieces and nephews, a children's Sunday School class, or a neighborhood Bible class in your home. *(SPEECH / BIBLE / ART / COMMUNITY SERVICE)*

L. Help your younger siblings memorize Bible verses each week. Have them recite them for you at the end of the week. Is there some way you can encourage and reward them for their hard work and successful memorization? *(BIBLE / TEACHER ED.)*

M. Write Bible quiz questions to ask the family at mealtimes. *(WRITING / BIBLE)*

N. Help correct papers for your family's or another family's homeschool, or for a classroom teacher. *(READING / MATH / WRITING / TEACHER ED.)*

O. Make your own instructional video or documentary. Ask your father or older sibling to videotape you as you demonstrate a skill or teach your younger siblings how to perform a cleaning job or a magic trick. Or teach them about an area of history or science, complete with stories, pictures, and demonstrations. *(SPEECH / TEACHER ED.)*

P. Ask permission to be the "Answer Man" for a day! Help your parents answer the many questions that your younger siblings ask all day! Or find some other harried mother who would like help answering "why" all the time. *(LOGIC / FAMILY / RESEARCH)*

Q. Organize and lead games for younger children at church while their parents visit after the service. *(P.E. / MUSIC / DRAMA, ETC.)*

R. Organize activities for pre-school children to do while Mom homeschools other members of the family. Play outside with your little brothers or sisters. Lead them in a game, or teach them simple lessons for school *(P.E. / MUSIC / ART / DRAMA / ETC.)*

S. Teach another child an area in which you are skilled -- carpentry, animal husbandry, sports, gardening, musical instruments, drawing, etc. *(HOME SKILLS / ART / MUSIC / ETC.)*

T. Attend a homeschool curriculum fair with your father and mother. Plan ahead before you go. Discuss your budget. List subjects for which you need to view and/or purchase materials. List specific companies' booths that you want to see. Examine curriculum with them. Ask your father questions as you shop. *(FINANCES / CONSUMER EDUCATION / TEACHER ED.)*

U. Under your parents' direction, write up long-term plans for teaching a year of science, history or art to a primary grade child. *(TEACHER ED.)*

V. Ask your parents if you can be involved in the selection of your school curriculum for the next year.

- List each subject to be studied.

- Find out what your budget is.

- Search online to compare features of different materials, read reviews, talk to homeschooling parents and students, and, if possible, examine actual copies of the material from other homeschoolers, or at a store or curriculum exhibit.

- How can you save money? Can you find used copies of any of your first choices? Can you borrow from other homeschoolers or from the library? Can you sell materials you no longer use to earn money for new materials? Can you share materials and expenses with another family and take turns using them? If not, do you need to change plans to stay within your budget?

- Discuss your recommendations with your parents. If they approve your choices, purchase the materials. If they have suggestions or concerns, continue your research and offer new recommendations.

(RESEARCH / MATH / TEACHER ED.)

W. Pretend you are the father in a family. What subjects do you think are important to teach in your homeschool? Do you want your sons' and daughters' schooling to be exactly the same? How much do you think you should spend on homeschooling materials each year? How can you save money in your schooling? *(FAMILY / TEACHER ED.)*

X. Help teach a Sunday school class or help with a boys' club at your church.
(BIBLE / P.E. / ART / TEACHER ED. / COMMUNITY SERVICE)

Y. Tutor a child in a school subject you understand well. *(TEACHER ED.)*

Z. Take community and store-sponsored classes that will prepare you to better teach your children in the future. Use what you have learned to serve others in your church and neighborhood. *(ARTS & CRAFTS / P.E. / ETC.)*

AA. Host a special "workshop" for a group of homeschooling friends. Display a special collection, teach a craft, or lead a cooking session. *(SPEECH / TEACHER ED. / COMMUNITY SERVICE)*

BB. Study and compare various approaches to teaching (i.e., classical, unit studies, "unschooling"). Outline the basic characteristics of each approach. What are the basic differences? Which approach do you think is the best? Write an essay explaining your reasons. *(RESEARCH / TEACHER ED.)*

CC. If you are homeschooled, write an essay describing the advantages of education at home. Submit your writing to the editor of the local newspaper, or to a homeschooling newsletter or magazine for possible publication. *(EDUCATION / ENGLISH COMPOSITION)*

DD. Study Jesus' teaching methods as recounted in the Gospels. How did He teach His followers? How did He teach those who disagreed with Him? List the various ways He taught. What can you learn from them that you can apply in your own teaching? *(BIBLE / RESEARCH / WRITING)*

EE. Write a paper discussing the advantages and disadvantages of using computers in education. *(ENGLISH COMPOSITION / TEACHER ED.)*

Advanced

FF. Under your parents' guidance, teach your siblings a subject in your homeschool (or assist in another family's homeschool). *(FAMILY / TEACHER ED.)*

GG. Study the Proverbs. How do they teach Scriptural truths? How can you apply these techniques to your teaching? Write an essay explaining your ideas. *(BIBLE / RESEARCH)*

HH. Complete the study "Commit to Christian Education" in Chapter 7 of *Prepare Thy Work*, by Daniel Forster. *(BIBLE / RESEARCH / EDUCATIONAL PHILOSOPHY / TEACHER ED.)*

II. Study the parables as teaching tools. What common elements do they have in their approach to teaching truth? How can you apply the principles of parables and storytelling to your teaching? *(RESEARCH / BIBLE / LITERATURE)*

JJ. Interview the fathers of homeschooling families. What roles do they play in their home schools? What advice can they offer you for the future? What do they do to support and encourage their wives? What do they do to motivate their children? What problems have their families encountered in homeschooling? What benefits have there been? Organize your notes from these interviews into a report that you can share with other young men and with young fathers. *(FAMILY)*

KK. Attend a homeschool workshop or seminar or listen to the tapes at home. Write a report on how you can implement what you have learned. *(ENGLISH COMPOSITION / TEACHER ED.)*

LL. Study different learning styles -- visual, auditory, kinesthetic. Which style best suits you in your studies? If you have siblings, try to identify the learning style of each child. Compare your conclusions with that of your parents. *(RESEARCH / TEACHER ED.)*

MM. Prepare a lesson teaching the same topic for each of the three basic learning styles, varying your methods according to the learning style. Use your plans to teach students with differing learning styles. *(RESEARCH / TEACHER ED.)*

NN. Lead a young men's Bible study. *(BIBLE / TEACHER ED. / COMMUNITY SERVICE)*

OO. Volunteer as a teacher's aide in a private Christian school one day a week. *(TEACHER ED. / COMMUNITY SERVICE)*

PP. Ask your parents if there is an area of schooling that they would like to include in your family's homeschool, or that they would like to offer at home as a supplement to out-of-home classroom schooling. If they don't have the time and energy to add this to their schedule, offer to do it yourself! Plan and teach the subject at least once a week. *(FAMILY / TEACHER ED.)*

QQ. Read Chapter 6, "A Perpetual Relay of Truth," and Chapter 8, "An Educational Control," in *What Is a Family?* by Edith Schaeffer. Outline the main points of these chapters. *(EDUCATION / FAMILY / WRITING)*

RR. Listen to the recordings of Gregg Harris's *Basic Home Schooling Workshop*. Take notes. Discuss the talks with your parents. (An MP3 download of this workshop is available at *www.noblebooks.org*.) *(FAMILY / TEACHER ED.)*

SS. Design your own independent study unit for school. Do all your own planning, scheduling, research, etc. *(TEACHER ED.)*

TT. Read *A Biblical Psychology of Learning,* by Ruth Beechick and outline its basic content. *(READING / WRITING / TEACHER ED.)*

UU. Read *When You Rise Up: A Covenantal Approach to Homeschooling,* by R.C. Sproul, Jr. Discuss the book with your parents. According to the author, what is the goal of education? Who should teach our children? What should they be taught? *(BIBLE / EDUCATION)*

VV. Read *Recovering the Lost Tools of Learning* and *Repairing the Ruins*, both by Douglas Wilson. Write a paper summarizing the message of these books. *(HISTORY / EDUCATION)*

WW. Write a paper summarizing your educational philosophy, including principles you have appreciated from any books you read in projects TT through VV. *(EDUCATION / ENGLISH COMPOSITION)*

XX. Research *Homeschool Legal Defense Association*. What qualifications are there for homeschooling families? What are the costs? What are the benefits of membership? *(RESEARCH / LAW / TEACHER ED.)*

YY. Read *College Without Compromise,* by Scott and Kris Wightman. What have you learned from this book that you could put into action in preparation for your career and for teaching your own children? What is your opinion about college? When do you think a college education is necessary? *(FAMILY / TEACHER ED.)*

ZZ. Read *Accelerated Distance Learning,* by Brad Voeller. Research the resources that the author lists for credit-by-exam options, distance learning programs, internships, test taking, and independent study. *(COLLEGE PREP. / TEACHER ED.)*

Additional ideas:

Parents:

Consider and discuss with your son the following questions:

- Is **he** teachable?

- Is he diligent in his own studies?

- Does he initiate learning on his own, through his own reading and research, etc.?

- Can he schedule his own schoolwork?

- Can he explain a basic procedure clearly to someone else?

- Can he clearly recount an event or narrate a story he has heard or read?

- Can he teach a new skill to a younger child?

- Has he taken advantage of opportunities to teach younger children -- Sunday School classes, clubs, at home, etc.?

- Does he grow impatient when trying to explain an idea or procedure to someone else?

- Has he ever been involved in selecting school curriculum -- his own or someone else's?

- Does he show enthusiasm and creativity in teaching?

- Can he plan a week's assignments for himself or another student?

- Is he prepared to guide and direct any homeschooling that his future family may choose to do?

Notes and comments:

Home Skills

"But if any provide not for his own, and especially for those of his own house, he hath denied the faith, and is worth than an infidel" (1 Timothy 5:8).

Part of every son's education needs to include basic training in the skills he will need around the home – general knowledge about car, yard and house maintenance, and at least minimal acquaintance with basic plumbing, electrical work, and carpentry. Some knowledge in these areas will potentially save them money and enable them to better care for the physical needs of their families.

Seek the help of other men in your church and family to train your sons in areas where you lack knowledge. Perhaps you could learn together from a skilled man who is willing to train you both in these areas! Purchase a good "fix-it-yourself" manual that you can refer to when maintaining your home, and teach your son to seek counsel from others and information from books and online when things break and need repair.

Beginner projects are listed at the beginning of each section within this chapter, with projects becoming progressively more challenging.

A. Select verses from the list below, and use some or all of the following suggestions to help you study and better understand their meaning (easier verses are listed first, in italics):

1) Copy the passage.

2) Read it in several different translations of the Bible.

3) Read the passage and several of the verses before and after it to gain a better understanding of the context of the passage.

4) Rewrite the passage in your own words. What does it mean?

5) Record a specific way in which you can change your actions or attitudes based on the teaching of this passage.

6) Memorize the passage.

Genesis 1:26
Genesis 1:28
Daniel 2:38
Hebrews 2:7-8
(BIBLE / SPEECH)

B. Help your parents with whatever they are doing. Ask them to teach you the proper way to do the job. *(HOME SKILLS / FAMILY / ETC.)*

C. Join a 4-H Club in an area of skill that you will be able to use in your home. *(ANIMAL HUSBANDRY / AGRICULTURE / ETC.)*

D. Help promptly repair broken and malfunctioning items in your home. *(HOME SKILLS)*

E. Take advantage of opportunities to help people who are building or remodeling their own houses. Learn as much as you can while you work with them. *(CARPENTRY / CONSTRUCTION / HOME SKILLS)*

F. Collect how-to books on different aspects of home and yard maintenance, gardening, and animal husbandry. *(RESEARCH)*

Animal husbandry:

G. Faithfully feed a pet or barnyard animal each day. *(ANIMAL HUSBANDRY / ZOOLOGY)*

H. Care for an animal's house, pen, or bed, keeping him clean and healthy. *(ANIMAL HUSBANDRY / ZOOLOGY)*

I. Eventually assume total responsibility for some livestock (i.e. buy feed, repair housing, give or arrange medical care, sell products such as eggs, milk, etc.) *(MATH / SCIENCE / BUSINESS ED. / RESEARCH / VETERINARY SCIENCE)*

J. Help build shelters and put in fences for animals that your family raises. *(CARPENTRY / CONSTRUCTION)*

K. Raise ducks, chickens, goats, cows, honeybees, rabbits, sheep, and other animals that will provide a source of food and/or income. Keep track of what the animals produce, the cost of feeding and housing them, your sales, and your profit or losses. *(RESEARCH / MATH / BUSINESS ED.)*

L. Learn to identify various breeds of a particular animal and explain their unique characteristics, strengths and weaknesses. *(ANIMAL HUSBANDRY / TAXONOMY)*

M. Compare prices of and ingredients in various types of feed. Which feed is the best deal? Can you save by buying in larger quantities? *(SCIENCE / CONSUMER EDUCATION)*

N. Learn how to give routine shots and how to treat simple wounds and diseases in animals. *(VETERINARY SCIENCE)*

O. Learn to mix your own feed for the livestock you raise. *(RESEARCH / ANIMAL HUSBANDRY)*

Carpentry:

P. Learn to hammer a nail into a piece of wood. *(CARPENTRY)*

Q. Use a screwdriver to help your father assemble or disassemble something. *(RESEARCH / HOME SKILLS)*

R. Learn basic care and use of tools. *(HOME SKILLS / SCIENCE)*

S. Learn how to use a hand saw. *(CARPENTRY)*

T. Build a fort in your backyard. *(CARPENTRY / CONSTRUCTION / ENGINEERING)*

U. Assist your father in a simple repair job. Get the tools he needs, help him with the work, ask questions, put all tools away, and finish any other clean-up. *(HOME SKILLS)*

V. Build projects with woodworking kits (i.e., birdhouse). *(CARPENTRY / MATH)*

W. Collect a basic set of carpentry tools suitable for simple household repair jobs. *(CARPENTRY / HOME SKILLS / CONSUMER EDUCATION)*

X. Design a simple carpentry project. Draw up plans, figure measurements and materials, and estimate costs. *(MATH / ENGINEERING / RESEARCH / ART)*

Y. Help Dad in building shelves, pens, fences, playhouse, fort, etc. *(MATH)*

Z. Work with an experienced carpenter. If possible, work on the job with him for a period of time, or spend evenings in the shop with a woodworking hobbyist. *(CAREER EDUCATION)*

Automotive:

AA. Help your father wash your car. *(HOME SKILLS)*

BB. Watch your father check the oil in your car. *(HOME SKILLS / SCIENCE)*

CC. Learn basic functions of a car engine. *(MECHANICS / SCIENCE)*

DD. Learn the names and uses for basic automotive tools. *(READING / RESEARCH)*

EE. Acquire a collection of tools for simple car maintenance and repair. *(HOME SKILLS / MECHANICS)*

FF. Learn maintenance basics (i.e. checking tire pressure, air filter, fluid levels, anti-freeze, changing oil). Do this with Dad or with another mechanically-minded man. *(MECHANICS / SCIENCE / HOME SKILLS)*

GG. Learn how to change a flat tire. *(MECHANICS)*

HH.   Learn how to put snow chains on tires. *(MECHANICS)*

II.   Learn how to use jumper cables to jump start/recharge a dead car battery. *(MECHANICS)*

JJ.   Study a book on basic car safety and maintenance. *(READING / RESEARCH)*

KK.   Help your father with any family car repairs. *(RESEARCH / MECHANICS)*

LL.   Observe a skilled mechanic at work when your family's car goes into the shop for repairs. *(MECHANICS)*

MM. Purchase a "junker" and restore it for yourself or for a family that needs a car. *(MECHANICS / RESEARCH / SCIENCE)*

NN.   Arrange to assist or apprentice under a car mechanic or hobbyist. *(CAREER EDUCATION)*

Appliance Repair:

OO. Learn how to safely operate the washer and dryer, dishwasher, and microwave. *(HOME SKILLS)*

PP.   Learn basic maintenance skills (cleaning, oiling, etc.). *(HOME SKILLS)*

QQ. Learn how to find operating and repair instructions for appliances online. *(COMPUTER SKILLS / RESEARCH)*

RR.   Work with your father or someone who does many of his own repairs while doing maintenance and repairs on washers, dryers, etc. *(SCIENCE / RESEARCH)*

SS.   Read a book on simple appliance repair. Refer to it the next time you have an opportunity to help repair something. *(READING / RESEARCH)*

TT.   Observe an appliance repairman. Try to make arrangements to work with him for an extended period of time as an assistant or apprentice. *(CAREER EDUCATION)*

UU. Choose an appliance you will need in your future household. Study consumer guides to help you compare the quality, price, and warranties of different brands. Which one would you buy? *(MATH / CONSUMER EDUCATION / FINANCES)*

VV.   Read about the advantages and disadvantages of extended warranties on appliances. *(RESEARCH / CONSUMER EDUCATION / FINANCES)*

Electrical:

WW. Ask your parents to teach you how to safely handle electrical cords and appliances. *(SAFETY / HOME SKILLS)*

XX. Learn how to properly install batteries in a flashlight. *(HOME SKILLS / SCIENCE)*

YY. Learn how to change a light bulb. *(HOME SKILLS)*

ZZ. Learn how to turn off electrical power at the main switch. *(HOME SKILLS / SAFETY)*

AAA. Learn how to repair broken electrical cords and replace plugs. *(SCIENCE / SAFETY / HOME SKILLS)*

BBB. Work with a skilled electrician to learn basic principles for repair. *(CAREER EDUCATION)*

CCC. Learn how to replace a light switch. *(SCIENCE)*

Plumbing:

DDD. Learn how to use a plunger to unstop a toilet. *(HOME SKILLS)*

EEE. Learn basic maintenance skills (cleaning drains, replacing washers, etc.). *(HOME SKILLS / SCIENCE)*

FFF. Learn how to protect pipes from freezing. *(RESEARCH / HOME SKILLS / SCIENCE)*

GGG. Learn how to turn off the water supply at the main valve. *(HOME SKILLS / SAFETY)*

HHH. Work as an assistant or apprentice to a plumber or do-it-yourselfer. *(CAREER EDUCATION)*

III. Learn how to do basic repairs on your toilet. *(HOME SKILLS / SCIENCE)*

Gardening:

JJJ. Order a seed catalog from a garden seed company. Mark the flowers and vegetables that you think would be fun to grow. *(RESEARCH)*

KKK. Ask your parents for your own little section of garden in the family garden or in the flower beds around the house. Plant seeds, weed, water, and enjoy. *(HORTICULTURE)*

LLL. Plant a small flower garden. Pick flowers to take to your mother and to share with grandparents and neighbors. *(HORTICULTURE)*

MMM. Learn how to care for, clean, sharpen and maintain tools. *(RESEARCH / SCIENCE)*

NNN. Help weed garden and flower beds. *(HORTICULTURE)*

OOO. Become an "expert" on the cultivation of one or two particular vegetables. Study their planting, care, fertilizing, harvest, etc. Plant and care for those crops. *(RESEARCH / AGRICULTURE)*

PPP. Learn which plants need which types of fertilizer. *(SCIENCE / AGRICULTURE)*

QQQ. Work with your parents while planning the garden for the year -- what to plant, how much to plant, where to plant it, ordering or going to the store for seeds, etc. *(BOTANY / MATH / FINANCES)*

RRR. Learn how to safely operate a lawn mower, edger, weed-eater, and rototiller. *(SAFETY / HOME SKILLS)*

SSS. Accept the responsibility of keeping the lawn mowed and trimmed. Try to mow the lawn before your parents have to remind you. *(HOME SKILLS)*

TTT. Mix your own organic fertilizer for use on your garden. *(SCIENCE / MATH)*

UUU. Work together in pruning fruit trees, berry and grape vines, bushes, etc. *(BOTANY)*

VVV. Work with your parents in learning about and using various methods of disease, pest, and weed control. *(SCIENCE / ENTOMOLOGY / RESEARCH)*

WWW. Learn how to propagate plant cuttings, harvest and save seeds, divide bulbs, etc. Share your plants and bulbs with family and neighbors. *(BOTANY / RESEARCH)*

XXX. Raise one "cash crop" -- something from your garden that you can sell (flowers, Indian corn, pumpkins, herbs, berries, etc.), or something that can be used to create a marketable product (strawflowers, herbs, etc.) Keep records of expenses, sales and profits. *(FINANCES / BUSINESS ED. / MATH / BOOKKEEPING / AGRICULTURE)*

YYY. Start your own transplants from seed. *(BOTANY)*

Additional ideas:

Parents:

Consider and discuss with your son the following questions:

- Can he perform basic household maintenance jobs?

- Does he put tools away in their proper place after using them?

- Does he take proper care of the tools he owns or uses?

- Does he work alongside you, learning skills necessary as a husband and father?

- Does he have a basic understanding of safety rules?

- Is he faithful in caring for pets? His room? His personal possessions?

- Is he faithful in caring for family belongings, furniture, car, etc.?

- Does he take initiative in fixing a problem when he sees it?

- Does he take advantage of opportunities to work with or observe skilled repairmen, carpenters, etc.?

- Does he know how to obtain the information he needs in order to take care of household repairs and projects?

Notes and comments:

And to knowledge,

TEMPERANCE

Self-Control: The Body

"But I keep under my body, and bring it into subjection: lest that by any means, when I have preached to others, I myself should be a castaway" (1 Corinthians 9:27).

The follower of Christ is called to lay down his life and his own desires in order to serve His Lord and his brothers. A father and husband is called to lay down his life in order to lovingly serve his family. The ability to rule over our own bodies -- choosing to do what is best, and choosing to do things we do not necessarily feel like doing -- will prepare us to exercise self-discipline in other areas of life. It will also enable us to better rule over others after we have learned to rule over ourselves.

A strong, healthy body enables us to better carry out the work God has given us to do. Our sons will need to learn the basic principles and habits of good health to fully serve the Lord as husbands and fathers.

A well-groomed body will not detract from our message of the Good News as we live in obedience to Christ. Man does "look on the outward appearance." We want others to see a body that is a fit "temple of the Holy Ghost."

Our sons will be more self-sacrificing husbands, more diligent workers, and more faithful fathers, if **we** are faithful to pass on to them the heritage of a disciplined life. We must call on them continually to do things they do not **feel** like doing. We must bring them alongside us, training them to do what is right, and letting them enjoy the blessings of self-control. And we must not shield them from the natural consequences of choosing to let their feelings rule.

A. Select verses from the list below, and use some or all of the following suggestions to help you study and better understand their meaning (easier verses are listed first, in italics):

1) Copy the passage.

2) Read it in several different translations of the Bible.

3) Read the passage and several of the verses before and after it to gain a better understanding of the context of the passage.

4) Rewrite the passage in your own words. What does it mean?

5) Record a specific way in which you can change your actions or attitudes based on the teaching of this passage.

6) Memorize the passage.

1 Corinthians 3:16
1 Corinthians 6:19-20
1 Samuel 16:7
Proverbs 6:12-13
Matthew 5:29-30
Romans 6:12-13
Romans 12:1-2
1 Corinthians 9:25-27
(BIBLE / SPEECH)

Beginner

B. Stay in bed during parent-appointed naptimes and bedtimes. Go to the bathroom and finish other duties beforehand so you won't need to get up when you should be in bed. *(TIME MANAGEMENT)*

C. Learn to brush your teeth and take a bath or shower by yourself without being reminded. *(TIME MANAGEMENT)*

D. Set and observe regular hours for going to bed and getting up. *(TIME MANAGEMENT)*

E. Practice sitting still for at least fifteen minutes a day. You can listen to a tape, but do not read, draw, play with toys, or anything else that requires movement. *(P.E.)*

F. Learn to stand still with good posture. *(P.E.)*

G. Use the chart on page 173 to help you be faithful in personal hygiene. Check off each task as you complete it each day. Perhaps you can work toward a goal to help you be consistent. *(TIME MANAGEMENT / HEALTH)*

Intermediate

H. Learn good grooming habits. Wash and comb hair, clean and trim nails, bathe, launder clothes, etc. **without being reminded.** *(PERSONAL HYGIENE / MANNERS)*

I. Ask others to help you see any annoying physical habits you have, and work to reform your behavior, with God's help. *(MANNERS)*

J. Observe people in a crowd. Watch their posture, eyes, clothes, and walk. What do these things communicate? Try to draw a picture of a confident, self-disciplined person, and another picture of a sluggardly person, based on your observations. Or write lists of descriptive words comparing the two. *(ART / WRITING / SOCIAL SKILLS)*

K. Find ways to help others while also getting exercise (i.e., mowing the widow neighbor's lawn, biking to the store for an elderly couple, taking a disabled person for a walk in his/her wheelchair). *(P.E. / COMMUNITY SERVICE)*

L. Participate in an individual or team sport on a regular basis, or perform tasks at home which require heavy labor. *(P.E.)*

M. Study the section on "The Face" in *Man in Demand*, by Wayne and Emily Hunter (pages 29-35). *(HEALTH)*

N. Study the section on "Hair" in *Man in Demand*, pages 36-41. *(HEALTH)*

O. Study the section on "Exercise" in *Man in Demand*, pages 50-52. *(HEALTH / P.E.)*

P. Study the section on "Clothing" in *Man in Demand*, pages 54-57. *(MANNERS)*

Q. Go through the checklists on pages 68-72 in *Man in Demand*. *(HEALTH / MANNERS)*

R. Study Chapter 13, "The Importance of Controlling the Flesh," and Chapter 26, "The Sacredness of the Body" in *Christian Manhood*, by Gary Maldaner. *(BIBLE)*

S. Complete the exercises on pages 50-53 in *Man in Demand*, by Wayne and Emily Hunter.

T. Practice good posture when standing and sitting. Ask your parents to correct you when you are slouching. *(MANNERS / HEALTH)*

U. Get some form of exercise every day. Set up a regular exercise or workout program and follow it faithfully. *(P.E. / HEALTH)*

V. Read biographies of successful athletes who exercised great self-discipline in training and competing. Keep a list of the principles you observe about self-control as you read these books. *(LITERATURE / HISTORY / WRITING)*

W. Notice the times when you are tired. Think back over the past few hours or days. Are there areas where you failed to exercise proper self-control which are now causing you to be tired -- not enough sleep, improper diet, frenzied activity, etc.? Keep a journal of these observations and adjust your habits based on what you have learned. *(RESEARCH / WRITING)*

X. Study the section on "Posture" in *Man in Demand*, by Wayne and Emily Hunter, pages 21-26. (This book focuses on a young man's physical appearance and manners, and relates them to his spiritual needs. The book's physical appearance initially put us off, but it does contain a lot of useful material.) *(MANNERS / HEALTH)*

Y.   What does the Bible call the body? Read 2 Corinthians 5:1, Job 4:19, 1 Corinthians 3:16 and 6:15, 19, and other verses you can find that refer to the body or the flesh. Make a list of all the things to which the body is compared. Then write down the reason you think the Bible makes each comparison, and how you can apply this in your life. *(BIBLE / LOGIC / READING)*

Z.   Study Matthew 5:29-30 and Matthew 18:8-9, in their contexts. How could you "cut" off your hand if it sinned? Your ears? Or "pluck" your eye? *(BIBLE / READING)*

AA.   Make a list of ways to help yourself exercise self-control when you struggle with sins related to specific parts of your body. *(BIBLE / RESEARCH)*

Advanced

BB.   Memorize Questions No. 137-139 in the *Westminster Larger Catechism. (BIBLE)*

CC.   Take responsibility for a job in your home that requires physical labor (lawn mowing, yard care, construction, excavation, etc.).

DD.   Study the brevity of life. Look up the word "life" in *Nave's Topical Bible*, and read the verses in the subsection entitled "Brevity and Uncertainty of." To what is our life likened? Note each passage you read, along with your observations. *(BIBLE / RESEARCH / WRITING)*

EE.   Write a paper explaining how a person could make his body -- health, appearance, physical fitness, athletic abilities, etc. -- an idol. *(BIBLE / ENGLISH COMPOSITION)*

FF.   Susanna Wesley once said that, "whatever increases the strength and authority of your body over your mind -- that thing is sin to you." Write an essay expanding on this thought. *(ENGLISH COMPOSITION)*

GG.   Study Matthew 5:29-30. Read commentaries on these verses. What do they mean? How should they be applied? Write an essay explaining the passage.

HH.   Write a paper commenting on the following statement by Elisabeth Elliot in *Discipline: The Glad Surrender*:

"More spiritual failure is due, I believe, to this cause than to any other: the failure to recognize this living body as having anything to do with worship or holy sacrifice. This body is, quite simply, the starting place. Failure here is failure everywhere else."

How does this statement relate to Romans 12:1-2? How is our body related to worship? How does failure to discipline the body affect our spiritual life?

Additional ideas:

Personal Hygiene Checklist

(See instructions in Project G.)

TASK	1	2	3	4	5	6	7	8	9	10	11	12	13	14	15	16	17	18	19	20	21	22	23	24	25	26	27	28	29	30
M. Wash ce																														
M. Brush eth																														
M. Comb ir																														
M. Wash ce or bathe																														
M. Brush eth																														
M. Clothes t away or in undry																														
nce a week: im and clean ils																														

Parents:

Consider and discuss with your son the following questions:

- Does he practice good hygiene? Does he have to be reminded?
- Does he exercise self-discipline in going to bed and getting up at regular times?
- Does he get plenty of exercise?
- Does he treat his body as "the temple of the Holy Ghost"?
- Does he sit in a polite fashion?
- Does his physical appearance and posture communicate self-discipline and confidence?
- Does he rule his body so that it does not offend others?
- Is he often tired?
- Is he often ill?
- Are there specific things he can do to improve his health and energy level?
- Can he hold still, without wiggling and fidgeting?
- Does he have nervous habits (such as nail biting) that he should overcome?
- Does he walk, dress, talk or look at others in a way that would lead to temptation in his own life?
- Does he walk, dress, talk or look at others in a way that would cause them to be tempted?
- Does he give **enough** thought to his physical appearance?
- Does he give **too much** thought to his physical appearance?
- Are bodily exercise and sports more important to him than "spiritual exercise"?

Notes and comments:

Self-Control: The Appetite

"Blessed art thou, O land, when thy king is the son of nobles, and thy princes eat in due season, for strength, and not for drunkenness" (Ecclesiastes 10:17).

Exercising self-control in eating and drinking will yield the fruit of a clearer mind and a healthier body for serving our Lord and others.

We can start teaching our sons self-discipline over their appetites when they are very young. We parents must resist the temptation to easily quiet a child by putting something in his mouth. A mother may be tempted to nurse a baby or toddler every time he is restless or out of control, instead of teaching the child other appropriate means of quieting himself. Parents may, in the interest of getting a child to eat, cater to his tastes or even offer him special foods instead of teaching him to eat, or at least try a bite of what is put before him.

In general, a regular schedule of meals is preferable to constant snacking. The allowance of continual snacking trains a child to expect immediate gratification. It is better for the body and for teaching self-control in eating habits, to train a child to wait for meal times.

Appetites also involve more than food and drink. Sons need to learn self-control over their appetites for entertainment and pleasure, as well. More attention will be given to this area in "Conquering Laziness."

A. Select verses from the list below, and use some or all of the following suggestions to help you study and better understand their meaning (easier verses are listed first, in italics):

1) Copy the passage.

2) Read it in several different translations of the Bible.

3) Read the passage and several of the verses before and after it to gain a better understanding of the context of the passage.

4) Rewrite the passage in your own words. What does it mean?

5) Record a specific way in which you can change your actions or attitudes based on the teaching of this passage.

6) Memorize the passage.

   Psalm 145:15
   Proverbs 21:17
   Proverbs 25:16

1 Corinthians 10:31
Ephesians 5:18
Proverbs 20:1
Proverbs 23:2
Proverbs 23:21
Proverbs 23:29-35
Proverbs 30:8
Proverbs 31:4-7
(BIBLE / SPEECH)

Beginner

B. Read with your parents 1 Corinthians 10:31. What should be our purpose as we live our lives? What should our purpose be when we eat and drink? How can we eat and drink for God's glory? Talk with your parents about some specific ways you can glorify God when you eat and drink. *(BIBLE / HEALTH / MANNERS)*

C. Read with your parents the story of Esau in Genesis 25. What was Esau willing to give up just because he was hungry? Act out this story in your playtime. *(DRAMA / BIBLE)*

D. Read with your parents Proverbs 23:29-35. What happens to the person who drinks too much wine? Illustrate this passage. *(BIBLE / ART)*

E. Eat what is given to you at meals and scheduled snack times and do not ask for food at other times of the day. Eat enough at meals so that you won't be hungry later. *(HEALTH)*

F. Read with your parents the story of the Israelites in Numbers 11. What did they complain about? What did they wish they had? What was God already giving them? Were they thankful for it? What did God say to Moses? What did He give the people? What happened next? Do you ever want something different to eat than what God and your parents provide? What should you do? *(BIBLE)*

Draw a picture of this story, or have fun acting it out with your family and friends. *(BIBLE / ART / DRAMA)*

G. Read with your parents Philippians 3:17-21. How can a person's "belly" become his god? *(BIBLE / HEALTH)*

H. Illustrate Proverbs 23:2 and post it in the dining room or on the refrigerator. *(BIBLE / ART)*

I. If you spend time on the computer or watching a movie, agree with your parents on a time limit and stop when the limit is reached. *(TIME MANAGMENT)*

Intermediate

J. Look up "glutton" and "gluttony" in *Strong's Concordance.* Read each verse that is listed (in the context of its surrounding verses), and take notes. What do you learn about overeating? Summarize what you have found into a short paper. *(BIBLE / RESEARCH / FOREIGN LANGUAGE)*

K. Study the section entitled "Eating for Physical Fitness," in *Man in Demand,* by Wayne and Emily Hunter, pages 42-46. *(HEALTH)*

L. Study the health hazards of overeating and being overweight. How does lack of self discipline in this area affect one's body? Make a list of your findings. *(RESEARCH / HEALTH)*

M. Keep a log of time spent on the computer and watching television. Add up your time each day and at the end of the week. How much time have you spent? Compare this to the time you spend working, interacting with people, studying your Bible, and learning new useful skills. Do you need to make any changes? Set goals and work to reach them. Ask someone to hold you accountable, if necessary.

N. Read Proverbs 25:27. Write an essay on the similarity of eating too much honey and boasting about oneself. *(BIBLE / WRITING)*

O. Read and study Psalm 104:14-15. Discuss these verses with your father. What does God cause to grow for man? What is man to do with the things that grow? What is the purpose of wine, oil, and bread? How can we abuse these things? *(BIBLE)*

P. Do a topical Bible study on drunkards and winebibbers. (Start by looking up the words "drunkard" and "drunkenness" in *Nave's Topical Bible*.) What happens to the drunkard? What should the believer be filled with instead of too much wine? Discuss your study with your father. *(BIBLE / RESEARCH)*

Q. Study the chapters on "Gluttony" and "Drunkenness" in *For Instruction in Righteousness,* by Pam Forster. *(BIBLE / HEALTH)*

R. Read 1 Corinthians 5:11. Study the meaning of each of the nouns in this verse. With whom are we not to keep company? Does this mean we should never associate with them or talk to them? Read some commentaries on this verse.

Write a short paper that summarizes what you learn and how this verse should affect your life. *(BIBLE / ENGLISH COMPOSITION)*

S. Read the book of Exodus. Note each time the Israelites are disciplined for complaining and disobedience. What are they complaining about? How many of these instances are related to food and drink? What can you learn from this? *(BIBLE)*

T. Read a book on nutrition or some specific aspect of healthy eating. Write down ways in which the information you have acquired will affect your eating habits. *(READING / HEALTH)*

U. Study the practice of fasting in the Bible by reading the verses listed under "fasting" in *Nave's Topical Bible*. Note your observations as you read. On what occasions did people fast in the Bible? What condition of heart accompanied fasting? Write a paper that summarizes the principles of fasting as seen through your study. *(BIBLE / HEALTH / WRITING)*

V. Complete the Bible study *Key Principles of Biblical Fasting,* by Kay Arthur and Pete DeLacy. Do this study with your father, if possible. *(BIBLE)*

W. Skip one meal a week, and devote that time to prayer. Keep a record of your requests and God's answers. *(DEVOTIONS / WRITING)*

Advanced

X. If you are part of a social network on the computer, or if you read blogs or play computer games, set a time limit for how long you are on these sites each day. Complete your other duties before looking at these sites. *(TIME MANAGEMENT / COMPUTER SKILLS)*

Y. Read Chapter 7, "Discipline of the Body," in *Discipline: The Glad Surrender,* by Elisabeth Elliot. Summarize what the author says about fasting. Read the rest of the book, if you haven't already. I*(READING)*

Z. Study Romans 13:13-14. Study the meaning of each noun and verb, using Strong's concordance to identify and define words. What does each of the words mean? How do the words relate to each other? What are we to put on instead of these sins? *(BIBLE / FOREIGN LANGUAGE)*

AA. Keep a diet diary in which you record all you eat throughout the day for several days. Look for patterns of overeating or unhealthy eating habits. When are you most apt to eat out of boredom, or simply for pleasure? Take steps to exercise more self-control in this area. *(HEALTH / WRITING)*

BB. Looking over the same diet diary as described in project AA above, study the nutritional content of all you have eaten. Based on recommended daily allowances (RDA), what should you eat more of, less of? Write down your conclusions, and work at making changes in your eating habits. *(HEALTH / SCIENCE / WRITING)*

CC. Study the chapter on "Overeating" in *A Homework Manual for Biblical Living, Vol. 1,* by Wayne Mack (pages 130-131). *(BIBLE / HEALTH / WRITING)*

DD. If you overeat or are overweight, commit to a change in eating and exercise habits. Research what is included in a healthy diet and how many calories are reasonable for your age and weight. Keep a log of all you eat each day and how many calories you consume. Look for helps that encourage life style changes, not quick, temporary diets. *(NUTRITION / HEALTH)*

EE. Read *A Hunger for God: Desiring God through Fasting and Prayer,* by John Piper. Write a review of the book to share with others. What are the main points of the book? Are they biblically sound? In what ways will the book benefit other readers? Then write a short summary statement of how this book will affect your life and actions. *(READING / WRITING)*

FF. If you spend a great deal of time playing video games, watching television, or browsing online, read *Hope and Help for Video Game, TV, and Internet "Addiction,"* by Mark Shaw. Use the practical helps in the appendix to help you develop a plan for change. *(READING)*

GG. If you or your parents feel that you have or are approaching some form of addiction (eating, drinking, drug abuse, sex, internet use, etc.), do at least one of the following:

- Enroll in the free courses, "The Lord's Table" or "New Wine," at *www.settingcaptivesfree.com*.

- Read *The Heart of Addiction,* by Mark Shaw, and complete the companion workbook.

- Read *Addictions: A Banquet in the Grave,* by Edward Welch. Complete the "Practical Theology" sections at the end of each chapter.

Additional ideas:

Parents:

Consider and discuss with your son the following questions:

- Does he eat in moderation, or does he eat more than he needs for nourishment and strength?

- Does he eat a balanced diet, or does he favor certain foods while neglecting others?

- Does he snack a lot between meals?

- Is satisfying his physical appetite more important to him than getting spiritual nourishment from God's Word and fellowship?

- Does he use good manners at the table?

- Does he wait at the table until all are served, or does he begin eating as soon as he is served?

- Can he quietly and patiently wait for a meal to be ready, or is he in the kitchen begging between meals?

- Does he seek more than his share at a meal?

- Does he indulge in an excess of sweets and junk food?

- Does he want to eat whenever he is bored?

- Does he keep company with friends who over-indulge in food or drink?

- Does he exercise self-discipline in other areas, strengthening himself to be self-disciplined, as well, in his eating and drinking habits?

- Is he discontent in other areas of his life?

- Is he indifferent or lukewarm in his walk with Christ?

- Is he using food as a comfort or means of satisfaction when experiencing frustrations or fears?

Notes and comments:

Self-Control: The Thought Life

"...bringing into captivity every thought to the obedience of Christ. (2 Corinthians 10:5b).

Scripture tells us that our actions are the result of our thoughts. Our thoughts are the fruit of what we have put into our hearts. The Christian cannot have a lazy, indifferent mind. Faith requires an active renewing of our minds, a choosing to think differently, a putting our trust in God and His Word.

It is imperative, then, to diligently help our sons to guard their minds and hearts. Television and reading material may be introducing ungodly teaching and role models that we would never consciously bring into our homes. We must pray for God's guidance and for a sensitive spirit in these areas. To "avoid all appearance of evil" is the simplest advice in this matter. If there is any question about a particular book or program, it should be turned off and discussed. Because you do not perceive it as a temptation to you does not mean that it will not cause your children to stumble.

The task of previewing all reading material that an active reader might devour is time-consuming. Rely on recommendations of trusted friends and reviewers. Peruse books from the library before your sons read them. Teach your sons to be discerning. Train them to detect humanism and false teaching by talking to them about what they read and watch.

Make Bible reading and serious Bible study a priority in your home. The best defense against unavoidable temptation in our thoughts is to fill our hearts and minds with God's Word. Constantly seek to apply God's wisdom to the everyday situations in your home. Memorize Scripture together with your children. Put the words of Scripture on the walls of your home.

A. Select verses from the list below, and use some or all of the following suggestions to help you study and better understand their meaning (easier verses are listed first, in italics):

1) Copy the passage.

2) Read it in several different translations of the Bible.

3) Read the passage and several of the verses before and after it to gain a better understanding of the context of the passage.

4) Rewrite the passage in your own words. What does it mean?

5) Record a specific way in which you can change your actions or attitudes based on the teaching of this passage.

6) Memorize the passage.

   Proverbs 4:23

   Proverbs 23:7a

   Matthew 5:8

   Deuteronomy 6:5-6

   1 Samuel 16:7

   Psalm 19:14

   Proverbs 14:30

   Matthew 5:27-28

   Luke 6:45

   Romans 12:2

   Romans 16:19

   2 Corinthians 10:4-5

   Philippians 4:8

   James 1:14-15

   (BIBLE / SPEECH)

Beginner

B. When your parents read the Bible to you, try to think of what it means and how you can apply it in your life. Listen carefully. *(BIBLE / DEVOTIONS)*

C. Draw a picture of a soldier (or purchase a flannelgraph "Christian Soldier," Christian soldier paper dolls, or a Christian Soldier action figure). Dress him in his "armor of God." When you sin in your thoughts, read Ephesians 6:13-17. Which piece of armor did you fail to use in combating temptation in this situation? Confess your sin to God, accept His forgiveness, and put your armor back on! (See Doorposts' *Bible Times Paper Dolls* which includes an "Armor of God" doll) *(ART / BIBLE)*

D. When you are tempted to think of what you **don't** have, stop and make a list of all the things you **do** have. Thank God for them, and trust Him to provide all that you need. *(WRITING)*

E. Pray when you are tempted to worry or be afraid.

F. Read with your parents Luke 6:45. Draw a picture to illustrate this verse and post it on a wall in your house. *(BIBLE / ART)*

G. Read with your parents Philippians 4:8. Make a list of the categories of things we are supposed to think about. Then write down specific ideas of things to think about for each of these categories. *(BIBLE / WRITING)*

H. Make a list of the kinds of sinful thoughts you sometimes have. Look at Philippians 4:8 and identify which area you are failing to think about. (For example, if you are thinking you would like to take a toy away from someone, you are failing to think about things that are just.) *(BIBLE / WRITING)*

Intermediate

I. Ask one of your parents to approve a book before you read it. Ask them what standards they use to judge the quality of a book and look for those qualities as you read. *(READING)*

J. List all the ways you can think of that we sin in our thoughts (i.e., bitterness, resentment). In which of these areas are you especially tempted? Pray for God to help you. Memorize verses to help you change. *(WRITING / BIBLE)*

K. Luke 6:45 says that good and bad actions are the result of the "treasure of our hearts." Spend a day paying special attention to what you are putting into your heart. Write down everything you did that brought thoughts into your heart -- watching TV, reading, listening to music, talking with others. Be specific. How long did you spend at each activity? What was heard or said?

Then look over the list. Do you need to make some changes? Are you bringing more "evil treasures" into your heart than "good treasures"? Write down specific plans for change. Share them with your parents, and take action! *(WRITING / MATH)*

L. Study Chapters 12 and 40 in *Christian Manhood,* by Gary Maldaner. These chapters discuss television viewing and its relationship to one's thought life. *(BIBLE)*

M. Read and study 2 Corinthians 10:3-5. What do these verses mean? Read them in several translations of the Bible. Then make a poster to put on your wall that includes the words of these verses and photographs or drawings to illustrate them. *(BIBLE / ART)*

N. Study Colossians 3. Outline the chapter. What does it say about our minds? What things does it identify as "earthly"? What does it identify as "things above" or things we are supposed to "put on"? Why are we to set our minds on "things above"? What is supposed to rule in our hearts (our thoughts and feelings)? *(BIBLE)*

O. Refer to these helpful resources when choosing books to read:
- *Books Children Love,* by Elizabeth Wilson and Susan Schaeffer Macaulay
- *Books that Build Character,* by William Kilpatrick and others
- *The Book Tree,* by Elizabeth MacCullum and Jane Scott
- *Honey for a Child's Heart,* by Gladys Hunt
- *Honey for a Teen's Heart,* by Gladys Hunt

(READING / LITERATURE)

P. Explore the Christian movie review sites listed below. Look at reviews on each site for the same movie and compare them. Which site do you like best?
- *www.movieguide.org*
- *www.thefish.com*
- *www.christiananswers.net*
- *www.pluggedin.com*

(COMPUTER SKILLS / WORLDVIEWS / RESEARCH)

Q. Ask one of your parents if you can search with them for a Christian review before your family watches a movie. *(RESEARCH)*

R. Keep a list of movies and books that are recommended to you by trustworthy friends and family members. Also look at the list of recommended movies at the back of *Disciplines of a Godly Family,* by R. Kent and Barbara Hughes. Refer to your movie list when your family wants to watch a movie. Read a Christian review of the movie before watching it. *(RESEARCH)*

S. Write out a covenant with yourself. Make a commitment about how you will use your eyes and ears. Write what you will not allow yourself to look at or listen to and what you plan to do when you are confronted with these things. Ask your parents, friends, and siblings to help keep you accountable to this commitment. Memorize one key verse that you can always recall and believe when you encounter temptation. *(WRITING)*

T. Search online for the lyrics to some of your favorite songs. Read the words carefully. Have your parents read them. Are the words and the messages of the songs ones that please God? Do they help you think rightly about the world? Do you need to make any changes? Discuss this with your parents. What do they think? *(MUSIC)*

U. Explore *www.Christianradio.com* or other sites for free Christian music online. Listen to this or other Christian music that will encourage godly thinking throughout the day. *(MUSIC)*

V. Examine any magazines, blogs, websites, and social networks you regularly read. Are they building up your mind or tearing it down? Do any of them tempt you to sin in your thoughts? Ask your parents for their input. Discontinue reading any which do not measure up to the list given in Philippians 4:8. Replace them with reading material that does meet the criteria of Philippians 4:8. *(JOURNALISM / COMPUTER SKILLS / WORLDVIEWS)*

W. Read Chapter 2, "God, My Heart, and Media," and Chapter 3, "God, My Heart, and Music," in *Worldliness: Resisting the Seduction of a Fallen World,* edited by C. J. Mahaney. Discuss the discussion questions at the back of the book with your father. Use the time, heart, and content questions in Chapter 2 to help you evaluate your use of media. Read the rest of the book, if you haven't already done so. *(READING / ART / MUSIC)*

X. Study the chapter entitled "Sinful Thought Life" in *For Instruction in Righteousness,* by Pam Forster. *(BIBLE)*

Y. Write down the times and places when you are most tempted in your thoughts. Rearrange your life to help avoid these times when possible. Write down a specific plan. Choose to submit to the Holy Spirit's control when you must face these situations. Pray for His help. *(WRITING)*

Z. Study and memorize Ephesians 4:22-24. Then discuss with your parents how a person can be "renewed in the spirit of [their] mind[s]." Look at the rest of the verses in the chapter. Are all these instructions part of being renewed in the spirit of our minds? List each instruction. What does Paul tell us **to do**? What does he say we should **not do**? What does the first verse of chapter 5 say in conclusion? *(BIBLE / WRITING)*

Advanced

AA. Ask your father to hold you accountable for your thoughts. Encourage him to ask you on a regular basis how you are doing and if there are areas for which you would like prayer. *(FAMILY / SOCIAL SKILLS)*

BB. Pinpoint any specific areas in which you are struggling with sinful thinking. Pray for God to show you areas in your life that may be contributing to your sinful thoughts. Outline a plan to help you make your thoughts more pleasing to God. What might you need to eliminate? What can you do to replace sinful thoughts with God-pleasing ones? Discuss your plan with your parents. *(WRITING)*

CC. Discuss with your parents the movies and television programs you watch. What is your standard? Do you or they think you are compromising in any areas? Would they like you to make changes? Discuss honestly with them the effect that your viewing has on your thoughts. *(ART / WORLDVIEW)*

DD. Read Chapter 8, "The Discipline of the Mind," in *Discipline: The Glad Surrender,* by Elisabeth Elliot. Expand on the statement, "The transformation of the mind produces a transformed vision of reality." What does the author mean? *(READING)*

EE. Study Matthew 22:37-39. What is the difference between the soul, heart, and mind? Read commentaries. In what specific ways can you obey these verses? *(BIBLE / RESEARCH)*

FF. Study the word "mind" in the Bible. Take notes as you read verses that include this word. Then study your notes. What does God say about our minds? Summarize your findings in a short paper. *(BIBLE / ENGLISH COMPOSITION)*

GG. Study the word "heart" in the Bible. What does the word mean? What does Scripture tell us about the heart? What commands are given? Outline your findings. *(RESEARCH / BIBLE / FOREIGN LANGUAGE)*

HH. Read Chapter 6, "Discipline of Mind," in *Disciplines of a Godly Man,* by R. Kent Hughes. Complete the "Food for Thought" section at the end of the chapter, and note any of the recommended books that you would like to read. Read the rest of this book, if you haven't already done so. *(READING / LITERATURE)*

II. Read Appendix C, "Personal Reading Survey," in *Disciplines of a Godly Man,* by R. Kent Hughes. Create a list of books you would like to read, based on this survey. Set a goal of reading at least one of them over the next few weeks. *(READING / LITERATURE)*

JJ. Memorize Questions No. 137-139 in *The Westminster Larger Catechism.* *(BIBLE)*

KK. Read Sinclair Ferguson's *Read Any Good Books?* How do our reading choices affect our thoughts? Write a summary of its message. *(READING / ENGLISH COMPOSITION)*

LL. Read *Renewing Your Mind in a Mindless World,* by James Montgomery Boice. Read and discuss it with your father, or ask a friend to read it so you can discuss it together. *(READING)*

MM. Read *Total Truth,* by Nancy Pearcey. Complete the study guide at the back of the book to help you master the major worldview themes presented in the book, and to test yourself on what you have learned. *(WORLDVIEW /SCIENCE / POLITICS / APOLOGETICS / RELIGION)*

NN. Study the section entitled "Changing Sinful Thought Patterns" in *A Homework Manual for Biblical Living, Vol. 1,* by Wayne Mack. *(BIBLE / READING / WRITING)*

Additional ideas:

Parents:

Consider and discuss with your son the following questions:

- Does he listen to music that promotes godly thinking?
- Is he careful about what he reads and what he views on television and in movies?
- Does he cheerfully accept your guidance in his reading and viewing habits?
- Is he reading and memorizing Scripture to equip his mind with God's truth?
- Is he accountable to anyone for his reading, internet, and video habits?
- Does he have filters for his internet access?
- Does he control his eyes, or does he allow them to dwell on things that will lead to lustful thoughts and desires?
- Does he spend a lot of time in idle daydreaming?
- Does he make wise use of free time? Does he have too much free time?
- Do his words reveal bitterness, pride, and other "secret" sins of the heart?
- Does he freely approach you with questions about sensitive or personal subjects?
- Does he frequently get excited about ideas without ever doing anything else about them?
- Do his thoughts seldom end in action?
- Is he fairly stable in his thinking or does he change views frequently?

Notes and comments:

Self-Control: The Tongue

"Let no corrupt communication proceed out of your mouth, but that which is good to the use of edifying, that it may minister grace unto the hearers" (Ephesians 4:29).

A husband and father must become a master at building up rather than tearing down. Part of his job as leader of his family will be to guide his children and wife toward maturity. This will require reproof and instruction. If this is done in a sarcastic, impatient, or proud manner, those under him will be tempted to ignore him or rebel against him. If reproof outweighs encouragement children will quickly become discouraged.

If he has gained no self-control over his words, he will be more apt to "provoke his children to anger." Let's set a godly example in this area as we reprove and lead our children in a gentle, loving manner.

A. Select verses from the list below, and use some or all of the following suggestions to help you study and better understand their meaning (easier verses are listed first, in italics):

1) Copy the passage.

2) Read it in several different translations of the Bible.

3) Read the passage and several of the verses before and after it to gain a better understanding of the context of the passage.

4) Rewrite the passage in your own words. What does it mean?

5) Record a specific way in which you can change your actions or attitudes based on the teaching of this passage.

6) Memorize the passage.

   Psalm 34:13
   Psalm 141:3
   Proverbs 4:24
   Proverbs 15:1
   Proverbs 6:16-19
   Proverbs 10:11
   Proverbs 10:19
   Proverbs 10:31-32
   Proverbs 13:3
   Proverbs 15:28

Proverbs 29:11
Proverbs 29:20
Ephesians 4:29
Ephesians 4:31
James 1:26
(BIBLE / SPEECH)

Beginner

B. Tell each person in your family something you appreciate about them. *(SPEECH)*

C. Practice being quiet for a designated amount of time (naptime, school time, during a short car ride, etc.)

D. Illustrate Proverbs 13:3 and post it on a wall in your house. *(BIBLE / ART)*

E. Learn how to ask forgiveness when you wrong one of your siblings or disobey your parents. Do this each time you sin against someone. *(SOCIAL SKILLS / MANNERS)*

F. For a day, try to stop and think every time before you speak. If you don't think God will be pleased with what you are going to say, don't say it. *(SPEECH / SOCIAL SKILLS)*

G. Read with your parents Proverbs 6:16-19. List the things that God hates. Think about each thing, and how you might be sinning in these ways. Confess these sins to God. Confess to others who are involved. Then change! *(BIBLE / READING / WRITING)*

H. Role play different situations with your parents or siblings. If someone says something hurtful to you, what should you say? If they say something in an angry voice, how should you respond? If someone gossips to you, what should you say? etc. *(DRAMA / MANNERS)*

I. 1 Peter 3:9-10 instructs us to not return evil for evil or railing for railing. Instead we are to return a blessing. Discuss with your parents how you can do this. Think of specific ways you can bless those who do evil against you. Write your ideas down. Refer to these ideas when you are tempted to speak unkindly to someone who has been unkind to you. *(BIBLE / WRITING)*

J. Read with your parents verses on the tongue, mouth, and lips. Make a notebook of pictures illustrating each proverb, and write the verses below each picture. Or use the pictures and verses as posters throughout the house. Use some or all of the verses listed below, in addition to others you find:

Ephesians 4:25   Proverbs 12:16

Psalm 141:3	Proverbs 12:18
Proverbs 17:14	Proverbs 16:28
Proverbs 25:9	Proverbs 17:9
James 1:26	Proverbs 18:8
Philippians 1:27	Proverbs 26:18-19
Proverbs 11:12	Proverbs 26:20-21
Proverbs 11:13	

(BIBLE / RESEARCH / ART)

Intermediate

K. Study Matthew 12:36-37. Ask ahead for a parent or friend to write down all the idle or unkind words you speak throughout a day (without telling you that they are doing it). Or they can tape record your words. Give an account to God for your words at the end of the day. *(BIBLE)*

L. Make a project of seeking to encourage others with your tongue for an entire day. How hard did you have to work at it? Write down what you have learned. *(WRITING)*

M. Study Chapter 19, "What Do Your Words Show About Your Character?" in *Christian Manhood,* by Gary Maldaner. *(BIBLE)*

N. Conduct this experiment. Ask someone to listen carefully to your speech throughout the day. Have them place a bean in one jar whenever they hear you use your tongue in a wise and edifying way. Have them place a bean in another jar when they hear you use your tongue in a rude, discouraging, or ungodly way. Which jar is fullest at the end of the day? What can you do to improve? Discuss specific goals for improvement. Confess your sin to God and to those you have wronged. *(WRITING)*

O. Write a list of ways to build someone up (edify) with words. In what areas can you encourage another person? What could you say instead of negative words? ("I struggle with that same problem. This verse has been a help to me," or "I am thankful for all the times you help me", etc.). *(SPEECH / WRITING / SOCIAL SKILLS)*

P. Study James 3. Write down everything it says about the tongue. Write a short summary of what you have learned from this passage. *(BIBLE / READING / WRITING)*

Q. List specific instructions from Scripture that God gives regarding the use of the tongue. List each instruction, along with its Scripture reference. (Look up

"Speaking" in *Nave's Topical Bible* for help finding verses.) Use the form on page 194. *(BIBLE / RESEARCH / WRITING)*

R. Study the following words in your Bible. Summarize in a paper what you learn about each word:

Busybody
Contention
Flattery
Lying
Meddling
Murmuring
Speaking
Talebearer

(BIBLE / RESEARCH / FOREIGN LANGUAGE)

S. Study the chapters on the "Sins of the Tongue" in *For Instruction in Righteousness,* by Pam Forster. *(BIBLE / RESEARCH / READING)*

T. Keep a journal. Write down each time you have used your tongue to tear someone down. Write down the date, the circumstances, who was involved, what you said, and the date you asked forgiveness. (See form on page 195.)
(WRITING)

U. Think of a person whose gracious speech you admire. Talk to him or her. How did they mature in the control of their tongue? What advice can they give you? Write a summary of your interview. *(SPEECH / WRITING)*

V. Study examples in the Bible of those who misused their tongues. In *Nave's Topical Bible,* look for "Instances of" under the following headings:

Boasting
Falsehood
Flattery
Murmuring
Slander
Talebearer

Write down each person and their sinful use of the tongue. Then note the consequences of their sin. (See form on page 196.) *(BIBLE / RESEARCH / WRITING)*

Advanced

W. Memorize Questions No. 144 and 145 in the *Westminster Larger Catechism.*
(BIBLE)

X. Read Chapter 11, "Discipline of Tongue," in *Disciplines of a Godly Man,* by R. Kent Hughes. Complete the "Food for Thought," "Application/Response," and "Think About It!" sections at the end of the chapter. *(SPEECH / BIBLE / SOCIAL SKILLS)*

Y. Write an essay entitled "What I Have Gained by Arguing." *(ENGLISH COMPOSITION)*

Z. Think about a relationship you have that is troubled by sinful speech patterns. List things you are doing that make the relationship challenging, practices that you know are offensive or discouraging. Pray about these sins, confess them, and commit to change. Ask forgiveness of the person. *(SOCIAL SKILLS)*

AA. Identify a specific sin of the tongue that is particularly tempting for you. Prayerfully design a plan to help you grow in this area.

- Study the sin in Scripture. Note its consequences.
- Study its positive counterpart in Scripture. (For example, honesty would be the positive counterpart of falsehood.) What blessings are associated with it? List verses you can memorize to help you resist the temptation to sin in this way.
- Find books to read that will help you grow more in this area.
- Seek counsel from others.
- Write down specific actions you can take.
- Pray each day for grace to improve.
- Work with someone who is willing to ask you questions and hold you accountable.

(BIBLE / RESEARCH / WRITING / SOCIAL SKILLS)

BB. Study the chapter on "Communication" in *A Homework Manual for Biblical Living, Vol. 1,* by Wayne Mack (pages 32-37). *(BIBLE / WRITING)*

CC. Study page 13, "Improving Your Speech" in *A Homework Manual for Biblical Living, Vol. 2,* by Wayne Mack. *(BIBLE / WRITING)*

Additional Ideas:

Biblical Instruction About Our Speech

(See instructions in Project Q.)

WHAT WE SHOULD DO	REFERENCE	WHAT WE SHOULD NOT DO	REFERENCE

Journal of Sinful Speech

(See instructions in Project T.)

DATE	CIRCUMSTANCES	PERSON INVOLVED	WHAT WAS SAID	DATE ASKED FORGIVENESS

Sinful Speech in the Bible

(See instructions in Project V.)

PERSON	REF.	SINFUL USE OF TONGUE	CONSEQUENCES

Parents:

Consider and discuss with your son the following questions:

- Does he criticize others?

- Does he mock others?

- Is he sarcastic in his speech?

- Does he tell the truth about someone's faults or wrongdoings with the intent of harming his reputation or getting him in trouble?

- Does he gossip about others?

- Does he call other people names?

- Does he use unkind words toward his siblings?

- Does he use flattery to manipulate others?

- Does he show respect to you with his words?

- Is there often a harsh or disrespectful tone in his voice?

- Does he use God's name in vain?

- Does he ever use crude or profane language?

- Does he tell lies?

- Does he stir up strife and contention?

- Does he have the habit of arguing?

- Does he whine?

- Does he grumble and complain?

- Does he monopolize a conversation?

- Does he speak too much about himself?

- Does he ask forgiveness when he has wronged another person?

- Are his words characterized by a desire to build others up or to tear them down?

Notes and comments:

Self-Control: Finances

"For which of you, intending to build a tower, sitteth not down first, and counteth the cost, whether he have sufficient to finish it?" (Luke 14:28).

We must train our sons to manage their money well. We may have limited resources or we may have much, but God is the giver of it all and we are called to be faithful and thankful stewards of whatever He has given. Living within our means will glorify God. The wise handling of money will enable your future daughters-in-law to stay home to manage their households and care for your grandchildren. Discipline in finances will help bring peace and contentment to a household. Many marital and family problems can be traced back to foolishness and disagreement in financial matters.

Give your sons the opportunity to budget their own money -- money that they had to work to earn, not just a welfare allowance! Let them learn that they will have to be diligent in working if they are to be faithful in providing for their families. Help them set up a budget based on sound Biblical principles of money management and help them work within it. Do not allow them to spend money that they do not have, unless you are trying to give them a real-life illustration of the pitfalls of going into debt!

Involve them in your money matters. Let them help with bill paying, checkbook balancing, household budgeting. Require them to set aside a specified percentage of their money for long-term savings in preparation for their own futures. Teach them to be wise buyers and generous givers.

A. Select verses from the list below, and use some or all of the following suggestions to help you study and better understand their meaning (easier verses are listed first, in italics):

1) Copy the passage.

2) Read it in several different translations of the Bible.

3) Read the passage and several of the verses before and after it to gain a better understanding of the context of the passage.

4) Rewrite the passage in your own words. What does it mean?

5) Record a specific way in which you can change your actions or attitudes based on the teaching of this passage.

6) Memorize the passage.

   Proverbs 10:22

Proverbs 11:28
Proverbs 22:7
Proverbs 27:1
Proverbs 27:23
Philippians 4:19
Deuteronomy 8:18
Deuteronomy 15:6
1 Samuel 2:7
Proverbs 22:26-27
Proverbs 30:8-9
Matthew 6:19-21
Luke 16:13
James 4:13-14
(SPEECH / BIBLE)

Beginner

B. Ask your parents if you can do a special job for pay. Save what you earn after tithing. *(FINANCES)*

C. Arrange with your parents to earn something each week when you do your chores well. Learn the connection between working and earning money. *(FINANCES / CAREER ED.)*

D. Put something in your church's offering each week. *(FINANCES)*

E. Pray with your family about an item your family needs. Pay attention to how God provides.

F. Read with your parents Philippians 4:19. Draw an illustration to show the meaning of the verse. *(BIBLE / ART)*

G. Use Doorposts' *Service Opportunities Chart* to help organize extra jobs you can do in your household for pay. Use what you earn to help support a missionary or bless someone in need. *(FINANCES)*

H. Study Doorposts' *Stewardship Street* with your parents. Set up your savings boxes, and divide any money you earn or receive into different budget categories. *(BIBLE / MATH / ART / FINANCES)*

I. Read with your parents Dave Ramsey's money-related storybooks for children. *(READING / FINANCES)*

J. Work through Dave Ramsey's *Financial Peace, Jr. for Kids* with your parents. *(FINANCES)*

K. Start saving 20% of what you earn. Put it in a special jar or piggy bank, and keep an account of how much you have saved. *(FINANCES / MATH / ACCOUNTING)*

L. Save part of your allowance or earnings toward a specific goal. For example, if a toy you would like costs ten dollars, commit to saving one dollar every week until you can buy it. *(FINANCES / MATH / ACCOUNTING)*

M. Save some of your money throughout the year and use it to buy Christmas and birthday gifts for your siblings. Pray before you go shopping and ask God to help you make the best use of your money. *(FINANCES)*

N. Help your mother clip coupons for items she needs to buy for the family. *(FINANCES / CONSUMER EDUCATION)*

Intermediate

O. Make a list of all the ways you can think of to save money in your home. *(WRITING / FINANCES)*

P. Keep a savings account in the bank. After you have saved enough, invest in a certificate of deposit or other forms of investment. *(MATH / FINANCES)*

Q. Go through *Money Matters for Kids,* by Larry Burkett. Put the principles into action with your own money. *(FINANCES / READING)*

R. Study Deuteronomy 15:4-6. What principles does this passage teach about borrowing? Write a short summary and explanation of the passage. *(BIBLE / FINANCES)*

S. Study ads in magazines and newspapers. How do they present their product? To what do they appeal? Clip several ads, paste them onto paper, and label them with explanations of their sales techniques. *(RESEARCH / WRITING / MARKETING / CONSUMER EDUCATION)*

T. What does the Bible say about "being surety" for someone? What is "surety"? Write out your findings. *(BIBLE / WRITING / RESEARCH)*

U. Design a prudent budget for the money you earn and receive. Think through which categories you should include, and what percentage of your earnings you should place in each category. *(MATH / FINANCES)*

V. Study the chapters on "Wastefulness/Carelessness" and "Borrowing" in *For Instruction in Righteousness,* by Pam Forster. *(BIBLE)*

W. Study the Bible to find out what practices in life can lead to poverty. (Start in the book of Proverbs, or look up the words "poor" and "poverty" in *Nave's Topical Bible*) *(BIBLE / RESEARCH / FINANCES)*

X. Select an item you would like to buy, or imagine an item that you might buy for your household someday. Do some comparison shopping. Call different stores to compare prices. Look at different models or brands of the item. Which one is better quality? Which one will last longer? Which one should you buy? *(CONSUMER EDUCATION / MATH / RESEARCH)*

Y. Study Abraham, Job, Solomon, Hezekiah, and Zaccheus. What was their attitude toward money? Did they use or abuse it? How? *(BIBLE / RESEARCH / FINANCES)*

Z. Study the parable of the rich man in Luke 12:16-21. Read commentaries about the passage. Write a short essay explaining its meaning and its application to your life. *(BIBLE / ENGLISH COMPOSITION)*

AA. Study the parable of the talents in Matthew 25:14-30. Write a short essay explaining its meaning and its application to your life. *(BIBLE / ENGLISH COMPOSITION)*

BB. Invest some of your savings into a business venture or project that will help you earn more money (i.e. lawnmower and tools for a lawn maintenance business). Keep track of your expenses, your income, and your profits (or loss). *(BUSINESS EDUCATION / MATH / WRITING)*

CC. Study the Bible to see what it says about borrowing and lending. Write a paper to summarize your findings (Start by looking up the terms "debt," "debtor," "borrowing," and "lending" in *Nave's Topical Bible*). *(BIBLE / RESEARCH / ENGLISH COMPOSITION)*

DD. With your parents' guidance, take charge of paying the family's bills. *(FAMILY / FINANCES / ACCOUNTING)*

EE. Research what the Bible says about **taxes**. Write out your findings. *(BIBLE / RESEARCH / GOVERNMENT / WRITING)*

FF. Ask your father to tell you your family's monthly income. Set up an imaginary budget for your family based on that amount. Compare it with your family's actual budget. Did you overlook some expenses? Did you underestimate costs? Did you allocate too much money in some areas? Discuss your "budget" with your father. *(FINANCES / BOOKKEEPING)*

GG. Set up a budget, using envelopes to divide your earnings into different categories. *(FINANCES / MATH / ACCOUNTING)*

HH. Discuss credit cards with your parents. What advantages are there in possessing one? What disadvantages? What dangers? Would you ever choose to use one? *(FINANCES)*

II. Read the book *The Tightwad Gazette,* by Amy Dacyczyn. Make a list of the good ideas you find. Read other books designed to help families save money. Keep notes from each book and file them for future reference. *(FINANCES / READING)*

Advanced

JJ. What things do you normally spend money on that you would be willing to forego in order to save money or cut back on spending? Make a list. Eliminate at least two of these expenses from your regular spending, and save that money to give to missionaries or a needy family. *(FINANCES / WRITING)*

KK. Complete the Bible study *Money and Possessions: The Quest for Contentment,* by Kay Arthur and David Arthur. Do this study with your father or with a group of young men. *(BIBLE / READING)*

LL. Write a paper entitled, "The Advantages and Disadvantages of Renting and Buying". Base your conclusions on careful research and thought. Interview homeowners and renters for their views. *(RESEARCH / SPEECH / ENGLISH COMPOSITION / FINANCES)*

MM. Complete the studies in Chapter 4, "Finances" in *Prepare Thy Work*, by Daniel Forster. *(BIBLE / RESEARCH / FINANCES)*

NN. Compare the actual cost of buying a new car versus buying a used car. How much value does the new car lose as soon as it is purchased and driven off the lot? How much is added to the sticker price of the car when you include the interest on a loan? How much money might you anticipate spending on repairs for either car? *(CONSUMER EDUCATION / FINANCES / RESEARCH)*

OO. Make a list of tools and training that you could invest in now as a young man that would better prepare you for your future. Also make a list of the things you do now that you could eliminate or minimize in order to give you more time for profitable training for the future. Use these lists to guide you as you seek to better prepare for the future. *(WRITING / FINANCES / CAREER EDUCATION)*

PP. Listen to Doug Wilson's lecture series, *Living with Money.* Discuss the talks with your father. *(FINANCES)*

QQ. Read *Using Your Money Wisely*, by Larry Burkett. *(READING / FINANCES)*

RR. Study *Money, Banking and Usury*, by Vic Lockman. Outline its basic content. *(READING / FINANCES / WRITING)*

SS. Under your father's oversight, manage the household bills for a month. *(FINANCES / HOME SKILLS)*

TT. Under your father's oversight, balance the family's checkbook for a month. *(FAMILY / ACCOUNTING/ MATH)*

UU. Open your own checking account, along with a debit card, and use it responsibly, keeping accurate records and balancing it regularly. Learn to check the balance and transaction history on the internet. *(FINANCES / ACCOUNTING / COMPUTER SKILLS)*

VV. Assist your father in filing your family's tax return, or complete a tax return for an imaginary family's income. Or if you have your own business, fill out a return for your income (even if it is not required). *(FINANCES / MATH / ACCOUNTING)*

WW. Study the advantages and disadvantages of certificates of deposit, T-bills, stocks and bonds, mutual funds, gold and silver, etc. In which would you choose to invest your money? *(RESEARCH / FINANCES)*

XX. Learn about mortgages. How much is actually paid on a house when you have a 7-year mortgage, a 30-year mortgage, etc.? Use an online mortgage calculator, enter real house prices, the present interest rate, different lengths for the loan, and varying amounts of down payment. What did you learn? How much can you save by paying a larger down payment? How much can you save by paying off the loan in a shorter amount of time? *(MATH / FINANCES)*

YY. Discuss with your father your family's health, car, and life insurance policies. What does "deductible" mean? What is "liability"? What is "comprehensive"? Research the meaning of insurance terms, and write a definition for each one. *(FINANCES / WRITING / LANGUAGE)*

ZZ. Think through your position on whether you will want your wife to take a paying job. Will you want her to work inside the home, outside the home, before children are born, after children, during periods of financial crisis or when you are out of work? Write out your convictions, supporting them with Scripture. *(BIBLE / WRITING / FAMILY)*

AAA. Study through the chapter on "Finances" in *A Homework Manual for Biblical Living, Vol. 1,* by Wayne Mack (pages 75-81). *(BIBLE / WRITING / FAMILY)*

BBB. Read Chapter 12, "Stewardship," and Appendix 8 in *The Exemplary Husband,* by Stuart Scott. Discuss what you learn with your father. What principles will you apply to your own finances? *(FINANCES)*

Additional ideas:

Parents:

Consider and discuss with your son the following questions:

- Can he perform mathematical operations accurately?

- Does he earn the money he has?

- Is he a hard worker?

- Does he tithe faithfully?

- Does he have a savings account?

- Does he place a proper value on money or does he spend it thoughtlessly?

- Is he miserly or greedy?

- Does he share what he has been blessed with?

- Does he want to spend more money than he has?

- Does he make purchases impulsively?

- Is he able to sacrifice immediate pleasure in order to save his money for a more valuable future purchase?

- Does he pray before he makes purchases?

- Does he study and research before making major purchases?

- Does he look for sales, used items, overstocks, and other means of saving money on a purchase?

- Does he spend money on things he really doesn't need?

- Does he spend money on things that he quickly tires of?

- Does he know how to talk to a salesman without being unduly swayed?

- Is he creative in thinking of different ways to obtain items without spending money?

- Does he think he has to spend every cent that comes his way, or is he able to save?

- Does he have a budget?

- Is he easily swayed by advertising?

- Is he grateful for the items you purchase for him? Does he take care of them?

- Does he waste the possessions he has through carelessness or neglect?

- Does he lose things and then expect to easily purchase another of the same item?

- Does he spend too much money on entertainment and pleasures so that he does not have enough for necessities and giving?

- Is he often out of money?

- Does he seek work when he needs money or does he want to borrow from others?

- If he has his own checking account, does he keep it balanced?

- Does he take care of any financial responsibilities in a prompt and orderly way?

- If he drives, does he pay for his own insurance?

Notes and comments:

Self-Control: Emotions

"He that hath no rule over his own spirit is like a city that is broken down, and without walls" (Proverbs 25:28).

From the moment a child is born, one of the challenges of his parents is to help him bring his emotions under control. The little baby must learn to quiet himself and not fret while waiting to have his needs met. The toddler must learn to not grow angry when he must wait or when he does not get what he wants. The young child must learn to control his emotions when playing with others. He must learn to trust God and not be afraid. The teenager must learn to control himself and not sin, even in the midst of the wide emotional swings that often accompany adolescence. Depression, moodiness, emotional attachments to young ladies, and worries about friendships are all opportunities to help our sons grow in self-control.

We as parents must be faithful in teaching our children to control their emotions. A young man who has not gained rule over his own spirit will not be able to successfully rule the family God puts under him. His uncontrolled passions will hurt and anger his wife and children. If his emotions rule he will live a life based not on principle, but on feelings.

A. Select verses from the list below, and use some or all of the following suggestions to help you study and better understand their meaning (easier verses are listed first, in italics):

   1) Copy the passage.

   2) Read it in several different translations of the Bible.

   3) Read the passage and several of the verses before and after it to gain a better understanding of the context of the passage.

   4) Rewrite the passage in your own words. What does it mean?

   5) Record a specific way in which you can change your actions or attitudes based on the teaching of this passage.

   6) Memorize the passage.

   Psalm 46:10
   Psalm 131:2
   (BIBLE / SPEECH)

B. Memorize some of the following verses about anger:

Proverbs 12:16
Proverbs 14:29
Proverbs 16:32
Proverbs 19:11
Proverbs 19:19
Proverbs 20:3
Ecclesiastes 7:9
Matthew 5:22
Colossians 3:8
(BIBLE / SPEECH)

C. Memorize some of the following verses about discouragement:
Psalm 94:19
Galatians 6:9
Psalm 42:5
Psalm 55:2
Revelation 21:4
(BIBLE / SPEECH)

D. Memorize some of the following verses about worry and anxiety:
Romans 8:28
1 Peter 5:7
Luke 12:22-31
Matthew 6:34
Philippians 4:6-7
(BIBLE / SPEECH)

Beginner

E. Read with your parents Proverbs 25:28. What does this verse mean? What were walls around cities for in Old Testament times? What could happen without the walls around the cities? Draw a picture to illustrate this proverb. Put it on your wall. Look at it when you are tempted to not exercise self-control. *(BIBLE / ART)*

F. Act out Proverbs 25:28 with your Legos or other building materials. *(BIBLE / CONSTRUCTION / DRAMA)*

G. Ask your parents to tell you a story of a time when one of them gave in to sinful emotions. What happened? What do they wish they had done differently?

H. Role play with your parents: How should you respond when you are tempted to be angry? What should you say to someone who has provoked you? What should you do if a situation is irritating or difficult? *(SOCIAL SKILLS / DRAMA)*

I. With your parents read the story of David's response to Nabal in 1 Samuel 25. Why was David angry? What was he going to do? Who appealed to him? What did she say? How did he respond? What happened next? Act out this story with your friends and family or with toys. *(BIBLE / DRAMA)*

J. Keep a jar of beans in the kitchen, along with 2 empty jars. Label one empty jar "Rule My Spirit" and the other "Not Rule My Spirit." As you go through the day, add a bean to the "Rule" jar whenever you rule your spirit in a tempting situation. Put a bean in the "Not Rule" jar whenever you fail to rule your spirit. Which jar is fullest at the end of the day? Do you need to ask God for help and power to bring your spirit into subjection to his rule? *(MATH)*

K. Work with a "buddy" who gently helps you see when you are not ruling your spirit. Thank him for his help. *(SOCIAL SKILLS)*

L. Write out and illustrate verses to put up on the wall around your house. Choose verses from the memory verses that will encourage you to obey God in the area of emotion in which you are most tempted. *(BIBLE / RESEARCH / ART / WRITING)*

M. Whenever you become angry, return to the person you wronged, confess your sin, and ask his forgiveness. *(SOCIAL SKILLS)*

Intermediate

N. Think about your friends. Are there any who do not rule their spirits as they should? Study Proverbs 22:24. Do you need to spend less time with certain friends? Are you picking up any bad habits from quick-tempered friends? How are you being influenced by your friends? How can you encourage them to exercise more self-control? Make a list of ideas. *(BIBLE / WRITING)*

O. Keep a journal. In it record each incident when you are tempted to become angry or when you did become angry. Write down what you did and what you should have done. Find a verse you can memorize to help you combat this sin. (Use the form on page 214.) *(WRITING / BIBLE / RESEARCH)*

P. Interview your parents and other adults, asking them to recount times in their lives when they have been tempted to become angry, discouraged, worried or afraid. What were the circumstances? What was their response? What were the results? Write a short essay summarizing your findings. Or write a short story recounting one of the stories you were told. *(SPEECH / HISTORY / ENGLISH COMPOSITION)*

Q. Look up "Despondency, Instances of" in *Nave's Topical Bible,* and read the stories of different people in the Bible who were despondent. Use the chart on page 215 to record your observations as you read. Why were they discouraged? What should they have done differently? *(BIBLE)*

R. Study the chapters on "Anger," "Faint-heartedness," "Depression," "Fear," and "Worry" in *For Instruction in Righteousness,* by Pam Forster. *(BIBLE / READING)*

S. Study an area of emotion that is a particularly weak area for you. Read related passages in the Bible. What can you do to gain victory over this area? Pray for God's grace and wisdom, write out some goals, and start working on them. *(BIBLE / RESEARCH)*

T. Make a list of what you are tempted to worry about. Pray over this list each day, and write down the answers God gives to your prayers. Review this list of answered prayers when you are tempted to worry. *(WRITING)*

U. Look up "Anger, Instances of" in *Nave's Topical Bible,* and read the stories of the different men of the Bible who were angry. Use the chart on page 216 to help you record your observations as you read. Why were they angry? What were the results of their anger? *(BIBLE)*

V. Study the life of Samson. How was his life influenced by his lack of emotional self-control and wisdom about women? Summarize in a short essay what you learn from his life and how it will affect your relationships with young ladies. *(BIBLE / SOCIAL SKILLS)*

W. Read *Emotional Purity: An Affair of the Heart,* by Heather Arnel Paulsen. Discuss the book with your father. *(SOCIAL SKILLS)*

X. Read *I Kissed Dating Goodbye,* by Joshua Harris. What principles and ideas stand out most to you in this book? What will you do differently after reading it? *(SOCIAL SKILLS)*

Advanced

Y. Read Chapter 13, "The Discipline of Feelings," in *Discipline: The Glad Surrender,* by Elisabeth Elliot. Outline the chapter. What is the relationship between the will and the emotions? What is the relationship between self-control and Spirit control? Discuss this with one of your parents. *(READING / CHARACTER TRAINING)*

Z. Study what the Bible says about **guarding our hearts.** List all the ways you can think of that you can guard your heart. (For help finding verses, look up **heart** in *Strong's Concordance*.) *(BIBLE / RESEARCH / WRITING)*

AA. Study the following topics in the Bible. What does the Bible say about them? What happens to the person who sins in these ways?

Anger

Fear

Grief

Discouragement

Worry

(BIBLE / RESEARCH)

BB. Do word studies on the following words. What do they mean? How do they affect our lives? What are their blessings?

Meekness

Courage

Faith

Joy

Trust

How do each of these words relate to the emotions listed in the project before this one? *(BIBLE / RESEARCH / FOREIGN LANGUAGE)*

CC. Study Proverbs 25:28. Where are your "walls broken down"? What can you do to build them back up again? Write an essay on the meaning of this verse and its application to your life. *(BIBLE / ENGLISH COMPOSITION)*

DD. Study the section on "anger" (pages 1-13) in *A Homework Manual for Biblical Living, Vol. 1,* by Wayne Mack. *(BIBLE / WRITING)*

EE. Study the section on "anxiety and worry" (pages 14-15) in *A Homework Manual for Biblical Living, Vol. 1,* by Wayne Mack. *(BIBLE / WRITING)*

FF. Read Chapter 18, "A Husband's Regret: Anger," and Chapter 19, "A Husband's Regret: Anxiety and Fear," in *The Exemplary Husband,* by Stuart Scott. Follow the steps outlined to govern both of these emotions. *(READING / CHARACTER TRAINING)*

Additional ideas:

Journal of Uncontrolled Emotions

(See instructions in Project O.)

DATE	WHAT I DID	WHAT I SHOULD HAVE DONE	VERSE TO MEMORIZ

Bible Characters Who Gave In to Discouragement

(See instructions in Project Q.)

ERSON	REF.	SITUATION	ACTIONS	RESULTS

Bible Characters
Who Did and Didn't Rule Their Emotions

(See instructions in Project U.)

PERSON	REF.	SITUATION	ACTIONS	RESULTS
Cain	Genesis 4:5-8			
Simeon and Levi	Genesis 49:5-7			
Moses	Exodus 16:7-8			
Gideon	Judges 7:7-23			
Balaam	Numbers 24:10-11			
David	1 Samuel 25			
Ahab	1 Kings 21:4			
Job	Job			
Peter	Matthew 26:69-74			
Disciples	Matthew 8:26			

Parents:

Consider and discuss with your son the following questions:

- Does he lose his temper easily?

- Does he grow angry when others disagree with him?

- Does he hit other children who are not doing things his way?

- Does he pout and sulk when he doesn't get his way?

- Does he cry easily when disappointed?

- Does he throw tantrums?

- Does he become overly emotional when disciplined?

- Does he only obey you when he feels like it?

- Is he moody?

- Does he give up quickly when things don't go right?

- Does he worry and fret?

- Is he overly fearful of certain things?

- Does he trust God to protect him and provide for him?

- Are his manners ruled by his emotions?

- Are his decisions governed by his emotions?

- Is he prone to discouragement or depression?

- Can he keep himself under control?

Notes and comments:

Self-Control: Manners

"And as ye would that men should do to you, do ye also to them likewise" (Luke 6:31).

Manners are a demonstration of our willingness to obey God in humbling ourselves and exalting others. A Christian with poor manners does not glorify God before an unbelieving, watchful world.

It is important for our sons to learn to make others more important than themselves. This is at the heart of good manners. If others are more important, they will more selflessly serve their families. They will be more effective witnesses in the community as they "grow in favor with God and man." They will more willingly set aside their own desires for the greater purpose of serving their Lord.

Manners do not come automatically -- at least not **good** ones! We must set an example of selfless, "others-centered" living. But we must also actively train and rehearse our children in acts that put the needs and feelings of others before their own.

A. Select verses from the list below, and use some or all of the following suggestions to help you study and better understand their meaning (easier verses are listed first, in italics):

1) Copy the passage.

2) Read it in several different translations of the Bible.

3) Read the passage and several of the verses before and after it to gain a better understanding of the context of the passage.

4) Rewrite the passage in your own words. What does it mean?

5) Record a specific way in which you can change your actions or attitudes based on the teaching of this passage.

6) Memorize the passage.

   Luke 6:31
   Romans 12:10
   1 Peter 2:17
   Proverbs 25:17
   Matthew 7:12
   1 Corinthians 13:4-5

Philippians 2:3
1 Peter 3:8
(BIBLE / SPEECH)

Beginner

B. Read *If Everybody Did,* by Jo Ann Stover. *(SOCIAL SKILLS)*

C. Say "please" every time you ask a favor today. Say "thank you" every time someone does something for you. Keep a "scorecard." How many times did you say these words throughout the day? Do this several days and see if your "score" improves. Then make it a habit every day! *(MANNERS / SOCIAL SKILLS)*

D. Wait until everyone is served before eating at mealtimes, and make sure you pass the food to the person next to you. *(MANNERS / SOCIAL SKILLS)*

E. Read with your parents Proverbs 25:17. How can you apply this verse when you go to visit at someone else's house? Draw a picture to illustrate this proverb. *(BIBLE / MANNERS / ART)*

F. Practice using your napkin politely at the dinner table today.

- Unfold it and place it on your lap.

- Wipe your hands on the napkin when it is in your lap.

- Dab your mouth frequently with it. If you must leave the table during the meal, place it on your chair.

- When you are finished with the meal, place it loosely to the left of your plate.

(MANNERS / SOCIAL SKILLS)

G. Look into the eyes of the person you are talking with throughout the day today. You will be honoring them and showing interest in what they say. Practice this habit every day. *(MANNERS / SOCIAL SKILLS)*

H. Learn to answer the telephone politely. Ask your father or mother to call your phone so that you can practice answering it correctly. *(SOCIAL SKILLS / SPEECH)*

I. Ask your mother or father to evaluate how your posture is when standing and when sitting. Sit and stand straight and tall. *(SOCIAL SKILLS / P.E.)*

J. Learn to introduce yourself and others to another person politely. Role play with your parents and siblings. *(SOCIAL SKILLS / SPEECH)*

K. Learn how to properly receive a compliment or praise. *(SOCIAL SKILLS)*

L. Learn how to politely seek the attention of someone who is busy or involved in conversation with someone else. *(SPEECH / SOCIAL SKILLS)*

M. Spend a day specifically working on the practice of seeking the desires of others above your own. Write down each incident in which you let others go before you. Then seek to make putting others first a daily practice. *(SOCIAL SKILLS)*

N. Ask your grandma to come to lunch. Be a good host when she is there.

- Greet her at the door.
- Take her coat.
- Offer her a drink of water or a cup of tea.
- Visit with her.
- Pull her chair out for her at the table.
- Serve her food.
- Offer her seconds.
- Eat politely.

(MANNERS / SOCIAL SKILLS)

O. See how many times in a day you can initiate good manners before your mother or father have to remind you. Keep track. Then see if you can improve your "score" tomorrow! *(MANNERS / SOCIAL SKILLS)*

P. Spend a day watching for opportunities to open doors for your sisters, mother, and other ladies. Then make it a regular habit! *(MANNERS / SOCIAL SKILLS)*

Q. Write thank you notes for gifts you have received for Christmas or your birthday. *(HANDWRITING / ENGLISH COMPOSITION)*

R. Study and practice proper table manners. Ask someone in your family to point out to you when you are not being polite at the table. *(SOCIAL SKILLS / FAMILY)*

Intermediate

S. With your parents, complete the activities in *Manners Made Easy,* by Judy Hines Moore. *(MANNERS / SOCIAL SKILLS)*

T. Discuss one section each day with your parents from *365 Manners Kids Should Know.* Try to practice what the lesson taught throughout the day. *(MANNERS / SOCIAL SKILLS)*

U. Write a thank you note to someone who has shown hospitality to you. Try to think of specific things they have done to make you feel loved and welcomed in their home, and thank them for these acts of kindness. *(WRITING / MANNERS)*

V. Work with your brothers and sisters in role-playing how you would practice good manners in different situations:

- Greeting a guest at the door
- Serving others at the meal table
- Interrupting a person who is talking or working
- Being a gracious guest at someone else's home
- Leaving a message on an answering machine
- Excusing yourself when you need to get around someone
- Politely sneezing, coughing, etc.
- Politely conversing with a new acquaintance

(DRAMA / SOCIAL SKILLS / FAMILY)

W. Call a store to see if they carry a particular product that you or a family member is interested in buying. Have one of your parents listen to you, and give you feedback on how well you did. *(SPEECH / SOCIAL SKILLS)*

X. Study Nabal in 1 Samuel 25, and Hanun in 2 Samuel 10:1-5. How did they practice bad manners? What were the results? What can you learn from these two stories? *(BIBLE / READING / SOCIAL SKILLS)*

Y. Study the chapter on "Bad Manners" in *For Instruction in Righteousness,* by Pam Forster. *(BIBLE)*

Z. Study Philippians 2:3-4. Make a list of ways you can apply this passage to being a gracious guest. *(WRITING / BIBLE / MANNERS)*

AA. Study a basic book of manners. Write down specific habits of politeness you would like to develop. Start practicing! *(SOCIAL SKILLS / WRITING)*

BB. Study the section on "Perfecting Your Manners" (pages 75-79) in *Man in Demand,* by Wayne and Emily Hunter. *(SOCIAL SKILLS)*

CC. Study the life of Jesus in the Gospels. What can you learn from Him about how to treat other people? Look at his example as a guest, as a friend, as a teacher, etc. Use the form on page 224 to record each Scripture reference, the incident, a description of how He treated others, and a specific way you can apply this to your own life. *(BIBLE / RESEARCH / WRITING)*

DD. Study and observe good manners that men show to women. Make a list and practice these manners. Open doors, allow them to go before you, stand when they enter a room, etc. Remember: your sisters and mother are women who qualify for this treatment! *(SOCIAL SKILLS / RESEARCH / WRITING)*

EE. Make a list of the habits you have that annoy people or that do not put the comfort of others ahead of your own comfort. (Ask someone to help you if you cannot think of any bad habits you have!) Write down specific ways you can change these behaviors, and then start putting your ideas into practice. *(SOCIAL SKILLS / WRITING)*

FF. Think about people you enjoy being with. Observe their behavior. What polite habits are they practicing? How do they treat others? Do they show honor to others above themselves? Compare your behavior to theirs. Are there any good qualities you could emulate in your life? Write down your observations and your specific plans for change in your own life. *(RESEARCH / WRITING)*

Advanced

GG. Search for *Credenda Agenda* online and go to the PDF archives. Find Doug Wilson's article, "Manners for Boys," in Volume 12, No. 3 and read it. What three categories of manners does Mr. Wilson delineate? Is there any area that you need to improve in? Formulate a plan to help you improve. *(RESEARCH / MANNERS / SOCIAL SKILLS)*

HH. Take your mother, grandmother, or sister out to dinner. Open doors for her, take her coat, seat her, order for her if she prefers for you to, and pay the bill. Initiate pleasant conversation throughout the meal. *(MANNERS / SOCIAL SKILLS)*

II. Read an etiquette book or search online for advice when preparing to attend a special event. You will be more comfortable and considerate if you know how to conduct yourself. What rules do you need to remember in order to properly honor those around you? Take notes if necessary. *(MANNERS / SOCIAL SKILLS)*

JJ. Complete a Bible word study on the phrase, **one to another.** *(BIBLE / RESEARCH / FOREIGN LANGUAGE)*

KK. Complete a Bible word study on the words, **courteous** and **kindness.** *(BIBLE / RESEARCH / FOREIGN LANGUAGE)*

LL. Study Scripture to find verses that give the Biblical basis for specific polite practices. For instance, is there a verse that suggests that we should show honor and preference to those that are older than we are? To serve others first? To speak when our mouths are not full at the table? List at least ten common rules of etiquette and a verse to go with each one. *(BIBLE / RESEARCH / SOCIAL SKILLS / WRITING)*

Additional ideas:

Jesus' Treatment of Others

(See instructions in Project CC.)

REF.	INCIDENT	HOW HE TREATED OTHERS	APPLICATION TO MY LIFE

Parents:

Evaluate your son in the following areas:

- Does he seek to treat others as he would want to be treated?

- Does he seek to honor others above himself?

- Does he desire to bring glory to God by living a gracious, thoughtful life?

- Does he practice good manners at the table?

- Does he show honor to sisters, his mother, and other women by seating them, assisting them, letting them go first, opening doors, etc.

- Does he show honor to the elderly?

- Does he interrupt only when necessary and does he do it properly?

- Does he speak clearly and politely?

- Does he excuse himself when he should?

- Do other people enjoy his company?

- Is he polite in the way he sits, stands, walks, and looks at others?

- Does he express proper thanks when someone has served him or given him something?

- Does he recognize ownership of others' belongings?

- Does he have habits or behave in ways that make those around him uncomfortable?

- Does he seek to make others comfortable and at ease, or does he worry about his own self-consciousness and comfort?

- Does he practice good etiquette -- following all the rules -- without having the proper spirit of humility and love for others?

- Are you often embarrassed by his behavior when hosting company, visiting the homes of others, shopping, speaking with other adults, etc.?

- Is he confident in social situations, or would training in proper etiquette make him more comfortable?

Notes and comments:

Self Control: Conquering Laziness

"But if any provide not for his own, and specially for those of his own house, he hath denied the faith, and is worse than an infidel" (1 Timothy 5:8).

Laziness is a true enemy to a productive, obedient life of service to God. God has put us on earth for a purpose. We are to subdue the earth and take dominion. That takes work. We can't be lazy followers of Christ.

A boy needs to take hold of this mission, and understand the dominion mandate that he has be given. With an understanding of the mission God has given him, and a vision for your family's particular mission, he can be a powerful influence, even as a young boy.

Besides wasting many potentially productive years in his youth, a lazy boy will most likely become a lazy, undisciplined man that wastes much of his adulthood as well. His parents and siblings will suffer with him while he is a boy. His future family will suffer with him as a husband and father.

Laziness leads to poverty. Slothfulness in spiritual things will lead to poverty of the soul, and laziness in physical things will result in financial poverty. A lazy person only does what he **feels** like doing. As the leaders of their future families, and as servants to potential employers, our sons will be called on over and over again to be faithful in duties that they will not always **feel** like doing.

So our job is an important one. We must be faithful (and not lazy) in driving any slothful spirit out of our sons. We must give them plenty of opportunities to work, and we must be diligent in training them to work whole-heartedly and "unto the Lord," because they are ultimately serving the Lord Jesus, and He is glorified when we give our best.

A. Select verses from the list below, and use some or all of the following suggestions to help you study and better understand their meaning (easier verses are listed first, in italics):

1) Copy the passage.

2) Read it in several different translations of the Bible.

3) Read the passage and several of the verses before and after it to gain a better understanding of the context of the passage.

4) Rewrite the passage in your own words. What does it mean?

5) Record a specific way in which you can change your actions or attitudes based on the teaching of this passage.

6) Memorize the passage.

Proverbs 10:26
Proverbs 14:23
Proverbs 18:9
Proverbs 21:17
Proverbs 22:29
Proverbs 27:1
Proverbs 28:19
1 Corinthians 4:2
Philippians 4:13
Ecclesiastes 10:18
Colossians 3:22-23

(BIBLE / SPEECH)

Beginner

B. Dramatize the following proverbs with your family. If you can, act it out for another family or friends and see if they can guess which proverb you are acting out.

Proverbs 10:26	Proverbs 26:13
Proverbs 12:27	Proverbs 26:14
Proverbs 13:4	Proverbs 26:15
Proverbs 21:25	Proverbs 26:16

(BIBLE / DRAMA)

C. Illustrate the following proverbs. Write the chapter number in the corner of the page, but not the verse. Put them together in a book and give to other people. See if they can identify which proverb each illustration represents as they read through the correct chapter of Proverbs.

Proverbs 12:24	Proverbs 20:4
Proverbs 15:19	Proverbs 22:13
Proverbs 18:9	Proverbs 24:30-34
Proverbs 19:24	

(BIBLE / ART)

D. Get up each day by a certain time, whether you feel like it or not. Get up as soon as your parents wake you, or set an alarm. *(TIME MANAGEMENT)*

E. Do at least one thing that you don't want to do each day.

F. Raise a pet or livestock. Take full responsibility for the care and feeding of your animal(s). Do not expect anyone else to do your chores for you. *(ANIMAL HUSBANDRY)*

G. Read with your parents Chapter 58, "God's Children Work" in *Leading Little Ones to God,* by Marian Schoolland. *(BIBLE / READING)*

H. Read with your parents the Fourth Commandment in Exodus 20:8-11. How many days did it take God to create the world? What did He do when He was finished? How many days of the week are we supposed to work? How many days do we rest? *(BIBLE)*

I. Ask one of your parents to help you make a daily checklist. List each regular task or activity you do each day, make columns for each day of the week, and check off each task when complete. *(TIME MANAGEMENT)*

J. Do at least two jobs that are not required of you today. Pick jobs that will make someone else's day easier for them.

K. Work for pay on extra jobs around the house. Ask your parents to pay you if you do a good job, and to make you their slave (to work more without pay) if you do a slothful job. *(BUSINESS ED. / FINANCES)*

L. With your parents or older siblings, volunteer to help another family move, or help with some other group project. Be sure to do your share of the work and more! *(COMMUNITY SERVICE)*

Intermediate

M. Study Ephesians 5:16. Read some commentaries on this verse. What does it mean to "redeem the time"? Why should we? What changes can you make to better redeem the time? Make a list and use it to help you improve. *(BIBLE)*

N. Establish a regular daily schedule to help you be more diligent with your time. Write it down and post it in your room. *(WRITING / MATH)*

O. Read Proverbs 6:6-11. Then study ants. Set up an ant colony to observe. Read all you can about ants. Write or give an oral report about ants. What can you learn from the ants that will affect the way you work? *(BIOLOGY / BIBLE / SPEECH / ENGLISH COMPOSITION)*

P. With your parents, go through *The Go-to-the-Ant Chart* from Doorposts. Write down specific goals to work on after you have finished studying it. *(BIBLE / WRITING / ART)*

Q. Watch your father. Write down each task he performs throughout the day. (You may need to ask him to tell you about his time at work.) How does his diligence bless you and your family? Thank him for his labors. *(FAMILY)*

R. Volunteer to take responsibility for at least one of the jobs your father normally does each day. Designate a specific time for doing the job so that you don't forget. *(HOME SKILLS, ETC.)*

S. Ask your parents to hire you for extra jobs around the house or at your father's place of business. Work hard and get paid. Be lazy and get fired! *(BUSINESS ED. / FINANCES / HOME SKILLS)*

T. Read Ephesians 5:8-10. How are we saved? Why are we saved? Are you accomplishing the work that God has prepared for you to do? *(BIBLE)*

U. Make a list of the chores and responsibilities you will commit to finishing each day before spending time in leisure activities. Post it on a wall near the toy shelves, computer, TV, or other recreational areas. *(TIME MANAGEMENT)*

V. If you play computer games or watch television, set a time limit for yourself or limit your time to what your parents have established. Put a timer in the area and set it when you start. Quit when it goes off. *(TIME MANAGEMENT)*

W. Ask your parents to list the areas in which they see a lack of diligence in your life. Ask them if they think you are investing time in activities that are not worthwhile. Work together on a plan to help you grown in diligence. *(TIME MANAGEMENT)*

X. Start the day with a list of the specific tasks you need to complete. Note times, when appropriate. Check each job off of your list as you complete it. Take satisfaction in reviewing your list of completed jobs at the end of the day, and carry any that are unfinished to tomorrow's list. Make this a habit each day, and notice how much more you get done. *(WRITING / TIME MANAGEMENT)*

Y. Pay for your own clothes after a certain age. Earn the money to pay for them, and shop for bargains. *(FINANCES / CONSUMER ED. / MATH)*

Z. Study Ephesians 4:28. What are we supposed to do instead of stealing? Why? If we don't work, what will we be tempted to do? *(BIBLE)*

AA. Study Chapter 7, "Diligence," in *Christian Character,* by Gary Maldaner. *(BIBLE)*

BB. Read Genesis 1:27-28. What did God tell Adam to do after he created him? Study the term "take dominion." Use a concordance and commentaries to help you. What does it mean? How do we do it? Discuss this with your parents. *(BIBLE)*

CC. Study faithful men from history who had to be diligent to succeed in their fields: inventors, athletes, musicians, soldiers, etc. Write a report on each man you study. *(HISTORY / SCIENCE / P.E. / MUSIC / ART / ETC.)*

DD. Study faithful, diligent men in the Bible: Joseph, Nehemiah, Jacob, Daniel. How did God use each of them? How did they affect others around them? What obstacles did they face? Recount at least one of the stories for your family at the meal table. Discuss the blessings of their diligence. *(BIBLE / WRITING)*

EE. Study in the Bible what happens to the lazy man. List each verse you find and what it says. Start by looking up "Laziness" in *For Instruction in Righteousness,* by Pam Forster, or look up the terms "slothfulness" and "idleness" in *Nave's Topical Bible.* Summarize your findings. *(BIBLE / RESEARCH / WRITING)*

FF. Study what the Bible says about the rewards of diligence. Write down each Bible reference, and what the verse says about diligence. Start by looking up "Laziness" in *For Instruction in Righteousness,* by Pam Forster, or look up the terms "industry" and "diligence" in *Nave's Topical Bible.* Summarize your findings. *(BIBLE / RESEARCH / WRITING)*

GG. Ask your parents to grant you full responsibility over an area in your household. You should be totally responsible without any reminders. Enjoy the blessings of diligence, or the cursings of laziness. *(FAMILY / HOME SKILLS)*

HH. Write an essay on Proverbs 10:26. How can a lazy person be like vinegar on our teeth and smoke in our eyes? Use commentaries to help you study, and give specific examples. *(BIBLE / ENGLISH COMPOSITION)*

II. Read with your father *Created for Work: Practical insights for Young Men,* by Bob Schulz. Try to read at least one section each day together, and discuss the questions at the end of each section. *(READING)*

JJ. Interview business owners and managers of businesses. What are they looking for in their employees? What qualities are most valuable to them? Write a report of your findings. *(BUSINESS ED. / SPEECH / WRITING)*

Advanced

KK. A system for organizing your time may help you use it more wisely. Research different time management systems. Look at different types of planners, calendars, and electronic organizers at an office supply store or online. What style do you like best? How much space do you want for each day's notes? What size will work best for you? What is most practical and most affordable? Buy a system you can afford, and start using it every day. *(RESEARCH / TIME MANAGEMENT)*

LL. Read *Redeeming the Time,* by Steven Maxwell. Discuss with your father Chapter 2, "Whose Time Is It?," Chapter 3, "Vision," and Chapter 12, "Prune Out the Time Robbers."

- Discuss your father's vision for your family.
- Write your own vision statement.
- Make a list of "time robbers" in your life, and a plan for eliminating them.

(READING / TME MANAGEMENT)

MM. Study 1 Corinthians 6:19-20. Study the words "price" and "glorify" using *Strong's Concordance.* Study other verses that use these same words. (For further instruction on how to perform word studies, see various teaching resources in "Bible Skills, pages 125-131.) Why should we glorify God with our bodies and spirits? How can we do this? Write a paper outlining what you have learned in your study and how you can practically apply these verses. *(BIBLE)*

NN. Read Chapter 12, "The Discipline of Work," in *Discipline: The Glad Surrender,* by Elisabeth Elliot. Discuss it with your father, and read the rest of the book if you haven't already. *(READING)*

OO. What things are you **not** doing that you know God wants you to do? What is keeping you from doing them? Make a list. Then review the list. Are any of the reasons legitimate? What can you quit doing to make more time for the things you need to do? Commit to putting those things aside. *(TIME MANAGEMENT)*

PP. Read Chapter 12, "The Discipline of Work," in *Disciplines of a Godly Man,* by R. Kent Hughes, and complete the activities at the end of the chapter. Read the rest of the book about manly disciplines if you haven't already. *(READING)*

QQ. Read *God at Work: Your Christian Vocation in All of Life,* by Gene Edward Veith. Outline each chapter and discuss the book with your father. How does God minister to others? Why does our work matter? What are you different callings, and are you diligently fulfilling each of them? *(READING)*

RR. Read *Manly Dominion,* by Mark Chanski. If possible, organize a book study group. Read a chapter each week and discuss what you have learned and what you can apply. *(READING / SOCIAL SKILLS)*

SS. Hire brothers or sisters to do a job for you. Tell them you will pay them all the same, no matter what they do. (Remember, you can pay them with something besides money.) How hard does everyone work? Hire them for another job, and pay them according to how much of the job they complete. Do they work differently this time? Write a short essay explaining why this happens. How does this relate to economics throughout history? *(BUSINESS ED. / GOVERNMENT / HISTORY)*

TT. Commit to some sort of regularly scheduled volunteer work. *(COMMUNITY SERVICE)*

Additional ideas:

Parents:

Evaluate your son in the following areas:

- Does he have a sense of purpose in life?

- Does he have clearly defined goals that he works diligently to reach?

- Does he cheerfully work toward fulfilling the goals of your family?

- Does he generally do his best?

- Does he not abandon a task until it is completely finished?

- Does he work well when no one is watching?

- Does he work hard, even when he knows there will be no pay or tangible reward for his labor?

- Does he perform the tasks he is responsible for without someone telling him to do so?

- Does he put his things away when finished with them, or when he won't be using them for a period of time?

- Does he check over his work to make sure it is complete before reporting to the person who assigned the task?

- Does he take good care of his belongings?

- Is he careless in his work?

- Does he waste time?

- Does he procrastinate?

- Does he quit when a job becomes boring or difficult?

- Does he complain about the work he is given?

- Does he make excuses for not starting a task?

- Does he make excuses for his unfinished work?

- Does he get easily distracted from his work?

- Does he talk more than he works when given a task to complete?

- Is he lazy about putting away clothes and keeping his room clean and orderly?

Notes and comments:

Self Control: Fleeing Temptation

"Flee also youthful lusts: but follow righteousness, faith, charity, peace, with them that call on the Lord out of a pure heart" (2 Tim. 2:22).

Our sons will confront temptation all their lives. They will have many temptations as young boys, as young men, and as adults. Part of our job as parents is to teach them how to resist the many temptations they will confront.

When our sons are young and under our direct authority, we can guard them from many of the outside influences that would lead them into temptation. We can choose to not expose them to certain types of music, reading material, television programs, etc. We can limit the amount of free time they have, which will reduce the opportunity for certain types of temptation.

During this period, we can teach them from Scripture to respond properly to temptation. We must teach them to **flee** temptation. We are told that God will always provide a "way of escape".

If we constantly point this out in the daily temptations that occur -- temptations to be angry, resentful, proud, lazy, fearful, deceitful, cruel -- we will be helping to build a pattern into our sons' lives that will be there when they are away from our oversight. If a boy has learned to flee from the temptation to hit his brother, if he has learned to look for the way to escape from the temptation to lie to his parents, he will be ready to do the same when faced with other temptations as a young man moving toward independence.

It is helpful to bring your sons to an understanding of temptation as a test. It is an opportunity to test our faithfulness to God, our commitment to righteous living, our trust in His promises, our knowledge and understanding of Scripture.

We need to develop relationships with our sons that will build their trust in us. If they trust us and do not fear rejection or over-reaction, they will feel free to come to us with their struggles and temptations. We will be given the privilege of knowing their inner thoughts and the opportunity to give counsel and direction. And we will be able to join with them in prayer for strength and obedience to God's Word.

A. Select verses from the list below, and use some or all of the following suggestions to help you study and better understand their meaning (easier verses are listed first, in italics):

   1) Copy the passage.

2) Read it in several different translations of the Bible.

3) Read the passage and several of the verses before and after it to gain a better understanding of the context of the passage.

4) Rewrite the passage in your own words. What does it mean?

5) Record a specific way in which you can change your actions or attitudes based on the teaching of this passage.

6) Memorize the passage.

Proverbs 27:12
Matthew 26:41
Romans 6:14
Philippians 4:13
James 4:7
1 Peter 1:15
1 Peter 5:8
Romans 6:6
1 Corinthians 6:13
1 Corinthians 10:12-13
2 Corinthians 5:10
Galatians 6:7-8
1 Timothy 5:22
Hebrews 2:18
Hebrews 4:15-16
James 1:12

(BIBLE / SPEECH)

Beginner

B. Read with your parents Chapter 61, "God's Children Learn to Say 'No'" in *Leading Little Ones to God,* by Marian Schoolland. *(BIBLE / READING)*

C. Read with your parents James 1:12. Illustrate the verse. *(BIBLE / ART)*

D. Discuss 1 Corinthians 16:13 with your parents. Memorize the verse and say it aloud whenever you are tempted to sin. *(BIBLE)*

E. Read with your parents Luke 4:1-13, the story of Jesus being tempted in the wilderness. What did the devil do and say to Jesus? How did Jesus respond? What did He do to fight against the devil's temptations? Act out this story with a friend or family member, or with your toys. *(BIBLE / DRAMA)*

F. Read with your parents a story about Joseph in Genesis 39. What did Joseph do when Potiphar's wife tried to tempt him? What can you learn from his example? Draw a picture to illustrate this story. *(BIBLE / ART)*

G. Pray together each day with your parents about your areas of temptation. Review your day before bedtime. Did God give you strength and grace to do better? *(FAMILY)*

H. With your family, study Betty Lukens' *The Christian's Armor.* Use the flannelgraph figures to help you memorize Ephesians 6:11-17. Then use your "Sword of the Spirit" to fight against the devil when he tempts you. *(BIBLE)*

I. Work with your father to make a wooden sword. (Doorposts' *Armor of God Patterns* includes instructions for making a sword, if you need help.) Paint it silver or gold and use a permanent felt pen or paints to write 1 Corinthians 16:13 on it. *(CARPENTRY / ART)*

J. Read and discuss with your parents 1 Corinthians 10:13. Draw a picture to illustrate this verse and post it on a wall in your house. When you are tempted to sin, look for the way to escape that God has provided. *(BIBLE / ART)*

K. When you face a temptation today, pray for God's help and recite a verse to help you be strong. Make a commitment to memorize a certain number of verses each week so that you will be well-armed with verses. *(BIBLE / SPEECH)*

Intermediate

L. Make a commitment to read and study your Bible **every day**. Keep a journal of what you are learning. *(BIBLE / READING / WRITING)*

M. Memorize Ephesians 6:11-17. When you are tempted, recite these verses to yourself and think about which pieces of armor you need to use against this sin. *(BIBLE)*

N. Study men and women in the Bible who resisted temptation. What were the blessings of obedience in their lives? List each character, the Bible references, and the results in their lives. (Look under "temptation" in *Nave's Topical Bible.*) Use the form on page 242. *(BIBLE / RESEARCH / WRITING)*

O. Study men and women in the Bible who yielded to temptation. What were the cursings of disobedience in their lives? List each character, the Bible references, and the results in their lives. (Look under "temptation" in *Nave's Topical Bible.*) Use the form on page 243. *(BIBLE / RESEARCH / WRITING)*

P. Ask your parents to help you make, and pray for you to keep, covenants with yourself and God in areas of particular temptation. Write out your covenant. *(WRITING)*

Q. Establish a "buddy" to whom you can be accountable in your areas of weakness and temptation (your parents, a friend, or another adult.) Meet together or call each other. Pray together. *(SOCIAL SKILLS)*

R. Pray for wisdom in discerning the "besetting" sins in your life (sins that you have a particular weakness and bent toward). Keep a journal and write down the areas in which you are struggling, Scripture passages and quotes from helpful books, and commitments and goals. *(WRITING)*

S. Do a topical Bible study on the area of temptation with which you struggle most. What does God say will happen to one who yields to temptation in this area? *(BIBLE / RESEARCH)*

T. Study the chapters in *For Instruction in Righteousness,* by Pam Forster, that deal with the areas of sin that you find most tempting. *(BIBLE / READING)*

U. Write up a list of questions to help you examine yourself for sin each evening. You could use the Ten Commandments as a standard for writing out your questions (i.e., Did I want other people's things today? Did that lead to arguing and fighting?). *(WRITING)*

V. Work together with your mom and/or dad on an area of common temptation (i.e., anger, unkind speech). Study the Bible together, pray for each other, plan your day, review your day, remind each other when you are succumbing to the temptation, confess your sin to each other. *(FAMILY / BIBLE)*

W. Study Chapter 23, "Purity," in *Christian Character,* by Gary Maldaner. *(BIBLE)*

X. Study "Understanding Sex Morality" in *Man in Demand,* (pages 58-61), by Wayne and Emily Hunter. *(BIBLE / READING)*

Y. *The Westminster Shorter Catechism* defines sin as "any want of conformity unto or transgression of the law of God." Think over the areas in which you are most likely to sin. In which ones do you transgress God's law by doing what Scripture says not to do? In which ones are you failing to conform to God's law by not doing what He says to do?

Make a list of these sins, repent, and pray for the Holy Spirit's strength to overcome them.

Make plans to start doing the things you haven't been doing, and confess your sins to those you have wronged. *(WRITING)*

Z. Study *Free from Bondage God's Way*, Kay Arthur's inductive study on Galatians and Ephesians. *(BIBLE / WRITING)*

AA. Write down a list of the specific sins you commit. Then write down specific ways of escape for each area. (What actions can you take to flee temptation in each of these areas?) Also list a verse you can memorize to help you in resisting this sin. (See form on page 244.) *(WRITING / BIBLE / RESEARCH)*

BB. Read *The Purity Principle,* by Randy Alcorn. List the author's strategies for resisting temptation, and write down commitments you are making. Ask your father or a friend to hold you accountable. *(READING)*

Advanced

CC. Read Chapter 2, "The Discipline of Purity," in *Disciplines of a Godly Man,* by R. Kent Hughes. Read the rest of the book if you have not already done so. *(READING)*

DD. Complete the Bible study *A Man's Strategy for Conquering Temptation,* by Bob Vereen. Do this study with your father or with a group of young men and their fathers. *(BIBLE)*

EE. Memorize the answers to Questions No. 137-139 in the *Westminster Larger Catechism.* Study these answers carefully. Look up definitions to words you don't understand. Discuss them with your father. Do you need to repent of any of these sins? Why do you think the writers of this catechism included idleness, gluttony, and drunkenness as sins related to adultery? *(BIBLE)*

FF. Read and outline the contents of *Spiritual Warfare in a Believer's Life,* by Charles Spurgeon. Copy quotes from this book into a journal that you can reread when struggling with temptation. *(READING / WRITING)*

GG. Read *The Enemy Within,* by Kris Lundgaard. Consider and discuss the questions at the end of each chapter. If possible, study this book with a group men. *(READING)*

HH. Organize a book study for a group of young men, and go through *Respectable Sins: Confronting the Sins We Tolerate,* by Jerry Bridges. Use the companion study guide to direct your personal study and your activities with the study group. *(READING / SOCIAL SKILLS)*

II. Study Jesus' response to temptation as you read through the Gospels. Write down the reference for each time He is tempted. Then write down the situation and the results. (See form on page 245.) *(BIBLE / WRITING / RESEARCH)*

JJ. Study the first chapter of James. What does it teach us about temptation? What is the source of sin? Why do we sin? What are the results of sin? Write a summary essay about sin based on James 1. *(BIBLE / READING / WRITING)*

KK. Do word studies in the Bible on the following words related to sexual sin:

Lust
Adultery
Concupiscence
Incontinency
Lasciviousness
Lewdness
Wantonness

(BIBLE / RESEARCH / WRITING / FOREIGN LANGUAGE)

LL. Do a topical study in the Bible on the **strange woman**. (Look up "strange woman" in *Strong's Concordance*.) With what is she compared? How is she described? What are the results of following after her? Write a short essay on your findings. *(BIBLE / WRITING / FOREIGN LANGUAGE)*

MM. Study the effect of "strange women" on the lives of various men in the Bible. Look up "Adultery, Instances of," in *Naves Topical Bible*. Who resisted them? Who yielded to them? What were the results? Use the form on page 246.
(BIBLE / RESEARCH)

NN. Read *Sex Is Not the Problem (Lust Is): Sexual Purity in a Lust-Saturated World*, by Joshua Harris. Discuss the book with your father. Follow the author's outline for designing a plan to deal with temptation. Also work through the appendix, "The Path of Repentance." *(READING)*

OO. Complete the study "Flee from Lust" in Chapter 2 of *Prepare Thy Work*, by Daniel Forster. *(BIBLE / RESEARCH / VOCATIONAL TRAINING)*

PP. Read *Passion and Purity*, by Elisabeth Elliot. Write a paper to summarize what you have learned, and how it will affect your behavior. *(READING / ENGLISH COMPOSITION)*

QQ. Read through the following verses and then write out a list of wholesome, godly activities to share with friends:

Romans 13:13-14
Romans 14:13

Galatians 6:7-8
Philippians 4:8
Colossians 3:16-17, 23
1 Timothy 4:12
(BIBLE / READING / WRITING / FAMILY)

RR. Write out biblical guidelines outlining the type of girl you will want to marry. Are you treating young ladies in a way that acknowledges that they are someone's future wife? Are you protecting their emotional and physical purity for the husbands? *(WRITING / BIBLE / RESEARCH)*

SS. Read *I Kissed Dating Goodbye,* by Joshua Harris. Discuss the book with your father and with friends. Do you agree with the author? *(READING / SOCIAL SKILLS)*

TT. Write a paper entitled "The Disadvantages of Dating." *(ENGLISH COMPOSITION)*

UU. Write a paper entitled "The Disadvantages of Going Steady." *(ENGLISH COMPOSITION)*

VV. Study the chapter entitled "Sex Problems" (pages 164-165) in *A Homework Manual for Biblical Living, Vol. 1,* by Wayne Mack. *(BIBLE / WRITING)*

WW. Read the chapter on the "Sixth Petition" in *The Lord's Prayer,* by Thomas Watson. Outline its main thoughts. *(READING / BIBLE / WRITING)*

XX. Read *Precious Remedies Against Satan's Devices,* by Thomas Brooks. Outline its basic content. *(READING / BIBLE / WRITING)*

YY. Read Part 4, "Experiencing Oneness," in *The Family: God's Weapon for Victory,* by Robert Andrews. Outline each chapter in this section of the book. *(READING / BIBLE / FAMILY)*

ZZ. Read Chapter 20, "The Husband's Regret: Lust," in *The Exemplary Husband,* by Stuart Scott. Outline the chapter and the steps toward repentance and change. *(READING / BIBLE / FAMILY)*

AAA. Read and discuss with your father all or portions of *Fidelity: What It Means to Be a One-Woman Man,* by Douglas Wilson. (Your father may want to select specific chapters that are appropriate for your present station in life.)

Additional ideas:

Men and Women Who Resisted Temptation

(See instructions in Project N.)

REF.	PERSON	HOW THEY OBEYED	RESULTS

Men and Women Who Yielded to Temptation

(See instructions in Project O.)

REF.	PERSON	HOW THEY DISOBEYED	RESULTS

Ways of Escape from Temptation

(See instructions in Project AA.)

SIN	WAY TO ESCAPE	VERSE TO MEMORIZE

Jesus' Response to Temptation

(See instructions in Project II.)

EF.	HOW HE WAS TEMPTED	HIS RESPONSE	RESULTS

Effects of "Strange Women" on Men in the Bible

(See instructions in Project MM.)

REF.	MAN	WOMAN	YIELD	RESIST	RESULTS

Parents:

Consider and discuss with your son the following questions:

- Does he believe in the activity of Satan and the spiritual conflict in which we are involved?

- Does he understand Satan's tactics?

- Is he on guard against Satan?

- Does he know the Bible well enough to use it as a defense against temptation?

- Does he pray for God's help in resisting sin?

- Does he memorize Scripture and review what he has memorized enough to keep it in his mind?

- Does he try to avoid tempting situations?

- Are his friends ones who will lead him into wrongdoing, or encourage him in righteousness?

- Does he spend a great deal of unchaperoned time with friends?

- Does he use his free time in a profitable way?

- Does he have too much free time?

- Does he spend too much time alone?

- Does he spend too much time on the internet?

- Is he careful about what kind of music he listens to, what movies he watches, what websites he visits?

- Does he have filters on his computer?

- Do you have a way to track what he is looking at on the computer?

- Does his life lack self-control in other areas?

- Does he blame others for his sins?

- Does he confess sin and accept God's forgiveness when he has fallen?

- Is he grieved at displeasing God when he sins, or has he become calloused and indifferent?

Notes and comments:

And to temperance,

PATIENCE

Faithfulness in Performing a Job

"He that is faithful in that which is least is faithful also in much: and he that is unjust in the least is unjust also in much" (Luke 16:10).

Our sons will need to work hard in order to fulfill God's purpose for their lives. They will labor to support themselves, and they will labor to provide for their wife and family. If they have learned to be faithful and diligent workers, they will be valued employees or hard-working entrepreneurs, equipped to care for their families and creative enough to weather most any economic setback.

The best place to learn how to work is at home! We need to give our children plenty of practice in learning to do a job cheerfully, thoroughly, and efficiently. When they work in the home, they are not only helping us carry the work load; they are training to be good workers outside your home.

Teach your children to work diligently at household chores and personal responsibilities. Hire them for extra jobs around the house. Train them well, and then require high-quality work.

One of the child's chief occupations includes the duties of being a student. Treat your son's education as his daily job, and teach him good work habits while he applies himself to learning.

A. Select verses from the list below, and use some or all of the following suggestions to help you study and better understand their meaning (easier verses are listed first, in italics):

1) Copy the passage.

2) Read it in several different translations of the Bible.

3) Read the passage and several of the verses before and after it to gain a better understanding of the context of the passage.

4) Rewrite the passage in your own words. What does it mean?

5) Record a specific way in which you can change your actions or attitudes based on the teaching of this passage.

6) Memorize the passage.

   Ecclesiastes 9:10a
   1 Corinthians 4:2
   Galatians 6:9
   Proverbs 22:29

Proverbs 28:20
Matthew 25:23
Colossians 3:22
(BIBLE / SPEECH)

Beginner

B. Read and discuss with your parents Proverbs 22:29. Draw a picture to illustrate it and post it in a place where you have a regular chore to do. *(BIBLE / ART)*

C. Read about Jeroboam with your parents in 1 Kings 11:28-39. Why did Solomon notice Jeroboam? What did he do for him? What did the prophet tell Jeroboam? *(BIBLE)*

D. Read and discuss with your parents Ecclesiastes 11:4-6. *(BIBLE)*

E. Working with your parents, write up a checklist of duties that must be completed by a certain time each day. Be sure to follow and complete the checklist on time without reminders. *(WRITING)*

F. Ask for menial household tasks. Perform them cheerfully and diligently. *(HOME SKILLS)*

G. Accept full responsibility for a task in your household. Do it without being reminded. *(HOME SKILLS)*

H. Make a list of tasks to accomplish before breakfast or lunch each day. Don't eat until they are done. *(TIME MANAGEMENT)*

I. Learn to initiate work on chores by reading a posted list of duties, and beginning these tasks without being told. *(READING)*

J. Report for school on time and work hard until designated break times. Don't waste time during school hours. Show respect to your teacher. Do your best at all times. *(TIME MANAGEMENT)*

K. Volunteer to help when you see that your father has more work and chores than he can keep up with in your home. *(HOME SKILLS / FAMILY)*

Intermediate

L. Plan ahead for an outing that will take place tomorrow. Find out when you need to leave and what you need to bring. Set out any items you need to take with you, have your clothes ready ahead of time, and get dressed early enough to be ready on time. *(TIME MANAGEMENT)*

M. Find out what time dinner will be. Finish and clean projects up before dinner. Then arrive in the kitchen early enough to help take food to the table. *(TIME MANAGEMENT)*

N. Practice faithfulness in your school work, or in assignments for Sunday school or Bible studies. Try to be done ahead of time, and give yourself extra work when you have not completed your goal by the deadline. *(TIME MANAGEMENT)*

O. If possible, go to work with your father or watch him do his work at home. What does he do? How does he do his work? Does he spend time doing other things, or does he concentrate on his work? Help him if you can. *(CAREER ED. / TIME MANAGEMENT)*

P. Study Chapter 5, "Dependability," in *Christian Character,* by Gary Maldaner. *(BIBLE)*

Q. Study Chapter 37, "How Can I Be a Good Worker?" in *Christian Manhood,* by Gary Maldaner. *(BIBLE)*

R. Work with your father in his vocation. Go with him to work or work with him at home. *(CAREER ED.)*

S. Read *Money-Making Ideas for Kids,* by Todd Temple and Melinda Douros, and other books with ideas for kid-operated businesses. Choose one idea and do it! Keep a journal. How much money did you invest? How much money did you earn? What problems did you encounter? *(FINANCES / WRITING / BUSINESS ED.)*

T. Study the chapter entitled "Unfaithful Employee" in *For Instruction in Righteousness,* by Pam Forster. *(BIBLE)*

U. Design a work evaluation form that asks questions about the quality of your work. Give this to your "bosses" (Mom, Dad, employers) to fill out. Do this every month at home, every 3 months with an employer outside the home, or each time you perform an "odd job" around the neighborhood. Discuss the results with your parents. *(WRITING / BUSINESS ED.)*

V. Write a resume. Why should someone hire you? What work experience do you have? What good character traits do you possess? *(WRITING / BUSINESS ED.)*

W. Interview a business owner. What qualities does he value most in an employee? Do you possess these qualities? *(BUSINESS / CAREER ED.)*

X. Interview a business owner. What qualities does he believe a self-employed person most needs to succeed? Do you possess these qualities? *(BUSINESS / CAREER ED.)*

Y. Design a character reference form. Ask people who know you to evaluate your character by answering these questions. Discuss the results with your parents. What can you do to improve? *(WRITING)*

Z. If possible, go to work with someone who has the type of work you think you might be interested in pursuing. Observe what he does, help him if you can, ask him questions when possible. What kind of training did he have for this job? *(BUSINESS / CAREER ED.)*

AA. Read *Common Sense Business for Kids,* by Kathryn Daniels and Anthony Maybury. Does this give you any ideas for a business you could start? *(BUSINESS ED.)*

BB. Study in the Bible the men who were faithful in their job calling. Write down the references that tell about the man, what he did and the results of his faithfulness. Start by looking up "Faithfulness, Instances of" in *Nave's Topical Bible*. (Use the form provided on page 257.) *(BIBLE / RESEARCH / WRITING)*

CC. Write a business plan for a real or hypothetical business you could run. How much money will it take to get started? How will you market your service or product? How much will you charge? How will you keep records? *(BUSINESS ED. / RESEARCH)*

DD. Observe the men that you know. Who among them do you think are especially faithful in the jobs that God has given them? Why? How do they exhibit faithfulness? List these character qualities. Examine your own character. Are these traits visible in your life? Write out a plan that will help you grow in these areas. Discuss these ideas with your parents. *(WRITING)*

Advanced

EE. Interview a man who has been working for many years in one field of work. What has he found to be satisfying in his work? What was challenging? When has he felt like giving up or quitting? How has God used his occupation to help him mature? Write a summary of your findings or a transcript of your interview. *(SPEECH / CAREER ED. / WRITING)*

FF. Interview a man who has worked for the same employer or owned the same business for many years, perhaps for his entire years of employment. What were the advantages of being loyal to the same employer, or sticking with the same job all those years? Write your findings.   *(SPEECH / BUSINESS ED.)*

GG. Interview a man who has worked in multiple fields of work, started multiple businesses, or sold one or more businesses during his lifetime. What were his reasons for changing jobs or starting a new business? What advantages or disadvantages did he encounter? Write your findings.   *(SPEECH / BUSINESS ED.)*

HH. Take a job aptitude test that helps to pinpoint your character qualities, skills and interests. Use these findings as a tool while you seek to discern the vocation to which God has called you. Make a list of all the jobs you can think of that use these interests and traits.   *(CAREER ED. / WRITING)*

II. Go through *Finding the Career that Fits You*, by Lee Ellis and Larry Burkett. *(CAREER ED.)*

JJ. Complete the study "Accept Responsibility" in Chapter 2 of *Prepare Thy Work*, by Daniel Forster. *(BIBLE / RESEARCH)*

KK. Do a topical study of God's faithfulness in the Bible. Write a paper summarizing your study. How can you reflect God's faithfulness in your work habits?   *(BIBLE / RESEARCH / ENGLISH COMPOSITION)*

LL. When accepting regular employment, make and keep a commitment to the employer for at least one year, if possible.

MM. Read Chapter 5, "Bringing Home the Bacon," in *Redeeming the Time*, by Steven Maxwell. Discuss the chapter with your father, and read the rest of the book if you haven't already. *(READING)*

NN. Read Chapter 12, "A Nice Little Family Business," in *All the Way Home*, by Mary Pride. Outline its basic content.   *(READING / BUSINESS ED.)*

OO. Complete the studies in Chapter 3 "Vocation" in *Prepare Thy Work*, by Daniel Forster. *(BIBLE / RESEARCH / CAREER ED.)*

PP. Establish a small business that will give you opportunities to work for people outside your home (lawn mowing, pet-sitting, etc.).   *(BUSINESS ED. / FINANCES / MATH)*

QQ. Read *Your Work Matters to God,* by Doug Sherman and William Hendricks. Outline the main thoughts of the book, and discuss it with your father. *(READING)*

RR. Read Chapters 1-10 in *Manly Dominion,* by Mark Chanski. Outline the chapters as you read. *(READING / CAREER ED. / WRITING)*

SS. Study the chapter entitled "Work" (pages 201-202) in *A Homework Manual for Biblical Living, Vol. 1,* by Wayne Mack. *(BIBLE / WRITING)*

TT. Listen to as many talks as you can from Vision Forum's *The Best of the 2006 Entrepreneurial Boot Camp for Christian Families.* Listen with your father, if possible, and discuss each talk after listening to it. *(BUSINESS / CAREER ED.)*

UU. Watch Vision Forum's *Venture Academy DVD Training Series.* This is a comprehensive, but expensive set of DVDs that address the many issues of business entrepreneurship. If you cannot locate these DVDs to borrow, consider financing the purchase of it in one of the following ways:

- Organize a men's study group or conference and charge each person attending to help defray the costs of the DVDs.

- If you already have the beginnings of a small business operation, purchase the DVD set as a business expense.

- Rent the DVDs out to others to help defray the cost.

- Use long term savings that you may have accumulated for possible college or vocational training. Start a business instead of using the money to attend college.

- Start a short-term business venture or do odd jobs for friends and neighbors in order to purchase the course.

- Ask your local library or church's library to consider purchasing the set.

- Find several Christian businessmen who are willing to finance the purchase of the set, and agree to pay them back if you learn enough from the series to start a profitable business.

  (BUSINESS / CAREER ED.)

VV. If you hope or plan to operate your own business, read Larry Burkett's *Business by the Book,* answering the questions in the book's included study guide, and taking notes to file for future reference. *(BUSINESS / CAREER ED.)*

Additional ideas:

Faithful Workers in the Bible

(See instructions in Project BB.)

WORKER	REF.	WHAT HE DID	RESULTS

Parents:

Consider and discuss with your son the following questions:

- Does he stick with a job until it is done?

- Does he take pleasure in a job well done?

- Can you tell him to do something and **know** that he will do it?

- Can he complete a list of tasks without constant reminders?

- Does he quit when a job becomes difficult, tedious, or boring?

- Does he do thorough work? School work? Chores?

- Can people count on him when he commits himself to a task?

- Is he punctual?

- Does he waste time?

- Is he easily distracted?

- Is he faithful in completing school work and other assignments?

- Does he give up easily?

- Is he working toward goals that will better prepare him for a vocation?

- Does he understand the importance of having a job that produces income?

- Does he only work when being watched?

- Does he quit working when he doesn't receive encouragement or praise?

- Does he complain about the work, or does he work cheerfully and thankfully?

- Does he have a reputation for being a hard worker?

Notes and comments:

Faithfulness in the Church Body

"And let us consider one another to provoke unto love and to good works: Not forsaking the assembling of ourselves together, as the manner of some is; but exhorting one another: and so much the more, as ye see the day approaching" (Hebrews 10:24-25).

Fellowship with other Christians and a firm commitment to a specific body of believers will lead each of us to greater maturity (if we choose to associate with other believers who are serious about studying and obeying God's Word).

As parents, we need the support of other like-minded believers as we train up our children. Our sons will benefit from the wisdom of others within the church and see that the standards that we embrace are the standards of others as well.

We need to involve our sons in the life of the entire church. Discuss the sermons together, minister to other church members together, serve in the church together, and discuss important issues with adults of the church together.

As parents, make a firm commitment to an organized group of believers. Then demonstrate the preciousness of that fellowship by faithfully attending services, loyally upholding your leaders, and practically loving your brothers and sisters in Christ.

A. Select verses from the list below, and use some or all of the following suggestions to help you study and better understand their meaning (easier verses are listed first, in italics):

1) Copy the passage.

2) Read it in several different translations of the Bible.

3) Read the passage and several of the verses before and after it to gain a better understanding of the context of the passage.

4) Rewrite the passage in your own words. What does it mean?

5) Record a specific way in which you can change your actions or attitudes based on the teaching of this passage.

6) Memorize the passage.

   Psalm 119:63
   Psalm 122:1
   Psalm 133:1
   Acts 2:42

Psalm 27:4
Psalm 35:18
Psalm 84:2
Psalm 111:1
Romans 12:4-5
Colossians 3:16
Hebrews 10:24-25
Hebrews 13:7
1 John 1:7

(BIBLE / SPEECH)

Beginner

B. Read with your parents Part 13, "About God's Church" in *Leading Little Ones to God,* by Marian Schoolland. *(BIBLE / READING)*

C. Be ready every Sunday morning to leave for church on time. Set out everything you need on Saturday night. Don't dawdle in the morning. Get yourself ready and then help younger siblings get dressed. Help your parents take things to the car. *(TIME MANAGEMENT)*

D. Memorize a song you sing at church. Then sing it heartily with the congregation during your worship service. *(MUSIC)*

E. Pray each day for your pastor and church leaders.

F. Help older people in the parking lot at your church. Help them carry things. Help them find seats. Move carefully around older people so that you don't make them uncomfortable or endanger them. *(SOCIAL SKILLS)*

G. Help clean up papers and other items in the sanctuary after your church's worship service. Volunteer to be responsible for this job every Sunday. *(COMMUNITY SERVICE)*

H. Sit quietly in church. Join in the singing. Listen to the Scripture reading. Listen as carefully as you can to the sermon, and take notes by drawing simple pictures to illustrate the stories and text of the sermon. Explain your pictures to your parents after the service or when you get home. *(ART / MUSIC)*

Intermediate

I. Think of ways you can minister to other believers in your church body. Make separate lists for your pastor(s), teachers, widows, children, singles, mothers, fathers, ill, elderly, etc. Then begin to minister! *(WRITING / COMMUNITY SERVICE)*

J. Take notes during the sermon and discuss it with your parents on Sunday afternoon. *(SPEECH / BIBLE)*

K. Keep a notebook of the notes you take on the sermon. Write down something that you can take action on each week. Share this goal with someone else. Evaluate your progress at the end of the week. *(WRITING / BIBLE)*

L. Write thank you notes to your pastor and teachers at church. Thank them for their work and tell them specific ways that God has used their faithful service in your life. *(ENGLISH COMPOSITION / HANDWRITING)*

M. Make a commitment to a ministry within the church -- anything from janitor work to typing the bulletins to teaching a Sunday School class, etc. *(COMMUNITY SERVICE)*

N. Become more familiar with the Church's history and with the leaders and believers who have worked to build the Church over the years. Research the major events of church history and make a timeline to show them. *(HISTORY / READING / ART)*

O. Study what the Bible says about resolving differences between you and others. Study Matthew 7, Matthew 18, and other passages. Write out the steps you should take when you have a disagreement with or see sin in the life of another believer. Practice these steps when necessary. *(BIBLE / SOCIAL SKILLS)*

P. Read the verses in *Nave's Topical Bible* under the headings, "Fellowship, of the Righteous" and "Communion of Saints." List what these verses instruct us to do with other believers. Review the list. Are there ways in which you are failing to fulfill your responsibility to other Christians, especially in your own church fellowship? List areas in which you need to improve, and specific actions you can take. *(BIBLE / RESEARCH / WRITNG)*

Q. Study in the Bible what the believer's responsibility is to the authority of leaders in your church. Read under the heading, "Church, Duty of, to Ministers," in *Nave's Topical Bible.* Write a paper summarizing your findings. *(BIBLE / RESEARCH / WRITING)*

R. Read *Growing Up Christian,* by Karl Graustein, a book written specifically for young people who have grown up in the church. Discuss the questions for each chapter with your parents. *(BIBLE / FAMILY / CHARACTER TRAINING)*

S. Read *Stop Dating the Church: Fall in Love with the Family of God,* by Joshua Harris. Explain the main points of the book to your parents or to a friend. How will this book affect your involvement in the Church? *(READING)*

Advanced

T. Read Chapter 11, "The Importance of the Church," in *Instructing a Child's Heart,* by Tedd and Margy Tripp. Why is the Church important to the family and the training of children? Discuss this with your parents. *(READING / FAMILY)*

U. Study in the Bible the roles of elders and deacons. List their qualifications and responsibilities. Are these qualities present in your life? *(BIBLE / RESEARCH / WRITING)*

V. Study in the Bible what the believer's responsibility is to the authority of leaders in church. Write your findings. *(BIBLE / RESEARCH / WRITING)*

W. Complete the study "Be Part of the Church Body" in Chapter 1 of *Prepare Thy Work,* by Daniel Forster. *(BIBLE / RESEARCH)*

X. Help with a children's Sunday school class or club at church. *(TEACHER ED.)*

Y. Attend congregational meetings in your church.

Z. Work alongside an adult in his regular church ministry. *(COMMUNITY SERVICE)*

AA. To what is the Church compared in Scripture? Study the verses listed in the form on page 264. Identify the comparison and note reasons why you think God compares the Church to each of these things. *(BIBLE / RESEARCH)*

BB. Study the role of women in the New Testament church. *(BIBLE / RESEARCH)*

CC. Read *Critique of the Modern Youth Ministry,* by Chris Schlect. Do you agree with the author's conclusions? Discuss the book with your father. *(READING)*

DD. Study the practice of communion in the Scriptures. Start with the Old Testament Passover, and then the New Testament Lord's Supper. What is commanded? What does it picture? Write up your findings. *(BIBLE / RESEARCH / WRITING)*

EE. Study Christ's relationship to the church as it is compared in the Bible to a bridegroom and bride. *(BIBLE / RESEARCH)*

FF. Read *What Is a Healthy Church Member?,* by Thabiti Anyabwile. Complete the "For Further Reflection" sections at the end of each chapter. What are the ten marks of a healthy church member? Discuss the book with the pastor or other men at your church. *(READING)*

GG. Read Chapter 14, "The Discipline of Church," in *Disciplines of a Godly Man,* by R. Kent Hughes. Complete the "Food for Thought," "Application/Response," and "Think About It!" sections at the end of the chapter. *(READING)*

HH. Listen to *Reforming the Church in the 21st Century,* a collection of interviews by Kevin Swanson with Dr. R. C. Sproul, Douglas Phillips, Douglas Wilson, Dr. Gary Cass, and Douglas Pagitt. Write an essay that summarizes what you think is wrong with the 21st century Church and what we should do to fix it. *(CURRENT EVENTS / BIBLE / ENGLISH COMPOSITION)*

II. Read Chapter 18, "Churchmanship," in *Manly Dominion,* by Mark Chanski. Outline each main point and discuss them with your father or pastor. *(READING)*

JJ. Study pages 116-117, number 6, "The Relationships of Early Christians," in *A Homework Manual for Biblical Living, Vol. 1,* by Wayne Mack. *(BIBLE / WRITING)*

KK. Read *Why We Love the Church: In Praise of Institutions and Organized Religion,* by Kevin DeYoung and Ted Kluck. Write a summary of the book and share it with others you think would benefit from reading the book. *(READING)*

LL. Read *The Crisis of Caring: Recovering the Meaning of True Fellowship,* by Jerry Bridges. Outline the main points of the book. How will this book affect your life and your commitment to your church body? *(READING)*

MM. Become more familiar with the history of the Church and the great leaders and faithful believers who have been part of it. Read and outline a book on church history (i.e., *The Church in History,* by B.K. Kuiper or *Christianity Through the Centuries,* by Earle Cairns). *(READING / HISTORY)*

Additional ideas:

Pictures of the Church
(See instructions in Project AA.)

REFERENCE	TO WHAT IS THE CHURCH COMPARED?	WHY?
John 10:16		
1 Cor. 3:16		
Eph. 1:22-23		
Eph. 2:16-18		
Eph. 2:19-22		
Eph. 3:15		
Eph 5:25-28		
1 Pet. 5:2-4		
Rev. 19:7		
Rev. 21:2		
Rev. 21:9-27		

Parents:

Consider and discuss with your son the following questions:

- Does he make an effort to apply what he has learned at church?

- Are his best friends people from church?

- Can he accurately review the sermon with you?

- Does he look forward to fellowshipping with his friends at church?

- Does he have a worshipful attitude at church?

- Does he serve others in the church with the gifts God has given him?

- Does he have a desire to hear Scripture being taught?

- Does he sit and listen attentively?

- Does he pray for the needs of others in the church body?

- Does he seek to serve others in the church body?

- Does he complain about going to church?

- Does he make excuses to avoid attending church?

- Does he leave the church service often to get drinks, go to the bathroom, etc.?

- Is he seeking to develop the qualities required of an elder or deacon?

- Does he admire men of your church congregation?

- Does he exercise any leadership within your church?

Notes and comments:

Perseverance in Trials

"Watch ye, stand fast in the faith, quit you like men, be strong" (1 Corinthians 16:13).

Our sons can learn much about faith and perseverance by watching our response when we encounter the many tests of life. Do we despair when we realize we are too weak and helpless to withstand trials, or do we turn to the Source of all strength? Do we boldly approach the throne of grace for the gift of God's mercy and grace, or do we become panicky, hopeless, or bitter?

As parents who love our children enough to lead them to maturity, we must resist the temptation to shield them from trials and adversity. We must not lead our children to believe that God is treating them unfairly. Help them turn to God and His Word, but do not step in to remove the problem. Do not rob your child of the opportunity to see God's great power and faithfulness. Much growth and refining take place in the furnace of adversity. And that growth will better equip our sons to lovingly lead their families through the inevitable trials and challenges that God will call them to share.

A. Select verses from the list below, and use some or all of the following suggestions to help you study and better understand their meaning (easier verses are listed first, in italics):

1) Copy the passage.

2) Read it in several different translations of the Bible.

3) Read the passage and several of the verses before and after it to gain a better understanding of the context of the passage.

4) Rewrite the passage in your own words. What does it mean?

5) Record a specific way in which you can change your actions or attitudes based on the teaching of this passage.

6) Memorize the passage.

   1 Chronicles 16:11
   Psalm 34:19
   Psalm 37:24
   Psalm 57:7
   Psalm 119:67
   Psalm 119:71
   Psalm 119:75

Proverbs 24:10
1 Corinthians 16:13
Galatians 6:9
2 Timothy 2:3
James 5:13
Psalm 23:4
Jeremiah 29:11
Jeremiah 32:17
Lamentations 3:32-33
Matthew 19:26
John 10:28-29
Romans 5:3
Philippians 1:6
2 Timothy 2:12
Hebrews 12:1-4
1 Peter 1:6-7
1 Peter 4:12-13
(BIBLE / SPEECH)

Beginner

B. Read with your parents Chapter 55, "God's Children Trust Him," Chapter 63, "God's Children Suffer for Him," and Chapter 64, "God's Children Look for What Is Coming," in *Leading Little Ones to God,* by Marian Schoolland. *(BIBLE / READING)*

C. Listen to tapes or watch a videotape of *Pilgrim's Progress.* Count all the trials Christian goes through. Does he give up? What is his reward for persevering? Act out some of the story of Christian when you play. *(LITERATURE)*

D. Read with your parents the story of Joseph in Genesis 37-47. Count how many times bad things happened to Joseph. What did he do each time he was wronged? Read Joseph's response to his brothers in Genesis 45:4-8. What did he say about what his brothers had done? How did God use his sufferings for good? *(BIBLE)*

E. Draw a series of illustrations to picture Joseph's life as it is recounted in Genesis 37-47. Start by showing him in the special robe his father gave him. Then show what his brothers did to him. What happened next? Show each trial and what happened after each trial. End with Joseph's family settled in Egypt. Bind your pictures into a booklet form, or draw the pictures in a series of comic strip scenes. *(BIBLE / ART)*

F. Act out the story of Joseph's life during your play time. *(BIBLE / DRAMA)*

G. Read with your parents the first two chapters of the book of Job. Tell the story back to your parents. How did Job respond to the trials that God allowed in his life? Draw a picture to illustrate this story. *(BIBLE / SPEECH / DRAMA)*

H. If a sibling or friend is unkind to you, be patient with them and show kindness. *(SOCIAL SKILLS)*

I. Think of at least one difficult situation being experienced by you or your family. Pray for God to give you strength to persevere. *(FAMILY)*

J. Ask your parents and grandparents to tell you stories of God's faithfulness in difficult times in their lives. Choose a story to write down and illustrate. *(FAMILY / ART / WRITING)*

K. Make a "Cloud of Witnesses" book. Read Hebrews 11:1-32, and make a page for each person who is listed in this passage. Write down the person's name and draw a picture on each page that will help you remember the person's faith and perseverance. *(BIBLE / ART)*

Intermediate

L. With your parents, explore *www.kidsofcourage.com*. Learn about Christians who suffer for their faith in Jesus.

- Sign up to receive their quarterly newsletter and share it with the family at meal times.
- Do some of the suggested activities and download free activity books.
- Use the maps to learn more about countries with persecuted Christians.
- Watch videos related to the persecuted Church.

(CURRENT EVENTS / GEOGRAPHY)

M. Study a man in the Bible who persevered (Abraham, Noah, Joseph, Moses, Job, for instance). Write a paper or give a report explaining each of his testings, his responses, and the results of his perseverance. *(BIBLE / READING / RESEARCH / WRITING / SPEECH)*

N. Study Hebrews 11:1-32 with your family. Make a list of each person whose faith led them through trials. Write down the person's name, what happened to him, the reference where the account is found in the Bible, and what happened to him after the trial. (Use the form provided on page 274.) Make your own book, with an illustrated page for each of the people you learn about. *(BIBLE / HISTORY / WRITING / ART / RESEARCH)*

O. Study Hebrews 11:33-39 with your family. Think of at least one person from the Bible to illustrate each of the trials listed here. List the trial, the person, the Bible reference where the story is found, and the results. (Use the form on page 275.) Make a book with illustrated pages for each person. *(BIBLE / HISTORY / WRITING / ART / RESEARCH)*

P. Read *Pilgrim's Progress.* Make a list of Christian's many testings and trials. How did he respond to each one? What did he do after yielding to temptation? What was the reward for his perseverance? Write an essay discussing trials and suffering as portrayed in *Pilgrim's Progress.* *(LITERATURE / ENGLISH COMPOSITION)*

Q. Ask God to help you see someone in your church family who is going through trials. Make a list of all the ways you could support and encourage them during their time of testing (prayer, cards, meals, baby-sitting, etc.). Put your list into action! *(FAMILY / WRITING)*

R. Read several accounts from *Extreme Devotion,* published by The Voice of the Martyrs. What kinds of trails were faced? Did the sufferer persevere? Did he give up? Recount the stories to your parents. *(READING / HISTORY / GEOGRAPHY)*

S. Study how gold is refined and how it is used. Then do one of the following:
- Discuss with your parents what you learn and how it relates to suffering.
- Make a small illustrated book explaining what you learn.
- Write an essay comparing the refining of gold with the refining of our faith through trials.
- Give a short talk for your family explaining the relationship between the refining of gold and the refining of our character through trials.

(SCIENCE / BIBLE / ENGLISH COMPOSITION / ART / SPEECH)

T. Pray today when difficulties come your way. Work on making it a habit to pray instead of complaining or becoming discouraged.

U. When you are going through a time of difficulty, write down all the possible outcomes (good and bad) of this trial. What is the worst thing that might happen? Now look at your list. Is there anything there that God is not in control of? He is in control of **everything** that comes into our lives. Choose to trust and obey. *(WRITING)*

V. Read about Christians who are or have been persecuted for their faith in other countries. Write a report about what you have learned from their lives, or explain what you have learned to your family at the dinner table one evening. *(HISTORY / READING / SPEECH / GEOGRAPHY / CURRENT EVENTS)*

W. Study the Psalms with your parents. Write down everything you learn about testing and trusting God. *(BIBLE / WRITING / RESEARCH)*

X. Memorize Psalms that will give you courage in times of testing. *(BIBLE / SPEECH)*

Y. Read biographies of the many famous and productive men who did not give up in the face of adversity and failure. Write a short paper or talk with your parents about the value of perseverance. *(HISTORY / READING / ENGLISH COMPOSITION)*

Z. Keep a record of times of testing and their outcome. How did you respond? How did God prove Himself faithful? Keep a journal of these events and your responses. *(WRITING)*

AA. Study the chapters on "Faint-heartedness" and "Depression" in *For Instruction in Righteousness,* by Pam Forster. *(BIBLE)*

BB. Write a list of men and women in the Bible who were tested and afflicted for their good. Write down the person's name, the Bible references that tell about him, how he was tested, and the good results that came from the testing. Start by looking up "Afflictions, Made Beneficial" in *Nave's Topical Bible.* (Use the form on page 276.) *(BIBLE / RESEARCH / WRITING)*

CC. Interview an elderly person or a person who has spent much of his life suffering from illness or other chronic problems. Learn from their perseverance. When have they felt like giving up? What happened in the times when they did give in to despair? What has given them the strength to persevere? What have they learned in their suffering? Report your findings. *(SPEECH / WRITING)*

DD. Read *Trial and Triumph: Stories from Church History,* by Richard Hannula. Retell the stories to your family during meal times. *(READING / HISTORY / SPEECH)*

EE. Explore Voice of the Martyrs' website at *www.persecution.com.* Learn more about Christians who are suffering for their faith:

- Subscribe to receive VOM's email news alerts about persecuted Christians. Share the news your receive with your family at the dinner table.

- Sign up to receive weekly prayer updates and share those during family worship each week.

- Donate part of your earnings to support the work of Voice of the Martyrs.

(CURRENT EVENTS / GEOGRAPHY / DEVOTIONS / FINANCES)

FF. Read *Foxe's Book of Martyrs.* Write an essay on "perseverance" as demonstrated in the lives of these saints who persevered unto death. *(HISTORY / ENGLISH COMPOSITION / READINGS)*

GG. Study the sufferings of Jesus by reading through the Gospels, Isaiah 53, and Philippians 2. List each way in which Jesus suffered, what His response was, and what the results of His obedience were. What can you learn from His example? (Use the form on page 277.) *(BIBLE / RESEARCH / WRITING)*

Advanced

HH. Complete the Bible study, *Living Victoriously in Difficult Times,* by Kay Arthur and Bob and Diane Vereen. Study this with your father or lead a study for a group of young men. *(BIBLE)*

II. Do a topical study on the **sovereignty of God**. Write a summary of your study. *(RESEARCH / BIBLE / WRITING)*

JJ. Do a topical study on **God's strength.** Write a short essay on God's strength and how it relates to our own suffering and trials. *(RESEARCH / BIBLE / ENGLISH COMPOSITION)*

KK. Go through each verse listed on page 278, "God's Reasons for Allowing Us to Suffer." Read each verse and write down what it says about the reason for suffering. When you are suffering or going through times of testing, review this list. Ask God to reveal to you His reasons for your suffering. Thank Him for His love, even when you do not understand His reasons. *(BIBLE / RESEARCH / WRITING)*

LL. Interview a godly man whose life you admire. Ask him about the suffering and trials that God has brought into his life. What experiences helped him to learn the most in his life? Write a transcript of your interview or a summary of your conversation. *(SPEECH / WRITING)*

MM. Study Psalms 69 and 102. List what David says about his afflictions. Note his response to affliction. What does he remember about God's character? What actions does he pray God will take? What does he say he will do? Write an essay applying David's example to your own life. *(BIBLE / READING / WRITING)*

NN. Study 1 Peter and the book of James. Mark in your Bible all the references to suffering, temptation, trials, testing, affliction. What does God say about testing in these passages? Write an essay on suffering, as explained in these passages. Why do we suffer? How should we suffer? What is the purpose of suffering? What are its results? *(BIBLE / RESEARCH / ENGLISH COMPOSITION)*

OO. Read Chapter 13, "Discipline of Perseverance," in *Disciplines of a Godly Man,* by R. Kent Hughes. Complete the "Food for Thought," "Application/ Response," and "Think About It!" sections at the end of the chapter. *(READING)*

PP. Read the book *How to Profit from Our Afflictions*, by Thomas Boston. Outline its main points or write a book report on it. *(READING / WRITING)*

QQ. Read *All Things for Good*, by Thomas Watson. Outline its main points, or write a short paper explaining how the truths in the book apply to your own life. *(READING / WRITING)*

RR. Study the chapter on "Suffering" (pages 170-172) in *A Homework Manual for Biblical Living, Vol. 1,* by Wayne Mack. *(BIBLE / WRITING)*

Additional ideas:

Faith in the Bible

(See Project N for instructions.)

PERSON	WHAT HAPPENED	REFERENCE	RESULTS

More Faith in the Bible

(See Project O for instructions.)

TRIAL	PERSON	REFERENCES	RESULT

Testing for Our Good

(See Project BB for instructions.)

PERSON	REFERENCES	HOW TESTED	GOOD RESULTS

Jesus' Response to Suffering

(See Project GG for instructions.)

REFERENCE	HOW HE SUFFERED	HIS RESPONSE	RESULTS

God's Reasons for Allowing Us to Suffer

(See Project KK for instructions.)

John 9:1-3

John 11:1-4

2 Corinthians 4:7-11

Psalm 119:71

Isaiah 26:9

Psalm 78:34

Deuteronomy 4:30-31

Jonah 2:1

Psalm 119:67

Luke 15:16-18

Psalm 32:3-5

Psalm 66:10-12

Psalm 17:3

1 Peter 1:6-7

2 Corinthians 12:7

2 Chronicles 7:13-14

Ecclesiastes 7:2-3

Isaiah 48:10

Romans 5:3

James 1:2-3

1 Peter 2:20

Hebrews 12:10-11

John 15:2

Acts 11:19-21

Philippians 1:12-14

2 Timothy 2:9-10

Parents:

Consider and discuss with your son the following questions:

- Does he understand that God has a purpose for his affliction?

- Does he trust God?

- Does he view trials as a test of his faith and a means of helping him mature?

- Does he turn to God in prayer when tested?

- Does he find comfort from Scripture when tested?

- Does he use his own trials to help him remember to pray for those who are going through much greater testings?

- Does he use his trials to remind him of the sufferings Jesus experienced in order to save him?

- Does he learn from his trials in order to better minister to others who are being tested?

- Does he give up as soon as something becomes hard?

- Does he complain and whine when things go wrong?

- Is he afraid to try something that might result in failure?

- Does he become bitter when going through trials?

- Does he feel sorry for himself when going through difficulties?

- Does he gossip or slander when he has been wronged by someone?

- Does he give up if something doesn't work out right the first time?

- Does he dwell on his problems?

Notes and comments:

Finishing What We Start

"Being confident of this very thing, that he which hath begun a good work in you will perform it until the day of Jesus Christ" (Philippians 1:6).

God finishes what he starts. He promises to work out His holy plan in each of our lives. "The Lord will perfect that which concerneth me" (Psalm 138:8a).

If we are going to be an accurate reflection of God's character, we will also finish whatever we start whenever it is possible. When our sons start a "good work" they need to learn to keep working until that job is finished. We can encourage them when they encounter difficulties. We can come alongside, showing empathy and offering support. We can discourage them from starting new projects and accepting additional responsibilities until they have fulfilled their earlier commitments.

We should reward and encourage them when they finish projects -- especially ones that have required a commitment over a long period of time and ones that have been exceptionally difficult.

If a son never learns to persevere in the face of difficulties or boredom, he will flounder as a believer. The Christian life is a battle. We must fight a good fight before we finish our course. We must constantly press on toward the goal.

A. Select verses from the list below, and use some or all of the following suggestions to help you study and better understand their meaning (easier verses are listed first, in italics):

1) Copy the passage.

2) Read it in several different translations of the Bible.

3) Read the passage and several of the verses before and after it to gain a better understanding of the context of the passage.

4) Rewrite the passage in your own words. What does it mean?

5) Record a specific way in which you can change your actions or attitudes based on the teaching of this passage.

6) Memorize the passage.

   Proverbs 22:29
   Matthew 24:13
   Philippians 1:6
   Psalm 138:8

Luke 14:28-30
2 Timothy 4:7-8
Hebrews 12:1
(BIBLE / SPEECH)

Beginner

B. Read with your parents the story of Noah in Genesis 6-9. How much work would it have been to make the ark? What would have happened if Noah had not obeyed God and if he had not finished the ark? What did God accomplish through Noah's work? Make an ark out of cardboard boxes and fill it with stuffed animals and food. Invite your siblings to join you in your ark and pretend the floods have arrived. Act out the rest of the story of the flood. *(BIBLE / DRAMA)*

C. Read the story of Nehemiah with your parents. What job did Nehemiah begin? What challenges did he have while he was working? Use Legos or other building materials and toys to act out the story of Nehemiah and the Jews rebuilding the walls of Jerusalem. *(BIBLE / DRAMA)*

D. Every time one of your parents gives you a job to do, report back to them when you have finished. Start doing this every day if you haven't already been doing so. *(CAREER EDUCATION)*

E. Do your chores today without stopping to do anything else before you are finished. How long did it take you to finish? Do the same thing again tomorrow, and the next day, until it becomes a habit. *(TIME MANAGEMENT)*

F. When you are playing today, be sure to clean up one project or set of toys before getting out new ones. Make this a habit every day.

G. Plant a small section of garden. Keep a journal of its growth. Write down when you plant your seeds and transplants, when seeds begin to sprout, when you weed, when you fertilize, when you harvest your crops and pick your flowers. How long did it take from seed to harvest for each plant? *(SCIENCE / BOTANY / WRITING)*

H. Practice the "Turn-and-Look Rule." Whenever you are leaving a room, or whenever you think you have finished a job, **turn** around **and look.** Is there anything you need to clean up or finish so that you leave the room clean and/or the job complete? Do whatever needs to be done! *(HOME SKILLS)*

I. Do you have projects that you have put aside before you finished them? Get one out and finish it today.

J. Read and discuss with your parents Hebrews 12:1. Who are the "cloud of witnesses"? Draw a picture to illustrate this verse. *(BIBLE / ART)*

K. Read and discuss with your parents Philippians 1:6. What does this verse mean? What good work has God begun in you? *(BIBLE)*

Intermediate

L. Study Chapter 6, "Determination," in *Christian Character,* by Gary Maldaner. *(BIBLE)*

M. Make a commitment to clean up one project before starting another. Your parents will probably be happy to help you keep this commitment. Ask them to help you see when you have not cleaned up behind yourself, and to design some form of discipline that will encourage you to remember next time! *(HOME SKILLS)*

N. Select a major long-term project to work on together with one of your parents. Keep a journal of its progress -- dates you work on it, what you did, etc. See the project through to completion. *(WRITING)*

O. Learn to complete school projects, art projects, etc. Keep a record of the projects you start, and write down the date of their completion, or the reason for not completing them. Are your reasons good ones? If not, go back and finish the project! *(WRITING)*

P. Keep a notebook or portfolio of major projects you have completed. For those projects that cannot be stored in your portfolio, include photographs. *(PHOTOGRAPHY / ART)*

Q. Look up the words "finish" and "finished" in a concordance. Read each verse. What do you learn about finishing from these verses? Share what you have learned with your family at family worship time, or write a short paper explaining your findings. *(RESEARCH / BIBLE / SPEECH / WRITING)*

R. Plan a new project that you might do someday or a project that your parents would like you to complete. How much time might it take? Will it require purchasing materials? Do you have the money? How will you earn the money? Do you need to do research? Will this prevent you from being faithful to commitments in other areas?

Think the entire project through and discuss your plans with your parents. Can they think of anything you didn't think of? If you conclude that the project is practical, and if you have enough time and resources to complete it, start and finish it.

Use this planning format for any new project you think about starting. (Use copies of the "Project Planning" form on page 285.) *(BUSINESS ED. / WRITING)*

S. Start a record sheet to note the commitments you make. Note the date you make the commitment, what you are going to do, and later record the date when you have fulfilled your obligation. Make a covenant with yourself to always keep your commitments -- even when it is hard! *(WRITING)*

Advanced

T. Select a major long-term project to complete by yourself. Keep a journal of its progress. *(WRITING)*

U. Study the creation account in Genesis. What can you learn about **finishing** from this account? Discuss this with your family, or write a paper about it. *(BIBLE / SPEECH / ENGLISH COMPOSITION)*

V. Write an essay on the following topic: What is wasted when a project is not completed? *(ENGLISH COMPOSITION)*

W. Study Philippians 3:13-14. Read commentaries on the verses and write an essay summarizing the meaning of this verse and its application to your life. *(BIBLE / ENGLISH COMPOSITION)*

X. Study what the Bible says about "divorce." How does divorce relate to not finishing what we start? Write an essay about divorce and the failure to persevere. *(BIBLE / FAMILY / ENGLISH COMPOSITION)*

Additional ideas:

Project Planning Worksheet

(See instructions in Project R.)

Project title: _____

Description of proposed project: _____

_____

_____

Estimated time to complete: _____

Materials needed: _____

_____

_____

Purchase cost of necessary materials: _____

_____

_____

How I will pay for materials: _____

_____

_____

Research required: _____

_____

_____

Value of this project (Is it worth the time it will require? What will it accomplish?

Who will benefit from it?): _____

_____

_____

Will it distract me from more important concerns and responsibilities? _____

_____

Parents:

Consider and discuss with your son the following questions:

- Does he have a short attention span?
- Does he leave toys and other items all over a room or yard when he is finished using them?
- Does he quit when something becomes boring or difficult?
- Does he give up when he makes a mistake?
- Is he willing to start over when something goes wrong?
- Does he keep working until a project is completed?
- Does he often leave a job done carelessly or unfinished?
- Does he become distracted and wander away to something else when given a job?
- Does he count the cost before starting a project or making a commitment?
- Does he consider his schedule and other commitments before accepting new responsibilities?
- Does he clean up his work space after a messy job?
- Does he have many half-finished projects around the house?
- Can he keep persevering on a long-term project over an extended period of time?
- Does he abandon friendships when there is a problem or does he go to the person and work things out?

Notes and comments:

And to patience,

GODLINESS

Consistently Meditating on God's Word

"As newborn babes, desire the sincere milk of the word, that ye may grow thereby" (1 Peter 2:2).

We should help instill in our sons the desire for consistent daily meditation on God's Word. This should go beyond simple reading, and extend into deeper study and reflecting on the application of Scripture's principles and truths.

To be a true man of God, to be a godly husband and a wise father -- indeed, to even please God -- our sons must learn to feed on God's Word and apply it to their lives. It is God's Word that leads to changed hearts and actions. God's Word enlightens, convicts, protects from sin, gives wisdom and guidance. If we fail to lead our sons constantly to God's Word, our other efforts will be in vain.

In addition to your regular family worship time you might consider a regular Bible reading time each day while your children are young. Set aside this time each evening for your children to spend in individual Bible study time. Each child can have his own Bible. The younger children have Bible story picture books. In our household we attempted to get picture books that used actual Scripture text or that were very accurate to Scripture. We were not using "devotional" books with "application" stories during this time, but Scripture itself at a level that the child could understand.

Each child spent time alone with his Bible, and one of us read with one child and the other read with another child. We rotated each night, so that each child was with Mommy or Daddy at least twice during the week. These were often rich times of questions and discussion, and helped to establish a regular routine of Bible reading as the children grew older.

A. Select verses from the list below, and use some or all of the following suggestions to help you study and better understand their meaning (easier verses are listed first, in italics):

   1) Copy the passage.

   2) Read it in several different translations of the Bible.

   3) Read the passage and several of the verses before and after it to gain a better understanding of the context of the passage.

   4) Rewrite the passage in your own words. What does it mean?

   5) Record a specific way in which you can change your actions or attitudes based on the teaching of this passage.

6) Memorize the passage.

> *Psalm 1:2*
> *Psalm 4:4*
> *Psalm 19:14*
> *Psalm 26:2*
> *Psalm 63:5-6*
> *Psalm 119:15*
> *Psalm 119:59*
> *1 Peter 2:2*
> Psalm 143:5
> Hebrews 11:6
> *(SPEECH / BIBLE)*

Beginner

B. Ask your father what he will be reading during family worship. Try to find the passage in your Bible and have it ready when you gather together to worship. *(BIBLE / MUSIC / DEVOTIONS)*

C. Ask your father what he will be reading for family worship time tomorrow. Read the passage (or have someone else read it to you), and draw a picture to illustrate the passage. Show it to the family when your father reads the passage. *(ART / BIBLE / DEVOTIONS)*

D. Always pray before reading your Bible. Ask God to give you an understanding and willing heart as you read His Word. *(BIBLE)*

E. Read Scripture with one of your parents before you go to bed, and think over what you have read as you go to sleep. Do this each night if you haven't before this. *(BIBLE)*

F. Listen to a tape recording of Scripture reading while going to sleep. *(BIBLE)*

G. As soon as you can read, make a commitment to read your Bible **every day**. Do not eat until you have had your "spiritual breakfast". *(BIBLE / READING)*

H. Copy passages from the Bible and read aloud what you have copied. *(BIBLE / HANDWRITING)*

I. Copy passages from the Bible, inserting your name wherever you can to help you personalize the truths of the passage into your life. Or read the passage aloud doing the same thing. *(HANDWRITING / BIBLE)*

J. Set up a scene with Legos, Playmobil, dolls, stuffed animals, or other toys to demonstrate a particular proverb. Have the family guess which proverb you are illustrating. *(BIBLE / ART)*

K. Illustrate the Bible passage while your father reads it during family worship time. Show it to the family when he finishes reading. *(BIBLE / ART)*

Intermediate

L. Read a chapter of Proverbs each day. Select one verse that you can illustrate with a drawing. Show your illustration to the family at mealtime and see if they can identify the proverb. *(BIBLE / ART)*

M. Read a chapter of Proverbs every day. Talk about at least one verse from the chapter with another member of the family. *(BIBLE / READING)*

N. Identify Proverb illustrations in *Hidden Treasures: Searching for Wisdom,* by Pam Forster.

O. Dramatize a proverb with some of your family members. Let the rest of the family guess which proverb you are depicting. *(DRAMA / BIBLE)*

P. Start a journal for your Bible study notes and observations. *(WRITING)*

Q. Copy portions of the Bible:
- Proverbs - To complete in one year, copy 4 verses each weekday, and 2 on Saturdays.
- James -To complete in one year, copy 2 verses each week.
- Psalm 119 - Copy 1 verse each weekday to finish in less than a year

(BIBLE / HANDWRITING)

R. Meet together weekly with your father or mother to discuss what you have been learning in your personal Bible study. *(BIBLE / FAMILY)*

S. Find out what text your pastor will be preaching on next Sunday. Read it every day this week, and write down any thoughts you have about the passage. Notice if it helps you listen better during the sermon. *(BIBLE)*

T. Read through the entire Bible. Don't worry about reading the entire Bible in a year. Just keep reading, taking time to understand what you read, and persevering until you have finished. (If a parent or other family member also does this, you can encourage each other, discuss what you are learning, and explore your questions together.) *(BIBLE / READING)*

U.   Select one or two verses from the Bible to read. Keep rereading them, each time emphasizing a different word. Take the time to think about what you have read each time. Do you understand the verse differently as you emphasize different words? Try memorizing the verses after reading them several times. *(BIBLE / SPEECH)*

V.   Pick a verse to read. After reading it several times, read it in its context – the verses before and after the verse you are reading. Ask yourself why these verses are placed together. Does one verse make the others make more sense? Meditate on the verses together. *(BIBLE)*

W.   Read a passage of Scripture several times and then write a paraphrase of it in your own words. *(BIBLE / WRITING)*

X.   Read a passage. After reading it, thinking about the individual words, and paraphrasing it (as in Projects U through W, meditate on how you could apply the verse in your life. *(BIBLE / WRITING)*

Y.   Read a passage of Scripture and personalize it by putting the words "I," "we," and "us" into the sentences. *(BIBLE)*

Z.   Read a Psalm as a prayer today. Say it to God. Add details related to your own life. *(BIBLE)*

AA. Copy the following words on a 3 x 5 card and keep it in your Bible for easy reference. Ask yourself these questions as you read and record your answers in a notebook or journal.

   S – Is there a **sin** for me to avoid?

   P – Is there a **promise** for me to claim?

   E – Is there an **example** for me to follow?

   C – Is there a **commandment** for me to obey?

   K – Is there **knowledge** I can gain about God the Father, about Jesus, or about the Holy Spirit?

   (BIBLE)

BB. Using a parallel Bible (print version or online), read a passage in several different translations. What additional insights do you gain? Record your observations. *(BIBLE)*

CC. Read through the verses from Psalm 119 listed on page 295, and write down what each one says about the results of reading, studying, meditating on, and obeying God's Word. *(BIBLE / READING / WRITING)*

DD. Follow the instructions for topical studies of the book of Proverbs, as outlined in *Hidden Treasures: Searching for Wisdom,* by Pam Forster. Use the charts to aid in your study of the Proverbs. *(BIBLE)*

EE. Ask your father if you can try out the various Bible study methods (listed in Project HH) together as a family during family worship time. *(BIBLE / RESEARCH / WRITING / DEVOTIONS / TEACHER ED.)*

FF. Categorize the book of Proverbs. Use a separate page for each topic discussed in Proverbs, such as laziness, foolishness, anger, etc. Read through the book and list each Proverb under the separate categories. *(BIBLE / RESEARCH / WRITING)*

Advanced

GG. Use copies of the form on page 296 to help you apply what you read from the Bible in your daily life. Put these pages into a Bible study notebook. *(READING / BIBLE)*

HH. Learn to use various Bible study methods (topics for many of these studies are suggested throughout this book):

Character studies
Word studies
Inductive study of a book of the Bible
Outlines
Topical studies

(BIBLE / RESEARCH)

II. Study the word "meditate", using the instructions on pages 297-299 to guide you in your study." *(BIBLE / RESEARCH / WRITING)*

JJ. As you read your Bible each day, single out a verse or short passage that you can continue to think and pray about throughout the day. End your day by rereading those verses, and recording any thoughts you have had. *(BIBLE)*

KK. Pick a portion of Scripture and reread it every day for a week. Copy portions on cards that you can carry with you or place around the house to reread as you work. Do this together with a parent, sibling, or friend, and discuss what you have learned at the end of the week. *(BIBLE / HANDWRITING)*

LL. Think about a problem or circumstance in your life. Find Scripture that applies to it. How will these verses change the way you think or act? Write out the problem, the Scripture, and how you will apply this in your life. Keep these notes for easy reference. *(BIBLE / RESEARCH / WRITING)*

MM. Read Chapter 7, "Discipline of Devotion," in *Disciplines of a Godly Man,* by R. Kent Hughes. Complete the "Food for Thought," "Application/Response," and "Think About It!" sections at the end of the chapter. *(READING)*

NN. Complete the "Projects in Proverbs," in Appendix C of *Teach Them Diligently,* by Lou Priolo. Use this format to continue studying the Proverbs. *(BIBLE)*

OO. Study Vic Lockman's *Reading and Understanding the Bible.* Outline its basic content. *(READING / BIBLE / WRITING)*

Additional ideas:

The Results of Studying and Obeying God's Word

(See instructions in Project CC.)

Psalm 119:9-11

Psalm 119:101

Psalm 119:21, 118, 155

Psalm 119:80

Psalm 119:42

Psalm 119:28, 50, 93, 156, 159

Psalm 119:50, 52, 67, 71, 92, 107, 143

Psalm 119:38

Psalm 119:153, 155, 170

Psalm 119:24, 66, 104, 105, 130, 165

Psalm 119:98

Psalm 119:99

Psalm 119:100

Psalm 119:7, 164

Psalm 119:74

Psalm 119:111

Psalm 119:165

Applying God's Word in My Life
(See instructions in Project GG.)

Date:_____   Bible passage I read:_____

- What does it say?

- What does it mean?

- How can I apply it to my life?

- What specifically will I do?

- A week later: How have I done?

- -

Date:_____   Bible passage I read:_____

- What does it say?

- What does it mean?

- How can I apply it to my life?

- What specifically will I do?

- A week later: How have I done?

A Study on Meditation

(Project II)

This study is designed to help you learn how to use "Strong's Exhaustive Concordance" while studying the word "meditate." If you have access to "The Englishman's Hebrew Concordance of the Old Testament," it will also be useful, but the study can be done without it. You should be able to find online versions of "Strong's." **Be sure to use a King James Version Bible** *when doing this study, because the "Strong's" listings are based on the King James Version.*

1. Using *Strong's Concordance,* look up the word "meditate." You will find all the biblical references (in the King James Version) to the word. This is what you should see:

    Meditate   See also PREMEDITATE
    Ge   24: 63 went out to *m* in the field at the
    Jos   1: 8 shalt *m* therein day and night.   1897
    Ps   1: 2 his law doth he *m* day and night   "
          63: 6 *m* on thee in the night watches   "
          77: 12 I will *m* also of all they work, and   "
        119: 15 I will *m* in thy precepts, and have   7878
            23 thy servant did *m* in thy statutes.   "
            48 loved; and I will *m* in thy statutes.   "
            78 cause; but I will *m* in thy precepts.   "
          148 that I might *m* in thy word.   "
        143: 5 I *m* on all thy works; I muse on   1897
    Isa   33: 18 Thine heart shall *m* terror. Where   *"
    Lu   21: 14 not to *m* before what ye shall   *4304*
    1 Ti   4: 15 *M* upon these things; give thyself   *3191*

You should be able to see the Bible references, a portion of the verse with the word "meditate" indicated by an "m" in italics, and a number (at the far right). The number on the right is the number assigned to the original Hebrew or Greek word that was translated as "meditate" in these verses.

The number corresponds to numbers in the Hebrew and Greek dictionaries at the back of the concordance. Upright type is used for Old Testament words which will be found in the Hebrew dictionary. Italic type is used for New Testament words which will be found in the Greek dictionary. Notice that the first verse listed has no dictionary number. This is because the Hebrew word for "meditate" was not actually used literally in the original text.

2. Write down the reference of each of the verses listed. Then read each verse, paying attention to the context of each (the verses preceding and following it in the text). Next to each reference, note anything you learn about "meditate."

3. Then look up the numbers (at the far right) in the Hebrew and Greek dictionaries (back portion of the concordance). Be sure you use the Hebrew dictionary for the Old Testament words and the Greek dictionary for the New Testament words. If you look up 1897 in the Hebrew dictionary, you will find the following entry:

> **1897.** הָגָה **hagah,** *haw-gaw';* a prim. root; [comp.
> 1901]; *to murmur* (in pleasure or anger);
> By impl. to *ponder:* -- imagine, meditate, mourn,
> mutter, roar, X sore, speak, study, talk, utter.

- After the number, you will first see the original word as it is written in Hebrew. Then you will see the exact equivalent of the word in English letters, followed by the word's pronunciation, using standard English pronunciation markings.

- After the pronunciation, the "etymology" of the word is given. This is the history of the word, tracing it back to its root word or words. This information can be useful for those who want to make a more detailed study of the word and its origins.

- Next, in italics, is the meaning of the word. **Hagah** means "to murmur," and the words that follow in parentheses further clarify the meaning by telling us that this murmuring can be done in pleasure or in anger.

- The next phrase, "By impl. to *ponder,*" tells us that the implied meaning of the word is "to ponder."

Reading just this much already gives us a better understanding of the word "meditate." We can assume from this definition that when we meditate on Scripture we are pondering its words with pleasure.

4. Write down the words that follow the dash (--) in the dictionary definition (as shown in Step 3). These will be especially helpful to you as you continue this study. These words are other English translations of **hagah.** Translators did not always translate **hagah** with the English word "meditate."

Depending on the context and other factors, the translators sometimes translated it with the different words, which are all listed in this part of the definition. Sometimes **hagah** is translated as "imagine," sometimes as "mourn," sometimes as "mutter," etc.

5. Look up the word "imagine" in the concordance portion of *Strong's.* Skim through the dictionary numbers on the right side of the listing. Do you see any that list "1897"? Those verses include the same Hebrew word **hagah,** but in these verses the word has been translated as "imagine" instead of "meditate."

(Note: If you are working with an online version of *Strong's Concordance,* you may also have access to *Englishman's Concordance.* Your family may also have a print version of *Englishman's.* If so, use it for this study. You can simply look up "1897" and find a complete listing of all the verses that include the Hebrew word **hagah**. You will not need to find the number listed under separate English words in *Strong's*.)

Read the two verses that have 1897 assigned to them. Do they help you gain a better understanding of our word? It seems that both of these verses are using the word in a more negative sense, and are not directly related to our study of meditating on Scripture. But they help us better understand the original Hebrew word. Take notes on how the word is used in both verses.

6. Look up the next word, "mourn." Find the verses that are followed by "1897" and read them. Again, these may not relate directly to meditating on God's Word, but they do shed more light on the usage of the word **hagah**. Note the references and how the word is used.

7. Do the same thing with the word "mutter." For the purpose of this study, **stop after these words**. Do not look up "roar" or the words that follow the "x" in the definition.

8. Now go back to the original concordance listing for the word "meditate" (top of page 297). Do you see any other dictionary numbers listed? Look up "7878" in the Hebrew dictionary. Note its definition.

9. Write down each of the other English words that translators used for this particular word (the words that follow the "--")

10. Look up each of these words in the concordance and look for other verses that used the Hebrew word that is assigned the dictionary number "7878." (Again, if you have access to *Englishman's Concordance,* use it to locate all the verses that use this word.)

11. Write down the references and read the verses, continuing to note your observations.

12. If you care to continue, you can also look up the New Testament verses and their corresponding dictionary numbers, taking care to look for your definitions in the **Greek** dictionary.

13. You can also extend your study, if you choose, by completing this same process with the word "meditation."

14. Review and organize your notes. What can you learn about "meditate" as it relates to Scripture and God's law? In what other ways is the word used? What can you learn from these verses? On what other things are we tempted to ponder when we fail to meditate on God's Word? How will this study affect your daily life?

15. Summarize your conclusions in a short paper. Share your paper with a friend or sibling.

(For a more detailed study on how to use the Greek and Hebrew dictionaries in your studies, see *Beauty and the Pig,* by Pam Forster, and other Bible study materials from Doorposts.)

Parents:

Consider and discuss with your son the following questions:

- Is he reading a translation of the Bible that he can understand?

- Does he read the Bible daily? Does he have to be reminded?

- Does he have a **desire** to read God's Word?

- Is his life changed by the study of God's Word?

- Does Scripture have meaning to him?

- Is he noticeably convicted by God's Word?

- Does he listen carefully when the Bible is read aloud?

- Can he think of passages that apply to specific situations that occur in his life?

- Does he ask you questions about what he is reading in the Bible?

- Does he share insights with you from his Bible reading?

- Does he see **you** reading and studying your Bible?

- Does he look to the Bible for answers to his questions and problems?

- Does he think he doesn't have time to study the Bible?

Notes and comments:

Hiding God's Word in Our Hearts

"Thy Word have I hid in my heart, that I might not sin against thee" (Psalm 119:11).

We and our children are involved in a battle. But God has provided armor, if we are willing to put it on. We must not allow our children to wage war unarmed against "principalities, against powers, against the rulers of the darkness of this world, against spiritual wickedness in high places" (Ephesians 6:12). We must help them take up the sword that God has supplied -- His Word.

We need God's Word in our hearts and minds if we are going to successfully fight off the temptations of this world. Memorizing Scripture -- and faithfully reviewing it so we can continue to remember it -- arms us for the inevitable temptations we encounter throughout each day. With Scripture committed to memory, we have picked up the sword and placed it in its sheath. The Holy Spirit will help us remember to pull it out and use it.

Jesus, when He was tempted, answered Satan with the words of Scripture. He was able to counter the deceiver with the truth of God's Word. If we help our children weave Scripture into the fabric of their lives, they will, empowered by the Holy Spirit, be able to stand against temptation as well.

A. Select verses from the list below, and use some or all of the following suggestions to help you study and better understand their meaning (easier verses are listed first, in italics):

1) Copy the passage.

2) Read it in several different translations of the Bible.

3) Read the passage and several of the verses before and after it to gain a better understanding of the context of the passage.

4) Rewrite the passage in your own words. What does it mean?

5) Record a specific way in which you can change your actions or attitudes based on the teaching of this passage.

6) Memorize the passage.

   Deuteronomy 6:6
   Psalm 119:11
   Psalm 119:30
   Psalm 119:105

Psalm 19:7-11
(BIBLE / SPEECH)

Beginner

B. Pick one of the memory verses for this chapter. Draw a picture to help illustrate the meaning of the verse, and work on memorizing it as you draw. *(BIBLE / ART)*

C. With your parents' help, pick a verse to memorize. Repeat the reference and the verse after your parent says it. Then say it again, emphasizing a different word in the verse. Say it again, emphasizing yet a different word, and so forth until you can repeat the entire verse by yourself. *(BIBLE)*

D. Recite at least one memory verse during your family worship time today. *(BIBLE / SPEECH)*

E. Practice your verse with members of your family at the dinner table. Go around the table with each person saying the next word in the verse. *(BIBLE / SPEECH)*

F. Make a commitment to memorize a certain number of verses each week. Set a goal and reward yourself when you reach it, or ask your parents if you could work toward some special privilege. *(BIBLE)*

G. Ask someone to listen to you recite your memorized verses. Ask if he or she would be willing to listen to you once a week. *(BIBLE / SPEECH)*

H. Write out a memory verse, using pictures and symbols to represent as many words as you can. Quote the verse while only looking at your picture sentence. *(BIBLE / ART)*

I. Pick a verse from this chapter to memorize. As you memorize, discuss it with your parents. What does the verse mean? How can you apply it in your life? *(BIBLE)*

J. Recite a memory verse at the table each meal before you eat. *(BIBLE / SPEECH)*

K. Write each word of a verse on separate 3" x 5" cards to help you memorize the verse, shuffle the cards and put them back in order. *(HANDWRITING / BIBLE)*

L. Hand-copy Scripture passages. *(HANDWRITING / BIBLE)*

Intermediate

M. Set up a notebook with verses to memorize. Copy each verse, leaving space below each to illustrate the passage with a simple drawing. *(HANDWRITING / ART / BIBLE)*

N. Write a paraphrase of each verse you memorize. Don't memorize your paraphrase, but write it to help you gain a better understanding of the verse. *(BIBLE / WRITING)*

O. Keep a notebook of verses you want to memorize. Arrange topically, so that you can refer to the appropriate section when you need to. Illustrate the verses you are memorizing to help you remember them better. *(BIBLE / ART)*

P. Make a memory verse file box. Purchase a file box designed for 3" x 5" cards, some 3" x 5" cards, and some cards with tabs designed to fit in the file box. Label the tabbed cards with different categories of verses you are memorizing (i.e., salvation, temptation, praise, proverbs). Use the 3" x 5" cards to write verses on. When you have finished the verse, put the card in the correct section of your card box. Take cards out of the file each day for review and then re-file them. *(HANDWRITING / BIBLE)*

Q. Write each verse you memorize on a 3" x 5" card. Carry it with you throughout the day, memorizing while you wash dishes, take out the garbage, ride in the car, etc. When you have finished memorizing the verse, file it in your verse card file box. *(BIBLE)*

R. Review your past memory verses each day. Recite at least 5 "old" memory verses after you have worked on your "new" verse. Review different verses each day. *(BIBLE / SPEECH)*

S. Research online the recordings that are available of Scripture verses set to music. Write a list of options. Ask your parents if you can purchase one to use for helping your younger siblings memorize Scripture. *(BIBLE / MUSIC)*

T. Download free memory verse cards from *www.memoryversecards.com* to print out and use. Carry these with you and memorize verses as you work and play. *(BIBLE)*

U. Make a list of verses that are related to areas of weakness and temptation in your life. Work on memorizing and applying these verses. *(BIBLE / WRITING)*

V. Use an organized Bible memory program to help you memorize verses. (*MemLok, Navigators' Topical Memory System, Scripture Memory Fellowship,* etc.) *(BIBLE)*

W. Use a computer program such as *Memorize His Word* to help you memorize verses. Work on your verses each day before you do anything else on the computer. *(BIBLE)*

X. Help your siblings memorize Bible verses.

- Say the verse and have them repeat it.

- Write the verse on a white board. Have them read the entire verse, and then erase words and have them keep filling in the blanks as they read.

- Teach them hand motions or sign language for some of the words. Use these as cues while they are memorizing, or have them do the motions while they recite the words.

- Say some words, with them filling in words each time you stop.

- Give a reference and have them say the verse.

- Listen to them recite the entire verse alone. *(TEACHING / BIBLE)*

Advanced

Y. Set to music the words of a verse you are memorizing. Make up your own tune or use a familiar folk or hymn tune. Sing the verse to yourself throughout the day until it is memorized. *(BIBLE / MUSIC)*

Z. Make a tape recording of passages you want to memorize by reading the verses yourself. Read the entire passage once, then read it while leaving certain words out. Then leave more words out. Then read only the beginning word of each verse. When you listen to this tape, you can test your memory by supplying the missing words. Plug in your earphones and work on memorizing verses while mowing the lawn, jogging around town, etc. *(SPEECH / BIBLE)*

AA. Select verses for the family to memorize, and lead in memorizing them at the dinner table. *(BIBLE / RESEARCH / TEACHING)*

BB. Design a game to help you and your siblings memorize and review Bible verses. *(BIBLE / WRITING / ART / P.E. / ETC.)*

CC. Devise a system for recording memory verses the family has learned, for reviewing them, and for motivating reluctant memorizers. Use it! *(TEACHING / BIBLE)*

Additional ideas:

Parents:

Consider and discuss with your son the following questions:

- Can he recite more than a dozen verses?

- Can he recall the verses he has memorized?

- Can he still accurately recite verses six months after he first memorized them?

- Does he memorize the Scripture reference as well as the verse?

- Can he recite a verse after you give him the reference?

- Does he have a regular time each day in which he can work on memorizing verses?

- Does he have a list or plan that enables him to know which verse to memorize next after he has finished a verse?

- Can he explain the meaning of the verses he memorizes?

- Can he recall appropriate verses throughout the day that apply to various situations he encounters?

- Can he quote an appropriate verse if you ask him what God's Word says about a particular discipline problem? Can he explain how it relates to the situation?

- Does he pray for God's help as he works at memorizing Scripture?

Notes and comments:

Daily Communion with God in Prayer

"Rejoice evermore. Pray without ceasing. In everything give thanks; for this is the will of God in Christ Jesus concerning you" (1 Thessalonians 5:16-18).

What man will ever truly know God and His grace without the habit of daily, fervent prayer? We all seem to fall short in this area. We should desire to lead our children to the throne of grace -- to praise Him, to discern and submit to His will, to give thanks, to call on His power and grace to meet our needs and the needs of others.

A. Select verses from the list below, and use some or all of the following suggestions to help you study and better understand their meaning (easier verses are listed first, in italics):

1) Copy the passage.

2) Read it in several different translations of the Bible.

3) Read the passage and several of the verses before and after it to gain a better understanding of the context of the passage.

4) Rewrite the passage in your own words. What does it mean?

5) Record a specific way in which you can change your actions or attitudes based on the teaching of this passage.

6) Memorize the passage.

   Psalm 34:15
   Jeremiah 33:3
   Matthew 21:22
   Romans 12:12
   1 Thessalonians 5:17
   Hebrews 4:16
   Psalm 9:10
   Psalm 55:16-17
   Psalm 116:2
   Psalm 145:18-19
   Proverbs 3:5-6
   Romans 8:26
   James 1:5-7
   James 5:16
   1 John 5:14-15

   (BIBLE / SPEECH)

Beginner

B. Pray with one of your parents each night at bedtime.

C. Pray for one of your family members each day. Make a poster with each day of the week on it, and assign specific family members to specific days. Glue their pictures onto the poster, if you like. Be sure to pray for those people on those days, in addition to other times during the week.

D. Have a special time of prayer alone with Dad (and/or Mom) once a week. *(FAMILY)*

E. Read with your parents Part 12, "When We Pray to God" in *Leading Little Ones to God,* by Marian Schoolland. *(BIBLE / READING)*

F. Read with your parents the story of Elijah and the prophets of Baal in 1 Kings 18. What challenge did Elijah propose? What did the prophets of Baal do? What did Elijah have the people do to the altar before he prayed? What did Elijah pray to God? What happened? Act out this story with your playmates, or draw a series of pictures to illustrate it. *(BIBLE/ DRAMA)*

G. Read in Genesis 24 with your parents the story of Abraham's servant seeking a wife for Isaac. What did the servant pray? Did God answer his prayer? *(BIBLE / READING)*

H. Tell your family stories of times when God answered prayers you have prayed. *(SPEECH)*

I. Ask your parents and grandparents to tell you stories of times when God has answered their prayers. Turn at least one of the stories into a picture book, with your own illustrations. Give the book to the storyteller as a gift. *(FAMILY HISTORY / ART)*

J. Pray aloud and ask the blessing at your next meal.

K. With your parents, make a prayer notebook. Paste in pictures of your family members, friends, church leaders, and government leaders. Choose one or two people from the book each day and pray for them. *(FAMILY / GOVERNMENT)*

L. Pray aloud during family prayer times.

M. Ask your grandparents for specific ways you can pray for them, and then pray each day for them. *(FAMILY)*

N. What physical need does your family have? Does your father need a job? Does your family need a new car? Is someone sick? Have you lost something that you need to find? Pray with your family for these needs, and watch to see how God will answer. Share the answers to your prayers with friends and other family members, and thank God for His answers. *(FAMILY)*

O. Memorize the Lord's Prayer. *(BIBLE / SPEECH)*

Intermediate

P. Pray together as a family each day. Under the guidance of your parents, set up a prayer notebook or file box in which you can record your family's requests and God's answers. Present your needs to the Lord, and witness the faithfulness and power of God as He provides. Use copies of the prayer journal sheet on page 313, if desired. Make one page in your notebook for each general area of prayer, such as government leaders, family, church leaders, illness, etc. *(WRITING)*

Q. Interview people you know, especially the godly men you admire. Ask them about answered prayers in their lives. In what specific ways has God answered their prayers? Write down some of the stories these people tell you. Read them to the rest of your family. *(SPEECH / WRITING / ENGLISH COMPOSITION)*

R. Make a list of unsaved family members and friends. Pray for these people, and pray for opportunities to show love to them and to share the gospel with them. *(EVANGELISM)*

S. Study the "Lord's Prayer" with your family during family worship time. *(BIBLE / RESEARCH)*

T. Spend time alone each day in private prayer. Keep a journal of requests and answers. Use copies of the prayer journal sheet on page 313, if desired. (See project P for further instructions in using it.) *(WRITING)*

U. During your personal prayer time try to include each of these elements in your prayer:
- Praising God for specific attributes of His character
- Confessing your sins
- Thanksgiving to God for what He has done and what He promises to do
- Specific requests for God's work in your life and the lives of others

V. Write to and pray for missionary families. Read their prayer letters to learn of their specific needs and keep track of how God meets them. *(READING / WRITING / GEOGRAPHY)*

W. Complete the study, *Lord, Teach Me to Pray for Kids,* by Kay Arthur and Janna Arndt. *(BIBLE)*

X. Read biographies of missionaries, reformers, preachers, and historical figures. How did prayer influence their life and work? How did God answer their prayers? *(READING / HISTORY)*

Y. Make a commitment to faithfully pray for your parents and siblings. Ask them what they would like you to pray for, and be sensitive to God's leading when you should be part of His answer to your prayers! *(FAMILY)*

Z. Become prayer partners with your father. Share your heart and your requests. Pray together for one another. *(FAMILY)*

AA. Do a topical study on prayer. What is prayer? Why should we pray? What difference does prayer make if God is sovereign? Write a summary of your findings. *(BIBLE / WRITING / RESEARCH)*

BB. Study and make a list of all the promises about prayer in God's Word. Write down each reference and a brief summary of each verse. (Look up verses under "prayer" in *Nave's Topical Bible*.) *(BIBLE / RESEARCH / WRITING)*

CC. Write up lists of specific ways you can pray for friends, parents, teachers, government leaders, sick people, missionaries, etc. Use these lists to pray for a different group of people each day of the week (i.e., friends on Monday, government leaders on Tuesday). *(WRITING)*

DD. Study the prayers in the book of Psalms. How does David approach God? What are common elements in his prayers? Examine them carefully, and write down your observations. Write a paper to summarize what you have learned in your study. *(BIBLE / WRITING)*

EE. Read the Psalms as your own prayers to God. *(READING / BIBLE)*

FF. Study stories in the Bible that record God's answers to prayer (Joshua, Moses, David, etc.). List each incident you can think of (look under "prayer" in *Nave's Topical Bible)*, the Scripture reference for it, and the results of the prayer. Use the form on page 314. Review these stories when you are tempted to think that God doesn't care about you or your needs. *(BIBLE / RESEARCH / WRITING)*

Advanced

GG. Attend a young men's prayer meeting. If there are none in your church, neighborhood, or homeschool support group, start one! *(SOCIAL SKILLS)*

HH. Read *Hudson Taylor's Spiritual Secret,* by Dr. and Mrs. Howard Taylor. Write down each example of answered prayer in his life. *(READING / HISTORY / WRITING)*

II. Memorize Questions No. 98-107 in *The Westminster Larger Catechism.* *(BIBLE / DOCTRINE / SPEECH)*

JJ. Write out some of your prayers. Writing sometimes helps us to think more carefully. Write out a prayer about an area of temptation, about a friend, etc. *(WRITING)*

KK. Study the prayers in a book of written prayers. Read and pray one of them each day. *(READING)*

LL. Read Chapter 8, "Discipline of Prayer," in *Disciplines of a Godly Man,* by R. Kent Hughes. Complete the "Food for Thought," "Application/Response," and "Think About It!" sections at the end of the chapter. *(READING)*

MM. Study imprecatory Psalms. What are they? Which Psalms are considered imprecatory Psalms? Is it wrong to pray the imprecatory Psalms? Why or why not? How do we reconcile the commandment to not take vengeance on our enemies with the Psalms that pray for the writer's enemies to be judged? Can imprecatory Psalms be wrong if they are part of the inspired Word of God? Read reliable commentators and authors, and write an essay on these questions. *(BIBLE / ENGLISH COMPOSITION)*

NN. Choose one of the imprecatory Psalms to study. Read the Psalm carefully. What is the psalmist asking for? Read various commentators' writings. What does John Calvin say about it? Charles Spurgeon? Matthew Henry? Write an essay that explains the Psalm and summarizes what you have learned. *(BIBLE / ENGLISH COMPOSITION)*

OO. Read Dietrich Bonhoeffer's *Psalms: The Prayer Book of the Bible* (available free at *www.books.google.com*). Outline the book's contents, and make a practice of praying the Psalms each day. *(BIBLE / READING)*

PP. Read *If God Already Knows, Why Pray?,* by Douglas Kelly. Then write a paper discussing the relationship of God's sovereignty and our prayers. If God already knows what is going to happen, how do our prayers make any difference? *(READING / ENGLISH COMPOSITION)*

QQ. Study what the Bible says about prayers that will not be heard. Whom does God say He will not hear? Study verses that deal with this topic and write a summary of your findings. (Start by looking up "Wicked, Prayer of" in *Nave's Topical Bible*, or search for "prayer" in *Strong's Concordance.*) *(BIBLE / RESEARCH / WRITING)*

RR. Do word studies in the Bible on the following words:

Giving of thanks
Intercessions
Prayers
Supplications
(BIBLE / RESEARCH / FOREIGN LANGUAGE)

SS. Study Lessons 55-64 on the Lord's Prayer in *The Westminster Shorter Catechism for Study Classes,* by G.I. Williamson. *(BIBLE / DOCTRINE)*

TT. Read *Luther's Prayers*, edited by Herbert Brokering. Read these prayers occasionally for your personal prayer time. The second section of this book contains much helpful instruction about prayer, the Ten Commandments, and the Lord's Prayer. *(BIBLE)*

UU. Use Matthew Henry's *A Method for Prayer* to help you pray effectively in your prayer times. *(READING)*

VV. Attend the men's prayer group meetings in your church. *(SOCIAL SKILLS)*

WW. Study the role of the Old Testament priest, as described in the law and history sections of the Old Testament. Compare that role to the role fathers played in acting as priest in their family before the time of the Levitical priests (Noah, Job, Abraham, etc.) How did they act as priests in their homes? How can men, as husbands and fathers, act as priests in their homes today? Write an essay explaining your thoughts. *(BIBLE / HISTORY / ENGLISH COMPOSITION)*

Additional ideas:

PRARYER JOURNAL

_____

SUBJECT OF PRAYER

DATE   **REQUEST**   *ANSWER*   *DATE*

___   _____   _____   _____

___   _____   _____   _____

___   _____   _____   _____

___   _____   _____   _____

___   _____   _____   _____

___   _____   _____   _____

___   _____   _____   _____

___   _____   _____   _____

___   _____   _____   _____

___   _____   _____   _____

___   _____   _____   _____

___   _____   _____   _____

___   _____   _____   _____

___   _____   _____   _____

___   _____   _____   _____

___   _____   _____   _____

___   _____   _____   _____

___   _____   _____   _____

___   _____   _____   _____

___   _____   _____   _____

God's Answers to Prayer in the Bible

(See Project FF for instructions.)

INCIDENT	REFERENCE	RESULTS

Parents:

Consider and discuss with your son the following questions:

- Does he close his eyes and sit quietly during times of prayer?
- Does he have a regular time of prayer each day?
- Does he pray for guidance when he needs to make a decision?
- Does he pray for the needs of others?
- Do his prayers display a true reverence and love for the Lord?
- Does he share his concerns and prayer requests with you?
- Does he believe that God will answer his prayers?
- Does he notice when God answers his prayers?
- Does he express thankfulness in his prayers or does he only ask for things?
- Does he readily acknowledge the power of prayer?
- Does he think to pray when faced with difficulties or temptations?
- Will he pray aloud in a group?

Notes and comments:

Honoring God's Day of Rest

"If thou turn away thy foot from the sabbath, from doing thy pleasure on my holy day; and call the sabbath a delight, the holy of the Lord, honorable; and shalt honour him, not doing thine own ways, nor finding thine own pleasure, nor speaking thine own words: then shalt thou delight thyself in the Lord; and I will cause thee to ride upon the high places of the earth, and feed thee with the heritage of Jacob thy father: for the mouth of the Lord hath spoken it" (Isaiah 58:13-14).

God's work of creation lasted for six days. On the seventh day, He rested in the good work He had accomplished. In the same way, we have been commanded to work six days and rest on the seventh. This day of rest is a **gift**, not a burden. We are not being deprived; we are being given the gift of a day free of labor, a day when we cannot feel guilty for setting aside the duties and cares of the week in order to focus our attention on worshipping God and serving and fellowshipping with His children. We look back on a week of satisfying labor for Christ's kingdom, and we rest, knowing that God is in control, and that His plan will continue to be accomplished even while we sit at His feet and worship Him.

We should pray that our sons would willingly give up their own pleasure on this blessed Lord's Day, and enjoy a "day of delight" that is especially set apart for worship and fellowship with other believers. Our sons will be blessed for their obedience in this area, just as God promises they will be.

A. Select verses from the list below, and use some or all of the following suggestions to help you study and better understand their meaning (easier verses are listed first, in italics):

1) Copy the passage.

2) Read it in several different translations of the Bible.

3) Read the passage and several of the verses before and after it to gain a better understanding of the context of the passage.

4) Rewrite the passage in your own words. What does it mean?

5) Record a specific way in which you can change your actions or attitudes based on the teaching of this passage.

6) Memorize the passage.

> *Leviticus 19:30*
> *Psalm 118:24*

Habakkuk 2:20
Mark 2:27
Psalm 89:7
Isaiah 58:13-14
(BIBLE / SPEECH)

Beginner

B. Read Chapter 77 "Why We Go to Church" and Chapter 78 "How We Worship God in Church" in *Leading Little Ones to God* by Marian Schoolland. *(BIBLE / READING)*

C. Read with your parents Genesis 1:1-2:3. How long did it take God to create the world? What did He do when He was finished? Draw a picture of what He made each day. *(BIBLE / ART)*

D. Read with your parents Exodus 20:8-11. How many days are we supposed to work each week? How many days are we not supposed to work? Who is not supposed to work? Why? *(BIBLE)*

E. Memorize the 4th Commandment in Exodus 20:8-11. *(BIBLE)*

F. Go through your toys and set aside ones to put in a box just for Sundays. Bring these out each week to enjoy on Sunday.

G. On Saturday, set out your clothes and shoes, your Bible and offering, and anything else you need at church. *(TIME MANAGEMENT)*

H. Work with your parents to make a list of your duties on Sunday morning. What do you need to do, and who do you need to help to be ready to leave for church on time each Sunday? Illustrate the list, and post it in your room where you can refer to it on Sunday mornings. *(TIME MANAGEMENT / WRITING / ART)*

I. Invite a friend over for Sunday afternoon and show him hospitality as you share a worshipful day of rest together. Have a good time together sharing activities that will help you focus more on God and His Word. (Act out Bible stories, play with Bible-times soldiers, play Bible games together, read, take a walk, play music, etc.) *(BIBLE / DRAMA / READING / MUSIC / ART / ETC.)*

J. With your parents' guidance, help design and make special toys to put in a "Sunday box" for Sunday playtime only. *(ART / WOODWORKING / ETC.)*

K. Help shop in stores and mail order catalogs for toys, crafts, and books that would be appropriate for the "Sunday box." *(READING / RESEARCH / MATH / WRITING / CONSUMER EDUCATION)*

Intermediate

L. Make a list of all the things you can do to be prepared for Sunday before the day arrives. Schedule when you will do these things throughout the week and follow your schedule. Is Sunday morning more pleasant? *(WRITING / FAMILY)*

M. Spend the first part of each Saturday in preparation for Sunday. Before you pursue your other interests for the day, make sure you have finished preparing for Sunday (getting out clothes, Bible, tithe money, Sunday School assignments, etc.) *(TIME MANAGEMENT)*

N. Read through the activity ideas listed in *A Day of Delight,* by Pam Forster. Choose ones to do each Sunday.

O. Design a craft project for Sunday afternoon. Do this with the other children in your family, or with visiting children, while your parents have the opportunity to visit or rest. *(TEACHING / ART)*

P. Design and make a game based on a story from the Bible or one that helps teach about the Bible. Teach everyone how to play it on Sunday afternoon. *(TEACHING / BIBLE / P.E.)*

Q. With your father's guidance, plan activities and dinner for next Sunday afternoon. *(FAMILY / BIBLE)*

R. Help your younger siblings prepare for Sunday on Saturday morning, and help them get dressed and ready to leave on Sunday morning. *(FAMILY / HOME SKILLS)*

S. Seek to minister to the needs of at least one other person in your church family this Sunday. Try to reach out and help someone every Sunday. *(COMMUNITY SERVICE / SOCIAL SKILLS)*

T. Make breakfast on Sunday morning (or prepare as much of it as you can on Saturday) so that your mother can rest from her normal cooking duties on Sunday morning. Offer to do this every week. *(FAMILY / HOME SKILLS)*

U. Keep a notebook and take notes on the sermon each Sunday. Discuss what you have learned with your parents. *(BIBLE / WRITING)*

V. Write down any questions you might have about the sermon to discuss with your parents later in the day. *(BIBLE)*

W. Memorize Questions No. 115-121 in *The Westminster Larger Catechism.* *(SPEECH / BIBLE / DOCTRINE)*

X. Read Chapter 13, "The Lord's Day," in *The Shaping of a Christian Family,* by Elisabeth Elliot. How did the author's family observe the Lord's Day? Why? *(READING)*

Y. Study Scripture passages on the Sabbath and Lord's Day. Make a list of commandments that are issued. List the promises that are given. *(BIBLE / RESEARCH)*

Z. Make a list of activities that would be appropriate and edifying to the family for Sunday afternoons:

- What can you do together and with other families that will cause you to focus on Scripture?
- What can you do that will help you to minister to those in need? What can you do to praise and worship God?
- What can you do that will help you meditate and reflect on your life over the past week?
- What can you do to encourage fellowship among believers? What can you do to remember God's acts of creation?

(BIBLE / FAMILY / WRITING)

AA. Spend part of each Saturday evening preparing your heart for Sunday. Think over your past week. Ask God to reveal sins in your life. Confess these, repent of them, and make plans for actions that demonstrate your repentance. Reconcile with any people you may have offended. *(DEVOTIONS / SOCIAL SKILLS)*

Advanced

BB. Visit a sick or elderly person on Sunday afternoon. Take flowers. Read the Bible aloud and pray. Play music, or put a puzzle together with him. Find out if he would like to attend church with you next Sunday morning, and make arrangements to pick him up and take him with you. *(SOCIAL SKILLS / READING / MUSIC / COMMUNITY SERVICE)*

CC. Visit a rest home or retirement center on Sunday afternoon. Play a musical instrument in a common meeting area, or sing hymns with your family. Read the Bible to people. Chat with them, take them outside for a walk, etc. If your church oversees a worship service at the home, attend and participate in it. *(SOCIAL SKILLS / READING / MUSIC / COMMUNITY SERVICE)*

DD. Study Jesus' response to the Pharisees when they tried to impose their own self-righteous laws about the Sabbath. What were the Pharisees saying? What accusations did they make? What did Jesus say and do? *(BIBLE)*

EE. Study Isaiah 58:13-14. Study the meanings of key words in the passage and note how the same words are used in other passages in the Bible. Notice the "if" at the beginning of the passage and the "then" that calls our attention to the results of delighting in the Sabbath. Read commentaries on the passage. Then write an essay that summarizes the meaning and application of these verses to your life. *(BIBLE / GRAMMAR / ENGLISH COMPOSITION)*

FF. Study the following words in the Bible. Write a short essay summarizing the meaning of each word and how it relates to the Lord's Day.

Praise
Reverence
Worship

(BIBLE / RESEARCH / WRITING / FOREIGN LANGUAGE)

GG. Read *Making Sunday Special,* by Karen Mains. Discuss the book with your parents. In what ways could you change the way you spend your Sundays? *(READING)*

HH. Read *Celebrating the Sabbath: Finding Rest in a Restless World,* by Bruce Ray. Discuss with your parents the "Review" and "Response" questions at the end of each chapter. *(READING)*

II. Read Chapter 9, "Discipline of Worship," in *Disciplines of a Godly Man,* by R. Kent Hughes. Complete the "Food for Thought," "Application/Response," and "Think About It!" sections at the end of the chapter. *(READING)*

JJ. Write an essay that explains the relationship between the Old Testament Sabbath and the New Testament Lord's Day. As part of your research, read or re-read Chapter 3, "Sabbath or Lord's Day? Old Testament Roots," and Chapter 4, "Sabbath or Lord's Day? New Testament Flower and Fruits," in *Celebrating the Sabbath,* by Bruce Ray. *(BIBLE / RESEARCH / ENGLISH COMPOSITION)*

KK. Research the reasons for the change from Old Testament seventh day Sabbath-keeping to New Testament Lord's Day observance. Why did the day change? Write a paper summarizing your findings, or discuss the topic with your father. *(BIBLE / RESEARCH / ENGLISH COMPOSITION)*

LL. Read *The Lord's Day,* by Joseph Pipa. Write a summary and review of the book and ask if it can be published in your church's newsletter, if it has one. *(READING / ENGLISH COMPOSITION)*

MM. After the sermon each Sunday, think of at least one way in which you can apply what you have learned during the next week. Write it down in a notebook (perhaps your prayer journal), and on the following Saturday evening evaluate how well you have done. *(WRITING)*

NN. Study Lessons 41-42 in *The Westminster Shorter Catechism for Study Classes*, by G.I. Williamson. *(BIBLE)*

OO. Research the history of observing Sunday as a day of rest or worship in the United States. How did the early colonists treat Sunday? What are "blue laws"? When were blue laws repealed and why? What have been the cultural trends since that time? Do you think there is any relationship between a neglect of the Lord's Day and cultural decline? Why? *(HISTORY / RESEARCH)*

PP. Write a research paper on church attendance in present-day America (or in your native country). What percentage of people attends church at all? Do the statistics vary according to geographical locations? How many people attend Bible-believing, Trinitarian churches? What should we as Christians do with these statistics? *(RESEARCH / RELIGION / SOCIAL STUDIES)*

QQ. Read *The Taste of Sabbath: How to Delight in God's Rest*, by Stuart Bryan. Discuss the book with your father. What changes do you need to make in your thinking and activities related to the Lord's Day? *(READING / FAMILY)*

RR. Write an essay that discusses the relationship between our trust in God to provide for us and our willingness to rest from our work on the Lord's Day. *(BIBLE / RESEARCH / ENGLISH COMPOSITION)*

SS. Read Chapter 4 on the 4th Commandment in *The Ten Commandments*, by Thomas Watson. Outline its basic points. What can you apply to your life? *(READING / WRITING)*

Additional ideas:

Parents:

Consider and discuss with your son the following questions:

- Is he happy to see Sunday arrive?

- Is he thankful for the day of rest God has given him?

- Is Sunday a day of rest and celebration for him and the rest of your family?

- Is he willing to set aside his normal weekly activities to focus his Sunday on worship, fellowship, and Bible study?

- Does he use Sunday as an opportunity to minister to others?

- Does he help your family make Sunday a special day, different from others?

- Does he help prepare on Saturday so that Sunday can be a day of rest?

- Does he help the family leave on time on Sunday mornings?

Notes and comments:

Obeying God with the Tithe

"Honour the Lord with thy substance, and with the firstfruits of all thine increase: so shall thy barns be filled with plenty, and thy presses shall burst out with new wine" (Proverbs 3:9-10).

We should train our children, from the moment they begin to earn their first pennies at household chores, to recognize that all we have comes from the Lord. We can set an example for them by gratefully and obediently giving back to Him the portion that He tells us is His. What blessings await the obedient in this area!

A. Select verses from the list below, and use some or all of the following suggestions to help you study and better understand their meaning (easier verses are listed first, in italics):

1) Copy the passage.

2) Read it in several different translations of the Bible.

3) Read the passage and several of the verses before and after it to gain a better understanding of the context of the passage.

4) Rewrite the passage in your own words. What does it mean?

5) Record a specific way in which you can change your actions or attitudes based on the teaching of this passage.

6) Memorize the passage.

   Haggai 2:8
   Matthew 6:21
   Matthew 6:33
   Deuteronomy 8:18
   Proverbs 3:9-10
   Malachi 3:8-12
   2 Corinthians 9:6-7
   (BIBLE / SPEECH)

Beginner

C. Draw a picture to illustrate Proverbs 3:9-10. *(BIBLE / ART)*

D. Ask your parents what the tithe is used for in your church. *(FINANCES)*

E. If you don't earn any of your own money yet, help your parents put their tithe in the offering on Sunday. *(FINANCES)*

F. Whenever you get ten cents, put one penny of it into the offering on Sunday. *(MATH / FINANCES)*

G. Ask your parents to help you set aside one tenth of any money you earn. Keep it in a special container, and put it in the offering each week at church. *(MATH / FINANCES)*

H. Make a special bag or wallet to put your tithe money in to take to church.

I. Talk to your parents about tithing. Do they have stories about when they have chosen to tithe, and when they have chosen not to tithe? What were the results in both cases? Write one of their accounts into a short story. *(SPEECH / ENGLISH COMPOSITION / FINANCES)*

Intermediate

J. Look up all the verses you can find in the Bible about giving cheerfully. List each reference and summarize what it says. *(BIBLE / RESEARCH / WRITING)*

K. Do a topical study on the practice of tithing. Write a summary of your research. (Look up "tithes" in *Nave's Topical Bible*.) What laws governed the practice of tithing? Was tithing still practiced in the New Testament? *(BIBLE / RESEARCH / WRITING / FINANCES)*

L. Read about Hezekiah and Nehemiah both reinstituting the tithe in 2 Chronicles 31:2-6 and Nehemiah 13:10-14. How was the tithe used? Why did both men see the need to encourage the people to bring their tithes? *(BIBLE)*

M. Do a study on the difference between tithes and offerings. *(BIBLE / RESEARCH / VOCABULARY)*

Advanced

N. Study Haggai 1:5-6. How can we put our wages "into a bag with holes"? Write an essay about this topic. *(BIBLE / ENGLISH COMPOSITION / FINANCES)*

O. Study Malachi 3:6-12. How had the people robbed God? What was the result of their sin? What did God challenge them to do? What did He say He would do? Discuss this with your father, or write an essay about the meaning of these verses. *(BIBLE / ENGLISH COMPOSITION)*

P. What does God say about sacrificing to Him when we aren't humbling ourselves before Him and obeying Him? Read under the heading, "Offerings, unavailing when not accompanied by piety," in *Nave's Topical Bible*. *(BIBLE)*

Q. Read Chapter 16, "Discipline of Giving," in *Disciplines of a Godly Man,* by R. Kent Hughes. Complete the "Food for Thought," "Application/Response," and "Think About It!" sections at the end of the chapter. *(READING)*

R. Read *Giving and Tithing,* by Larry Burkett. Outline or summarize basic content. *(READING / BIBLE / WRITING / FINANCES)*

S. Read *Tithing and Dominion,* by Edward Powell and R. J. Rushdoony. If possible, read the book along with your father. Discuss each chapter together as you read. *(BIBLE / READING / FINANCES)*

T. Study Lesson 5, "Financing the Work of God's Kingdom," in *God and Government, Vol. 2,* by Gary DeMar. Talk over the questions for discussion with your father. *(READING / FINANCES)*

Additional ideas:

Parents:

Consider and discuss with your son the following questions:

- Does he understand that all that he possesses has been given to him by His loving Heavenly Father?

- Is he thankful for all the Lord has given him?

- Does he acknowledge that all that he has really belongs to God?

- Does he cheerfully give back to God a portion in tithes and offerings as a demonstration of his acknowledging God's blessing and ownership in his life?

Notes and comments:

Obeying God and His Delegated Authorities

"Submit yourselves to every ordinance of man for the Lord's sake: whether it be to the king, as supreme; or unto governors, as unto them that are sent by him for the punishment of evildoers, and for the praise of them that do well. For so is the will of God, that with well doing ye may put to silence the ignorance of foolish men" (1 Peter 2:13-15).

Our sons should, because of their respect for and obedience to God, respect and obey His delegated authorities. As parents, we must require our children to respect us as an authority placed over them by their loving heavenly Father.

Even when we recognize that, in our fallen state, we are not always respectable, we still must require respect for our position (and strive to become more respectable!). If we neglect this responsibility, we encourage our children to disrespect God as well as other earthly authorities.

Our sons, by their example, will teach their children how to respect his authority and all the other authorities in their lives. If his children do not see him showing proper respect to employers, government leaders, pastors, and law enforcement officers, they will be tempted to take his authority less seriously as well.

A. Select verses from the list below, and use some or all of the following suggestions to help you study and better understand their meaning (easier verses are listed first, in italics):

1) Copy the passage.

2) Read it in several different translations of the Bible.

3) Read the passage and several of the verses before and after it to gain a better understanding of the context of the passage.

4) Rewrite the passage in your own words. What does it mean?

5) Record a specific way in which you can change your actions or attitudes based on the teaching of this passage.

6) Memorize the passage.

   Exodus 20:12
   Lamentations 3:27
   1 Peter 2:17
   Psalm 111:10
   Psalm 143:10
   Ecclesiastes 4:13

Ecclesiastes 12:13
Ephesians 6:1-3
1 Timothy 6:1
Titus 2:9-10
Hebrews 13:17
(BIBLE / SPEECH)

Beginner

B. Read with your parents Chapter 57, "God's Children Obey" in *Leading Little Ones to God,* by Marian Schoolland. *(BIBLE / READING)*

C. Read with your parents about Abraham's obedience in Genesis 22. What did God tell Abraham to do? What did Abraham do? What did God do when Abraham proved that he trusted God and was willing to obey Him? Are you willing to obey God and your parents, even when you don't understand why they are asking you to do something? Act out the story with family and friends or with toys. *(BIBLE / DRAMA)*

D. Read with your parents the story of Jonah's disobedience and repentance in the book of Jonah. What did God tell Jonah to do? What did Jonah do? What happened to Jonah? What did Jonah do in the belly of the fish? What did he do after the fish spit him out onto land? Is God pleased when we disobey Him? *(BIBLE / READING)*

E. List 10 ways to show honor to your parents. Then do them! *(WRITING / FAMILY)*

F. Read *Honor Your Father and Mother: The Fifth Commandment for Little Ones,* by Pam Forster. Color the pictures, and draw more of your own, if you like. *(BIBLE / ART)*

G. Ask your parents to tell you a story about a time one of them chose to disobey God or one of His delegated authorities. What happened? *(FAMILY)*

H. Tell your parents and siblings a story of a time you chose to disobey and what the results of your disobedience were. *(SPEECH)*

I. Discuss with your parents:

Who, besides your parents, are the authorities in your life? Talk about specific ways in which you can better show honor and respect to each. Role-play with family members, different situations where you should show respect. Practice behaving in a respectful manner in each situation. Then put what you have learned into practice. *(MANNERS / DRAMA)*

J. Discuss with your parents: When is it right to disobey those who are older than you or who are in authority over you? *(SOCIAL SKILLS / FAMILY / GOVERNMENT)*

K. Read the story of Shadrach, Meshach, and Abednego in Chapter 3 of the book of Daniel. *(BIBLE / READING)*

L. Read with your parents Deuteronomy 28. Make a small illustrated book showing the blessings of obedience and the cursings of disobedience as they are outlined in this passage. *(BIBLE / WRITING)*

Intermediate

M. Read Deuteronomy 28. Draw up a chart contrasting the blessings of obedience with the cursings of disobedience. *(BIBLE)*

N. Study Chapter 21, "Obedience," in *Christian Character,* by Gary Maldaner. *(BIBLE)*

O. Study Chapter 14, "What Does It Mean to Be Submissive to Authority?" in *Christian Manhood,* by Gary Maldaner. *(BIBLE)*

P. Study God's chain of command. Chart out a "chain of command" for an enlisted private in the army. Who is directly in charge of him? Then who is in charge of that person, and the next person, etc.? Then do the same for other authority relationships -- for children, wives, husbands, workers, government leaders, church leaders, etc. Start with the lowest position, list the authority over him, then the authority over that person, etc. Who is over all other authorities? *(BIBLE / MILITARY / FAMILY / GOVERNMENT)*

Q. Study stories in the Bible of people who were obedient. List each person, the Bible references, how the person disobeyed, and the results in his life. You can find a list of references under "Obedience, Instances of" in *Nave's Topical Bible.* (Use the form on page 335.) *(BIBLE / HISTORY / WRITING)*

R. Study stories in the Bible of people who were disobedient. List each person, the Bible references, how the person disobeyed, and the results in his life. Look up "Disobedience to God, Instances of" in *Nave's Topical Bible.* (Use the form on page 336.) *(BIBLE / HISTORY / WRITING)*

S. Study Proverbs 10:1. List ways you can make your parents glad and ways you might cause your parents to grieve. Think of your habits, relationships, money, time, attitudes, etc. Use your list of ways to make your parents glad as a reminder of things you should be doing. Use your list of ways to bring them grief as a means of examining yourself for sinful actions and attitudes and avoiding such behavior.   *(BIBLE / WRITING / FAMILY)*

T. Make a list of everything about your father that is worthy of your respect. Think about his character, his physical attributes, his spiritual life, his mental abilities, his financial stewardship, his faithfulness to his wife and children, his loyalty in friendships, etc. Write down everything you can think of and then thank your father for all these things. Or write him a letter telling him all these things that you admire in him.   *(WRITING / FAMILY)*

U. Make a list of everything about your mother that is worthy of your respect. Think about her character, her physical attributes, her spiritual life, her mental abilities, her financial stewardship, her faithfulness to her husband and children, her loyalty in friendships, etc. Write down everything you can think of and then thank your mother for all these things. Or write her a letter telling her all these things that you admire in her. (Hint: Unless she has allergies, she'd probably like some flowers, too! Just a suggestion!)   *(WRITING / FAMILY)*

V. Do the same activity described in projects T and U, thinking about other authorities in your life. Think about teachers, pastors, grandparents, etc.   *(WRITING)*

W. Study the obedience of Abraham by reading the following passages. What did Abraham do when God told him to do something? What were the results? Write a short essay summarizing what you have learned about obedience from the life of Abraham.

Genesis 12:1-4

Genesis 17:23

Genesis 21:4

Genesis 22:12

Nehemiah 9:6-8

Acts 7:1-8

Hebrews 11:8-17

(BIBLE / ENGLISH COMPOSITION)

X. Study the chapters on "Disobedience" and "Defiance" in *For Instruction in Righteousness,* by Pam Forster.   *(BIBLE)*

Y. Study and list God's instructions to each of the following groups of people. Use a concordance and *Strong's Concordance* to aid you in your study. God will call you to obey Him in all or most of these areas as you live your life.

- Sons
- Workers and servants
- Citizens
- Church members
- Church leaders
- Fathers
- Government leaders

(BIBLE / FAMILY / BUSINESS / GOVERNMENT)

Z. Study Jesus' relationship to God the Father. Read the Gospels, writing down each time you see evidence of Jesus' submission to His Father. Then write down what you can learn from His example to apply in your own life. (Use the form on page 337.) *(BIBLE / WRITING / RESEARCH)*

AA. Study the lives of different sons in the Bible (Cain, Abel, Seth, Isaac, Jacob, Esau, Joseph and his brothers, Moses, Samuel, Eli's sons, Samson, Jonathan, Absalom, Amnon, Solomon, and Adonijah, as well as many others). Note Bible passages that refer to each of these men and the events in their lives. Record what each son did right or wrong and how his decisions and behavior affected his life and the lives of others. Write a paper that summarizes what you have learned about obedience and disobedience from these men. *(BIBLE / ENGLISH COMPOSITION)*

BB. Study what the Bible says about rebellious children. Look up "Children, Good" and "Children, Bad" in *Nave's Topical Bible.* What principles can you apply as you respond to the authority and leadership of your parents? *(BIBLE / FAMILY)*

CC. Study examples of those in the Bible who chose to openly question their authorities' right to rule over them (Miriam, Aaron, Dathan and Abiram, Absalom). Carefully read the accounts of their lives, giving special attention to the passages that describe their criticism of or resistance to their God-ordained authorities. Note all your observations. What did each person do wrong? What were their apparent motivations? What were the results in their lives and in the lives of those around them? *(BIBLE)*

DD. Read a page each day from *For This is Right*, by Pam Forster. Answer each question honestly, and copy at least one verse for each question. As God speaks to you about areas where you have not been fully obeying, ask forgiveness from God and from those you have wronged. *(BIBLE / FAMILY)*

EE. Design your own evaluation form that you can give to people who are placed in authority over you. Ask questions about how well you show respect, obey immediately, listen, speak to them, show initiative, etc. Give this form to teachers, employers, coaches, your pastor, and of course your parents. Read through the results with your parents. Design a plan to help you work on your weak areas. *(WRITING / FAMILY)*

FF. Read each of the following verses. Then list the promises that are given in these verses, and give an example from the Bible or from someone you know whose life illustrates the truth of each promise.

Exodus 20:12
Proverbs 1:8-9
Proverbs 4:1-10
Proverbs 6:20-22
Ephesians 6:1-3
(BIBLE / WRITING)

GG. Read each of the following verses. Then list the warnings that are given in these verses, and give an example from the Bible or from someone you know whose life illustrates the truth of each warning.

Proverbs 28:24
Proverbs 30:17
Mark 7:8-13
Romans 1:28-32
Galatians 6:7
1 Timothy 5:8
(BIBLE / WRITING)

Advanced

HH. Study and memorize Questions No. 124-133 in the *Westminster Larger Catechism*. Write a paraphrase of the answers. *(BIBLE / DOCTRINE / SPEECH / FAMILY)*

II. Design your own **Checklist for Sons**. Study the instructions God gives to sons and to believers in general. Write out these verses and compose questions based on each of these instructions that you can ask yourself each day or week.

For example, Eph. 6:1 says, "Children, obey your parents in the Lord, for this is right." You could ask yourself, "Did I please and obey God today by obeying my mother and father?"

Ask yourself these questions on a regular basis, and use them as an aid to confessing and repenting of the sin of rebellion. *(BIBLE / FAMILY / WRITING)*

JJ. Complete the study "Submit to God-given Authorities" in Chapter 2 of *Prepare Thy Work*, by Daniel Forster. *(BIBLE / RESEARCH / GOVERNMENT)*

KK. Write an essay on the following statement: Disobeying God is the result of failing to trust Him. Do you agree or disagree with this statement? Why or why not? Support your opinion with Scripture and personal anecdotes. *(BIBLE / ENGLISH COMPOSITION)*

LL. Do word studies on the following words:
Honor
Subjection
Submission

(BIBLE / WRITING / RESEARCH / FOREIGN LANGUAGE / VOCABULARY)

MM. Read Chapter 9, "The Discipline of Place," in *Discipline: The Glad Surrender,* by Elisabeth Elliot. Write a short essay expanding on the following quote from the book:

"What was Jesus' place? A servant. A slave. My bearing toward others arises out of my life in Him."
(ENGLISH COMPOSITION)

NN. Study Lesson 43 in *The Westminster Shorter Catechism for Study Classes,* by G.I. Williamson. *(BIBLE / FAMILY / GOVERNMENT)*

OO. Study Scripture and other reliable sources in order to answer the following question: When is it right to obey God rather than men? In what circumstances are we called to disobey the authorities over us? *(BIBLE)*

PP. What is the believer's responsibility to government authorities? Read the verses listed in *Nave's Topical Bible* under the headings, "Government, Duty of citizens to" and "Citizens, Duties of." *(BIBLE / GOVERNMENT)*

QQ. Discuss with your father and your pastor the question of civil disobedience. When is it biblical to disobey the government authorities over us? Do we have a biblical basis for disobeying those leaders who permit or tolerate evil? Do we have a biblical basis to disobey those who command us to do what God forbids? What about those who forbid us to do what God commands? What role does the legal system play in these decisions? What passages of Scripture guide us in these decisions? *(BIBLE / GOVERNMENT)*

RR. Read Chapters 1-3 and 6 in the book of Daniel. Note each instance of men choosing to obey God rather than men. What were the reasons for disobeying? Notice Daniel's method of appealing in the first chapter and the results. Note the three men's words of response when the king gave them the choice of bowing down to his image or being cast into the fire. What did God do when they refused and when Daniel later chose to disobey the king's command? Based on these examples, can you see some principles to apply when an authority has commanded you to act against your conscience and your beliefs? Write a paper summarizing your thoughts. *(BIBLE / GOVERNMENT / ENGLISH COMPOSITION)*

SS. Read and study Lesson 1, "A Biblical View of Authority," in *God and Government, Vol. 3,* by Gary DeMar. *(READING / BIBLE / GOVERNMENT)*

Additional ideas:

The Results of Obedience

(See Project Q for instructions.)

PERSON	REFERENCE	HOW HE OBEYED	RESULTS

The Results of Disobedience

(See Project R for instructions.)

PERSON	REFERENCE	HOW HE DISOBEYED	RESULTS

Jesus' Submission to God the Father

(See Project Z for instructions.)

INCIDENT	REFERENCE	WHAT JESUS DID	WHAT I CAN LEARN

Parents:

Consider and discuss with your son the following questions:

- Does he obey immediately without hesitation or dawdling?

- Does he obey without questioning, arguing or complaining?

- How does he do when he is placed under an authority that has been delegated by you (i.e., baby-sitter, teacher, older sibling)?

- Is he motivated by a desire to please God, or is he merely a man-pleaser?

- Does he understand that God is the final authority to whom we must all answer?

- Does he show honor to policemen, government officials, teachers, etc.?

- Does he speak respectfully to and about authorities?

- Does he seek to obey what he understands of God's Word?

- Does he seek to do what he knows you would want him to do even when you are not present?

- Does he have a cheerful, submissive attitude toward you and other authorities?

- Does he know how to properly appeal to an authority?

- Does he understand when it is appropriate to disobey an authority?

Notes and comments:

Recognizing and Repenting of Sin

"He that covereth his sins shall not prosper: but whoso confesseth and forsaketh them shall have mercy" (Proverbs 28:13).

How do our sons respond to correction? Are they defensive? Do they make excuses? Do they overlook their faults? Or do they grieve over their sin? Do they heed reproof? Is there repentance and a true desire to change? What kind of example do they see in our lives?

Refusal to accept correction, to admit sin, and to repent of it, does not lead to the life of blessing that we all would wish for our sons. "He who covereth his sins shall not prosper" (Proverbs 28:13). Our sons will not grow if they have not learned to acknowledge and repent of their sins. They will not experience true and joyful fellowship with God if they refuse to humble themselves, acknowledge their sin, and submit to the Holy Spirit's sanctifying work in their lives.

Refusal to acknowledge that Jesus paid for all his sins can lead to a life crippled by guilt. Attempting to change without the help of the Holy Spirit can lead to a life of frustration, pretense, and discouragement. Complete refusal to accept Christ's payment for his sins will lead to eternity in hell.

We must be faithful to train our children in this very important area.

A. Select verses from the list below, and use some or all of the following suggestions to help you study and better understand their meaning (easier verses are listed first, in italics):

   1) Copy the passage.

   2) Read it in several different translations of the Bible.

   3) Read the passage and several of the verses before and after it to gain a better understanding of the context of the passage.

   4) Rewrite the passage in your own words. What does it mean?

   5) Record a specific way in which you can change your actions or attitudes based on the teaching of this passage.

   6) Memorize the passage.

   Psalm 38:18
   Psalm 51:10
   Psalm 51:12
   Psalm 86:5

Psalm 130:3-4
Psalm 139:1
Proverbs 28:13
Luke 13:3
James 4:17
1 John 1:9
Psalm 19:12
Psalm 51:4
Psalm 51:17
Psalm 77:6
Psalm 139:23-24
Proverbs 1:24-33
Isaiah 55:6-7
Micah 7:19
(BIBLE / SPEECH)

Beginner

B. Read with your parents Parts 4, 5, and 11 in *Leading Little Ones to God,* by Marian Schoolland. *(BIBLE / READING)*

C. Read with your parents 2 Samuel 12. David sinned with Bathsheba and then killed her husband and married her. What story did the prophet Nathan tell David? How did David respond? What did Nathan say next? What did he say God would do? What did David say? What can you learn from David's example? *(BIBLE)*

D. Learn how to respond when your parents correct you or when you have sinned against one of your siblings. Say, "I was wrong. Will you forgive me?" Role-play different situations and practice acknowledging your sin and asking forgiveness. *(FAMILY / DRAMA)*

E. Act out what it means to repent: Walk one direction, and then turn around and run the other way. When we repent we have a change of mind along with a change of actions. When you repent of a sin, you change your mind and do something different – the right thing. *(DRAMA)*

F. Study the *Brother-Offended Checklist* together with your parents. Put it into practice in your home. *(BIBLE / FAMILY / SOCIAL SKILLS)*

G. If you have been unkind, repent. Acknowledge your wrong, ask forgiveness, and do the right thing – do something kind for them. *(SOCIAL SKILLS)*

H. Role-play with your family ways to demonstrate your repentance in the following situations. What would be the right thing to do in each situation?

- You hit your brother.
- You took something away from your little sister.
- You failed to complete your chores.
- You made fun of someone else.
- You disobeyed your mother.
- You became angry with a friend.

(FAMILY / SOCIAL SKILLS / DRAMA)

I. Read or recite the 10 Commandments tonight, and ask God to help you see the ways in which you have transgressed them throughout the day. *(BIBLE)*

Intermediate

J. Study stories of repentant men in the Bible. What happened to each of them? List each person, the Bible references that tell about him, what he did, how he was reproved, and the results of his repentance. Look up "Repentance, Instances of" and "Repentance, Exemplified" in *Nave's Topical Bible* (Use the form on page 344.) *(BIBLE / WRITING)*

K. Study stories of unrepentant men in the Bible. What happened to each of them? List each person, the Bible references that tell about him, what he did, how he was reproved, and the results of his unrepentance. If you need help, start by looking under "Stubbornness" and "Defiance" in *For Instruction in Righteousness,* by Pam Forster. (Use the form on page 345.) *(BIBLE / WRITING)*

L. Study the chapters on "Pride," "Self-Righteousness," and "Shifting Blame" in *For Instruction in Righteousness,* by Pam Forster. *(BIBLE)*

M. Study Psalm 51. What does David's example of repentance teach us? Write down what you learn about repentance from this Psalm. *(BIBLE / WRITING)*

N. Sin is defined as "any want of conformity unto, or transgression of, the law of God." When you are aware that you have sinned, think about whether you have failed to conform to one of God's laws or if you have gone against one of God's laws. Write down the sin, whether it is lack of conformity or transgression, and what law it violates. Then repent. *(WRITING)*

O. Study in the Bible what happens to the "hard-hearted" man who is unwilling to repent. List specific Bible verses. (You may want to look up "Heart, Instances of Hardened Hearts" in *Nave's Topical Bible*.) *(BIBLE / RESEARCH / WRITING)*

P.   Read and study Proverbs 1:24-31. What does the passage say will happen to the person who rejects wisdom and is unwilling to respond rightly to correction? *(BIBLE)*

Q.   When does Scripture require restitution for sins committed? Look for answers in the Bible to this question. (Start by looking up "restitution" in *Strong's Concordance*.) List each incident and the Bible reference. Make restitution when required. *(BIBLE / RESEARCH / LAW / WRITING)*

R.   Write down an area of sin with which you are struggling. Confess this sin to God. Now, with the Holy Spirit's guidance, write down steps to "turn" toward God and away from this sin. What are specific actions you can take that will demonstrate your repentance? *(WRITING / BIBLE)*

S.   Write down accounts of when you have admitted wrongdoing and asked forgiveness of others. *(WRITING)*

Advanced

T.   Subscribe to and read Navigators' daily email devotional *Holiness Day by Day*. *(BIBLE / DEVOTIONS)*

U.   Memorize Questions No. 28-29 in the *Westminster Larger Catechism*. *(BIBLE / DOCTRINE / SPEECH)*

V.   Find out which seven Psalms are considered "penitential." Study each one. Make copies of each and mark with one color all the things the psalmist asks God to do. Use another color to mark what he says he has done, and another to mark what he says he *will* do. What does he say he is like? What does he say God has or will do? *(BIBLE)*

W.   Read the penitential Psalms as prayers to God when you have sinned. *(BIBLE)*

X.   Study the word "repent." Use *Strong's Concordance* to locate each use of the word. Look up the number that is assigned to the Greek word for "repent" that is used in the New Testament. What does it mean? Read the verses that use this word. Summarize what you learn about repentance. *(BIBLE / RESEARCH / VOCABULARY / FOREIGN LANGUAGE)*

Y.   Do a word study on **holiness**. *(BIBLE / RESEARCH / VOCABULARY / FOREIGN LANGUAGE)*

Z.   Do a topical study on **pride**. Then write an essay on the sin of pride as it relates to unrepentance. *(BIBLE / RESEARCH / ENGLISH COMPOSITION)*

AA. Do a topical study on **repentance**. Then write an essay describing Biblical repentance. *(BIBLE / RESEARCH / ENGLISH COMPOSITION)*

BB. Repentance involves a hatred of sin, a sorrow for it, an acknowledgment of it before God, and a forsaking of it. Find Scripture passages that show each of these elements of repentance. Look up words like "repent," "turn," and "humble" in your concordance for help. *(BIBLE / RESEARCH / WRITING)*

CC. Study the meanings of the phrases, "quenching the Spirit" and "grieving the Spirit." Write definitions for both of these phrases. *(BIBLE / RESEARCH / VOCABULARY / WRITING)*

DD. Read *Respectable Sins: Confronting the Sins We Tolerate,* by Jerry Bridges. Go through the discussion guide with your father or with a group of other Christians. *(READING)*

EE. Read *The Ten Commandments,* by the 17th century Puritan, Thomas Watson. Or at least read Section IV, "The Way of Salvation." Outline what you have learned from this reading. *(READING / BIBLE / DOCTRINE / WRITING)*

FF. Read *The Doctrine of Repentance,* by Thomas Watson. Write a summary of the book or outline its main points. *(READING / BIBLE / DOCTRINE / WRITING)*

Additional ideas:

The Results of Repentance

(See Project J for instructions.)

PERSON	REF.	WHAT HE DID	REPROOF	RESULTS OF REPENTING

The Results of Refusing to Repent

(See Project K for instructions.)

PERSON	REF.	WHAT HE DID	REPROOF	RESULTS OF REPENTING

Parents:

Consider and discuss with your son the following questions:

- Has he ever come to a point of true salvation through Christ's death and resurrection? Is he born again? Does he acknowledge Christ's finished work on the cross, recognize that his sin has been paid for, and accept God's forgiveness that is made possible because of Christ's death and resurrection?

- Does he daily seek to put to death the sin that remains in his heart and actions?

- Is he afraid of sinning and displeasing God?

- Does he have a true understanding (as true as is possible on this side of heaven) of God's holiness and His holy standard?

- Does he deny, excuse, or defend himself when corrected for wrongs, or does he respond humbly to reproof?

- Does he justify what he has done based on what someone else has done to him?

- Does he willingly confess wrong and ask forgiveness of those he has offended?

- Is he honest in his acknowledgment and confession of specific sins?

- Does he readily confess his sin to God and ask His forgiveness?

- Does he obey God by making restitution when needed?

- Does he see his sin and then give in to despair and guilt, not accepting Christ's finished payment?

- Does he seek, with the help of the Holy Spirit, to turn from his sinful ways and obey God and His commands, or does he only acknowledge his sin and then continue in it?

- Does he appear to be grieved only because his reputation has been harmed, or is he grieved because he has sinned against God, and not brought glory to God in his actions?

- Does he appear to be grieved only because of the pain of chastisement that accompanies his sin, or is he grieved because he has transgressed God's holy standard?

- Does he realize and demonstrate by his actions that he is unable to "do better" in his own strength?

- Does he acknowledge God's right to rule and govern over him?

- Does he acknowledge your right as parents to rule and govern over him?

- Does he understand that God's law exists for our well-being?

Notes and comments:

Seeking and Accepting Counsel

"If any of you lack wisdom, let him ask of God, that giveth to all men liberally, and upbraideth not; and it shall be given him" (James 1:5).

We must set for our children an example of humililty, a willingness to recognize that we need wisdom beyond our own. We should constantly be going to God, asking for wisdom and searching Scripture for answers. And we should seek out counsel from pastors, parents, and friends, listening carefully and weighing their advice against the truth of Scripture.

God has ordained that believers live in community. Not only does He guide us through His Word, but He also guides us through the counsel of wise and humble brothers and sisters in Christ. He ministers to us through people, and will often use the greater wisdom and experience of others to help us see an issue more clearly.

We will need to teach our sons how to discern between wise counsel and foolish counsel. Help them evaluate the different words of counsel you receive, and teach them to compare the counsel they are given with the words of Scripture. Teach them to also evaluate the character of the person offering counsel.

Our sons will also need to learn to accept wise counsel or reproof offered to them when they haven't asked for it. A humble man will be grateful for the "wounds of a friend." Teach your sons to express gratitude for your correction and to humbly evaluate the sometimes painful feedback he receives from siblings, friends, teachers, coaches, and others. The boy who feels criticized when confronted with his weaknesses will most likely become the man who is too proud to value his wife's counsel and loving input.

Proverbs 15:12 tells us that "A scorner loveth not one that reproveth him: neither will he go unto the wise." The man who hates correction and refuses to seek counsel from the wise is a foolish man.

A. Select verses from the list below, and use some or all of the following suggestions to help you study and better understand their meaning (easier verses are listed first, in italics):

   1) Copy the passage.

   2) Read it in several different translations of the Bible.

3) Read the passage and several of the verses before and after it to gain a better understanding of the context of the passage.

4) Rewrite the passage in your own words. What does it mean?

5) Record a specific way in which you can change your actions or attitudes based on the teaching of this passage.

6) Memorize the passage.

> *Proverbs 12:15*
> *Proverbs 19:20*
> *Proverbs 27:6*
> Psalm 141:5
> Proverbs 1:5
> Proverbs 3:5-6
> Proverbs 9:9
> Proverbs 11:14
> Proverbs15:22
> Proverbs 18:15
> James 1:5
> *(BIBLE / SPEECH)*

Beginner

B. Read with your parents Exodus 18. What was Moses doing? What did his father-in-law advise him to do? Why? What does verse 24 say Moses did after his father-in-law talked to him? Act out this story with play figures or stuffed animals. *(BIBLE / READING / DRAMA)*

C. Before you listen to your parents read the Bible, pray for God to use His Word to teach you.

D. Ask your father to show you how to do something new today. Listen carefully to him, and do what he says. *(FAMILY / HOME SKILLS)*

E. Before your father leaves for work, ask him what he would like you to do with your day. Tell him what you did when he gets home. *(FAMILY)*

F. Read with your parents about Naaman in 2 Kings 5. What was wrong with Naaman? Where did he go? What did Elisha's messenger tell him to do? How did he respond to these instructions? Whose counsel did he listen to, and what happened after he did? What might have happened if he had not listened to their counsel and had not done what Elisha told him to do? Act this story out with toys in the bathtub, a wading pool, or even a mud puddle. *(BIBLE / DRAMA)*

G. Draw a picture to illustrate Psalm 141:5. *(BIBLE / ART)*

H. Say "thank you" next time one of your parents has to discipline you.

I. Ask your parents or grandparents to tell you stories about incidents in their lives when they chose to do something on their own without first getting the advice of others. What were the results? Draw a picture book to depict at least one of these stories. *(SPEECH / HISTORY / ART)*

J. Read about the Israelites' response to Joshua's counsel in Numbers 13:16-14:38. What report did Joshua and Caleb give to the people when they returned from spying in the land of Caanan? What did the rest of the spies report? How did the people respond? What did Joshua and Caleb say to them in Numbers 14:7-9? How did the people respond to their counsel? What happened because of this? *(BIBLE / READING)*

K. Ask your father to tell you a story about a time when he chose to get counsel from someone, and how God used that counsel to help and guide him. *(FAMILY HISTORY / SOCIAL SKILLS)*

L. Tell your siblings a story about a time you chose to ignore your parents' counsel and what the results were. *(FAMILY)*

Intermediate

M. Read and discuss with your parents Psalm 1:1-3. Who should we not walk, stand, or sit with? What should we delight in? How can you apply this verse in your life? *(BIBLE)*

N. Keep a journal in which you write down the bits of advice your father gives you throughout your youth. Also write down the results in your life when you followed his advice and when you rejected it. *(WRITING)*

O. Read about Rehoboam in 1 Kings 12. With what two groups of men did Rehoboam consult? What advice did both groups give him? Which one did he follow? Was the advice based on biblical truth? Why or why not? What were the results of following this advice? *(BIBLE)*

P. Read the book of Proverbs, noting the reference of each verse that says, "Listen, my son." Write down the advice that follows each of these admonitions. *(BIBLE / RESEARCH / WRITING)*

Q. Study James 1:5-8. What does it say about wisdom? What does it say our attitude should be when we ask God for wisdom? *(BIBLE / RESEARCH / WRITING)*

R. Study Chapter 20, "What Is Your Attitude Toward Counsel?" in *Christian Manhood.* *(BIBLE)*

S. Read through the book of Proverbs. List all the references to and descriptions of a foolish son and a wise son. How do they differ? What are the characteristics of each? Make a chart to summarize your findings. *(BIBLE / RESEARCH)*

T. Use an online or Bible software concordance to search for the words "own eyes." (Or use a regular concordance, look up the word "eyes" and look for verses in the list that have the word "own" before eyes.) How are the words used? How do these verses relate to a willingness to listen to the wisdom of God and others? Discuss this with your parents. *(BIBLE / RESEARCH)*

U. Read the verses under "Reproof" in *Nave's Topical Bible.* How, according to Scripture, does the fool or scorner respond to reproof? How does the wise man respond? Are you wise or foolish? What happens to the person who rejects instruction? What is better, someone who loves you enough to correct you, or the person who just tells you what you want to hear? Share what you have learned at your next family worship time. *(BIBLE / RESEARCH / DEVOTIONS)*

V. Interview adults asking them how they choose their counselors. How do they decide whom to go to for advice in spiritual matters, household matters, social problems, financial issues? What do they look for in a good counselor? Write a summary of your findings. *(SPEECH / WRITING)*

W. Read the verses under the topic heading, "Counsel," in *Nave's Topical Bible.* Summarize what they say about counsel, and how you will apply these verses in your life. *(BIBLE / RESEARCH)*

X. Think of a problem that you would like to find answers for in the Bible. Use the concordance and topical Bible to help you research the topic. Write out your findings. *(BIBLE / RESEARCH / WRITING)*

Y. Do a word study on **wisdom**. What is it? What Hebrew and Greek words are translated "wisdom"? In what ways are these words used? Write a definition of the word. *(BIBLE / VOCABULARY / FOREIGN LANGUAGE / WRITING)*

Z. Do a topical study on **wisdom**. What is its source? What is its value? What are the results of acquiring it? Write an essay on wisdom. *(BIBLE / RESEARCH / ENGLISH COMPOSITION)*

Advanced

AA. Do a topical study in the Bible on **counselors** and **guidance**. Write an essay on your findings. *(BIBLE / RESEARCH / ENGLISH COMPOSITION)*

BB. Keep a journal as you read through the Bible. Write down every command that is given and its reference in Scripture. When you have read the entire Bible, try to categorize all the commands you have listed. You will have a collection of God's instructions about many different topics that you can refer to for guidance. *(BIBLE / RESEARCH / WRITING)*

CC. Tape record interviews with your father on such topics as: "How To Be a Good Husband," "How To Be a Good Father," "How To Be a Good Worker," etc. *(SPEECH / FAMILY)*

DD. Study the **omniscience** of God. How does omniscience relate to seeking wisdom from God's Word? Summarize your study in a short written or oral report. *(BIBLE / RESEARCH / VOCABULARY / ENGLISH COMPOSITION / SPEECH)*

EE. Read books written to young men by fathers (i.e., *Letters to Young Men*, by W.B. Sprague, *The Letters and Lessons of Teddy Roosevelt for His Sons,* or *The Bible Lessons of John Quincy Adams for His Son*). Take notes on these books, and put what you learn into action. *(READING / FAMILY)*

FF. With your father, write letters of advice and counsel to your future sons and daughters. *(FAMILY / ENGLISH COMPOSITION)*

Additional ideas:

Parents:

Consider and discuss with your son the following questions:

- Does your son approach you for advice and guidance, or does he consistently "lean on his own understanding"?

- Does he know he can ask for counsel without you over-reacting to his questions?

- Does he honor your counsel over the counsel of his friends?

- Does he approach you with spiritual questions and concerns?

- Does he respond humbly to the counsel and correction of his father, or is he proud, inattentive, or defensive?

- Does he grow angry or sullen when corrected?

- Does he ignore your counsel?

- Does he purposely reject your counsel?

- Does he think he is smarter and wiser than you?

- Does he look to the Bible as the authority in all issues of life?

- Does he seek God's guidance through the study of His Word?

- Does he seek God's guidance through prayer?

- Does he know how to use the study tools to find answers in the Bible to his questions?

- Does he rest in the counsel of God's guidance and the counsel of godly men, or does he fret and try to manipulate circumstances to match his desires?

- Is he thankful for the counsel of others, or does he resent it?

- Does he resist asking for help when it is needed?

- Does he sometimes choose to follow poor counsel?

Notes and comments:

Being Content with God's Sovereignty

"Not that I speak in respect of want: for I have learned, in whatsoever state I am, therewith to be content" (Philippians 4:11).

We want to train our sons to be content with what God and we, by God's grace, have chosen to give them. We want to encourage them to trust God's sovereign plan for them, and to realize that all we really deserve is eternal condemnation. Anything beyond that is a gift that God has bestowed upon us and we should be grateful.

A. Select verses from the list below, and use some or all of the following suggestions to help you study and better understand their meaning (easier verses are listed first, in italics):

1) Copy the passage.

2) Read it in several different translations of the Bible.

3) Read the passage and several of the verses before and after it to gain a better understanding of the context of the passage.

4) Rewrite the passage in your own words. What does it mean?

5) Record a specific way in which you can change your actions or attitudes based on the teaching of this passage.

6) Memorize the passage.

   Proverbs 16:8
   Philippians 2:14
   Philippians 4:19
   Psalm 16:6
   Psalm 37:1
   Psalm 37:16
   Psalm 40:2
   Psalm 68:19
   Proverbs 19:3
   Proverbs 30:8
   Lamentations 3:39-40
   1 Corinthians 10:10
   Galatians 5:26
   1 Timothy 6:6-8
   Hebrews 13:5

   (BIBLE / SPEECH)

Beginner

B. Read with your parents Part 3, "All That God Does Is Good" in *Leading Little Ones to God,* by Marian Schoolland. *(BIBLE / READING)*

C. Copy Philippians 2:14 and draw a picture to illustrate it. Post it on a wall in your house. *(BIBLE / ART)*

D. Read with your parents the account of the Israelites and the waters of Meribah in Numbers 20. Why were the Israelites unhappy? What questions did they ask Moses? What did they wish they had? Had this happened to them before? Read Exodus 17:1-7. Did God provide what they needed that time? Could they trust Him to take care of them? Draw a picture of this story or act it out with friends or family. *(BIBLE / ART / DRAMA)*

E. For a day (or week) commit to not complaining. Even if you are unhappy with what you're told to do, the food you're served, etc., express your gratitude instead of complaining. *(MANNERS)*

F. Ask your parents to help you make a list of all the things you can think of that God has done for you. Consider spiritual, physical, and social areas, family, possessions, abilities, opportunities, etc. Can you trust Him to take care of you? Keep this list and continue to add to it. *(WRITING)*

G. Ask your mother to help you make a list of all the things you appreciate about your father. Then list ways in which you can express your thankfulness to him. Show him your gratitude by doing those things. *(WRITING)*

H. Ask your father to help you make a list of all the things you appreciate about your mother. List ways in which you can express your thankfulness. Put your ideas into action! *(WRITING)*

Intermediate

I. Make a commitment to read and study the Bible every day. Don't eat breakfast until you read. Focusing on God's Word leads to true contentment. *(BIBLE / DEVOTIONS / TIME MANAGEMENT)*

J. Make a commitment to pray every day. Don't go to sleep until you have had your private prayer time. Prayer helps us bring our desires into harmony with God's plan for our lives. *(DEVOTIONS / TIME MANAGEMENT)*

K. Keep a notebook in which you list all the promises you come across as you read your Bible. Thank God for being a faithful God who will keep His promises. *(WRITING / BIBLE)*

L. Study 1 Timothy 6:6. Write a short essay on this verse and how you can apply it in your life. *(BIBLE / ENGLISH COMPOSITION)*

M. Pray daily, setting aside time to specifically praise God for His character, His loving mercy, and His many blessings in your life. *(DEVOTIONS)*

N. Read along with your father *Practical Happiness: A Young Man's Guide to a Contented Life,* by Bob Schultz. Discuss each chapter together. What lessons can you apply to your own life? *(READING)*

O. Study the chapters on "Complaining," "Envy/Jealousy," and "Covetousness" in *For Instruction in Righteousness,* by Pam Forster. *(BIBLE)*

P. Study Chapters 2, 19, and 28 in *Christian Character,* by Gary Maldaner. *(BIBLE)*

Q. Study God's **sovereignty**. What does sovereignty mean? How does it affect our lives? Write an essay explaining the relationship between contentment and one's acceptance of God's sovereignty. *(BIBLE / RESEARCH / VOCABULARY / WRITING)*

R. Should a child of the King be discontent? List all the things you desire but do not have. Read through the list. Mark anything on the list that God would not be able to give you if He knew it was best for you. *(WRITING)*

S. What does the Bible say the believer's relationship should be to the world? Study this in the Bible, and write out your answer, supporting it with the verses you have found. *(BIBLE / RESEARCH / WRITING)*

T. Make a list of all the things about which you are discontent -- everything you can think of -- your appearance, circumstances, family, etc. Then list the sins of your heart that are at the root of these areas of discontent. Confess these sins to God, and to the people involved. Memorize verses that will help you combat these sins. *(WRITING / BIBLE / SPEECH)*

U. Read the verses under the heading "Contentment" in *Nave's Topical Bible.* Take notes and summarize what you have learned about contentment. *(BIBLE)*

V. Study verses under the heading "Covetousness" in *Nave's Topical Bible.* Write a paper on the consequences of covetousness. *(BIBLE)*

W. Study Lesson 15 in *The Westminster Shorter Catechism for Study Classes,* by G.I. Williamson. *(BIBLE)*

X. Study Philippians 4:19. Read the verse and emphasize a different word each time you read it. ("*My* God shall supply...," My *God* shall supply...," "My God *shall* supply," etc.) What do you learn as you read this way? Write an essay on the meaning of this verse. *(BIBLE / ENGLISH COMPOSITION)*

Y. Study what God says about "riches." How does this relate to discontent and covetousness? Write a summary of your study. *(BIBLE / RESEARCH / WRITING)*

Z. Read Chapter 4, "God, My Heart, and Stuff," by Dave Harvey, in *Worldliness: Resisting the Seduction of a Fallen World,* edited by C. J. Mahaney. Discuss with your father or friends the discussion questions in the back of the book for this chapter. If you haven't already, read the rest of the book. *(READING)*

AA. Study what the Bible says about the consequences of murmuring. See "Murmuring, Instances of" in *Nave's Topical Bible* and "Complaining/ Ingratitude" in *For Instruction in Righteousness,* by Pam Forster. (Use the form on page 360.) *(HISTORY / BIBLE / WRITING)*

Advanced

BB. Memorize Questions No. 146-149 in the *Westminster Larger Catechism.* *(BIBLE / DOCTRINE / SPEECH)*

CC. Study the history of the Israelites from Egypt to Canaan. List all mentions of their murmurings, the Bible reference, and the results of their discontent. (Use the form on page 361.) *(BIBLE / HISTORY / WRITING)*

DD. Study accounts in the Bible of people other than the Israelites who were discontent or covetous. What happened to them? List each person, reference, situation, and consequences. (Use the form on page 362.) *(BIBLE / HISTORY / WRITING)*

EE. Discontent can be described as a "questioning of God's goodness." Write an essay on this theme. *(ENGLISH COMPOSITION)*

FF. Read Chapter 11, "The Discipline of Possessions," in *Discipline: The Glad Surrender,* by Elisabeth Elliot. List and explain to one of your parents the four lessons about possessions that the author describes. *(READING / SPEECH)*

GG. Read *Learning to Be Happy,* by Jeremiah Burroughs. Outline the main ideas of the book, or write a paper explaining what actions you plan to take as the result of reading this book. *(READING / ENGLISH COMPOSITION)*

HH. Write an essay discussing the following quote from *The Rare Jewel of Christian Contentment,* by Jeremiah Burroughs: "You know how when you strike something soft it makes no noise, but if you strike a hard thing it makes a noise; so with the hearts of men who are full of themselves, and hardened with self-love, if they receive a stroke they make a noise, but a self-denying Christian yields to God's hand, and makes no noise." *(ENGLISH COMPOSITION)*

II. Martin Luther once said, "The sea of God's mercies should swallow up all our particular afflictions." Write an essay or present a speech on what you think this means. *(ENGLISH COMPOSITION)*

Additional ideas:

The Consequences of Murmuring and Complaining

(See Project AA for instructions.)

PERSON	INCIDENT	REFERENCE	RESULTS

The Results of the Israelites' Murmurings

(See Project CC for instructions.)

INCIDENT	REFERENCE	RESULTS

The Results of Discontent

(See Project DD for instructions.)

PERSON	INCIDENT	REFERENCE	RESULTS

Parents:

Consider and discuss with your son the following questions:

- Does he complain?

- Does he whine?

- Does he worry about someone else getting a bigger share of something than he does?

- Is he unpleasant when things don't go his way?

- Does he feel sorry for himself when he encounters difficulties?

- Does he strive with others to gain something he wants?

- Does he strive with others to protect what he believes are his rights?

- Does he want something after he sees someone else with it?

- Is he discontent with what he does have, always wishing for more?

- Does he envy the talents of others?

- Does he think he should have the same privileges as others?

- Does he harbor bitterness?

- Is he unhappy about things he cannot change -- appearance, family, role in life, etc.?

- Does he look for happiness in activities and things, instead of experiencing true happiness in his relationship to God?

- Is he happy when others succeed or are honored in special ways?

- Does he trust God to know and do what is best for him?

Notes and comments:

And to godliness,

BROTHERLY KINDNESS

Developing Godly Relationships

"This is my commandment, that ye love one another, as I have loved you" (John 15:12).

Learning how to develop godly relationships with acquaintances, close friends, and siblings will help prepare a son for godly relationships as an adult. These relationships will include a life-long friendship with his future wife and healthy, loving relationships with his children.

Through friendship and family life, he can learn much about honesty, true Christian love, forgiveness, loyalty, self-sacrifice, and patience. Much growth and sanctification takes place in the context of our relationships, and how we relate to other fallen human beings is an accurate measure of our relationship with God. 1 John 4:20-21 (ESV) boldly states, "If anyone says, 'I love God,' and hates his brother, he is a liar; for he who does not love his brother whom he has seen cannot love God whom he has not seen. And this commandment we have from him: whoever loves God must also love his brother."

We need to be faithful in teaching our sons to treat their friends and siblings in a loving, godly way. This is one of the major tasks of parenthood. We also need to teach them how to wisely select friends. If we choose to neglect this responsibility, our sons will be left unprotected from the potentially devastating effects of ungodly friendships.

A. Select verses from the list below, and use some or all of the following suggestions to help you study and better understand their meaning (easier verses are listed first, in italics):

1) Copy the passage.

2) Read it in several different translations of the Bible.

3) Read the passage and several of the verses before and after it to gain a better understanding of the context of the passage.

4) Rewrite the passage in your own words. What does it mean?

5) Record a specific way in which you can change your actions or attitudes based on the teaching of this passage.

6) Memorize the passage.

   Proverbs 16:28
   Proverbs 17:9

Proverbs 17:17
Proverbs 18:24
Proverbs 25:17
Proverbs 29:5
Romans 12:10
Psalm 1:1
Proverbs 3:27-28
Proverbs 25:21-22
John 15:12-14
Romans 15:1-2
Philippians 2:1-4
James 4:4
1 Peter 3:8-9
(BIBLE / SPEECH)

Beginner

B. Read with your parents Chapter 54, "God's Children Love One Another" in *Leading Little Ones to God,* by Marian Schoolland. *(BIBLE / READING)*

C. With your parents' help, list ten ways to show love to your friends. Put your ideas into action. *(WRITING / SOCIAL SKILLS)*

D. With your parents' help, list ten ways to show love to each of your siblings. Use your ideas right away. *(WRITING / FAMILY / SOCIAL SKILLS)*

E. Talk about your friends with your parents. Who are your best friends? Why do you like them? What problems do you sometimes have with them? *(FAMILY / SPEECH / SOCIAL SKILLS)*

F. Call up one of your friends and thank him for his friendship. Or make him a special card or gift that includes a thank you note. *(WRITING / SOCIAL SKILLS)*

G. Read with your parents the story of Jonathan and David's friendship in 1 Samuel 17 through 20.
- What had David just done before Jonathan became his friend?
- How did Jonathan respond?
- What did he give David?
- Since Jonathan was the king's son, what was he destined to one day become?
- Do you think he was worried about David taking his place?
- What did he do when his father wanted to kill David?

- What can you learn from Jonathan about being a friend?
- What can you learn from Jonathan about trusting God?

Act out with a sibling or friend the meetings between Jonathan and David, or act out the entire story, starting with David killing Goliath. *(BIBLE / DRAMA)*

H. Make a cartoon strip or small picture book illustrating the story of David and Jonathan from 1 Samuel 17-20. *(BIBLE / ART)*

I. Study with your parents *Rules for Young Friends,* by Gregg and Joshua Harris. Follow these rules when friends visit you, and when you visit at their houses. *(FAMILY / MANNERS)*

J. Read through the book of Proverbs with your parents, writing down all verses and observations about friendships and getting along with others. *(BIBLE / RESEARCH / WRITING)*

K. Write a letter to each of your siblings, expressing your thankfulness for all that they are to you as a brother or sister, and telling each one what you appreciate about them. *(ENGLISH COMPOSITION / FAMILY)*

L. Tell your family how you and your best friend became friends. How did you meet? What interests did you share? How did you get to know each other better? *(SPEECH)*

M. Tell another story to your family about a disagreement you once had with a friend or sibling, and how you resolved your differences. *(SPEECH)*

N. Study with your family *The Brother-Offended Checklist,* and put the biblical principles into action when disagreements arise. *(BIBLE / FAMILY / SOCIAL SKILLS)*

O. Study with your family *The Put On Chart.* Color and cut out the paper dolls. Memorize the verses. Look at the chart throughout the day to help you remember how God wants you to treat other people. *(BIBLE / FAMILY / SOCIAL SKILLS)*

P. Role-play with your family different relational situations. (What should you do when someone says something unkind to you? What should you do when a friend is doing something wrong and wants you to do it with him?, etc.) *(SOCIAL SKILLS / DRAMA)*

Intermediate

Q. Write or tell a story about how an ungodly acquaintance or friendship led you to get into trouble. What Biblical principles did you violate? *(WRITING / SPEECH)*

R. Write or tell a story about a time when God used a friend to help, encourage, or bless you. *(WRITING / SPEECH)*

S. Talk with your parents about your friends and acquaintances. What qualities do they value in your friends? What traits do they want to warn you about? What friendships are they pleased with? Do they prefer for you to limit the time you spend with other friends? Listen carefully to their advice. *(FAMILY / SOCIAL SKILLS)*

T. Be a friend to a person who **needs** a friend. Look for someone to befriend at church or in your neighborhood. Pray for him, encourage him, show acts of kindness. *(SOCIAL SKILLS)*

U. Read or listen to your father read the book of Proverbs. Write down every verse that tells us not to associate with a certain type of person. Note the reference and the type of person. Summarize your findings in a short essay. *(BIBLE / ENGLISH COMPOSITION)*

V. Read with your family *Making Brothers and Sisters Best Friends,* by Sarah, Stephen, and Grace Mally. Discuss each chapter together, take the self-evaluation quizzes, and put what you learn into practice. *(READING / SOCIAL SKILLS / FAMILY)*

W. Do a topical Bible study on **friends.** Describe a godly friend as he is described in Scripture. (Look up "friendship" in *Nave's Topical Bible.*) *(BIBLE / RESEARCH / WRITING)*

X. Study examples of both good and bad friendships in the Bible. List each, with references, and what you can learn from each. (Look up "Friends, False Friends" and "Friendship, Instances of" in *Nave's Topical Bible.*) *(BIBLE / RESEARCH / SOCIAL SKILLS)*

Y. Study Chapter 8, "Friendships with Boys," and Chapter 25, "Am I Building My Character Through My Relationships with Brothers and Sisters?" in *Christian Manhood,* by Gary Maldaner. *(BIBLE)*

Z. Write a paper explaining the meaning of Proverbs 13:20, or discuss the verse with your parents. How does this verse apply to your life? In what ways have you seen the truth of this verse displayed in lives around you? *(BIBLE / ENGLISH COMPOSITION)*

AA. Study the chapter on "Bad Friendships" in *For Instruction in Righteousness,* by Pam Forster. *(BIBLE)*

BB. Discuss with your parents how they would like you to handle friendships with girls. What guidelines can they offer you? What restrictions would they like to impose? *(SOCIAL SKILLS)*

CC. Make a list of standards for choosing godly friends. Base your list on Scripture's advice about friends. What qualities will you seek in a friend? What negative character traits should you avoid? Ask your parents to review your list and add any additional ideas they have. *(BIBLE / SOCIAL SKILLS / WRITING)*

DD. Study Chapter 20, "Loyalty," in *Christian Manhood*, by Gary Maldaner. *(BIBLE)*

EE. Listen to S. M. Davis's lecture, *Understanding the Blessings and Hazards of Friendships.* Listen for answers to the following questions:

- How does he define "friend"?
- How many friends do you need?
- How do you find and keep good friends?
- Why is it important to have the right kind of friends?
- How and why do people develop wrong friendships?
- How can you make sure you only develop right friendships?
- Should parents be friends with their children?
- Can guys and girls be close friends?

(BIBLE / SOCIAL SKILLS)

FF. Encourage a close friend to help you develop your character, as you also seek to help him in his growth. Ask him to tell you when you need correcting, and then accept it humbly and work to change. Humbly and prayerfully encourage him toward righteousness when he sins. *(SOCIAL SKILLS)*

GG. Study Psalm 1. List the ways, if any, that you are:

- Walking in the counsel of the ungodly
- Standing in the way of sinners
- Sitting in the seat of the scornful

Don't forget to consider what you watch and what you listen to. List ways you can turn from these sinful friendships and actions. *(BIBLE / RESEARCH / WRITING)*

HH. Observe a person who is a good and faithful friend to others. What character qualities does he possess? How many of these qualities do you think are present in your own life? Write down your thoughts. *(WRITING)*

Advanced

II. Study the third chapter of Colossians. Write down all the instructions that are given. Make one list for what we are to stop doing and another list of what we are supposed to do. Note any reasons given for these instructions. How many of these instructions relate to our relationships with other people? *(BIBLE)*

JJ. Listen to Douglas Phillips' talks on *Manly Friendships.* Discuss these with your father. *(SOCIAL SKILLS)*

KK. Study examples of bad friendships in the Bible. List each example, its Bible reference, how the friendship was bad, and what its results were. (Use the form on page 374.) *(BIBLE / RESEARCH / WRITING)*

LL. Read Chapter 5, "The Discipline of Friendship," in *Disciplines of a Godly Man,* by R. Kent Hughes. Complete the "Food for Thought," "Application/Response," and "Think About It!" sections at the end of the chapter. *(READING / SOCIAL SKILLS)*

MM. Read *Relationships: A Mess Worth Making,* by Timothy Lane and Paul David Tripp. Write a summary of each chapter and list specific points that stand out to you. What principles can you apply to improve the relationships you have? *(READING / SOCIAL SKILLS)*

NN. Read *The Peacemaker,* by Ken Sande. Use the application questions to help you apply what you have learned. Use Appendix A, "A Peacemaker's Checklist," to guide you as you resolve relational problems, and read Appendix C, "Principles of Restitution," to help you understand what the Bible says about making things right when something has been damaged or someone has been harmed. Use what you have learned from this book in the everyday challenges of relating to other people. *(BIBLE / READING / SOCIAL SKILLS)*

OO. Using a concordance, study the use of the Greek word, **philadelphia.** What does it mean? Give examples of this type of love from the Bible and from your own life. *(BIBLE / RESEARCH FOREIGN LANGUAGE / WRITING)*

PP. Read Part 1, "Friendship," in *Face to Face,* by Steven Wilkins. Outline the main points of each chapter and discuss them with a friend. *(READING / SOCIAL SKILLS)*

QQ. Read the section on friendship in Paul Jehle's *Dating vs. Courtship,* pages 73-81. Outline its basic content. *(READING / WRITING / SOCIAL SKILLS / BIBLE)*

RR. Read Chapter 17, "Conflict Resolution," in *The Exemplary Husband,* by Stuart Scott. Apply the principles of this chapter the next time you have a disagreement with someone. *(BIBLE / SOCIAL SKILLS)*

SS. Work through the material on "loneliness" in Wayne Mack's *Homework Manual for Biblical Living, Vol. 1 (*pages 107-118). These pages deal with how to be a good friend. *(BIBLE / WRITING / SOCIAL SKILLS)*

TT. Read *The Four Loves,* by C. S. Lewis. Write a paper summarizing the four different types of love. *(READING / ENGLISH COMPOSITION)*

Additional ideas:

Bad Friendships in the Bible

(See instructions in Project KK.)

PEOPLE WHO WERE FRIENDS	REF.	HOW THE FRIENDSHIP WAS BAD	RESULTS

Parents:

Consider and discuss with your son the following questions:

- Does he get along well with his siblings or is there constant bickering and seeking to protect his "rights"?

- Does he show kindness and gratitude to siblings and friends?

- Does he choose godly friends?

- Does he respect your counsel regarding his friendships?

- Does he seek to encourage and build up his friends and siblings?

- Do he and his friends share spiritual goals and ministries?

- Does he seek to befriend those who are lonely or less liked by others?

- Does he seek to serve in his friendships and in the family, or does he only seek his own selfish gain?

- Do he and his friends seek to serve and please God together?

- Is he willing to ask forgiveness when he wrongs someone?

- Is he quick to seek reconciliation when conflicts arise?

- Is he willing to work things out when he has been misunderstood?

- Is he easily offended?

- Is he willing to forgive when he has been wronged?

- Is he willing to humbly point out sin in the life of a friend?

- Does he expect perfection from his friends?

- Is he easily influenced by the opinions and actions of his siblings and friends, or does he stand up for what he knows is right regardless of what others think?

- Is he a loyal friend and brother? Does he stand alongside friends and siblings, encouraging and counseling them when things are difficult?

- Is he honest in his friendships?

- Does he show respect for the feelings and opinions of his friends and siblings? Is he careful with his words when he disagrees with them?

- Is he a trustworthy friend? Will he guard a confidence, or does he gossip and slander?

- Is he a loyal friend when his friends experience difficulties?

- Does he treat young ladies like sisters?

Notes and comments:

Protecting Others

"Or else how can one enter into a strong man's house, and spoil his goods, except he first bind the strong man? and then he will spoil his house" (Matthew 12:29).

God our Father is our all-powerful Protector. He is our Shield from all harm. "If God be for us, who can be against us?" (Romans 8:31)

God calls men, as His image bearers, to be protectors. Boys can be taught from an early age to accept their God-given role as protectors. That role has many faces. A son can learn to help and protect younger siblings. He can learn and practice gentlemanly manners toward his mother, sisters, and other women, honoring and showing deference to them. He can work to make your home a safer place and act as a defender in unpleasant or threatening situations. He can learn to anticipate potential dangers and help avoid or prepare for them.

Young men must also assume a protective role in their relationships with young women. Every young lady must be viewed as the future wife of someone else; she must not be defrauded or dishonored by self-serving young men. Sons should understand the power of their words and actions, and behave in a manner that will leave the hearts and bodies of young ladies pure and whole, ready to offer to their future husbands without regrets.

Men are also called to protect the helpless and oppressed, bringing God's justice to rule in His world. Our sons can learn to take compassionate action by working alongside the rest of the family in ministries and by looking around them and praying for specific ways to make a difference. This might involve helping a single mother, engaging in pro-life activities, assisting the homeless or those without food or work, helping to support orphans, ministering to those who are ill, or reaching out to those beyond our own borders.

A. Select verses from the list below, and use some or all of the following suggestions to help you study and better understand their meaning (easier verses are listed first, in italics):

1) Copy the passage.

2) Read it in several different translations of the Bible.

3) Read the passage and several of the verses before and after it to gain a better understanding of the context of the passage.

4) Rewrite the passage in your own words. What does it mean?

5) Record a specific way in which you can change your actions or attitudes based on the teaching of this passage.

6) Memorize the passage.

1 Peter 5:8
Matthew 12:29
1 Peter 3:7
(BIBLE / SPEECH)

Beginner

B. Ask your father to explain why men should honor and protect women. Why should you honor and protect women and girls? *(FAMILY / MANNERS)*

C. Pull out your mother's chair for her at mealtimes today. Don't sit down at the table until she sits down. Start doing this every day. *(FAMILY / MANNERS)*

D. Open and close the car door for your mother and sisters when you get in the car. Open the door for them and help carry things into the house when you return from your outing. *(FAMILY / MANNERS)*

E. Play with the baby and keep him safe and happy while your mother takes care of other children and does her work today. *(FAMILY / HOME SKILLS)*

F. Learn how to call 9-1-1, and in what circumstances you should call it. *(SAFETY)*

G. Ask your father to help you think of different ways you can show honor to your mother. Make a list. Illustrate it, if that helps you remember better. Then ask him to help you notice opportunities, and put your ideas into action. *(FAMILY / MANNERS / ART)*

H. Go out to breakfast or dinner with your parents and your grandmother or a sister. Watch your father show honor to your mother by helping her out of the car, taking her coat, opening doors, etc. Imitate him and do each of the same things for your grandmother or sister. *(FAMILY / MANNERS)*

I. Role-play with your family different situations that involve younger children, elderly people, disabled people, and women and children. How can you honor and protect each of the groups of people? What things *should* you do? What things should you *not* do? *(MANNERS / SOCIAL SKILLS / DRAMA)*

J. Learn to **see** the weak and helpless. Watch your youngest sibling for a day, or baby-sit for a family with very young children. Notice all the ways in which they need to be protected and all the potential dangers they come across. Then make a list of specific ways in which you can protect your younger siblings. *(FAMILY / SAFETY)*

K. Help your father draw a map of escape routes from different rooms in your house in case of fire. Practice with your siblings and parents the proper procedure you should follow if there is a fire started in your house. *(SAFETY / HOME SKILLS)*

L. Learn how to use a fire extinguisher. *(SAFETY / HOME SKILLS)*

M. Work with your parents to make lists of specific ways in which you can protect the following groups of people:
- Younger children at church
- Disabled people
- Your grandparents or other elderly people in your life

(SOCIAL SKILLS / MANNERS)

Intermediate

N. What things can you do (and not do) to make your home a safer place? Make a list and start putting it into action. *(SAFETY / HOME SKILLS)*

O. Study a book on manners. List out the specific rules that relate to:
- Women
- Elderly people
- Those who are younger than you
- Those who are weaker than you

(WRITING / MANNERS / SOCIAL SKILLS)

P. Study Chapter 10, "How Do You Treat the Women in Your Life?" in *Christian Manhood,* by Gary Maldaner. *(BIBLE)*

Q. Study Chapter 1, "Compassion," in *Christian Character,* by Gary Maldaner. *(BIBLE)*

R. Give a day of physical relief to your mother. Do her work for her so that she can rest or go out. *(FAMILY)*

S. Study examples of men in the Bible who were protectors of their families, the oppressed, and the ill, etc. List each man, the incident, the Bible reference, what he did, and the results. (Use the chart on page 383 for this study.)
- Abraham with Lot – Genesis 14

- Joseph with Mary and Jesus – Matthew 2:13-23
- Boaz with Ruth and Naomi – the book of Ruth
- Cornelius – Acts 10
- David with Mephibosheth – 2 Samuel 9

(BIBLE / RESEARCH / WRITING)

T. Study examples of men in the Bible who failed to protect women, their families, the oppressed, the ill, etc. List each man, the incident, the Bible reference, what he did, and the results. (Use the chart on page 384 for this study.)

- Lot in Sodom – Genesis 19
- Jacob with Dinah – Genesis 34
- David with Bathsheba – 2 Samuel 11
- Amnon with Tamar, David with Amnon – 2 Samuel 13
- Aachan – Joshua 7

(BIBLE / RESEARCH / WRITING)

U. Listen to *Women and Children First,* presented by Doug Phillips. Discuss the talk with your father. What can you learn and apply from it? *(FAMILY)*

V. Learn the basic rules of car safety. List the main rules a driver needs to observe. *(DRIVER EDUCATION / SAFETY)*

W. Learn how to handle roadside emergencies in order to help your mother if the need arises. Learn how to properly use jumper cables to charge a dead car. Learn how to change a flat tire. Learn how to deal with these emergencies in a safe way that doesn't endanger you or the passengers in the car. *(DRIVER EDUCATION / SAFETY / MECHANICS)*

X. Enroll in a self-defense class, or read a good book on self-defense and safety. Role-play the proper defensive response in various situations. *(P.E. / READING / SAFETY EDUCATION)*

Y. Read a good book on emergency preparation (i.e., *Just in Case: How to Be Self-Sufficient When the Unexpected Happens,* by Kathy Harrison), and make a list of actions to take and materials to gather to be properly prepared for a major emergency or natural disaster. *(SAFETY EDUCATION / HOME SKILLS)*

Z. Put together emergency kits to keep in each of your family's cars. Look for items recommended online or in books to include in the kits. *(SAFETY / HOME SKILLS)*

AA. With the aid of a good book on household safety, take a safety survey of your home. Where are potential dangers? What actions could be taken to make your home safer? Make a list of all dangerous areas and suggested remedies. *(SAFETY EDUCATION / WRITING / HOME SKILS)*

BB. Learn how to turn off the water, natural gas, electricity, etc. from its main source. Discuss with your father the situations in which you should turn off these utilities. *(HOME SKILLS / SAFETY EDUCATION)*

CC. Read *Generation Change,* by Zach Hunter. Seriously think about the "Brainstorm for Change" sections at the end of each chapter. What specific thing can **you** do to help change the world? *(READING)*

DD. Read *Take Your Best Shot,* by Austin Gutwein. Complete the "Take Your Best Shot" sections at the end of each chapter. Research some of the websites included in the "Ministry Resource Guide" at the end of the book. In what ways will this book change your life? Write down some ideas you can put into action. *(READING)*

Advanced

EE. Study God's role as **protector** as it is displayed in Scripture. With what objects is God compared? In what ways does He protect us? Whom does He protect? What can we learn about protecting others from His example? Summarize your study in a paper. (Look up "God, Preserver," and "God, His Preserving Care Exemplified" in *Nave's Topical Bible*.) *(BIBLE / RESEARCH)*

FF. Study Jesus' example of protecting and caring for the weak. Read through the Gospels, noting each interaction He has and how He responds to them. What can you learn from His example? Write a list of specific actions you can take based on this study. *(BIBLE / WRITING)*

GG. Study the phrase **weaker vessel** as it is used in 1 Peter 3:7. How can a husband honor his wife as the weaker vessel? Write a short essay answering this question. *(BIBLE / ENGLISH COMPOSITION)*

HH. Read *I Kissed Dating Goodbye,* by Joshua Harris, paying special attention to sections that address the emotional aspects of dating versus courtship. How could the practice of dating make it more difficult to protect a girl emotionally and physically? Write a short paper or discuss this question with your father. *(SOCIAL SKILLIS / PSYCHOLOGY / ENGLISH COMPOSITION)*

II. Research from reliable sources the advantages and disadvantages of owning a gun to protect those in your home. What is your opinion? Will you want a gun in your home? If so, complete Projects JJ and KK. *(RESEARCH / SAFETY)*

JJ. Study gun safety. List main safety rules to observe. *(SAFETY EDUCATION)*

KK. Obtain a hand gun, and enroll in a class on its use for self-defense. *(SELF DEFENSE)*

LL. Study the subject of life insurance. How can a life insurance policy be part of protecting your wife and family? Learn about the different types of policies, and their advantages and disadvantages. Which type would you select? *(RESEARCH / FAMILY / FINANCES)*

MM. Study the different options for health insurance and health care sharing ministries such as Samaritan Ministries and Medi-Share. What are the advantages and disadvantages of each option? Discuss these with your father and other knowledgeable men. Which type do you think you would use to help protect your family from unexpected health care costs? Why? *(RESEARCH / FAMILY / FINANCES)*

NN. Study the advantages and disadvantages of childhood vaccinations. Which ones are statistically safest? What are the risks involved in the various vaccines? How effective have they proven to be? Do you think you will want to vaccinate your children? Be sure to research both sides of the issue. Write a report that summarizes your research. *(RESEARCH / HEALTH / ENGLISH COMPOSITION)*

OO. Study the role of women in the military defense of a country. What does the Bible say about this? Should women participate in combat? Write a paper explaining your beliefs. *(BIBLE / ENGLISH COMPOSITION / RESEARCH / LAW)*

PP. In what specific ways will you need to protect your future wife? Make a list. In what ways can you be protecting her now, before you even know who she is? In what ways can you help protect the future wives of other men? *(FAMILY)*

QQ. In what ways will you need to protect your future children? Make a list. Can you do anything now that will better prepare you to protect them when you have a family? *(FAMILY)*

Additional ideas:

Men Who Protected Their Families

(See project S for instructions.)

NAME	REFERENCE	SITUATION	WHAT HE DID	RESULTS
Abraham with Lot	Genesis 14			
Joseph with Mary and Jesus	Matthew 2:13-23			
Boaz with Ruth and Naomi	Book of Ruth			
Cornelius	Acts 10			
David with Mephibosheth	2 Samuel 9			

Men Who Failed to Protect Others

(See project T for instructions.)

NAME	REFERENCE	SITUATION	WHAT HE DID	RESULTS
Lot in Sodom	Genesis 19			
Jacob with Dinah	Genesis 34			
David with Bathsheba	2 Samuel 11			
Amnon with Tamar	2 Samuel 13			
Achan	Joshua 7			

Parents:

Consider and discuss with your son the following questions:

- Does he take initiative in protecting his siblings and in steering them away from potential danger?

- Does he anticipate and take steps to avoid potential dangers?

- Does he recognize potentially tempting and emotionally harmful situations and take steps to protect himself and others from them?

- Does he know how to seek help in case of a medical emergency?

- Does he verbally defend his family and friends when they are criticized or slandered?

- Does his play reflect his God-given role as protector (i.e., pretending to be a policeman, soldier, father)?

- Does he display a difference in the way he plays with girls than with boys?

- Does he think of the safety of others when he is working and playing, or does he do foolish and careless things that could harm others?

- Does he protect girls his age by not playing roughly (if he is young) and by not being flirtatious and indiscreet (if he is older)?

- Does he guard his words and behavior in order to avoid emotionally or physically arousing young women?

- Does he seek to protect his mother and sisters?

- Does he seek to help his mother and other women and girls with physically demanding tasks?

- Does he seek to protect and assist the helpless?

- Is he knowledgeable in the basics of first aid and self-defense?

- Does he drive carefully?

- Is he actively involved in helping protect the weak and helpless in our society and throughout the world?

- Is he so overly concerned with safety that he is unwilling to take ordinary risks (like refusing to play a game because "someone might get hurt")?

Notes and comments:

Showing Hospitality

"Use hospitality one to another without grudging" (1 Peter 4:9).

God has extended hospitality, inviting us into his household of faith when we were strangers. He has commanded us to show the same love to others as we open our hearts and homes to them.

Although many of the tasks of extending hospitality naturally fall to the wife, our sons as heads of their households will be the leaders in opening their homes to others. They will set the tone of the household. They will help create the orderly and loving atmosphere that joyfully spreads to others outside the family.

We must set an example in this area, and we need to help our sons develop the attitudes and skills that will help them make their homes a "haven of rest" for others.

A. Select verses from the list below, and use some or all of the following suggestions to help you study and better understand their meaning (easier verses are listed first, in italics):

1) Copy the passage.

2) Read it in several different translations of the Bible.

3) Read the passage and several of the verses before and after it to gain a better understanding of the context of the passage.

4) Rewrite the passage in your own words. What does it mean?

5) Record a specific way in which you can change your actions or attitudes based on the teaching of this passage.

6) Memorize the passage.

   Romans 12:13
   Hebrews 13:1-2
   1 Peter 4:9
   Matthew 10:42
   Matthew 18:4
   Matthew 25:34-46

   (BIBLE / SPEECH)

Beginner

B. Read with your parents Genesis 18. Who was hospitable? List each thing he did for the three men. What were the results? Draw a picture to illustrate this story. *(BIBLE / ART)*

C. With your parents' permission, invite a friend to your house. Make him feel at home, play what he would like to play, and make sure he has a good time with you and your family. *(SOCIAL SKILLS / MANNERS)*

D. Role-play with your family how to greet and say good-bye to family, friends, and guests. Think of actions and words that will make them feel welcomed, honored, and loved. *(MANNERS / FAMILY / DRAMA)*

E. When your parents invite another family with small children to your house, get out toys you can share with them, and make sure they have a good time. *(SOCIAL SKILLS / MANNERS)*

F. When your family is expecting company:
- Help clean the house.
- Set the table.
- Help prepare the food.
- Think of activities that all will enjoy.
- Help clean up afterward.

(HOME SKILLS / SOCIAL SKILLS)

G. Who do you know who is lonely? Is there a child at church or school who has few friends? A widow who lives alone? Invite that person to your home. Do everything you can to make the time pleasant for them. Do what you can to become better friends with this person. *(SOCIAL SKILLS)*

H. Study a book of manners. List specific practices related to hosting company:
- How to greet the men, the women, and the children
- How to introduce people to each other
- How to help with coats and other belongings
- How to converse politely
- How to serve others
- How to make them feel at ease

(MANNERS / SOCIAL SKILLS / READING)

I. Pretend with your family that Jesus is a guest in your home. How would you treat Him? If He visited your church, what would you do to make Him feel welcome? Read Matthew 25:34-40. What does Jesus say about the kindnesses we show to others? *(BIBLE)*

J. Practice your skills as a host when your family has company over. Before they come, make a list of ways to make them feel at home, and then serve them in every way you can. *(MANNERS / WRITING)*

K. Invite a guest to your home. Pray and ask God to lead you to extend an invitation to someone that you would not normally invite, rather than someone you are already good friends with. Try to think of someone who might be lonely, someone in need, etc. Make them feel at home. *(SOCIAL SKILLS)*

Intermediate

L. Make a list of ways to be prepared for unexpected guests. Think about meals, sleeping areas, activities, etc. *(WRITING / SOCIAL SKILLS)*

M. Practice playing the part of the host at the family dinner table. Serve the food, make sure everyone has what they need, guide the conversation, etc. *(MANNERS / SOCIAL SKILLS)*

N. Discuss with your family what the difference is between **entertaining** and **hospitality**. What are the differences in motivation, preparation, whom you invite, etc.? *(FAMILY / SOCIAL SKILLS / BIBLE)*

O. Make a list of ways you can help when your family has unexpected guests or spontaneously invites someone for dinner. How can you help your father and mother? Your guests? Other family members? *(WRITING / FAMILY / MANNERS)*

P. Make a list of questions you can ask and things you can say to visitors in your church or home. Review your list so that you can recall it when you are tempted to not talk to a visitor because you don't know what to say. *(WRITING / SOCIAL SKILLS)*

Q. Plan and host a birthday party for one of your siblings or friends, or for one of your parents, grandparents, or other extended family members. *(FAMILY / SOCIAL SKILLS)*

R. When your parents have guests with younger children, help them feel at home while the adults visit. Play with them, bring out toys and games, serve snacks. After they leave, write down what you did with them. Did you show real hospitality? *(SOCIAL SKILLS / FAMILY / TEACHING)*

S. Think of someone who always makes you feel welcome and at home in their house. What does he or she do and say that makes you feel this way? Make a list of each thing you think of. *(SOCIAL SKILLS / WRITING)*

T. Make a list of ways to make visitors at your church feel welcome. Put your ideas into action. *(WRITING / SOCIAL SKILLS)*

U. Do a topical Bible study on **hospitality.** What does the Bible say about it? What is it? To whom should we show it? How should we practice it? (Look up "hospitality" in *Nave's Topical Bible* to get started.) *(BIBLE / RESEARCH / VOCABULARY / WRITING)*

V. Study 1 Peter 4:9. How might we show hospitality **with** grudging? Make a list and then next to each, write in a way to show hospitality **without** grudging. *(WRITING)*

Advanced

W. Be hospitable with your own family. Show kindness to your younger siblings. If you have your own room, make them feel welcome there. If you share a room, be a kind and pleasant roommate. Greet them cheerfully, give them your time, play the games they want to play. *(SOCIAL SKILLS / MANNERS)*

X. Read Hebrews 13:2. Study commentaries on this verse. Who entertained angels in Scripture? What were the results? *(BIBLE / RESEARCH)*

Y. Find examples of hospitality in the Bible. Who showed hospitality to Jesus? To the prophets? To spies? To extended family members? List each person, the Bible reference, who they hosted, and any results that might be related to the person's hospitality. (Use the form on page 392.) *(BIBLE / RESEARCH / WRITING)*

Z. Befriend a foreign student and welcome him into your home and family activities. *(FOREIGN LANGUAGE / GEOGRAPHY)*

AA. With your family, provide housing and meals for missionaries who are visiting your area during their furlough. *(HOME SKILLS / GEOGRAPHY)*

BB. Study Jesus' words in Luke 14:12-14. Write an essay explaining the meaning of this command and ways you might practically implement it in your life. *(BIBLE / ENGLISH COMPOSITION)*

CC. Read *Face to Face: Meditations on Friendship and Hospitality,* by Steve Wilkins. Outline each chapter. *(READING / BIBLE)*

DD. Consider the role of the husband as compared with the role of the wife in showing hospitality to others. Make lists of what you would consider to be the responsibilities of each. *(FAMILY)*

EE. Read *Making Room: Recovering Hospitality as a Christian Tradition,* by Christine Pohl. Write a summary of each chapter, and then write a summary of how this book will affect your practice of hospitality now and in your future home. *(READING)*

Additional ideas:

Hospitality in the Bible

(See instructions in Project Y.)

PERSON	REFERENCE	GUESTS	RESULTS

Parents:

Consider and discuss with your son the following questions:

- Does he show kindness and hospitality to those in his own family?

- Does he join you in cheerfully greeting guests?

- Does he make guests welcome in your home?

- Does he set aside his own plans when unexpected guests arrive?

- Is he gracious in making guests feel at home? Does he help with coats, make introductions, ask polite questions, draw children into his play, etc.

- Does he converse with guests in your home, or does he merely go on with his own activities?

- Does he keep his room tidy so that he and you will not be ashamed when you have guests?

- Does he show kindness to younger children of guests? Does he seek to keep them happy while the adults visit?

- Does he willingly share his belongings with young guests?

- Does he respectfully join into adult conversation?

- Does he initiate conversation with guests?

- Is he polite at the table?

- Is he trained in basic etiquette so that he is comfortable in social situations and when hosting others?

- Does he show kindness to visitors at church?

- Does he see his home as a center for reaching others for Christ?

- Does he understand that he is serving Jesus when he serves others and brings them into your home?

Notes and comments:

Providing for Those in Our Care

"But if any provide not for his own, and specially for those of his own house, he hath denied the faith, and is worse than an infidel" (1 Timothy 5:8).

Regardless of the feminist thinking of our age, God has given men the primary responsibility of providing for their families. The effectiveness and harmony of his future family will be greatly influenced by our son's commitment to faithfully work with God to provide for his family -- spiritually, emotionally, and physically. This will require strong character. To provide for others requires selflessness, diligence, perseverance, dependability, initiative, planning, and many other godly traits.

As parents, we also need to help our son put his vocation into proper perspective. Although this will be an important means of serving and glorifying God, as well as providing for his family, he may be tempted to overemphasize that portion of his life. This could lead to the neglect of his many other duties as husband and father.

A. Select verses from the list below, and use some or all of the following suggestions to help you study and better understand their meaning (easier verses are listed first, in italics):

1) Copy the passage.

2) Read it in several different translations of the Bible.

3) Read the passage and several of the verses before and after it to gain a better understanding of the context of the passage.

4) Rewrite the passage in your own words. What does it mean?

5) Record a specific way in which you can change your actions or attitudes based on the teaching of this passage.

6) Memorize the passage.

   Psalm 145:15
   Proverbs 12:11
   Proverbs 21:5
   Proverbs 28:19
   1 Thessalonians 4:11-12
   1 Timothy 5:8
   (BIBLE / SPEECH)

Beginner

B. Read with your parents the story of Ruth and Naomi in the book of Ruth. How did Ruth provide for her family? What had Boaz heard about Ruth before he met her? How did Boaz provide for his relatives? Draw a picture book to illustrate this story. *(BIBLE / READING / ART)*

C. Read with your parents Genesis 45-47, the story of Joseph when his brothers came to him in Egypt. How did Joseph provide for his father and his brothers and their families? Narrate the story back to your parents. *(BIBLE / READING / SPEECH)*

D. Read and discuss with your parents Proverbs 28:19. Draw a picture to illustrate the verse. *(BIBLE / ART)*

E. If you have a baby brother or sister, help feed him/her at mealtimes today. *(CHILD CARE)*

F. With your parents' permission, get a pet and take full responsibility for its care, remembering that this animal depends on you for its food, shelter, and health. *(ANIMAL HUSBANDRY / SCIENCE / CARPENTRY)*

G. Ask your father to tell a story of a time when God clearly provided for you and your family in a way that demonstrated His strength and His love. *(FAMILY HISTORY)*

H. Ask your father to tell you how he came to do the work he does. What experiences did God give him that prepared him for his work? What other jobs has he had? How did God lead him into this job? *(FAMILY HISTORY)*

I. Help your father do yard work or home maintenance for your grandparents. *(HOME SKILLS)*

J. "Adopt" an elderly neighbor or church member who has no family to care for him or her. Visit them. Encourage them. Help with their shopping, yard work, and household needs. Take them to church and on family outings. Invite them to your home for meals and holidays. *(FAMILY / CONSUMER EDUCATION / HOME SKILLS / COMMUNITY SERVICE / P.E.)*

K. Read with your parents 1 Timothy 5:8. What does this verse mean? *(BIBLE)*

Intermediate

L. Help your family provide for aging grandparents or great-grandparents. Help care for their yard, clean their house, and volunteer to run errands. If they live in your home, accept full responsibility for some part of their care. *(FINANCES / FAMILY / HEALTH / P.E.)*

M. Put an established percentage of all your earnings into long-term savings. Use this money to prepare yourself for being the earthly provider for your future family. Use it for job training, further education, purchasing land and/or house, equipping yourself with the tools you will need, etc. *(FINANCES / CAREER EDUCATION)*

N. Put an established percentage of all earnings into a "dowry" savings account. This should grow into a substantial sum of money that you will be able to give to your wife when you marry. It will become a form of life insurance for her, as well as money she can use to wisely invest as the Proverbs 31 woman did. (See projects JJ and KK for further expansion on this idea.) *(FINANCES / FAMILY)*

O. Put an established percentage of all earnings into a "living expense" fund. Use this money to contribute to the purchase of clothing and other necessary items. *(FINANCES / CONSUMER EDUCATION)*

P. Sponsor a child overseas. Help earn the money for his or her monthly support, write letters, send small gifts, etc. There are several organizations devoted to this purpose. **Compassion International** may be contacted at 1-800-336-7676, online at *www.compassion.com*, or by mailing to Compassion International, Colorado Springs, CO, 80997. *(GEOGRAPHY / WRITING / FINANCES)*

Q. Interview men, asking them to tell you of the ways God has helped them to provide for their families in times of difficulty. Tape record your interviews, or compile your data into a collection of short stories that testify to God's faithfulness in this area. *(SPEECH / WRITING / ENGLISH COMPOSITION)*

R. Interview husbands and wives in families where the wife stays home instead of going out to work. How does God provide for them? How do they economize? How do they manage on one income? How do the wife and children contribute to the family income? Write a report that summarizes your findings. *(FINANCES / FAMILY / WRITING)*

S. Study God's role as **Provider**. List verses you find on this subject, summarize each one, and then write a short essay that summarizes your entire study. (Look up verses listed under "Gifts from God" in *Nave's Topical Bible*.) *(BIBLE / RESEARCH / ENGLISH COMPOSITION)*

T. Study examples of men in the Bible who were providers. List each person, the reference, and what he did that provided for those who depended on him. (Use the form on page 401.) *(BIBLE / RESEARCH / WRITING / FAMILY)*

U. Discuss with your father the different ways he provides for your family. Are material possessions and money the only ways he provides? In what other ways does he act as a provider? *(FAMILY)*

V. Discuss the family budget with your father. How much money does it take to care for your family each month? In what ways does he work to reduce expenses? How does he handle emergencies and unexpected expenses? What role does prayer play in his providing for your family? How have the needs of the family changed over the years, and how has God been faithful to care for all of you? *(FINANCES / FAMILY / CONSUMER EDUCATION)*

W. Compare costs for various types of shelter -- apartment, mobile home, old home, new home -- and the costs of renting versus buying. Then list the advantages and disadvantages of each option. (You may need to interview some adults for some of this information.) Based on your research, write a short paper explaining what you would consider to be the best housing option for: (a) you and your wife when you first get married (b) your family as your children grow up. *(FINANCES / FAMILY / WRITING / CONSUMER EDUCATION)*

X. List ways to provide food for your family other than buying it from the store. Then list each option in order from most to least economical. *(CONSUMER EDUCATION / FINANCES)*

Y. List ways to provide clothing for your family other than buying it from a department store. Then list each option in order from most to least economical. *(CONSUMER EDUCATION / FINANCES)*

Z. Make a list of ways to reduce housing costs. *(FINANCES)*

AA. Make a list of ways to reduce utilities and telephone/internet costs. *(FINANCES / CONSUMER EDUCATION)*

BB. List all the elements of what you would consider the ideal house. Or look through magazines of house plans, and choose the house you think would be best for your future family. Explain the reasons for your choice. *(ARCHITECTURE / FAMILY / FINANCES / WRITING)*

CC. Establish an amount of money that you would like to earn each week. Then work to earn it by doing extra household chores (if your parents are willing to pay for them), odd jobs in your neighborhood, working for business owners in your church, setting up small business enterprises, etc. Establish a budget based on your projected weekly earnings. *(CAREER AND BUSINESS EDUCATION / FINANCES)*

DD. Make a list of all the areas in which you will be responsible for providing for your family. Discuss this list with your father. What can you do now to prepare for those responsibilities? *(FINANCES / FAMILY)*

EE. Decide with your parents the age at which they would like you to purchase your own clothing. Earn the money to do this. *(CAREER EDUCATION / CONSUMER EDUCATION / FINANCES)*

Advanced

FF. Take on an extra job in order to regularly provide for an orphan or orphanage or to contribute to a needy household in your church community. Set a goal of how much you need to earn, and work enough each month to keep your commitment. *(FINANCES / CAREER EDUCATION / COMMUNITY SERVICE)*

GG. Study what the Bible says about adult children providing care for their aging parents. What Biblical principles guide us in this area? List all Scripture passages that you find, and explain how they apply to this question. Then write a short essay summarizing your study. *(BIBLE / RESEARCH / WRITING / SOCIAL STUDIES)*

HH. Write a paper on 1 Timothy 5:8. What does this verse mean? Read different commentaries to gain a better understanding of the verse. In what ways can a person neglect to provide for his own family and relatives? How can a person be worse than an unbeliever? *(BIBLE)*

II. Read *The Gift of Work,* by Bill Heatley. Write a summary of the book and explain how it will affect your work. What is success? What is the purpose of work? How can you incorporate your faith into your workplace? *(READING / ENGLISH COMPOSITION)*

JJ. Study the **dowry** as described in the Bible. Read passages that recount the courtship and marriage of various couples. Who gave what to whom? What principles might we extract from these practices? *(FAMILY / BIBLE)*

KK. Read the section on the Biblical dowry as discussed in *Dating vs. Courtship* (pages 89-95), by Paul Jehle. Discuss the concept with your father. If you would like to start saving up money for a dowry, decide what percentage of your earnings will go into this fund. *(BIBLE / FINANCES / FAMILY)*

LL. What evidences of your ability to provide for a family will you demonstrate before marrying? Make a list. How much money will you want in savings? How much work experience will you have? Will you have your lifetime career established? Will you own land or a home? Will you have dowry savings for your wife? Show your list to your parents for their review. What would they recommend adding, deleting, or changing? *(WRITING / FINANCES / CAREER EDUCATION)*

Additional ideas:

Providers in the Bible

(See Project T for instructions.)

PERSON	REFERENCE	WHAT HE PROVIDED

Parents:

Consider and discuss with your son the following questions:

- Is he faithful in his household chores?

- Is he faithful in providing for animals entrusted to his care?

- Is he reliable? Does he complete tasks that others are counting on him to do?

- When he works for others are they satisfied with his work?

- Does he take care of the things you provide for him?

- Does he take your provision for granted, or does he express thankfulness?

- Does he pray for God's provision and for God's wisdom in obtaining needed items?

- Does he recognize God as the ultimate provider and source of all that we have?

- Does he take initiative in earning money when he needs it?

- Does he save a portion of his money or does he spend it all as he wishes?

- Does he budget his earnings into various spending and savings categories?

- Does he help purchase any of his own clothes or other necessities?

- Is he saving money for the future -- for vocational training, property, house, car, etc.?

- Is he setting aside money for a dowry to give to his wife?

- Does he help with the shopping? Does he have a good picture of the cost of clothing, food, etc.?

- Is he familiar with your family budget? Does he know how much it costs for your family to live each month?

- Is he wise and thrifty in his purchases, or does he spend his money with little thought, planning or research?

- Does he seek to save money by purchasing used items, waiting for sales, etc.?

- Does he spend carefully without becoming miserly with his money?

- Does he see the value of investing in good tools, books, etc. to help him in his tasks, or does he begrudge the expense?

- Does he understand the difference between **needs** and **desires**? Does he seek to spend his money only on desires while neglecting real needs?

- Is he preparing himself for a vocation? Does he have clearly defined vocational goals?

- Has he attempted any small money-making ventures?

- Does he focus his energies on play and self-centered activities? Does he resist and resent the work he must do?

- Does he recognize that work is a blessing from God and commanded by God?

- Is he seeking to grow in his spiritual life so that he will be prepared to provide spiritual and emotional support and leadership for his family?

Notes and comments:

And to brotherly kindness,

CHARITY

Giving to Those in Need

"I have showed you all things, how that so labouring ye ought to support the weak, and to remember the words of the Lord Jesus, how he said, 'It is more blessed to give than to receive'" (Acts 20:35).

Our sons will spend the majority of their adult years giving -- if we do our job right (and if they choose to respond correctly to our instruction)! They will give daily of themselves to their wives and children. They will give of themselves to their fellow believers in the church body. And as godly men, blessed by God, they will share those blessings with the needy around them.

We need to train our sons to become aware of the needs around them. Have them join you as you give of your time and energy to those in need. Work together. They will learn important lessons, and you will grow closer to each other as you serve the Lord together.

A. Select verses from the list below, and use some or all of the following suggestions to help you study and better understand their meaning (easier verses are listed first, in italics):

1) Copy the passage.

2) Read it in several different translations of the Bible.

3) Read the passage and several of the verses before and after it to gain a better understanding of the context of the passage.

4) Rewrite the passage in your own words. What does it mean?

5) Record a specific way in which you can change your actions or attitudes based on the teaching of this passage.

6) Memorize the passage.

Proverbs 3:27
Proverbs 19:17
Proverbs 21:13
Isaiah 1:17
Galatians 6:2
Psalm 82:2-4
Proverbs 25:20-22
Isaiah 58:10
Matthew 25:37-40
Acts 20:35

Galatians 6:10
James 1:27
James 2:15-16
1 John 3:17
(BIBLE / SPEECH)

Beginner

B. Read with your parents Chapter 56, "God's Children Give" in *Leading Little Ones to God,* by Marian Schoolland. *(BIBLE / READING)*

C. Read with your parents the account of Jesus feeding five thousand people in John 6. What did Jesus ask the disciples to do? What did they find to eat among all the people? What did Jesus do with the lunch that one boy was willing to share? Draw a picture to illustrate this story. *(BIBLE / ART)*

D. Read with your parents the story of the Good Samaritan in Luke 10:30-37. Who chose not to help the injured man? Who did help him? What did it cost him to help the man? Act out this story with your family and friends or with toys. *(BIBLE / DRAMA)*

E. Read and discuss with your parents Proverbs 25:20-22. Draw a picture to illustrate these verses. *(BIBLE / ART)*

F. Go through all your toys. Choose several to give to needy children, and place them in a box. Don't give your broken toys! Give toys you would like to receive! Include a note in the box. Help your mother deliver the toys to a family or to an organization that distributes them. *(WRITING / COMMUNITY SERVICE)*

G. Write down a list of needy people you know -- people who are sick, elderly, poor, overworked, discouraged, alone, etc. Then write down a list of specific ways you can give help to each of these people. Now do them! *(WRITING / COMMUNITY SERVICE)*

H. Visit people in the hospital or in rest homes, widows, orphans, the sick, and the elderly. Talk to them, read for them, play games with them, etc. Or call them on the telephone to give encouragement. *(COMMUNITY SERVICE / SOCIAL SKILLS)*

Intermediate

I. Make a list of all the different ways we can give to others (money, time, etc.) *(WRITING)*

J. Budget a specific proportion of your earnings for the purpose of giving to others in need. *(FINANCES)*

K. Study the chapters on "Insensitivity" and "Selfishness" in *For Instruction in Righteousness,* by Pam Forster. *(BIBLE)*

L. Study Chapter 10, "Empathy," and Chapter 13, "Generosity," in *Christian Character.* *(BIBLE)*

M. Read the newspaper looking for articles about people who have experienced tragedy or who have special needs that you might be able to meet. List each incident and write down what you could do to help in each situation. Then choose one and put your ideas into practice. *(CURRENT EVENTS / READING)*

N. Write cards and letters to those in your church who need spiritual and emotional encouragement. *(WRITING)*

O. Learn to take initiative in seeing the needs of others. Write a list throughout a week's time, listing all the needs you see in the lives of those you are with. Watch for spiritual, physical, emotional, financial, and social needs. At the end of the week, look over your list and write down ways you can serve God by helping to meet those needs. *(WRITING)*

P. Join your family in helping a single mother or family who would normally qualify for government welfare. Don't just give them everything. Think of Biblical ways to offer opportunities to earn income, ways to help them save money, ways to give physical and emotional support. *(FINANCES / GOVERNMENT)*

Q. Write letters to prison inmates. For addresses, contact Prison Fellowship at P.O. Box 17500, Washington, DC 20041 (also at *www.prisonfellowship.org*). *(WRITING)*

R. Volunteer to work in a food pantry or other ministry to the needy. Talk to the people who benefit from the ministry and express an interest in their lives. *(COMMUNITY SERVICE / SOCIAL SKILLS)*

S. Read through the Gospels. Look for ways that Jesus helped the needy. How did He treat the sick, the lonely, the poor, the widow and orphan, etc.? List each reference and Christ's action. What can we learn from His example? Use the form on page 412 to organize your findings. *(BIBLE / RESEARCH / WRITING)*

T. Read Matthew 25:31-46. List the ways we can serve Jesus by ministering to the needs of others. Then list specific ways you can help specific people in each of these categories. *(BIBLE / WRITING)*

U. Study the Bible, looking for examples of benevolence -- men and women who ministered to the needs of others. Write down each example, where it is given in Scripture, and what we can learn from each. (Use the form on page 413.) Look up "Beneficence, Instances of," "Kindness, Instances of," and "Love, Instances of" in Nave's Topical Bible. *(BIBLE / RESEARCH / WRITING)*

V. What does God say will happen to the person who is generous with others? Study this topic in the Bible, and list all the blessings of generosity. (Look up "liberality" in *Nave's Topical Bible*.) *(BIBLE / RESEARCH / WRITING)*

W. What does God say will happen to the person who is selfish or who oppresses or ignores the needy? Study this topic in the Bible and list each consequence of selfishness. (Look up "Poor, oppressions of" and the terms "selfishness" and "oppression" in *Nave's Topical Bible* and the chapter on "Selfishness/Greed" in *For Instruction in Righteousness,* by Pam Forster.) *(BIBLE/ RESEARCH / WRITING)*

X. Discuss with the deacons in your church the benevolent ministries of the church and how you can become involved. *(COMMUNITY SERVICE)*

Y. How are we supposed to treat the poor person? Research this topic in the Bible, and write a short essay to summarize your study. *(BIBLE / RESEARCH / ENGLISH COMPOSITION / SOCIAL STUDIES)*

Z. List out Old Testament laws as they relate to the poor. List each specific law, its reference, and how we might practically apply its principle to our present day. (Use the form on page 414.) Find these laws by looking up the word **poor** in *Strong's Concordance* and reading all the verses in Exodus, Leviticus, and Deuteronomy. *(BIBLE / SOCIAL STUDIES / RESEARCH / WRITING)*

Advanced

AA. Listen to *Defending the Fatherless,* by Douglas Phillips. List the ways the Church can enable single mothers to home educate their children.

BB. Read all the verses under the following topics in *Nave's Topical Bible.*

- Alms
- Beneficence
- Giving, Rules for
- Poor, Duty to

Take notes. Organize your observations into a paper on one of the following aspects of Christian charity and benevolence:

- Who should we give to
- Hypocrisy in giving
- Blessings of giving
- Giving in a way that strengthens the recipient
- The role of love in giving

(BIBLE / RESEARCH / WRITING)

CC. Write a paper explaining how our help should differ for the oppressed who have been **denied** the opportunity to work, compared to helping the slothful who **reject** the opportunity to work. Base your opinions on Scriptural principles. *(BIBLE / ENGLISH COMPOSITION / SOCIAL STUDIES)*

DD. Study the principle of **gleaning** as it is described in the Bible. Describe in a paper, or explain to your family, how this practice could be applied to the present day. *(BIBLE / SOCIAL STUDIES / FINANCES)*

EE. Do a study on the word **compassion** as it is used in the Bible. *(BIBLE / VOCABULARY / WRITING / RESEARCH)*

FF. Write a paper explaining why the present government welfare system is unbiblical. Offer several Biblical alternatives to replace the system. *(BIBLE / ENGLISH COMPOSITION / SOCIAL STUDIES)*

GG. Study how our help for our Christian brothers should differ from our helping the needy who are living in sin. Write a paper and support your opinions with Scripture. *(BIBLE / ENGLISH COMPOSITION)*

HH. Read the section on "Welfare and Benevolence" in *Giving and Tithing,* by Larry Burkett. *(FINANCES / SOCIAL STUDIES)*

II. Read George Grant's book, *Bringing in the Sheaves.* Outline the book's basic content. Discuss it with your father. *(READING / WRITING / SOCIAL STUDIES)*

JJ. Study Lessons 9, "The Cause of Poverty," and Lesson 10, "The Conquest of Poverty," in *God and Government, Volume 2*, by Gary DeMar. Talk over the discussion questions with your parents. *(READING / SOCIAL STUDIES / BIBLE)*

KK. Research the benevolent practices of the church in Geneva during John Calvin's time. Outline the basic approach of these believers to helping those in need. *(SOCIAL STUDIES / HISTORY)*

Additional ideas:

Jesus' Gifts to the Needy

(See instructions in Project S.)

REFERENCE	CHRIST'S ACTION	WHAT I CAN LEARN

Benevolence in the Bible

(See instructions in Project U.)

PEOPLE	REF.	WHAT THEY DID	WHAT I CAN LEARN

Old Testament Laws Regarding the Poor

(See instructions in Project Z.)

LAW	REFERENCE	APPLICATION TO TODAY

Parents:

Consider and discuss with your son the following questions:

- Does he see the physical needs of others around him?

- Does he notice needs and become involved in meeting them?

- Does he have compassion for those in need?

- Does his compassion lead to acts of kindness and mercy?

- Does he seek to comfort siblings when they are injured, disappointed, etc.?

- Does he seek to minister to the needs of those in his own family?

- Does he generally focus on others or himself?

- Is he sensitive to the emotional needs of others?

- Does he feel a burden for the spiritual needs of others?

- Does he save money specifically for giving to others?

- Does he give out of love for God or to impress others?

- Is he willing to give of his time to help others?

- Does he understand that giving a poor person everything he needs is not usually the best way to help him?

- Does he have a desire to follow Jesus' example in ministering to others?

- Does he cheerfully join with the family in serving and ministering to the needs of others?

- Is he a cheerful giver?

Notes and comments:

Communicating in a Godly Way

"Likewise, ye husbands, dwell with them according to knowledge, giving honour unto the wife, as unto the weaker vessel, and as being heirs together of the grace of life; that your prayers be not hindered" (1 Peter 3:7).

We have previously addressed the area of godly speech in the chapter entitled "Self-Control: The Tongue." Its focus is on control over sins of the tongue -- gossip, angry or impure words, criticism, etc.

This chapter focuses on positive communication, and on conversational skills and speech patterns that will help our sons learn to talk and listen at a deeper, more personal level. God has designed us to live with others, and to grow and learn in the context of relationships. Relationships are built on communication.

Our relationship with God and our communion with Him is foundational. Building on that groundwork, our relationships with others flourish when there is open, honest, loving, encouraging communication. If we aren't communicating with someone, our relationship will stagnate or die. If we aren't communicating in a godly way our relationships will suffer. Because we are sinners, we must be ready to repent and ask forgiveness when we have sinned against others, and just as ready to forgive when others have sinned against us.

If a young man has not learned to communicate in an open and honest, but also **loving** and humble way, he will struggle in his relationship with his wife and children. His family will need him to talk to them. They will also need him to listen to them – another aspect of communication which is just as important as talking. If he cannot communicate well, he will not be able to lead his family as effectively, and will not be able to teach them.

If he has developed bad habits of communication, it will affect his relationships outside the home as well. It may affect the quality of your relationship to him and his family. It will affect the closeness he will have to his church family and other brothers and sisters in Christ.

We need to train our son in this important area. Many of us may come from homes that have left us weak in communications skills. The first place, as always, that we need to start is in our own hearts. Where do we need to grow? In what ways are we sinning in our communication with others?

A book that is very helpful in pinpointing problems of communication in our families is Wayne Mack's *Your Family God's Way.* (We refer to it in Project VV.) We highly recommend it for parents to read and study.

A. Select verses from the list below, and use some or all of the following suggestions to help you study and better understand their meaning (easier verses are listed first, in italics):

1) Copy the passage.

2) Read it in several different translations of the Bible.

3) Read the passage and several of the verses before and after it to gain a better understanding of the context of the passage.

4) Rewrite the passage in your own words. What does it mean?

5) Record a specific way in which you can change your actions or attitudes based on the teaching of this passage.

6) Memorize the passage.

> *Proverbs 10:21*
> *Proverbs 12:18*
> *Proverbs 16:24*
> *Proverbs 18:13*
> *1 Thessalonians 5:11*
> *James 1:19*
> Proverbs 18:2
> Ecclesiastes 3:1 and 7
> Ecclesiastes 5:3
> 1 Corinthians 13:4-8
> 1 Peter 3:7
> *(BIBLE / SPEECH)*

Beginner

B. At the dinner table, tell your father all about your day. *(SPEECH)*

C. Have a special time each day to talk with your Dad or Mom. Snuggle at night, go for a walk, spend a few minutes together during naptime, etc. *(FAMILY)*

D. Read with your parents 1 Samuel 24. What had Saul tried to do to David before this story takes place? Narrate this story back to your parents. How did David respond to the opportunity to harm Saul? What did Saul say and do when he realized what David had chosen to do? What can you learn from this story? Act the story out during your playtime. *(BIBLE / SPEECH / DRAMA)*

E. Read and discuss with your parents Proverbs 12:18. Draw a picture to illustrate this proverb. Is your tongue a sword or health? *(BIBLE / ART)*

F. When you visit your grandparents, ask them to tell you a story about their childhood. Sit quietly and listen while they talk. Retell the story to a friend or sibling. *(SOCIAL SKILLS / MANNERS / SPEECH)*

G. Read with your parents Ephesians 4:29. Discuss the meaning of this verse with them, and talk about specific ways you can build someone else up. *(BIBLE)*

H. Role-play different conversational situations with your family. Practice the proper response when someone shares a disappointment with you. Act out what you should say when someone voices an opinion with which you disagree. What should you say when someone shares their dreams, speaks of their concerns, tells you of their successes, etc.? *(SOCIAL SKILLS / FAMILY / BIBLE)*

I. When you have sinned against someone, go to them and confess that you were wrong and ask their forgiveness. ("I was wrong for _____. Will you please forgive me?) *(SOCIAL SKILLS)*

J. In what other ways, besides talking, do we communicate with others? Discuss this with your parents. What things do we do with our face and the rest of our body? What actions can we take that communicate to others that we do or don't care about them? *(SOCIAL SKILLS / MANNERS)*

K. Hug someone in your family today and tell him you love him. Do this every day for every member of your family. *(FAMILY)*

L. When your parents discipline you for saying unkind words, think of more godly words you could have used in the situation and say them. *(MANNERS / SPEECH)*

M. Illustrate some of the following proverbs. Post them in your room as reminders of how you should use your tongue. Or bind them together into a booklet that you can review each day.

> Proverbs 12:25
> Proverbs 15:1
> Proverbs 15:4
> Proverbs 15:28
> Proverbs 16:24
> Proverbs 25:11

Proverbs 25:12

Proverbs 25:15

(BIBLE / ART)

N. Study *The Brother-Offended Checklist.* Use the biblical principles outlined in this book and chart to help you resolve disagreements in a godly manner. *(BIBLE / SOCIAL SKILLS)*

O. Pray each day for God's help in lovingly communicating with those people you associate with throughout the day.

P. Read a magazine or news article and talk about it with everyone at the dinner table. *(CURRENT EVENTS)*

Intermediate

Q. Say at least one encouraging thing to each person in your family today. Try to make this a habit every day. *(SOCIAL SKILLS / FAMILY)*

R. Devote a regular amount of time each day to conversing with God in prayer. Learning to honestly open your heart and soul to God will result in greater communication with people as well. *(DEVOTIONS)*

S. Each Sunday at church and at other social gatherings, initiate conversation with at least one person that you do not know well, and to whom you would not normally have spoken. *(SOCIAL SKILLS)*

T. Write out imaginary conversations that demonstrate proper interest in others, and proper responses to their comments. *(WRITING / SOCIAL SKILLS)*

U. Write accounts of at least two times when you have asked forgiveness of someone for the wrong you have done. How did the people respond to your request? *(WRITING / ENGLISH COMPOSITION)*

V. Search for scriptural principles that teach us how to be a good listener. List each principle and its Bible reference. (Look up the word "hear" and its derivative forms in *Strong's Concordance*.) *(BIBLE / MANNERS/ RESEARCH)*

W. Read Proverbs 18:13. How can you apply this verse in your life? Will it make a difference in how you interact with your siblings? Your parents? Your friends? *(BIBLE)*

X. Study James 1:19. Memorize this verse and say it to yourself every time you are tempted to interrupt or not pay attention to someone who is speaking to you. *(BIBLE / MANNERS)*

Y. Study Jesus' example as a listener. How did He listen and how did He respond? Read through one or more of the Gospels and list each situation, the reference, His actions, and what we can learn from His example. (Use the form on page 424.) *(BIBLE / RESEARCH / WRITING)*

Z. Read through the Gospels, noting all of Jesus' conversations. Write down everything you can learn from his example about conversing with others. *(BIBLE / RESEARCH / WRITING)*

AA. Meditate each day for a week on the verses listed in project M. At the end of each day, review the verses again and record any situations during the day when you chose to obey or disobey their teaching. Pray that God will help you remember and apply these verses. (Use the chart on pages 425-426 for this project.) *(BIBLE / WRITING)*

BB. Read good magazines, newspapers and books, and listen to good radio broadcasts in order to give yourself conversational material. Discuss what you have learned with your family at meal times. *(READING / CURRENT EVENTS / SOCIAL STUDIES)*

CC. Go through the chapter entitled "Acquiring Conversational Skills," in *Man in Demand*, pages 14-20. *(BIBLE/ SOCIAL SKILLS)*

DD. Read one of the many books available on conversing comfortably and politely with other people. Take notes. What are some good ways to start conversations? How can you communicate interest in the other person? Practice these tips with your own family and in other social situations. *(READING / SOCIAL SKILLS)*

EE. Study the first chapter of the book of Jeremiah. What excuse did Jeremiah give when God called him to be a prophet? What was God's response? What can you learn from this passage? Read through the rest of the book. Did God enable Jeremiah to speak clearly? *(BIBLE)*

FF. Study the account of God calling Moses in Exodus 3. Then review the rest of Moses' life. Was God faithful in enabling Moses to lead the Israelites? What can we learn from this passage about being fearful of speaking to others? *(BIBLE / RESEARCH)*

Advanced

GG. Make a list of questions you can ask other members of your family to engage them in conversation and to show interest in their lives (i.e., What did they do during the day? How are they progressing on a project? What have they made or drawn or written that they can show you?). Use this list to help you talk with your parents and siblings. Be sure to really listen and be interested when they answer your questions. *(WRITING / SOCIAL SKILLS)*

HH. Make a list of things you can share about yourself at the table or in the car with your family (i.e., what you are reading, what you learned from the sermon, what the people you work with are like). *(WRITING / SOCIAL SKILLS)*

II. Study Ephesians 4:26-27. Study the meaning of different key words, and read commentaries on the passage. Then write a paper summarizing what you have learned and how you will apply it in your life. How will obedience to this verse improve your future marriage? *(BIBLE / ENGLISH COMPOSITION)*

JJ. Read all the verses under "forgiveness" in *Nave's Topical Bible.* Take notes and then organize them into a summary essay. Why should we forgive others? How should we forgive them? How often should we forgive them? Why is forgiveness important for good communication? *(BIBLE / ENGLISH COMPOSITION)*

KK. Study the "Parable of the Sower" in Luke 8:4-15. What principles about listening can we glean from this story? Write a short paper explaining your answer. *(BIBLE / ENGLISH COMPOSITION)*

LL. Fill out the "Conversation Inventory" on page 427. Circle one number for each area of conversation: "3" if you think you talk **too much** about the topic, "2" if you think you speak about these areas the **right amount**, "1" if you feel you should talk about these subjects **more often**. Add up your score when you have finished. Give another copy of the page to one or both of your parents to complete about you. Add up their score(s). Compare your answers and scores. Do you all agree? In what areas do you need to make changes toward more honest and open communication? *(SOCIAL SKILLS / FAMILY)*

MM. Use the list in the "Conversation Inventory" on page 427 to help you think of questions you can ask other people when talking to them. *(SOCIAL SKILLS)*

NN. Copy the chart in Appendix Four, "Daily Reminder of How to Treat One Another," in *The Exemplary Husband,* by Stuart Scott. Post this in a prominent place and refer to it throughout the day to guide your actions and attitudes with your family. *(BIBLE / SOCIAL SKILLS)*

OO. Keep a journal in which you write your feelings, dreams, etc. Use it as a reminder of things to talk about with your parents. Write down advice and thoughts your parents share with you on these subjects. *(WRITING)*

PP. Read and study Proverbs 20:5. How could a husband apply this verse to his relationship with his wife? Discuss this with your father. *(BIBLE / FAMILY)*

QQ. Study 1 Peter 3:7. Explain the connection between a husband's communicating with his wife and his communication with God through prayer. *(BIBLE / FAMILY)*

RR. Write a paper explaining why it is important for a husband to converse (at a personal and meaningful level) with his wife. *(ENGLISH COMPOSITION / FAMILY)*

SS. Read *War of Words: Getting to the Heart of Your Communication Struggles*, by Paul David Tripp. If possible, read this book with your parents or others. Answer the "Getting Personal" questions at the end of each chapter. *(READING / SPEECH)*

TT. Work through the sections on communication, pages 23-37, in Wayne Mack's book, *A Homework Manual for Biblical Living, Vol. 1.* *(WRITING / BIBLE / SOCIAL SKILLS)*

UU. Read Chapter 16, "A Husband's Resolve: Good Communication," in *The Exemplary Husband*, by Stuart Scott. List the effects of good and bad communication, the six prerequisites to good communication, and four principles related to Christ's communication. *(SOCIAL SKILLS / WRITING)*

VV. Read all of Section 2, "Developing God-Honoring Family Relationships," in *Your Family God's Way*, by Wayne Mack. Complete all study and application assignments. This section is very helpful and includes the following chapters:

Chapter 4: "I Heard What You Didn't Say"
Chapter 5: "How to Hear What's Not Being Said"
Chapter 6: "Small Talk: The Silent Menace"
Chapter 7: "Enough Is Enough and Too Much Is Too Much"
Chapter 8: "Circuit Jammers to Family Communication"
Chapter 9: "To Tell the Truth"
Chapter 10: "Now You're Really Talking"
Chapter 11: "Getting Your Ears On"

(BIBLE / FAMILY / SOCIAL SKILLS / WRITING)

Additional ideas:

Jesus Listens

(See instructions in Project Y.)

INCIDENT	REF.	JESUS' ACTIONS	WHAT I CAN LEARN

Applying the Wisdom of Solomon

(See instruction in Project AA.)

Verse (ESV)	Sunday	Monday	Tuesday	Wednesday	Thursday	Friday	Saturday
"Anxiety in a man's heart weighs him down, but a good word makes him glad." Proverbs 12:25							
"A soft answer turns away wrath, but a harsh word stirs up anger." Proverbs 15:1							
A gentle tongue is a tree of life, but perverseness in it breaks the spirit." Proverbs 15:4							
"The heart of the righteous ponders how to answer, but the mouth of the wicked pours out evil things." Proverbs 15:28							

Verse	Sunday	Monday	Tuesday	Wednesday	Thursday	Friday	Saturday
"Gracious words are like a honeycomb, sweetness to the soul and health to the body." Proverbs 16:24							
"A word fitly spoken is like apples of gold in a setting of silver." Proverbs 25:11							
"Like a gold ring or an ornament of gold is a wise reprover to a listening ear." Proverbs 25:12							
"With patience a ruler may be persuaded, and a soft tongue will break a bone." Proverbs 25:15							

Conversation Inventory

(See instructions in Project LL.)

a. Facts and information	1	2	3
b. Ideas and opinions	1	2	3
c. Spiritual matters, Bible truths, prayer	1	2	3
d. How to apply God's Word to everyday life	1	2	3
e. Feelings and emotions	1	2	3
f. Desires and concerns	1	2	3
g. Plans and goals	1	2	3
h. Dreams and aspirations	1	2	3
i. Finances, material things, purchases	1	2	3
j. School	1	2	3
k. Work	1	2	3
l. Friends	1	2	3
m. Fears	1	2	3
n. Sports and recreation	1	2	3
o. Problems	1	2	3
p. Successes	1	2	3
q. Current events and politics	1	2	3
r. What you are reading, learning, etc.	1	2	3
s. News about others	1	2	3

Parents:

Consider and discuss with your son the following questions:

- Does he listen carefully to what the other person is saying to him?

- Does he think he already knows what a person is going to say before the person has a chance to finish expressing himself?

- Does he look at the person who is speaking to him?

- Does he interrupt with criticism, solutions, or opinions before hearing all of what someone is trying to say?

- Is he interested in what others have to say, or is he only anxious to voice his next thought?

- Does he, by his facial expressions and tone of voice, frequently communicate indifference to the thoughts and opinions of others?

- Does he acknowledge what people say to him, or does he act as though they never spoke?

- Does he seek to truly understand the feelings and thoughts of the person who is speaking to him?

- Does he ask questions that will help him better understand the thoughts of another person?

- Does he admit when he has wronged someone? Does he go to them to confess his wrong and ask forgiveness, or does he ignore the problem?

- Does he often communicate in a negative way with his posture, eyes, facial expressions, and clothing?

- Does he feel free to share his feelings and opinions? Does he do so in a gracious manner?

- Does he avoid certain topics of discussion instead of dealing with them as he should?

- Does he talk openly with you about his thoughts, feelings, goals, interests, etc., or is he hard to get to know?

- Does he ever talk to you at a personal level?

- Does he talk very little, the proper amount, or too much?

- Does he verbally express appreciation for the services and kindnesses of others?

- Does he encourage others with his words toward greater godliness and greater accomplishment?

- Does his tone of voice frequently communicate something other than what his words are saying?

- Does he have any distracting nervous habits (i.e. fidgeting, nail biting, jiggling the legs) when conversing with others?

- Does he speak clearly so that the people he is addressing are able to hear him, or does he mumble?

- Is he vague with his words, so that people easily misunderstand him?

- Can he explain something in a clear, understandable way, or does he leave his listeners confused?

- Is he timid and uncomfortable in conversing with people other than his best friends?

Notes and comments:

Serving Others with a Cheerful Heart

"But ye shall not be so: but he that is greatest among you, let him be as the younger; and he that is chief, as he that doth serve" (Luke 22:26).

Jesus reminded us that our lives are to be ones of service. "If I then, your Lord and Master, have washed your feet; ye also ought to wash one another's feet. For I have given you an example, that ye should do as I have done to you" (John 13:14-15).

The greatest among us will be the one who is willing to serve. A life that is devoted to serving others (seeking the best for them) will attract and inspire followers. A man who seeks to serve the Lord by faithfully serving his family will have a wife and children who delight in following him and take joy in serving alongside him.

Our job as parents is to train up sons who seek to **serve** rather than seeking to **be served**.

A. Select verses from the list below, and use some or all of the following suggestions to help you study and better understand their meaning (easier verses are listed first, in italics):

1) Copy the passage.

2) Read it in several different translations of the Bible.

3) Read the passage and several of the verses before and after it to gain a better understanding of the context of the passage.

4) Rewrite the passage in your own words. What does it mean?

5) Record a specific way in which you can change your actions or attitudes based on the teaching of this passage.

6) Memorize the passage.

> *Psalm 116:16*
> *Proverbs 29:23*
> *Matthew 20:28*
> Luke 17:10
> Luke 22:26-27
> John 3:14-16
> Philippians 2:4-8
> Hebrews 13:1-3
>
> *(BIBLE / SPEECH)*

Beginner

B. Do a job today that someone else in your family usually does. Surprise them! *(HOME SKILLS)*

C. Read with your parents John 13:1-17. What did Jesus do for the disciples? What did he tell the disciples they should do? What should we do if we are going to follow Jesus' example? Draw a picture to illustrate this story. *(BIBLE / DRAMA)*

D. Give your mother a foot rub at the end of the day. Bring her a glass of water or a cup of tea. Rub some lotion on her feet and massage them. When you are all done, put some nice warm socks on her feet. *(FAMILY)*

E. Ask your mother to show you how to polish a pair of your father's shoes. Shine them up and put them where he will find them next time he wants to wear them. Clean up after yourself. *(FAMILY)*

F. Help your brother or sister clean his/her room. *(FAMILY / HOME SKILLS)*

G. Devote a day to serving your father in every way you can. *(FAMILY)*

H. Devote a day to serving your mother in every way you can. *(FAMILY)*

I. Devote a day to serving your brother(s) in every way you can. If you have more than one brother, spend one day serving each. *(FAMILY)*

J. Devote a day to serving your sister(s) in every way you can. If you have more than one sister, spend one day serving each. *(FAMILY)*

K. Devote a day to serving your grandparents. If they do not live with you, go to their home and do all you can to help them. *(FAMILY)*

L. Read with your parents Luke 22:24-27. What were the disciples talking about? What did Jesus say to them? If we want to be the greatest, what does Jesus say we need to be? How does this work? Discuss this with your parents. *(BIBLE)*

M. Ask someone to help you today by writing down each time **you** serve someone else, and each time **someone else** serves you. How well did you do as a servant?

N. Prepare a special treat and serve it to everyone in the family room. Have a good movie ready to watch together while everyone enjoys your treat. *(FAMILY)*

Intermediate

O. Declare one day "Servant's Day" in your home. Do all you can to serve your family. *(FAMILY)*

P. Be "Mr. Fix-It" for a day! Do what minor repairs you can throughout the house, and have your siblings bring you broken toys for repair. *(HOME SKILLS / CARPENTRY)*

Q. Make a list of all the ways you can help others in your home. Make separate lists for each of these groups of people:

Father
Mother
Brothers
Sisters
Grandparents
(FAMILY / HOME SKILLS)

R. Make a list of ways to serve guests who come to your home. *(WRITING / MANNERS)*

S. Offer your services today (or on a regular basis) to:

A family with young children
A family with an ill or disabled parent
An elderly couple, widow or widower
(COMMUNITY SERVICE / HOME SKILLS / READING / P.E. / WRITING / ETC.)

T. Ask a deacon in your church for a regular job you can perform in order to serve your church body. *(COMMUNITY SERVICE)*

U. Study Philippians 2:5-11. List each thing Jesus did. Notice the "therefore" at the beginning of verse 9. What did God do? Why? How will Jesus be exalted? How do these verses relate to what Jesus said in Matthew 23:10-12? Write a paper on these verses and how they relate to your life. *(BIBLE / ENGLISH COMPOSITION)*

V. Write your own paraphrase of Philippians 2:3-11. *(BIBLE / VOCABULARY / WRITING)*

W. Study Jesus' example as a servant. Read through one or more of the Gospels and list each incident, the Bible reference, how He served, and what we can learn from His example. (Use the form on page 436.) *(BIBLE / RESEARCH / WRITING)*

X. Find all the names the Bible gives to God the Father and to Jesus. Write down each name and its Bible reference. Many of these titles denote a position that demands our reverence and obeisance (i.e., Master, King of kings). Circle each of these names. Review this list when you are tempted to want others to serve you. When we serve others we are serving our Lord! (To get started, you can look up "Jesus, the Christ: Names, Appellations and Titles of" in *Nave's Topical Bible*. You can also search online for "Names of God.") *(BIBLE / RESEARCH)*

Y. Study the lives of men and women in the Bible who cheerfully and faithfully served others. (Look under "Servant, Instances of Good" in *Nave's Topical Bible* and think of other Bible stories you know.) Write down their names, what they did, the Bible references, and what you learn from their examples. (Use the form on page 437.) *(BIBLE / RESEARCH)*

Advanced

Z. Read *Humility,* by C. J. Mahaney. Outline the book as you read it. Then write an essay summarizing the book, and explaining what you will do as a result of reading it. *(READING / BIBLE)*

AA. Do a topical study on **serving**. What is it? What are the rewards of serving others? How can we serve others? etc. Write a paper summarizing your study. *(BIBLE / RESEARCH / VOCABULARY / ENGLISH COMPOSITION)*

BB. Survey at least 20 different young and adult children. What do they appreciate most about their fathers? After compiling all your data, study to see how many of the things involve the willingness of fathers to serve their family. Mark each of those items. *(SPEECH / FAMILY / WRITING)*

CC. Complete the study "Serve Others" in Chapter 2 of *Prepare Thy Work*, by Daniel Forster. *(BIBLE / RESEARCH)*

DD. Study Colossians 3:24. What is the "inheritance" that we will receive as our reward for working heartily while we serve the Lord? Read commentaries on this verse and the verses around it. Then write a paper expounding on the meaning and application of the verse. *(BIBLE / ENGLISH COMPOSITION)*

EE. Study the Gospel of Mark. How does it portray Jesus as a servant? Note each time Jesus serves someone else. Write a paper to summarize your observations. *(BIBLE / RESEARCH / ENGLISH COMPOSITION)*

FF. Fill out the "Service Involvement" form on page 438. Based on your answers, do you think you need to become more involved in serving others? In what specific ways will you start to serve more? *(FAMILY / COMMUNITY SERVICE)*

GG. Read and meditate on Mary's response to the angel's message in Luke 1:38. Write a paper entitled "I Am His Servant." *(ENGLISH COMPOSITION)*

HH. Read Chapter 15, "Discipline of Ministry," and Chapter 18, "Discipline of Leadership," in *Disciplines of a Godly Man,* by R. Kent Hughes. Complete the "Food for Thought," "Application/Response," and "Think About It!" sections at the end of both chapters. *(READING / BIBLE)*

II. Read Chapter 13, "A Husband's Resolve: Humility and Service," in *The Exemplary Husband,* by Stuart Scott. Does your life exhibit any of the manifestations of pride listed in this chapter? Does it exhibit any of the manifestations of humility? What changes do you, with God's help, need to make? *(READING / CHARACTER TRAINING)*

JJ. Study Section I, "Usefulness in the Church" and Section J, "Usefulness in the Home," questions 1 and 3 (pages 188-192) in *A Homework Manual for Biblical Living, Volume 1*, by Wayne Mack. *(BIBLE / FAMILY / SOCIAL SKILLS)*

Additional ideas:

Jesus as a Servant

(See instructions in Project W.)

INCIDENT	REF.	HOW HE SERVED	WHAT I CAN LEARN

Servants in the Bible

(See instructions in Project Y.)

PERSON	REF.	HOW HE SERVED	WHAT I CAN LEARN

Service Involvement

(See instructions in Project FF.)

Type of Service _____ **If Involved_____ Approx. Hrs. / Month____**

1. Helping father in his occupation _____

2. Helping father with household duties, repairs, maintenance _____

3. Helping father with yardwork, livestock, garden, etc. _____

4. Helping mother with household duties, shopping, cleaning, cooking, etc. _____

5. Helping care for younger siblings (bathing, dressing, baby-sitting, etc.) _____

6. Helping with homeschooling (teaching, correcting, recordkeeping, etc.)_____

7. Visiting and caring for grandparents _____

8. Extending hospitality (and helping host)_____

9. Writing letters and cards of encouragement_____

10. Helping with music _____

11. Visiting people in nursing homes_____

12. Corresponding with missionaries _____

13. Ministering to families in need of help_____

14. Ministering to widows _____

15. Ministering to orphans and fatherless _____

16. Ministering to the sick _____

17. Ministering in nursing homes _____

18. Helping with children's work in church or homeschool support group _____

19. Teaching Sunday School: _____

20. Helping with church library _____

21. Helping with church camps _____

22. Counseling others _____

23. Helping in church nursery _____

24. Helping in other church tasks (ushering, cleaning, mailing, carpentry, etc.) _____

Parents:

Consider and discuss with your son the following questions:

- Does he desire to serve others like Jesus did?

- Does his love for the Savior motivate him to serve others?

- Does he view his purpose in life as gaining all he can for himself or of serving others in any way he can?

- Does he view others as more important than himself?

- Does he seek to give more than he receives?

- Does he look for ways to help others?

- Does he take initiative when he sees a need?

- Does he use the abilities and talents God has given him to help him serve others better?

- Does he resent doing "more than his share"?

- Does he serve with a cheerful attitude or does he complain?

- Does he take joy and satisfaction in serving others?

- Does he serve with a humble spirit, or does he seek the praise of others?

- Does he acknowledge and show gratefulness to those who serve him?

Notes and comments:

Giving Up Our Own Desires

"He that findeth his life shall lose it: and he that loseth his life for my sake shall find it" (Matthew 10:39).

Jesus said we must deny ourselves if we are going to follow Him. The godly man must give up his own desires in order to obey his Lord. A husband and father must frequently give up his own desires in order to better serve his family. An employee must deny his own pleasures to faithfully serve his employer.

Our purpose in life is to do the **Father's** will, not our own. By faithfully training our son to obey us without question, we teach him to honor our will over his own. This in turn will train him to honor God's will above all others.

A. Select verses from the list below, and use some or all of the following suggestions to help you study and better understand their meaning (easier verses are listed first, in italics):

1) Copy the passage.

2) Read it in several different translations of the Bible.

3) Read the passage and several of the verses before and after it to gain a better understanding of the context of the passage.

4) Rewrite the passage in your own words. What does it mean?

5) Record a specific way in which you can change your actions or attitudes based on the teaching of this passage.

6) Memorize the passage.

> *John 6:38*
> *1 Corinthians 10:24*
> *Philippians 2:4*
> Matthew 7:21
> Matthew 10:37-39
> Matthew 16:24
> Matthew 21:28-31
> Mark 3:35
> Galatians 2:20
> 2 Timothy 2:21
> 1 John 3:16
>
> *(SPEECH / BIBLE)*

Beginner

B. When you play today, let your playmates choose the activity. What would they like to do? Seek to please them (unless their wishes violate the teaching of your parents and Scripture). *(MANNERS)*

C. Read with your parents John 12:24-25. What does this passage mean? Plant some seeds in a small pot or milk carton. Water them and place the pot in a sunny window. What happens to these seeds that you buried? What happens to us when we are willing to die to our own desires? *(GARDENING / BIBLE)*

D. Read with your parents Genesis 13. Tell the story back to your parents. What was Abraham doing? How did he decide what land to have? Read Genesis 14. What happened to Lot in the land he chose? *(BIBLE / SPEECH)*

E. Read with your parents 1 Kings 21. What did Ahab want? Why? How did he respond when Naboth refused to sell to him? Was he willing to give up what he wanted? What did his wife Jezebel do next? What did the prophet Elijah say would happen to Ahab and Jezebel? Read 1 Kings 22:29-40. What happened to Ahab? Read 2 Kings 9:30-37. What happened to Jezebel? *(BIBLE)*

F. Proclaim one person in your family to be "Lord-for-the-Day." Let him decide what to eat, what to play, what to read, etc. throughout the day. Give up your own wishes in order to fulfill the wishes of your "lord." *(FAMILY / MANNERS)*

G. Tell or write a story about a child who always got his own way. Make sure you demonstrate biblical principles! *(SPEECH / WRITING)*

H. Read with your parents 1 Kings 17:8-24. Draw a picture to illustrate this story. What did Elijah ask of the woman? What was she about to do when he met her? What happened when she was willing to give up what she had in order to give it to Elijah? What happened later to her and her son? *(BIBLE / ART)*

I. Serve everyone else first at meals today. If you divide something in half, let the other person choose which half he would like *(MANNERS)*

Intermediate

J. Observe your father for a day. Write down every time you see him give up his own personal desires in order to serve God and his family more faithfully.
(FAMILY)

K. Join a sports or ministry team or serve on a group project together with your family. Give up your own desires for the harmony and effectiveness of the team. *(P.E.)*

L. If you take any kind of lessons -- music, ballet, sport or art lessons – practice today without any reminders. Learn to give up your own wishes in order to practice on a regular, disciplined basis. *(MUSIC / P.E. / ART)*

M. Study Christ's example of self-denial. List each reference and explain how He was denying himself. Then, next to each example, write down ideas of how you can follow His example in your own life. Look up "Jesus, the Christ: Example, An" in *Nave's Topical Bible* for a few references to get you started. (Use the form on page 447.) *(BIBLE / RESEARCH / WRITING)*

N. Read all the passages in the Bible that tell of Jesus calling the disciples. What was each of them doing? What did they give up to follow Jesus? Write an essay about their sacrifices and what you have learned from their examples. *(BIBLE / ENGLISH COMPOSITION)*

O. Study examples of people in the Bible who gave up their own desires. List each person, his actions, the Bible reference, and the results of his self-denial. Look up "Self-Denial, Instances of" in *Nave's Topical Bible*. (Use the form on page 448.) *(BIBLE / RESEARCH / WRITING)*

P. Study examples of people in the Bible who were unwilling to give up what they wanted, thinking only of themselves. List each person, his actions, the Bible reference, and the results of his self-centeredness. See "Covetousness, Instances of" in *Nave's Topical Bible* and "Selfishness/Greed" in *For Instruction in Righteousness,* by Pam Forster. (Use the form on page 449.) *(BIBLE / RESEARCH / WRITING)*

Q. Watch a baby or very young child for a period of time. How often do they fuss and cry when they are unwilling to give up their own desires? How do his parents teach him to submit to their desires? Take notes! *(FAMILY)*

R. Spend time in prayer and Bible study each day, seeking to discern God's desires for your life, and to align your desires with His. *(BIBLE / DEVOTIONS)*

S. Study *The Call to Follow Jesus,* Kay Arthur's inductive study on the book of Luke. *(BIBLE)*

T. Study the topic of **self-denial**. What does it mean? What does it require? What are its results? Write a short essay summarizing your study. *(BIBLE / RESEARCH / VOCABULARY / ENGLISH COMPOSITION)*

U. Study the topic of **peacemaking**. What is it? How does one make peace? What are the rewards of peacemaking? How does peacemaking relate to willingness to give up our own desires? Write a summary of your study. *(BIBLE / RESEARCH / VOCABULARY / WRITING)*

V. What were Jesus' teachings about denying one's self? Write out each verse that you can find. Insert, where appropriate, your name or the personal pronouns, "I," "me," "myself," etc. Read each verse aloud. *(BIBLE / RESEARCH / WRITING)*

W. Memorize several of the verses you listed on self-denial in the previous project. *(BIBLE / SPEECH)*

Advanced

X. Study the meaning of the phrase, "take up your cross." How does our crucifixion with Christ affect our need to deny ourselves? Write a summary of your study. *(BIBLE / VOCABULARY / WRITING)*

Y. Study in Jesus' prayer the phrase "not my will, but thine, be done" (Luke 22:42). Study other times in His life when Jesus speaks of doing the will of His Father. What does He mean? List Jesus' actions that demonstrate His willingness to perform the Father's will. *(BIBLE / RESEARCH / WRITING)*

Z. Study the parable of the two sons in Matthew 21:28-31. What do you learn from this story about self-denial and doing the Father's will? Write your own parable that illustrates the same principle. *(BIBLE / ENGLISH COMPOSITION)*

AA. Pray and fast as a means of giving up your own pleasure while seeking the will of your Heavenly Father. *(HEALTH)*

BB. Study the word **lord** as it is used in the Bible. What does the word mean? How is it used? Is Jesus your Lord? What do you need to change to be a better follower of Jesus? *(BIBLE / VOCABULARY / FOREIGN LANGUAGE)*

CC. Read Matthew 16:24-26. After studying the passage and reading commentaries on it, write your own paraphrase of the verses. *(BIBLE / WRITING)*

DD. Study Isaiah 58:13-14. What does this passage say about giving up our own pleasure? What is the reward for honoring God's will for us on His day of rest? Write a short paper on the relationship between submitting to God and His will for us and honoring the Lord's Day. *(BIBLE / ENGLISH COMPOSITION)*

EE. Read Chapter 14, "Exchange: My Life for His," in *Discipline: The Glad Surrender,* by Elisabeth Elliot. Write a short essay explaining the following quote:

"The goal of the cook – a perfect dessert – will not be attained without her first giving up her 'right' to do it her way, then studying the book and doing exactly what it says. When I am the cook, I surrender easily and happily to a pastry recipe by M. F. K. Fisher. I take her word for it that if I do this, I will end up with that." *(READING / ENGLISH COMPOSITION)*

FF. Do a Bible study on what it means when God "gives us up to our own desires." Write a short essay explaining this passage. *(BIBLE / RESEARCH / WRITING)*

GG. Read Chapter 4, "The Discipline of Fatherhood," in *Disciplines of a Godly Man,* by R. Kent Hughes. List the "Do Nots" and the "Do's" of fathering. Complete the "Food for Thought," "Application/Response," and "Think About It!" sections at the end of the chapter. *(FAMILY)*

HH. Read Psalm 37:4. What will God give us if we delight in Him? How does this relate to the call to deny ourselves when we follow Jesus? Read commentaries on this verse, and write a paper about the relationship between Psalm 37:4 and Mark 8:34-37. *(BIBLE / ENGLISH COMPOSITION)*

II. Read through the following points, quoted from *The Rare Jewel of Christian Contentment,* by Jeremiah Burroughs, on self-denial as taught by Jesus. Find Scripture passages to support each statement.

1. A person who denies himself learns to know that he is nothing.
2. I deserve nothing.
3. I can do nothing without Christ.
4. I am so vile that I cannot of myself receive any good.
5. We can make use of nothing when we have it, if God but withdraws Himself.
6. We are worse than nothing. By sin we become worse than nothing.
7. If we perish we will be no loss. God can raise up someone else in my place.

(BIBLE / RESEARCH / WRITING)

JJ. Read the *Golden Booklet of the True Christian Life,* by John Calvin. Take time to read each of the Scripture verses to which he refers. Write down notes on all that you learn about self-denial. Then write down specific ways to implement these new thoughts. *(BIBLE / READING)*

KK. Read *A Quest for More: Living for Something Bigger Than You,* by Paul David Tripp. Discuss with your father or with a friend how this book will change your life. What will you do differently as a result of reading this book? *(READING)*

Additional ideas:

Jesus' Example of Self-Denial

(See instructions in Project M.)

INCIDENT	REF.	HOW JESUS DENIED HIMSELF	WHAT I CAN LEARN

Self-Denial in the Bible

(See instructions in Project O.)

PERSON	ACTIONS	REF.	RESULTS

Self-Centeredness in the Bible

(See instructions in Project P.)

PERSON	ACTIONS	REF.	RESULTS

Parents:

Consider and discuss the following questions with your son:

- Does he recognize God as Lord of his life?

- Does he deeply desire to understand and fulfill God's desires for his life?

- Does he acknowledge that God's will is more important than his own selfish desires?

- Does he study God's Word in order to bring his desires into agreement with God's desires?

- Is he willing to deny his own desires in order to please and obey God?

- Is he willing to deny his own pleasures in order to minister to others?

- Is he willing to give up his desires in order to let others have their way?

- Does he want everybody to do what he wants when playing or working together?

- Is he often anxious about getting "his share" of something?

- Does he often argue with others in order to protect his "rights"?

- Is he willing to set aside immediate desires for future goals?

- Does he set aside his own desires in order to make peace?

- Does he set aside his own desires to properly honor God's day of rest?

Notes and comments:

Showing Patience and Forgiveness

"Looking diligently lest any man fail of the grace of God; lest any root of bitterness springing up trouble you, and thereby many be defiled" (Hebrews 12:15).

Life is full of opportunities to forgive! Just as we must constantly be seeking and accepting God's forgiveness for our sinful actions and attitudes, we must also be ready and willing to forgive the sins of others.

The family provides the perfect laboratory for learning obedience in this important area. If our sons learn to biblically reconcile their differences with others at home, they will be prepared to maintain healthy relationships with their wives, their children, their extended families, their fellow workers, and their brothers and sisters in Christ.

Bitterness cripples; to forgive as Christ forgives brings healing, growth, and blessing.

A. Select verses from the list below, and use some or all of the following suggestions to help you study and better understand their meaning (easier verses are listed first, in italics):

1) Copy the passage.

2) Read it in several different translations of the Bible.

3) Read the passage and several of the verses before and after it to gain a better understanding of the context of the passage.

4) Rewrite the passage in your own words. What does it mean?

5) Record a specific way in which you can change your actions or attitudes based on the teaching of this passage.

6) Memorize the passage.

Psalm 103:13
Psalm 120:1
Psalm 133:1
Proverbs 19:11
Psalm 119:23
Proverbs 25:21-22
Matthew 5:39-48
Matthew 6:14-15
Luke 6:36-37

Luke 11:4
Luke 17:3-4
Romans 12:17-21
Ephesians 4:31-32
Colossians 3:13
Hebrews 12:15

(BIBLE / SPEECH)

Beginner

B. Read with your parents Luke 23:32-34. What was happening to Jesus? What did Jesus say while it was happening? If Jesus could say this, can you forgive people for the wrongs they commit against you? Draw a picture to illustrate this story. *(BIBLE / ART)*

C. Read with your parents Luke 15:11-24. Narrate the story back to your parents. Who was sinning? What did he do wrong? Who was watching for him when he returned? What did the son say when he returned? How did the father demonstrate his forgiveness? Draw a comic strip to illustrate different scenes from this story, or act the story out during your playtime. *(BIBLE / ART / DRAMA)*

D. Study with your family *The Brother-Offended Checklist.* Read the related Bible stories. Then memorize the basic steps outlined on the chart, and role play them with your family. Use these steps when you have a disagreement with someone. *(FAMILY / BIBLE / SOCIAL SKILLS)*

E. Read and discuss with your parents Matthew 5:39-42. Draw a series of pictures to illustrate these verses. *(BIBLE/ ART)*

F. Read with your parents 1 Corinthians 13:4-7 in an easy-to-understand translation. Repeat each phrase after it is read, replacing the word "charity" or "love" with your name or the word "I." Do these verses describe you? If no, what can you do so they do? *(BIBLE / WRITING / VOCABULARY)*

G. Learn how to ask forgiveness of someone you have wronged. Practice with a sibling. Say, "I was wrong for _____. Will you please forgive me?" *(SOCIAL SKILLS / MANNERS)*

H. Learn how to grant forgiveness to someone who asks you to forgive them. Practice with a sibling. Say, "Thank you for asking. Yes, I forgive you." *(SOCIAL SKILLS / MANNERS)*

Intermediate

I. Keep a journal in which you note times when you become irritated and impatient with others. Using the form on page 457, record the situation in which you were irritated, the people involved, and how you expressed your annoyance, and what Scriptural principle you violated. Do you see any circumstances that are particularly troublesome for you? What can you do and think to become more patient at these times? *(WRITING / BIBLE / SOCIAL SKILLS)*

J. Study with your family the following chapters in *For Instruction in Righteousness,* by Pam Forster:

Revenge
Impatience
Bitterness
Hatred

(BIBLE)

K. Study Chapter 22, "What Should I Know About Offenses?" in *Christian Manhood,* by Gary Maldaner. *(BIBLE)*

L. Study Psalm 37:1-9. List each thing the psalmist says we are **not** to do, and the reasons why. List each thing we **should** do, and what he says the results will be. Memorize this psalm. *(BIBLE)*

M. Study *The Young Peacemaker,* by Corlette Sande, with your parents. Complete the activities and memorize the verse at the end of each chapter. *(SOCIAL SKILLS / BIBLE)*

N. Read the verses under the heading, "Patience," in *Nave's Topical Bible.* What commands are given? What promises are given? Note any other observations as you read. Then write an essay summarizing what the verses tell us about patience. *(BIBLE / ENGLISH COMPOSITION)*

O. Interview adults, asking them to tell you stories of times in their lives when they chose to be bitter against someone and times when they chose to forgive. Compare the endings of each story. Which ones are best? *(SPEECH)*

P. Read Romans 12:19. Think of examples from your own life of times when you resisted the temptation to take revenge on someone who had wronged you, and God then clearly punished the person for his wrongdoing. Tell this story to your family during dinner. *(BIBLE / SPEECH)*

Q. Study Matthew 5:43-44. When faced with an enemy (or someone with whom you have a disagreement):

- Write down specific ways to **bless** him. What kind words can you say to him?
- Write down specific ways to **do good** to him. What kind actions can you take on his behalf?
- **Pray** for him. Write down some of your prayers. Pray for God to change your heart toward him.

(BIBLE / SOCIAL SKILLS / WRITING)

R. Read the Gospels, noting all the examples of Jesus' forgiveness of those who wronged Him. Write down the Bible reference, how He was wronged, how he responded, and what you can learn from His example. (Use the form on page 458.) *(BIBLE / WRITING / RESEARCH)*

S. Find examples in the Bible of people who forgave others. List each person, the Bible references, how they were wronged, how they forgave, and what the results were. (Look up "Forgiveness, Instances of" in *Nave's Topical Bible*.) (Use the form on page 459.) *(BIBLE / WRITING / RESEARCH)*

T. Find examples in the Bible of people who were bitter or took revenge. List each person, the Bible references, how they were wronged, how they demonstrated their bitterness, and what the results were. Look up the chapters on "Bitterness" and "Revenge" in *For Instruction in Righteousness,* by Pam Forster, look up "revenge," "retaliation," and "vengeance" in *Nave's Topical Bible,* and/or think of other Bible stories you know. (Use the form on page 460.) *(BIBLE / WRITING / RESEARCH)*

U. Read of David's life in 1 and 2 Samuel. List each example of his forgiving spirit and reliance on God to avenge the evildoer. List the Bible reference, the wrong committed against him, his response, and the results. (Use the form on page 461.) *(BIBLE / RESEARCH / WRITING)*

V. After studying 1 Peter 2:20-24, write your own paraphrase of the passage. What did Jesus do instead of trying to get even with those who were sinning against Him? *(BIBLE / WRITING / VOCABULARY)*

W. Complete the study *Forgiveness: Breaking the Power of the Past,* by Kay Arthur and BJ and David Lawson. *(READING)*

Advanced

X. Read and study Romans 12:20. What does it mean to "heap coals of fire" on someone's head? List some specific ways you can "feed" and "give drink" to your enemies and those who have offended you. *(BIBLE)*

Y. Study the Sermon on the Mount in chapters 5 through 7 of Matthew. List and summarize each verse that teaches us something about the treatment of enemies and those who wrong us. Then write down a specific way that you can apply each truth in your daily life. *(BIBLE / WRITING)*

Z. Scripture tells us to forgive others in the same way that God has forgiven us. What has God forgiven in your life? Are you showing mercy to others in the same way He has shown mercy to you? Make a list of people you need to forgive. Ask God to help you forgive them, and go to those people, confessing your bitterness and asking their forgiveness. *(WRITING)*

AA. Study the parable of the debtor in Matthew 18:21-35. What does it teach about forgiveness? Write a paper explaining the meaning of this parable and its application to your life. *(BIBLE / ENGLISH COMPOSITION)*

BB. Read the Psalms, making a list of verses that express David's forgiving attitude toward those who wronged him and his trust in God to avenge the evil doer. Memorize some of these verses. *(BIBLE / WRITING / RESEARCH)*

CC. Find examples in the Bible of God's intervention for people who chose not to take revenge against the wrongdoings of others. List the incident, the Bible reference, how the person was wronged, how he responded, and what God did to punish the wrongdoer. (Use the form on page 462.) *(BIBLE / WRITING / RESEARCH)*

DD. Read the verses listed under "God, Judge and His Justice," in *Nave's Topical Bible.* Take notes. If God is a just God and a wise, all-knowing God, can we trust Him to judge perfectly? Do we need to take revenge against wrongdoers? Do we know everything that God knows about the situation? *(BIBLE / RESEARCH)*

EE. Do topical or word studies on the following subjects, writing a short summary of your studies, and explaining how you will apply your insights to everyday life.

Forbearance
Long-suffering
Forgiveness
(BIBLE / VOCABULARY / RESEARCH / WRITING)

FF. Read *How to Be Free from Bitterness,* by Jim Wilson, completing the study guide at the end of each chapter. Has this book revealed any areas of bitterness in your life? What will you do about it? *(READING)*

GG. Think of a person you know who is bitter. What fruits do you see in his life? Then think of a cheerful, forgiving person you know. What fruits do you see in his life? Compare the end results of these two contrasting outlooks. Then find Scripture verses that explain these results. *(BIBLE / RESEARCH)*

HH. Write an essay entitled "What I Have Gained by Holding a Grudge." *(ENGLISH COMPOSITION)*

II. Write an essay entitled "What I Have Gained by Forgiving a Wrong." *(ENGLISH COMPOSITION)*

JJ. Read Chapter 9, "Forgiveness," in *Relationships: A Mess Worth Making,* by Timothy Lane and Paul David Tripp. How does the author define forgiveness? What is the difference between an apology and asking forgiveness? Read the rest of the book if you haven't already done so. *(READING / SOCIAL SKILLS)*

KK. Read *The Peacemaker,* by Ken Sande. Use the application questions to help you apply what you have learned. Use Appendix A, "A Peacemaker's Checklist," to guide you as you resolve relational problems. Use what you have learned from this book to nurture healthy, godly relationships with your family and friends. *(BIBLE / READING / SOCIAL SKILLS)*

LL. Read Appendix 9, "Defining 'Love Covers,' 'Love Conceals,' and 'Overlooking a Transgression,'" in *Exemplary Husband,* by Stuart Scott. Compare the three phrases in a short essay. *(READING / BIBLE / WRITING)*

MM. Write an essay explaining Hebrews 12:15. Read different translations of the verse, and use commentaries and word studies to help you better understand its meaning. *(BIBLE / ENGLISH COMPOSITION)*

NN. Study the sections on "Interpersonal Relationships" and "Healing Broken Relationships" in *A Homework Manual for Biblical Living, Vol. 1,* by Wayne Mack. *(BIBLE / WRITING)*

OO. Read in Thomas Watson's *The Lord's Prayer*, the chapter on the fifth petition "as we forgive them that trespass against us." Outline its basic content, and note particular thoughts that you would like to implement in your life. *(READING / BIBLE / WRITING)*

PP. Read *From Forgiven to Forgiving*, by Jay Adams. Outline its main points, and put its principles into action. (Highly recommended!) *(READING / SOCIAL SKILLS / BIBLE / WRITING)*

Additional ideas:

"Impatience Journal"

(See instructions in Project I.)

SITUATION	PEOPLE INVOLVED	HOW I EXPRESSED ANNOYANCE	SCRIPTURE PRINCIPLES I VIOLATED

Jesus' Forgiveness

(See instructions in Project R.)

REF.	HOW HE WAS WRONGED	HIS RESPONSE	WHAT I CAN LEARN

Forgiveness in the Bible

(See instructions in Project S.)

PERSON	REF.	HOW THEY WERE WRONGED	HOW THEY FORGAVE	RESULTS

Bitterness in the Bible

(See instructions in Project T.)

PERSON	REF.	HOW THEY WERE WRONGED	HOW THEY SHOWED BITTERNESS	RESULTS

David's Forgiving Spirit

(See instructions in Project U.)

REF.	WRONG COMMITTED	HIS RESPONSES	RESULTS

God's Revenge

(See instructions in Project CC.)

INCIDENT	REF.	HOW PERSON WAS WRONGED	HIS RESPONSE	GOD'S RESPONSE TO EVILDOER

Parents:

Consider and discuss with your son the following questions:

- Is he willing to overlook the sins of others, recognizing that they do the same for him?

- Does he look for the positive traits in people or does he focus on the negative?

- Is he quick to forgive when asked?

- Is he willing to forgive a wrongdoer, even if the offender does not repent or ask forgiveness?

- Does he trust God with the outcome of wrongs committed against him?

- Does he listen carefully when rebuked or criticized and humbly examine his heart?

- When relational problems arise does he examine his own heart to see where he is at fault?

- When problems arise between him and others does he seek to change his own behavior, attitudes, and responses?

- Does he humbly repent and ask forgiveness of those he sins against?

- Is he quick to humbly repent to those he wrongs in your household?

- Does he grumble and gossip about wrongs committed against him?

- Does he resent and carry a grudge against someone who has offended him?

- Does he desire to restore a broken relationship?

- Does he desire peace and reconciliation or does he desire revenge?

- Is he willing to approach a person when he has been offended?

- Does he know when and how to bring up a disagreement in a gentle, non-combative way?

- Does he approach an offender quickly and prayerfully, or does he allow problems to "brew" and intensify?

- Does he follow the biblical steps outlined in Matthew 18 when approaching someone who has wronged him?

- Is he willing to approach a person more than once over an offense that needs resolving?

- Is he willing to trust God to punish a wrongdoer, or does he "take the law into his own hands"?

- Does he forgive and forget, or does he keep bringing up past offenses to the offended, to others, and to himself?

Notes and comments:

Sharing the Gospel

"And he saith unto them, 'Follow me, and I will make you fishers of men'" (Matthew 4:19).

We are commanded in Scripture to go into all the world and preach the gospel. Our first obligation is to our own family members. We want to make the gospel perfectly clear to our children, leading them to a saving knowledge of the Savior. We must then teach our saved children to have compassion for an unsaved world.

We can make them aware of and involved in foreign missions, but we also need to set an example for them as we reach out to our unsaved friends and neighbors. We must help them learn how to explain the gospel to others. We must train them so that they become "lights on a hill" in a dark world.

A. Select verses from the list below, and use some or all of the following suggestions to help you study and better understand their meaning (easier verses are listed first, in italics):

1) Copy the passage.

2) Read it in several different translations of the Bible.

3) Read the passage and several of the verses before and after it to gain a better understanding of the context of the passage.

4) Rewrite the passage in your own words. What does it mean?

5) Record a specific way in which you can change your actions or attitudes based on the teaching of this passage.

6) Memorize the passage.

> *Matthew 4:19*
> *Matthew 10:32*
> *Mark 16:15*
> Isaiah 55:11
> Matthew 28:19-20
> Luke 10:2
> John 4:35-37
> Acts 1:8
> Romans 10:13-15
> 2 Corinthians 6:2
> 1 Peter 3:15

1 John 5:10-12
(BIBLE / SPEECH)

At Home:

Beginner

B. Read with your parents Part 9, "How We Become Children of God," in *Leading Little Ones to God,* by Marian Schoolland. *(BIBLE / READING)*

C. Tell your parents how someone becomes a Christian. *(BIBLE / DOCTRINE)*

D. Use flannelgraph or your own illustrations to tell your siblings or young neighborhood children the story of Jesus' birth, life, crucifixion, resurrection and ascension. *(SPEECH / BIBLE / ART)*

E. Read and discuss with your parents the answers to Questions 21-59 in *The Catechism for Young Children with Cartoons,* by Vic Lockman. Memorize these questions and answers if you can.

F. Pray for the salvation of unbelieving friends and family members. Make a list in your prayer notebook. *(WRITING)*

Intermediate

G. Memorize verses that you would like to share when talking with someone about the Gospel and salvation. *(BIBLE / SPEECH)*

H. List at least five people you know who are unsaved. Pray for opportunities to show kindness and love to them, and for courage and opportunities to share the Gospel with them within the next two weeks.

I. Look over your list of people from project H. Think of common interests that you share or could learn to share with each person. Write them down next to each name. Make specific plans to start cultivating these common interests, using them as a "bridge" to gain each person's confidence and to give you opportunity to share Christ with them. *(WRITING / SOCIAL SKILLS)*

J. List the ways you make contact with non-Christian people (i.e. baseball team, your job at a fast-food restaurant). List at least one person from each of these places for whom you can begin to pray. Then list other ways that will help you come into contact with unbelievers. *(WRITING)*

K. Write your Christian testimony. How did you become a Christian? How has Jesus changed your life? Try to write something that isn't too "preachy" that you could share with someone in three minutes or less. *(WRITING)*

L. Outline a short series of verses that explain the way of salvation. Find a verse for each of the following points of the Gospel. Write out the verses and memorize them.

- All have sinned:
- The penalty for sin:
- Christ paid the penalty:
- We are saved by grace alone:
- We must receive Christ:
- Assurance of salvation:

(BIBLE / RESEARCH / WRITING)

M. Role-play the following situations with your family:

- Start a casual conversation with a stranger on a bus. Ask general questions or respond to their initial comments in a friendly way that leads to more conversation. Take advantage of opportunities to non-aggressively turn the conversation to spiritual matters.

- Answer the questions of a friend who has asked you why your life is different, why you seem so happy and peaceful.

- Lead an interested person through Scripture verses that explain how to become a Christian.

- Lead an interested person in praying a prayer of confession and acceptance of Christ as their Lord and Savior.

- Answer a skeptical unbeliever's questions about the gospel and Christianity.

(DRAMA / BIBLE / SPEECH)

N. Start a Bible club for children in your neighborhood. *(TEACHING / BIBLE / SPEECH)*

O. Study Jesus' example of evangelism. How did He tell others about Himself? How did he guide people to the point of repentance? Write down each incident, the Bible reference, what Jesus did and said, the results, and what we can learn from each example. (Use the form on page 474.) *(BIBLE / RESEARCH / WRITING)*

Advanced

P. Read *Don't Waste Your Life,* by John Piper. Use the free online study guide (at *http://www.desiringgod.org/media/pdf/books_dwyl/sgdwl_full.pdf*) to guide your daily reading and meditation on the message of this book. Or use the guide for study group discussion. *(READING)*

Q. List specific ways you can help a new believer grow in his Christian life. *(WRITING)*

R. Commit to establishing a growing acquaintance with one unbeliever. Take advantage of opportunities to make contact with him, and pray for opportunities to share the gospel with him. *(SOCIAL SKILLS)*

S. Write out the story of the gospel and how to become a Christian. Have a non-Christian acquaintance read it and evaluate how clearly you have explained the message of the gospel. Answer any questions your friend might have. *(ENGLISH COMPOSITION / BIBLE)*

T. Write out typical questions that skeptical unbelievers ask when approached with the gospel. (i.e., "How can God be a God of love when He allows so much pain and evil in the world?") Then think about Biblical answers you can give for each question. *(WRITING / BIBLE / RESEARCH)*

U. Read and study Chapters 6 through 18 in *The Westminster Confession of Faith.* Look online for a version with Scripture proofs, and read the verses. Explain to your father the following concepts:

The covenant of works

The covenant of grace

Christ as our mediator

Justification

Adoption

Sanctification

Perseverance of the saints

(DOCTRINE / BIBLE)

V. Read *Answers to Tough Questions,* by Josh McDowell to arm yourself with answers for skeptics. *(BIBLE / READING)*

W. Read Chapter 17, "Discipline of Witness," in *Disciplines of a Godly Man,* by R. Kent Hughes. Complete the "Food for Thought," "Application/Response," and "Think About It!" sections at the end of the chapter. *(READING)*

X. Find and list examples from the Bible of incidents when people met the physical needs of others before attempting to help them with their spiritual needs. Look at Isaiah, Paul, Peter, James and Jesus. *(BIBLE / RESEARCH / WRITING)*

Y. The Bible uses several different metaphors in reference to Christians. Read each metaphor and passage listed below and explain how we can be like each of these items.

- A fragrant aroma, 2 Corinthians 2:15
- A shining star, Philippians 2:15
- Light, Matthew 5:14
- A farmer, Matthew 13:1-43
- A bride, Ephesians 5:25-33
- A fisherman, Matthew 4:19
- Salt, Matthew 5:13
- A living letter that is read by all men, 2 Corinthians 3:2-3

(BIBLE / ENGLISH / WRITING / SCIENCE)

Z. Read *Evangelism and the Sovereignty of God,* by J. I. Packer. After reading and outlining the book, write a paper on the relationship between man's responsibility and God's sovereignty in reaching the unsaved with the gospel. *(READING / ENGLISH COMPOSITION)*

AA. Read *The Gospel and Personal Evangelism,* by Mark Dever. Discuss the book with your father or other Christian men. What is evangelism? Who should we evangelize? How should we evangelize? Why should we evangelize? How will this book affect your life? *(READING)*

BB. Read *Tell the Truth: The Whole Gospel to the Whole Person by Whole People,* by Will Metzger. What is the difference between man-centered and God-centered evangelism? How are evangelism and worship related to each other?

- If possible, start a study group with other young men, using the questions in Appendix C to direct your discussions.
- Study the training and role playing materials in Appendix A.
- Learn how to use the Gospel diagram, "Coming Home," in Appendix B.
- Practice sharing the gospel through the Bible stories listed in Section 3 of Appendix B.

(BIBLE / SPEECH)

CC. After reading all three of the above books on evangelism, write a review that compares them with each other. What are the strengths of each book? Which one did you find most helpful? How will each affect your thinking and actions? *(ENGLISH COMPOSITION)*

DD. Listen to Doug Wilson's *Biblical Evangelism* series of four lectures. Discuss what you hear with your father.

EE. Explore *www.mathiasmedia.com.au.* What materials could be helpful to you in your own life and in sharing the gospel with others?

- Study the "Two Ways to Live" presentation of the gospel, both for children and for adults. Practice using it with a family member.

- Note evangelistic studies you could use with an unbelieving friend or in a group study of unbelievers.

- Make a list of Bible study materials that you could use for your own study or for studying with a new believer.

- Listen to any audio materials that interest you.

(BIBLE / RESEARCH)

FF. Study with a new believer or with an unbeliever who is interested in the Bible *God, Are You There?,* by Kay Arthur. *(BIBLE)*

GG. Copy the headings for each chapter in this book. Next to each chapter title, write down how this area relates to being a good witness for Christ. Why is each area of character important in sharing the Gospel with unbelievers? *(WRITING)*

On the Mission Field:

Beginner

HH. Pray for a missionary family overseas. Listen to their prayer letters, put their picture up in your house, write letters of encouragement to them. *(READING / LETTER WRITING / GEOGRAPHY)*

II. Read with your parents Chapter 62, "God's Children Tell God's Story" in *Leading Little Ones to God,* by Marian Schoolland. *(BIBLE / READING)*

JJ. Read the book of Jonah with your parents. What did God tell Jonah to do? What did he do instead? What happened? What did Jonah do after he repented of his disobedience? What did Jonah do when God told him to go again? How did the people respond? Act this story out during your playtime, or draw a series of pictures to illustrate it. *(BIBLE / DRAMA / ART)*

KK. Pretend to be a missionary during your playtime. Make a house to live in, eat foreign food, share the gospel with your playmates. *(BIBLE / DRAMA / CONSTRUCTION)*

LL. Make extra money to help your family support a missionary family or a specific missionary project in another country. *(FINANCES)*

MM. Read missionary stories in the "Little Light" series by Catherine Mackenzie.

NN. Read *Missionary Stories with the Millers,* by Mildred Martin. *(READING / GEOGRAPHY)*

OO. With your family, read one chapter each week in *Operation World.* Find the country on a globe or world map, discuss the culture and spiritual needs of the people, and pray for the expansion of God's kingdom there. *(GEOGRAPHY)*

Intermediate

PP. Join your family (and possibly donate your room as a guest room) in hosting a missionary family who is home on furlough. Do all you can to make them at home, and learn all you can about the country where they serve, their ministry and their needs. *(GEOGRAPHY / SOCIAL SKILLS)*

QQ. Make a missionary bulletin board by posting a world map, and pinning up pictures of missionaries from different countries. Pray for a different family each day. Thank God for His answers to prayer. *(ART / GEOGRAPHY)*

RR. Write to the son of a missionary as a pen pal. Encourage him and find out how you can pray for him and help him in the work he and his family do. *(WRITING / SOCIAL SKILLS)*

SS. Ask a missionary to help connect you with an unbelieving boy with whom you can be a pen pal. Share your life with him. Tell him about Jesus. *(WRITING / SOCIAL SKILLS)*

TT. Earn and donate money to organizations that place Bibles in hotels, prisons, and foreign countries. *(FINANCES)*

UU. Read biographies of missionaries in the "Trailblazer Series."

VV. Read biographies of missionaries in YWAM's *Christian Heroes Then and Now* Series. Note the missionaries' prayer lives, their problems, their sacrifices, their means of presenting the gospel. *(HISTORY / READING)*

WW. Read several books and do other research in order to write a report on at least one missionary's life and ministry. *(READING / HISTORY / ENGLISH COMPOSITION)*

XX. Explore *www.operationworld.24-7prayer.com* to learn more about the needs of different countries throughout the world. *(GEOGRAPHY / SOCIAL STUDIES)*

YY. Read about Saul's conversion and calling in Acts 9. What did God say to Ananias when he was reluctant to go to Saul? *(BIBLE)*

ZZ. Read the verses under the heading "Mission" in *Nave's Topical Bible*. Take notes and write a short summary of what you learn from these verses. *(BIBLE)*

Advanced

AAA. Read biographies of missionaries throughout history. Take notes on different aspects of their lives and on how they recognized God's calling. *(READING / HISTORY)*

BBB. Explore *www.joshuaproject.net*. Pick at least one country to learn more about, using the information and resources available at this site. Share what you learn with your family at a meal time. *(RESEARCH / GEOGRAPHY)*

CCC. Read through the book of Acts.

- List the different men who were called to take the gospel to the Gentiles.
- Study Peter's sermon in Acts 2.
- List the miracles that occurred.
- Note the times when the Christians were called before authorities, arrested, or imprisoned, and how God worked in those circumstances.
- List the times when prayer is mentioned, and the answers to prayers.
- Study Stephen's speech.
- Note the occurrences of trials, persecution, and martyrdom.
- List the conversions that are mentioned.
- Look at a map that shows the missionary journeys of Paul.
- List each place Paul goes and what happens at each place.
- Study chapter 15's account of the Jerusalem Council.
- Study Paul's defense before Agrippa in chapter 26.

(BIBLE)

DDD. Host a foreign student in your home. As you befriend him, and as you consistently demonstrate before him a godly, self-sacrificing life, take advantage of opportunities to share the gospel with him. *(SOCIAL SKILLS)*

EEE. Pray daily for a missionary family. Email them with words of encouragement. Ask for specific ways to pray for them. If possible, go to visit and work with them. *(WRITING / MISSIONS)*

FFF. Read *From Jerusalem to Irian Jaya,* by Ruth Tucker, to gain a better understanding of the history of missionary work since the ministry of Paul. *(READING / HISTORY)*

GGG. Go with your family to serve with a missionary for a short period of time. Assist them in any way you can. *(MISSIONS / GEOGRAPHY)*

HHH. Travel to visit and work with a missionary that you and your family have been supporting and praying for over the years. Share your experience with your church family when you return. *(MISSIONS / GEOGRAPHY / SPEECH)*

III. Participate in a short-term missionary assignment in some other country. Study the language of the country before you go. *(FOREIGN LANGUAGE / GEOGRAPHY)*

Additional ideas:

Jesus' Evangelism

(See instructions in Project O.)

INCIDENT	REF.	WHAT JESUS DID & SAID	RESULTS	WHAT I CAN LEARN

Parents:

Consider and discuss with your son the following questions:

- Does he believe that Jesus died and rose again to pay for his sins?

- Has he chosen to make Jesus his Savior and Lord?

- Does he care about the lost souls around him?

- Does he truly believe that those who do not accept the Gospel are doomed to everlasting suffering in hell?

- Does he pray for unsaved friends and family?

- Does he pray for missionaries and for people who have never heard the gospel?

- Does he give some of his money to help the work of missionaries?

- Can he explain the basic elements of the Gospel?

- Can he take someone through key Scripture verses that explain the way of salvation?

- Does he tell others about his belief in Jesus?

- Does he take advantage of opportunities to share Christ with others?

- Does his life reflect a desire to obey God's commands?

- Is his life consistent with what he says about God and His Word?

Notes and comments:

Loving a Wife

"Husbands, love your wives, even as Christ also loved the church, and gave himself for it" (Ephesians 5:25).

The focus of this chapter is to help our son show true Christ-like love to his wife by remaining physically and emotionally pure throughout his youth. We should prepare him for his parents' involvement in the important decision of choosing a wife and helper. We must seek to protect him and his future happiness in marriage by helping him avoid the dangers and emotional pitfalls of youthful romance.

This can be accomplished if we reject the cultural practice of dating, and turn back to a biblical concept of courtship. This is a radical step for many, but one that can prepare our children for solid, life-long marriages. If the idea of parental involvement in the selection of a mate is new to you, read one or more of the many good books recommended in this chapter. They will help you see the wisdom in this approach.

We also want to help our son set standards for selecting his wife, and we want to help him discern when he is ready, with God's help, to protect and provide for a wife. If we have raised our sons to humbly submit to God's leading in his life, the period of preparation and courtship should be a rich time of blessing for the entire family.

A. Select verses from the list below, and use some or all of the following suggestions to help you study and better understand their meaning (easier verses are listed first, in italics):

1) Copy the passage.

2) Read it in several different translations of the Bible.

3) Read the passage and several of the verses before and after it to gain a better understanding of the context of the passage.

4) Rewrite the passage in your own words. What does it mean?

5) Record a specific way in which you can change your actions or attitudes based on the teaching of this passage.

6) Memorize the passage.

   Proverbs 18:22
   Romans 13:10

Genesis 2:23
1 Corinthians 7:1-5
1 Corinthians 11:3
1 Corinthians 13:1-8
Ephesians 5:22-33
Colossians 3:19-21
1 Peter 3:7
(BIBLE / SPEECH)

Beginner

B. Read with your parents the story of God creating Eve for Adam in Genesis 2. What did Adam say when he saw her? *(BIBLE)*

C. Pray regularly with your parents for the spiritual growth of the young girl who will someday become your wife. Pray, too, for the spiritual growth of the boy (you!) who will become her husband! *(FAMILY)*

D. Read with your parents *The Princess and the Kiss,* by Jenny Bishop. Talk with your parents about this story. *(READING)*

E. Read with your parents *The Squire and the Scroll,* by Jennie Bishop. Talk about this story with your parents. *(READING)*

F. Talk to your parents about their plans for helping you find a wife when you are ready. *(FAMILY)*

Intermediate

G. Study Ephesians 6:1-3. What do these verses say will happen when you obey and honor your father and mother? Keep a journal throughout your entire childhood and youth in which you record the many times that things "go well with thee" after you have chosen to honor the wishes of your parents. Review this list when you are tempted to question their judgment in matters of courtship and marriage. Trust God to lead you through their counsel. *(BIBLE / WRITING / FAMILY)*

H. Study 1 Corinthians 13:1-8. List each thing that this passage says love **does**. Then list everything the verses say love **does not do**. Next to each of these listings, write an antonym that describes the opposite of these qualities of love. Now you have a list of words that describes love, and you have a list of words that describes the opposite of love -- hatred, self-centeredness, and bitterness. Which list best describes you? In what areas do you need to change so that you will love the way God describes? *(BIBLE / WRITING / VOCABULARY)*

I. Write your own paraphrase of 1 Corinthians 13:1-8. *(BIBLE / VOCABULARY)*

J. As a family, make a list of all the husbands and wives that are mentioned in the Bible. Then mark each couple with a plus (+) sign if they served God effectively as a team, or minus (-) sign if they together sinned against God. Mark with an asterisk (*) if one spouse obeyed God while the other did not. Then write a brief explanation of why you marked each couple as you did. *(BIBLE / RESEARCH / FAMILY / WRITING)*

K. Research the history of courtship and the history of dating. Write a paper comparing the two practices, and the way they have been practiced throughout history. *(HISTORY / ENGLISH COMPOSITION / FAMILY)*

L. Read biographies of Christian couples. How did the Lord bring their lives together? What part did prayer play in their meeting and marrying? *(HISTORY / READING)*

M. Work with your parents in outlining the character qualities, the financial state, the occupational attainments, etc. that they would like to see present in your life before you consider courtship. *(WRITING / FINANCES / CAREER EDUCATION)*

N. Study the practice of presenting a dowry to a bride as it is mentioned in Scripture. Then read "God's Law of the Dowry" (page 89-94) as explained in *Dating vs. Courtship*, by Paul Jehle. Start saving a substantial percentage of your earnings as a dowry to give your future wife. Set a goal of how much money you would like to have in this dowry before marriage. *(FINANCES / BIBLE)*

O. Listen to *Timeless Bible Teachings of the Bride Price*, by S. M. Davis. Summarize the speaker's main points. Do you agree with him? Do you think a suitor should pay a bride price to the young lady's father or to the young lady? *(BIBLE / HISTORY)*

P. Complete the studies in Chapter 5, "Dowry" and Chapter 6, "Courtship" in *Prepare Thy Work*, by Daniel Forster. *(BIBLE / RESEARCH / FAMILY / SOCIAL SKILLS)*

Q. Study Chapter 44, "Friendships with Girls," in *Christian Manhood*, by Gary Maldaner. *(BIBLE / SOCIAL SKILLS)*

R. Read *Dating vs. Courtship,* by Paul Jehle, with your father. Discuss its content with him. *(BIBLE / FAMILY / SOCIAL SKILLS)*

S. Make two lists, one entitled "The Dangers of Dating" and the other entitled "The Advantages of Dating." Discuss your lists with your parents, inviting them to add their own thoughts. Do the dangers outweigh the advantages? *(WRITING / FAMILY)*

T. Make two lists, one entitled "The Disadvantages of Courtship" and the other entitled "The Advantages of Courtship." Discuss your lists with your parents, inviting them to add their own thoughts. Do the dangers outweigh the advantages? *(WRITING / FAMILY)*

U. Study in the Bible the following examples of people who practiced courtship before marriage. What can you learn about courtship and preparation for marriage from these examples?

Ruth
Isaac and Rebekah
Jacob and Rachel
David and Michal

(BIBLE / RESEARCH / FAMILY / SOCIAL SKILLS)

V. Study in the Bible the following men who chose their own wives without heeding the counsel of God or parents. What were the results of their decisions?

Esau
David
Samson
Solomon

(BIBLE / RESEARCH / FAMILY / SOCIAL SKILLS / HISTORY)

W. Read *I Kissed Dating Goodbye,* by Joshua Harris. If possible, read this together with your parents and discuss each chapter. What principles will you adopt in your own preparation for marriage? *(SOCIAL SKILLS)*

X. Write a covenant with your parents, making a commitment to be accountable to them, allowing them to protect you and work with you in discerning God's perfect mate for you. Vow that you will not marry without their blessing. You may purchase a special certificate for this purpose or write out your own. *(FAMILY / WRITING)*

Y. Study 1 Corinthians 13:1-8. Write down how each phrase relates to courtship (i.e., How will you not "seek your own" as you wait on God for a mate?). Then write down how each phrase will relate to loving your wife in marriage. *(BIBLE / WRITING / FAMILY / SOCIAL SKILLS)*

Z. Do a topical study from Scripture on the role of the husband in the family. List each responsibility he has, and the Scripture reference that mentions it. *(BIBLE / RESEARCH / FAMILY / WRITING)*

AA. Do a topical study from Scripture on the role of the wife in the family. List each responsibility she has, and the Scripture reference that mentions it. *(BIBLE / RESEARCH / FAMILY / WRITING)*

Advanced

BB. Read with your father *Her Hand in Marriage,* by Douglas Wilson. Discuss together what principles from this book you can apply in your own life and your plans for marriage. *(READING / SOCIAL SKILLS)*

CC. Read Voddie Baucham, Jr.'s book, *What He Must Be to Marry My Daughter.* In what areas do you need to work to meet the standards presented in this book? Make a list of goals and practical steps to take to reach your goals. *(READING)*

DD. Complete the studies "Know What Biblical Marriage Is" and "Set High Goals" in Chapter 7 of *Prepare Thy Work*, by Daniel Forster. *(BIBLE / RESEARCH / FAMILY)*

EE. Do word studies on **phileo**, **agape**, and **eros**. How do these three kinds of love differ from each other? Write a summary of your study and how it relates to courtship and your future wife. *(BIBLE / FOREIGN LANGUAGE / FAMILY / WRITING)*

FF. Look for examples in the Bible of men and women who were working when God brought their mates to them. List each person, the Bible reference, and what they were doing when they met their future mate. What can we learn from this pattern in Scripture? *(BIBLE / RESEARCH / WRITING / FAMILY)*

GG. Study the story in Genesis 24 of Abraham finding a wife for Isaac. Read the story carefully, paying attention to all conversations and actions. What can you learn from this account that relates to waiting on God to provide your future wife? Write a short paper on this theme. *(BIBLE / HISTORY / FAMILY / WRITING)*

HH. Write down the title of each chapter in this book. Then go through the list and write down how each character quality is important in preparing for marriage. *(WRITING)*

II. Study Proverbs 31:10-31. Although this passage is held up as a standard for women, remember that it is the counsel of a mother to her son. This passage describes the virtuous woman whose worth will be "far above rubies," as she "does [you] good and not evil all the days of her life."

- List the **actions** of a virtuous woman.
- List what the passage says the virtuous woman **does not do**.
- List the **thoughts** of a virtuous woman.
- List **adjectives**, based on this passage, that describe the virtuous woman.
- List what she does in regard to: **food, clothing, business**, and **outreach**.
- List what it says about her **speech**.
- List what it says about her **relationship to her family**.
- List what it says about her **husband**.

(BIBLE / WRITING / FAMILY / FINANCES)

JJ. Study all the passages in the Bible about the "strange woman." List all the ways Scripture describes her. What is she like? Now, next to each of these negative qualities, list a word that describes a contrasting character quality.

(BIBLE / WRITING / VOCABULARY / SOCIAL SKILLS)

KK. Find verses that tell how a man can protect himself from the strange woman.

(BIBLE)

LL. Read *Passion and Purity*, by Elisabeth Elliot. Write down insights you gain from the book. *(BIBLE / HISTORY / FAMILY)*

MM. Read *Getting Serious About Getting Married,* by Debbie Maken. If possible, read this book together with several other single men and their fathers. What is the main thesis of this book? Do you agree with it? Talk about the questions in the discussion guide at the back of the book. Will you do anything different based on what you have learned in this book? *(READING)*

NN. Read biographies of single men that God used in a special way for His service.

(READING / HISTORY)

OO. Study and list all the passages from the Bible that teach about the call to single life. Then write a summary that explains the purpose of singleness as designed by God for some people. *(BIBLE)*

PP. If you are courting, work with your father and the father of the girl you are courting to design projects that you and she can work on as you get to know each other better. *(FAMILY / SOCIAL SKILLS / COMMUNITY SERVICE)*

QQ. Make a list of questions and topics that you will want to discuss with your future wife before marriage (children, goals, etc.) *(WRITING / FAMILY)*

RR. Study *Preparing for Marriage God's Way*, by Wayne and Nathan Mack. (Highly recommended!) *(BIBLE / FAMILY)*

SS. Read Part 5, "Selecting a Mate," in *The Family: God's Weapon for Victory,* by Robert Andrews. Discuss the content of these chapters with your father. Go over the discussion questions at the end of each chapter. *(FAMILY)*

TT. Study the concept of the "year of exclusion" as it is described in Deuteronomy 24:5. How might you want to apply this principle to the first year of your married life? *(BIBLE / FAMILY)*

UU. Listen to Douglas Wilson's series entitled *Husbands and Wives.* Take notes and outline the message of these tapes. *(FAMILY / BIBLE)*

VV. Carefully study Ephesians 5:22-33.

- Look up the meaning of words.
- Make lists of instructions to wives and to husbands.
- Look for the stated reasons for certain instructions.
- Note the parallels between the husband/wife relationship and the relationship of Christ and the church.
- Write a short summary of your study and then paraphrase the passage in your own words.

(BIBLE / WRITING / VOCABULARY)

WW. Read, study, and discuss with your father several of the following books about marriage, family life, and being a husband:

- *The Complete Husband,* by Lou Priolo
- *Disciplines of a Godly Man,* by R. Kent Hughes
- *The Exemplary Husband,* by Stuart Scott
- *Family Driven Faith,* by Voddie Baucham
- *The Family: God's Weapon for Victory,* by Robert Andrews
- *Federal Husband,* by Douglas Wilson
- *For a Glory and a Covering,* by Douglas Wilson
- *Manly Dominion,* by Mark Chanski
- *A Sacred Foundation,* by Michael Farris
- *Strengthening Your Marriage,* by Wayne Mack
- *The Godly Home,* by Richard Baxter

(READING / FAMILY)

Additional ideas:

Parents:

Consider and discuss with your son the following questions:

- Has he learned to submit to your counsel and discipline, knowing that God is directing his life through you?

- Does he have a relaxed attitude toward the discovery of his future mate? Does he trust God to bring her to him at the right time?

- Is he willing to submit to your guidance and counsel concerning the selection of his life partner?

- Is he willing to not marry until he has your blessing?

- Is he more concerned about future marriage than he is about faithfully serving God in his present state as a single young man?

- Is he actively seeking to grow in his Christian life, and to prepare himself for the privilege and responsibility of marriage?

- Is he careful to guard himself from sexual temptation as presented in music, books, artwork, media, and social contact?

- Is he aware of the characteristics of a "strange woman," and does he know how to respond if he encounters one?

- Does he have clearly defined standards to guide him in the selection of a wife?

- Does he show proper respect and honor to his mother?

- Does he come to you with questions about sex?

- Does he have a Biblical understanding of the purpose of sex?

- Does he understand the physical aspects of puberty and sex?

- Is he willing to approach the father of a girl before initiating any sort of relationship with her?

- Is he willing to save himself emotionally, as well as physically, for the woman he will marry?

- Is he willing to remain single if that is God's calling for him?

Notes and comments:

Other Books from Doorposts

Bible Study Forms on CD for Plants Grown Up and Polished Cornerstones

We offer this CD for the many parents who prefer to print copies of these study forms straight from their computer, rather than making trips to a copy machine. All the forms from both books are indexed on one disc for quick printing on your home printer. Planning sheets and parental evaluation questions are included too!

Polished Cornerstones

Like **Plants Grown Up**, but for daughters! A 497-page book full of goals and projects especially designed for parents and their daughters. Choose from hundreds of activities and Bible study ideas to help your daughters prepare for their future roles as friends, homemakers, wives, mothers, church and community members. One copy works for all daughters of all ages! Spiral-bound. 51 chapters on:

Loyalty	Listening	Contentment
Thrift	Prudence	Submission
Goals	Diligence	Stewardship
Speech	Single Life	Hospitality
Purity	Manners	Encouragement
Mercy	Teaching	Home Skills
Justice	Courtship	Peacemaking
Respect	Mothering	& much more!

For Instruction In Righteousness

A topical guide for parents, listing Scripture on over 50 common areas of sin. Each chapter gives Bible verses that tell about the sin, what the Bible says will happen to a person who indulges in that sin, parallel ideas for discipline, simple, instructive object lessons based on Scriptural teaching about the sin, verses that explain how God blesses those who resist the sin, parallel ideas for rewards and encouragement, fully quoted memory verses, Bible stories that illustrate obedience and disobedience.

This book can be used as a handy reference in discipline, and for family worship times, parents' personal Bible study, unit studies, counseling, character training, and Bible study projects for older children. Available in spiral or 3-ring binding. See our website for free sample pages.

If-Then Chart

This is a chart designed to help you be more consistent in disciplining your children. The chart is divided into 3 columns. The left-hand column lists common areas of misbehavior (arguing, complaining, etc.), each illustrated with a simple cartoon. The center column gives a Scripture verse related to each sin. The third column is blank, for you to write in the agreed-upon consequences for each misbehavior. An instruction sheet offers suggestions for discipline. This chart has made discipline much easier in our home!

The Blessing Chart

This chart is designed to help you acknowledge and reward godly attitudes and behavior, in a way that is patterned after Scripture. Based on the ideas listed in **For Instruction in Righteousness**, this chart comes with a list of ideas for rewards that relate to God's rewards in our lives. The left-hand column lists good character qualities, with cartoon drawings. The center column quotes Scripture verses that tell how God blesses us when these qualities are present in our lives. The third column is blank, for you to write in the agreed-upon rewards for positive behavior. This chart offers a good balance for Moms like me who specialize in seeing what the kids are doing wrong!

The Put On Chart

Doorposts' newest chart, with its companion study book and paper dolls, is designed to help your family "put on" the character qualities of God's children. Based on Colossians 3:12-14, it will lead you in studying what the Bible says about compassion, kindness, humility, meekness, patience, forbearance, forgiveness, and love. The illustrated chart associates each quality with a piece of clothing, providing object lessons that help younger children understand how they can put on this quality.

The Brother-Offended Checklist

A chart-and-book set that helps teach your children to follow Scriptural instructions when responding to those who have wronged or offended them. It instructs the offender regarding confession and repentance of sin. The chart is illustrated in cartoon-strip style, with steps for the offended and the offender to follow when they have a disagreement. The book expands on each step and refers to illustrative Bible stories, and gives Scriptural principles to help parents act as righteous judges when dealing with disagreements among family members and friends. It also includes memory verses to arm your child against temptation.

Checklist For Parents

A series of 25 questions designed to **help parents examine themselves in light of God's Word**. Organized under 6 areas of responsibility (love, prayer, instruction, protection, provision, and example), each question is followed by Scripture verses which explain what God requires of us as parents. Use as a tool for prayer times, Scripture memorization, preparing your children for parenthood.

For This Is Right

Over 350 questions, each followed by Scripture, which help children and their parents explore the meaning and practical application of the Fifth Commandment, "Honor thy fathers and thy mothers..." Designed for parent and child study and to help sons and daughters prayerfully evaluate their attitudes and actions.

Honor Your Father and Mother

Patterned after **For This Is Right**, this book is designed to use with small children. Simple questions and accompanying Bible verses are paired with line drawings (suitable for coloring) to help a child understand obedience.

Prepare Thy Work

Material to help young men properly prepare for courtship, marriage, and raising a family. Addressing doctrine, vocation, finances, family vision, and more, this book includes Bible studies, evaluation questions, counsel from godly men, discussion topics, practical projects, recommended reading material, and study questions.

A Day of Delight

Dozens of creative ideas to help make Sunday a unique and joyous day of rest and celebration for the whole family (even Mom!). Ideas for preparing for Sunday throughout the week, making mealtimes special but easy, creating a treasure chest of special Sunday-only toys and books, and lots of ideas for toys, games, activities, and projects that focus on Scripture, fellowship, and meditation. Good source of ideas for family worship times, too!

The Mighty Acts of God

Collection of ideas to inspire some **simple** drama times in your family. Ideas for easy costumes (including patterns for almost-instant tunic and cape), simple props, fun meals to go with some Bible stories, and Scripture references and suggestions for acting out over 50 Bible stories. These are **simple** ideas -- no scripts, no rehearsals -- just quick, spontaneous family play times that help teach Scripture's truths. Also includes ideas for acting out Bible stories with Legos, Playmobil, Fisher-Price, building blocks, stuffed animals, dolls, and other toys.

As Unto the Lord

This unique book for women includes:

- A **short set of questions** for daily review. These are designed to help wives prayerfully examine their attitudes and actions with the goal of quickly pinpointing areas of sin for further thought, Bible study and repentance.

- An **in-depth, expanded series** of almost 200 questions, each followed by Scripture which explains what God commands of us as wives. These are patterned after **The Westminster Larger Catechism's** teaching on the Fifth Commandment and are ideal for personal study when you know you're straying from God's design for wives; for study with daughters as they learn to submit to parents and prepare to submit to their future husbands; as a group study with other wives; as counseling material or a helpful gift for a discouraged or rebellious wife or for a young bride as she seeks to fulfill her new role as wife.

- Suggested **Bible study topics and other projects** to aid a woman in reaching the mature godly womanhood to which God has called her.

Family Circles

A kit of materials to help you assemble a life-changing visual aid for your family. Helps you plan for individual time with each child during the day -- for special projects, prayer, Bible study, bed-time snuggling, etc. Children love this project!

The Armor of God Patterns

Simple patterns and instructions for making a cloth "Breastplate of Righteousness," "Helmet of Salvation," "Belt of Truth," and "Shoes of the Gospel of Peace." Also a wooden "Sword of the Spirit" and "Shield of Faith." These are **simple** and **sturdy**!

Service Opportunities Chart

A chart to simplify chore assignments in your household. Divided into 20 sections, you can list up to 40 of your most frequent chores. We provide 56 cartoon illustrations that you can color, cut, and glue next to each chore listing. The right-hand side of the chart can be left blank, or you can write in wages if you choose to pay for chores. Movable name stickers allow you to assign different chores each day to each child. A simple, flexible, inexpensive system.

Stewardship Street

Discusses 7 suggested budget categories for children, gives patterns and instructions for making a "street" of savings boxes out of milk cartons. Each box looks like a different house, store, or business along a street. Also includes patterns for making a memory visual that will help your children memorize verses that tell about God's plan for our money, and a record-keeping form for figuring percentages of earnings for each budget category. We've seen wonderful results with our children, using this system.

Watchwords

12 verses written in beautiful hand calligraphy to help you remember, discuss, and apply Scripture in your family's everyday activities. Frame and hang these verses throughout your house; we tried to include ones that would be appropriate in all different areas of the house. Verses include: Gal. 6:9, Ps. 101:3, Ps. 90:12, Ps. 141:3, Pr. 31:25-27, Ps. 121:3, Eph. 4:26, I Cor. 14:40, Ps. 127:4, Pr. 17:1, Lk.6:31, Pr. 20:3. On cream parchment paper.

Hidden Treasures

Bring Proverbs to life for your whole family. This new book is full of materials and ideas to help you discover the wisdom of Proverbs. **Hidden Treasures** contains 90 prize-winning drawings from our Illustrated Proverbs contest (out of over 500 entries), plus lots of study material for verse-by-verse, chapter-by-chapter, and topical studies. Charts are included for recording your findings. It also includes object lessons, activities, and suggestions for applying what you learn. Suitable for all ages.

Beauty and the Pig

Clear, easy-to-follow instructions teach young people how to **study** the Bible. Studies focus on Proverbs 11:22 and other passages that teach about godly beauty and discretion.

Learn how to use a concordance; how to study a specific verse, passage, or entire book of the Bible; how to study a particular word or topic; and how to study the lives of different people in Scripture. These studies are appropriate for both young ladies and young men.

Includes word studies on "beauty" and "discretion," verse studies of Proverbs 11:22 and I Peter 3:3-4, topical study on modesty and "strange women," concordance study on contentiousness, book studies of Esther and Ruth, character study of Sarah, topical study on good works, chapter study of 1 Samuel 25. It also includes suggestions for 32 other related studies.

Ruby Doll Kit

Make a delightful family of pocket-sized dolls for your daughter while you teach her basic hand-sewing skills, study portions of Proverbs 31, and enjoy times of good fellowship together. Kit includes all fabrics and materials to make "Ruby," the Proverbs 31 woman, in her purple silk and tapestry, and her husband "Victor" and their family of children, all clothed in scarlet.

Bible studies deal with an overview of Proverbs 31, kind speech, diligence, and reaching out to the needy. Lots of fun and learning!

Goldie Doll Kit

Based on Proverbs 11:22, "As a jewel of gold in a swine's snout, so is a fair woman which is without discretion," this new doll-and-Bible-study kit teaches young ladies about true, godly beauty. In the style of the traditional "topsy-turvy" doll. 12-inch-tall Goldie has two personalities! Turn her one way and she's a pretty young lady. Flip her over and she becomes a pig with a gold ring in her nose!

The doll body is made of knit fabric. The girl is dressed in cotton calico trimmed with satin ribbon and lace, and the pig wears coarse cotton with ragged edges and hand-sewn patches. "Wiggle" eyes and a "gold" ring attached to her pink button nose give the pig extra personality.

Simple sewing instructions and all materials (except stuffing, needle, thread, and optional trims) are included. This doll involves more sewing than our Ruby doll, but construction methods are simple enough for the novice seamstress. For durability, we recommend machine-sewing the doll body, but clothes could be made by hand, if desired.

Boxed kit includes patterns and instructions, **Beauty and the Pig** Bible study, and all basic materials except stuffing, needle, thread, and optional trims.

Go-to-the-Ant Chart

This chart arms parents with Scripture for working with any child that needs training in diligence and faithfulness. Verses for easy reference on every area of laziness we could think of. Take your child to the chart, identify his slothful action or attitude, read what God says about it, and pray for His strength to obey.

For more information, sample pages, ordering, or to request a free catalog, please visit our website at:

www.Doorposts.com

Call us at (888)-433-4749
or write to 5905 SW Lookingglass Dr., Gaston, OR 97119